D0060298

CREATORS AND DISTURBERS

CREATORS AND DISTURBERS

Reminiscences by Jewish
Intellectuals of New York

Drawn from conversations with
BERNARD ROSENBERG and
ERNEST GOLDSTEIN

Columbia University Press
New York   1982

Library of Congress Cataloging in Publication Data
Main entry under title:

Creators and disturbers.

  Includes index.
    1. Jews—New York (N.Y.)—Biography.
  2. Jews—New York (N.Y.)—Intellectual life.
  3. New York (N.Y.)—Biography.   4. New York
  (N.Y.)—Intellectual life. I. Rosenberg,
Bernard, 1923–   II. Goldstein, Ernest,
1933–
F128.9.J5C79   973'.04924 [B]   82-4281
ISBN 0-231-04712-6   AACR2

Columbia University Press
New York   Guildford, Surrey

Copyright © 1982   Columbia University Press
All rights reserved
Printed in the United States of America

Clothbound editions of Columbia University Press books are Smyth-
sewn and printed on permanent and durable acid-free paper.

To Helen and Sarah Helen

CONTENTS

Introduction   I

PART I. THE EUROPEAN IMMIGRANTS   25

1. The Yiddish Writer and His Audience   27
   Isaac B. Singer

2. From a Russian *Stetl* to the Founding of *Midstream*   45
   Shlomo Katz

3. The Historian of the Holocaust at YIVO   61
   Isaiah Trunk

4. The Tragedy of the German Jewish Intellectual   75
   Hans Morgenthau

5. The Jewish Novelist in New York—An Émigré   87
   Soma Morgenstern

6. Jazz—The Jewish-Black Connection   95
   Dan Morgenstern

7. The Radical Émigré in the Metropolis   113
   Henry Pachter

PART II. THE NEW YORK NATIVES   135

8. From the Lower East Side to "Over the Rainbow"   137
   Yip Harburg

9. The Intellectual and the ILGWU   155
   Gus Tyler

10. The Yiddish Influence on American Theater   176
    Harold Clurman

11. "New York Jew"   194
    Alfred Kazin

12. The Scholar as Chancellor   210
    Gerson Cohen

13. The Teaching of the Holocaust   227
    Irving Greenberg

14. Psychoanalyst in New York   234
    Joel Kovel

15. The Spirit of the New York Labor Movement   246
    Victor Gotbaum

16. The Range of the New York Intellectual   264
    Irving Howe

17. The Writer in Greenwich Village   288
    Grace Paley

18. The Music of the City   299
    Barry Brook

19. "The Architect from New York"   311
    Percival Goodman

20. The Rabbi's Daughter as Judge and Humanist   330
    Justine Wise Polier

PART III. FROM BEYOND THE HUDSON   349

21. An Activist Critic on the Upper West Side   351
    Midge Decter

22. The Sociologist on the Cutting Edge   368
    Joseph Bensman

23. The Educational Critic in New York   388
    Diane Ravitch

24. The New York Publishing World   401
    Ted Solotaroff

Index   421

CREATORS AND DISTURBERS

INTRODUCTION

WHEN ALFRED NORTH WHITEHEAD described his most intense graduate students at Harvard University, he referred to their "Jewish energy." This book is about a major source of that energy. It is about New York and the Jewish intellectuals who did so much to form the city which in turn formed them.

The reader will be confronted with a multiplicity of relationships connecting the cultural and social life of those intellectuals and the milieu in which they were able to thrive. This mosaic (or Mosaic) is based upon interviews conducted in depth and over an extended period with some of the most gifted intellectuals—including some part-time intellectuals—in New York and in the world. It is not celebrity-centered. Any general reader will find that the contents page presents a mixture of familiar and unfamiliar names. But all of them are instantly recognizable within their special spheres.

We focus upon the intimate experiences and principal preoccupations of an intelligentsia embedded in a specific subcultural and contracultural environment. How does the individual identify himself? What do intellectuality and Jewishness mean to men and women who work within the bounds of a metropolis that, however far gone in physical decay, is still indispensable to them? Our book is designed to clarify these questions with all the specificity and particularity of personal life histories.

The New York Jewish intellectuals whose testimony we have recorded represent a wide variety of perspectives, occupations, and interests including fiction, journalism, psychoanalysis, history, philosophy, theology, sociology, political science, theater, economics, and free-floating criticism. Some of our witnesses made their way out of ghettos in Manhattan, Brooklyn, and the Bronx. Others grew up in the hinterlands, and a few are European refugees. Despite their heterogeneity, they take a common stance

I

with regard to New York, each fixing upon a particular aspect of the metropolis that enchants or encapsulates them.

The image of the Jew as a twentieth-century urban archetype had been defined in the Paris of Proust's Swann, the Dublin of Joyce's Bloom and the Prague of Kafka's Joseph K. The Jews of modernity are preeminently city people. Despite their differences, it is this that gives them their family resemblance. Even in the ancient world, Jews helped to swell population centers like Alexandria, Antioch, and Jerusalem. Later on, if expelled from a feudal city, they usually wound their way back into its environs. Consigned to the East European Pale of Settlement, they broke out of it. Whenever possible, Jews migrated to the metropolis, usually to the largest metropolis within their reach.

Jewish emancipation was a child of the Enlightenment. It therefore dovetailed with the overall secularization of Western society. Freely mingling in the city, many children of traditionalistic ghetto Jews began to develop a secular, nonconformist, radical intelligentsia. Everywhere they were disturbers of the intellectual peace. Harnessing energy that had been confined for centuries, these Jews moved quickly toward the higher reaches of every intellectual, academic, scientific, and artistic field they were permitted to enter.

That the explosion of Jewish energy in these areas also coincided with the rise of great cities made upward Jewish mobility an urban phenomenon. Jews left their distinctive stamp on the culture of Berlin as well as that of Vienna, Warsaw, Prague, Budapest, Paris, and London. They borrowed, contributed, and carried ideas with them. They bore whole movements of philosophic thought, aesthetic practice, and scientific theory.

Slowly at first, and then with a rush, these movements reached the United States. The earliest Jewish settlers, a few hundred Sephardim fleeing the Inquisition, were followed by a small wave of immigrants from Germany. Each group produced its share of distinguished families: the Cardozos, the Brandeises, the Schiffs, the Sulzbergers. These and other "grandees" worked their way up through commerce, finance, the press, philanthropy, and the law. But even they were long barred by academic quotas that amounted to an unwritten *numerus clausus*, from the elite higher education that their children or grandchildren were to enjoy.

Virulent anti-Semitism in Eastern Europe brought Jews called Ashkenazim to New York. That port of entry, a focal point of mass migration for a hundred years, proved congenial to the largest number of Jewish émigrés. Hardships notwithstanding, more than half of them remained in New York City where they created a rich Yiddish culture whose many uses, past and present, are written all over our record. That world of internal conflict laced with ideological friction was animated by drama, poetry, art, and music. Impoverished Jews, in an array of occupations largely related to their training as tailors, soon organized to fight the "bosses," small businessmen who were generally also Jewish. They thereby gave major impetus to the overall American trade union movement. Many were attracted to political reform and radical innovation. The legacy of their struggle has become a vital part of American civilization.

But it was only after the Great Depression, especially after World War II (the last "good" global war), that Ashkenazic Jews began to leave an inextinguishable mark upon the culture of New York and that of North America at large. Novelists like Norman Mailer, Bernard Malamud, Saul Bellow, and Phillip Roth, often referred to but only indirectly represented in these pages, seemed for a while to be the literary voice of America.

Among our premier critics were such men as Alfred Kazin and Irving Howe (both of them speaking straightforwardly to us in this book), along with the late Lionel Trilling. Ted Solotaroff, an accomplished editor and writer, characterizes Trilling as the Jewish Matthew Arnold. Be that as it may, Trilling was the first person of his extraction to become a professor of English literature at so exalted a seat of learning as Columbia University. He was a genteel practitioner of his high art, and a New York Jew to the core.

For a few decades the Jewish star shone brightly in and out of our best universities. But we regard it as a serious mistake to equate the literary intellectuals—even though, as Irving Howe points out, their interests have always been more than literary—with all New York City intellectuals. (One could quibble about the meaning of intellectuals, a word totally lacking in precision, but it would be an arid exercise.) It seems to us that our colleague Lewis Coser is entirely correct when he writes in his book on intellectuals, *Men of Ideas* (1965) that

Few modern terms are as imprecise as the term intellectuals. Its very mention is likely to provoke debate about both meaning and evaluation. To many it stands for qualities deeply distrusted and despised. To others it connotes excellence aspired to but not often achieved. To some, intellectuals are impractical dreamers who interfere with the serious business of life. To others they are the antennae of the race.

The best we can do is to agree with Henry Pachter's definition that intellectuals are people who read outside their field. The empirical fact is that American-born scholars like Meyer Schapiro, Robert K. Merton, Paul A. Samuelson, Morris Cohen, and Ernest Nagel bestrode their fields. Of these, Meyer Schapiro, even more a Jewish renaissance man than Trilling was an elegant Englishman, may be said to haunt those who have eloquently talked their way into this book.

Driven by the Nazi scourge, many renowned artists arrived at approximately the same time* as an even larger contingent of natural and social scientists. While all of them found refuge in the United States, a large proportion remained in and around New York. They enriched a variety of disciplines immeasurably—most spectacularly nuclear physics, as evidenced in the Manhattan Project, which was sparked by a famous letter that Albert Einstein (a German Jew) signed and Leo Szilard (a Hungarian Jew) wrote and sent to President Roosevelt. Without that technological undertaking, subsidized by a secret Congressional appropriation of two billion dollars, Nazi Germany would have developed atomic bombs before the United States—an outcome whose fateful consequences one would rather not imagine. Jews of American birth who played a major role in the Manhattan Project included J. Robert Oppenheimer and Isidor Isaac Rabi, the latter an octogenarian who at this writing is still very active. Rabi was awarded

---

* For an analysis of painters and sculptors in this context, see *The Vanguard Artist*, by Bernard Rosenberg and Norris Fliegel. (Quadrangle Books, 1965. Reissued by Arno Press in 1979.)

the Nobel Prize in 1944 for research in nuclear physics, quantum mechanics, and magnetism. Starting in 1937 as a professor of physics at Columbia University, he was also chairman of the general advisory committee of the U.S. Atomic Energy Commission. No one more appropriately belongs in a galaxy of New York intellectuals than such a man. But possibly because he is the author of *My Life and Times as a Physicist* and, more recently, of a series in the *New Yorker* that also delineates his Jewish persona, he was unavailable for further conversations with us.

Although only echoes of the story Rabi might again have told are to be apprehended in what follows, this is the kind of gap we hope to fill in subsequent volumes. Meanwhile, thinkers like Hans Morgenthau (ailing at the time we met him, now no longer alive) and Henry Pachter (also recently deceased), both German Jews living in this country thanks to Hitler, vividly recreate their lives as engagé social scientists. That these two men of learning supply a strong and deep contrast is not the least of their contributions. If born and bred New Yorkers dominate our scene, Morgenthau and Pachter from central Europe, like Shlomo Katz from Tsarist Russia and Isaiah Trunk from prewar Poland, provide angles of vision that help us to see—or hear—the genus under observation.

But there is one other regional point of view, that of Midge Decter, Diane Ravitch, Joseph Bensman, and Ted Solotaroff, which cannot be ignored. It happens that second and third generation American Jews have been drawn magnetically to New York from small and middle-sized cities. Some, subject to the vicissitudes of academia, went west of the Hudson to Berkeley, Chicago, Cambridge, even to Texas. Others took off for Hollywood, and yet others settled in the state of Israel. Most nevertheless continued to regard New York as their cultural and spiritual home.

To a significant extent, by the late fifties the culture of New York became "Jewish," and world culture became "American." For Jews, only Jerusalem loomed large as a competitive culture capital. Hitler had seen to that. Jerusalem (and all of Israel), however, began to develop a particularistic and nationalistic culture, while New York remained the cosmopolitan capital of an "enlightened" secular Diaspora.

This unique Diaspora engendered problems of its own. A secular Jewish culture is, by definition, stripped of its sacred or manifestly Jewish content. A sizable percentage of Jews born on the Lower East Side of Manhattan gained a special identity by leaving the ghetto that impeded their acculturation. Later, many of them tended to experience a longing for the roots they had relinquished. And Judaism as a religion, with assistance from the remnants of European Orthodoxy, showed surprising resilience. The relative success of this religion in all three of its denominations—Orthodox, Conservative, and Reform—is implicit in statements made by their spokesmen: Rabbis Greenberg, Cohen, and the late Stephen Wise through his daughter. Their success has been a mixed blessing to these cultivated Jews. They are aware that they are viewed with some hostility by those who have fared less well and by those who now perceive Jews as a group that blocks *their* success. Just so, New York has provoked the hostility of non–New Yorkers. The extent of that hostility became particularly apparent during a nearly fatal fiscal crisis in the 1970s. Seldom has the destiny of Jews been so closely linked to the fate of a city. (Again, only Jerusalem is of comparable importance.)

The articulateness of our respondents in the open-ended tandem interview—three-way conversations rather than unilateral interrogations—allows us to contemplate brief biographies and to develop themes in which (according to Irving Howe) the Jewish experience "undercuts ideology." The trauma of the New York City teachers' strike, which had little effect except to scar its principals and bystanders, illustrates the point: Gerson Cohen, head of the Jewish Theological Seminary, traveled around the country .lecturing on the origin of pogroms, while other Jewish leaders took to the streets and broke down the school doors. Underneath these diametrically opposed actions, and the anxiety that accompanied them (each an expression of the Jewish jitters), is the East European *shtetl* (small Jewish town) experience recalled by Shlomo Katz: "One day it was 'unquiet' in town, not quite a pogrom yet, but rumors of an impending one. My mother was always nervous about this, so she ordered us, 'Stay indoors!'" Underneath the hullabaloo occasioned by chronic crises is Harold Clurman's description of why he hollers:

[On the Lower East Side] I had some of the most wonderful discussions—I never could get to bed. To this day, I go to bed at three in the morning because when I was a kid all I used to hear in my home, starting at nine o'clock, after dinner, were these violent (they seemed violent, but they were really very friendly) discussions about American politics, about Russia, about literature, about art. . . . The first play I ever did, independently, was *Awake and Sing*. People asked me, "Why did you have three characters talking at the same time?" I said, "Because in my family everybody was a disputer. I was the youngest. In order to be heard I had to yell louder than anybody else. As a result I have never stopped shouting."

And underneath much of the passion conveyed to us is Justine Polier's description of her father, Rabbi Stephen Wise, fighting Hitler abroad and at the same time being harrassed by fellow Jews in America.

Despite many unfortunate conditions that now disfigure their city, the projective question "Why New York?" generated a rich harvest of responses. For Harold Clurman and "Yip" Harburg, their city is the theatrical center of America; the ballet and the availability of friends like Meyer Schapiro hold Irving Howe; Midge Decter is immersed in the intellectual life of the Upper West Side; for Isaac Singer it is the readers of *The Forward*; in Soma Morgenstern's eyes, New York is the only place to be free; for Shlomo Katz it is the universe of Jewish and other magazines; for Grace Paley, the neighborhoods; for Joel Kovel, the ambience of advanced psychoanalysis; to Dan Morgenstern the city is jazz land.

It is New York's physical and cultural setting that grips a type of person who even now refuses to join the general exodus of over 600,000 middle-class Jews. If Greenwich Village has held Grace Paley for most of her adult life and the Upper West Side continues to exercise its fascination over others, a worldly man like Hans Morgenthau compared his part of Madison Avenue to "the beautiful Rue St. Honoré in Paris." Similarly, for Joel Kovel, who values the range of human associations, even those that occur by chance, it is also a matter of friends and colleagues. A walker (like Alfred Kazin, Henry Pachter, and Yip Harburg), a jogger, and a bicycler, Kovel says of the streets that they "are a book."

Paley is also fond of the streets but, characteristically, she loves to observe passengers on the subway with its kaleidoscopic "subway culture." Irving Howe defends "the myth of New York," insisting that it makes all the difference:

By the myth I mean a group of interesting people. A myth isn't a lie; it's a reality that takes on a kind of enlarged character. After a while it became clear to me that I belonged to a generation called the New York intellectuals. These people don't necessarily have to see, or talk to, one another. They still have certain kinds of common experience.

Again, and more graphically, in explanation of why he would "find it terribly hard to leave" New York:

You can take the same group you find interesting here and put them in Stanford and they're not interesting. You can take a group of people from Stanford and put them here and they become more interesting. . . . The atmosphere shapes the people, it shapes one's life.

Percival Goodman, the architect, professor, and writer, spurns as an idiot's invention a term like "the Big Apple." To him in his youth, the city was "a nice big oyster": "All you had to do was get your knife in and turn it and there was the nice big oyster to eat." Goodman's imagery suggests what he himself calls the sense of unlimited opportunities that enlivened his existence and that of his celebrated brother Paul. It was and is a good place for experimental artists of the avant-garde engaged in their endless search for new visions.

Nevertheless, we find respondents in our group who speak warmly of continuity and tradition. Goodman, who cares about the preservation of old buildings, is such a person. But no more so than Victor Gotbaum, a labor leader striving to better the conditions of his members, for whom the New York tradition signifies "nineteen hospitals available to the sick poor," and "the highest monetary rate for people on relief," or "looking after the aged." Representing municipal workers, Gotbaum takes as much pride in the needle trades tradition as we might expect from Gus Tyler, Vice President and resident intellectual of the International Ladies Garment Workers Union. But it is Tyler who expresses concern about the dangers to that tradition and Gotbaum who declares: "If trade unionism transcends its necessary bread-and-butter operations we have Dubinsky (a founder of the ILGWU) and the New York atmosphere to thank for a large part of it." For him, as for Tyler and for most of the political respondents in this book, the New York tradition is a social welfare tradition, a social democratic tradition, and a tradition of hospitality. Hence Gotbaum says, "I don't think it's an accident that so many people came here and found roots in New York."

Quite naturally, it is New York's literary tradition that Alfred Kazin finds most compelling. In his well-documented move from Williamsburg across the Brooklyn Bridge—a famous metaphor in the poetry of Walt Whitman and Hart Crane—Kazin felt the appropriateness of F. Scott Fitzgerald's assertion that once he had "slid" across that bridge into Manhattan, "anything could happen." Besides, "the city directly represented an important historical and literary tradition," that of Melville and Whitman, of Henry James, and Edith Wharton. This is the tradition that spurred a twenty-seven-year-old child of the Russian-Jewish ghetto to write *On Native Grounds*, his masterly interpretation of American literature.

In Rabbi Irving Greenberg's experience, a transplanted religious and ethnic tradition has mattered most. When he began to teach a then unrecognized academic course on the Holocaust, Greenberg relied on the booksellers and bookstores of New York City, but:

Partly for the lack of an adequate literature we had to bring survivors in to talk. Their presence, their stories had a tremendous effect. In Oshkosh, or wherever, you couldn't do that, but New York has so many survivors with so many different experiences. And some of the kids were themselves children of survivors.

Greenberg gave his course at Yeshiva University, which is itself a unique religious and secular institution.

On the other hand, Joel Kovel studied at the Albert Einstein College of Medicine because of its extraordinary psychiatric program. At that college a special cultural coalescence had taken place:

Einstein inherited certain fruits of the Holocaust. An incredibly beautiful psychoanalytic culture had developed in central Europe. It was dispersed. Key figures ended up in New York: Hartmann and Kris and Lowenstein

and many others. . . . Einstein was the place to be if you were a young
psychiatrist interested in psychoanalysis, as I had become by that time.

Kovel tried living in Seattle and found it pleasant but lacking in
the collegial stimulation of New York: "The place was just too
bland. The sense of opposition that makes New York what it is
was missing. I remember walking through the shopping centers;
people looked the same; they were all lined up like a cross-section
of the consumer society." The qualities of irony and complexity
which typify so many of our subjects seemed to Kovel, as to the
others, more abundant in the city they could not long abandon.
Its special difference had been bred into them. Kovel speaks for
many when he praises his Brooklyn neighborhood and his com-
panions on the street: being around "bright kids" and sensing
"an enormous amount" of intellectuality that eclipsed school
(where "we were smarter than our teachers and we knew it") as
a formative influence.

But libraries were the single resource that meant most to these
New Yorkers. Barry Brook, musical from an early age, found a
circle of friends with whom to attend concerts which were more
varied and frequent in New York than anywhere else in America.
And the same friends were with him when he went to "the 58th
Street Music Library on Saturdays to listen to records." The library had thousands of scores that could be studied or rented by
those who might wish to use them for amateur or school orchestras:

It had tables where music copyists spent hours upon hours, every day,
taking things down and copying them out for publishers who put out
works that originated in other editions. They were copying for republication. . . . I was drawn there because of the great riches the library
held. . . . I don't know if it was unique in this country but it was surely,
exceptional.

When twelve years old or so, the precocious Irving Howe,
in a sickbed at the time, sent his father to the library to bring
home the collected poems of Milton, Wordsworth, and Keats. As
Howe recalls it, the librarian apparently looked at his immigrant
father "with considerable disbelief, for which I don't blame her.
'What the hell's going on here—this man with a Jewish accent

comes for the collected poems of Milton, Wordsworth, and Keats.' But she gives them to him. I guess she has some idea of these crazy Jewish kids." Those books were not set aside. On the contrary, they were consumed. "I was laid up for about six weeks, and in a feverish condition I read just about all of those three poets."

Nor can it have been entirely a matter of happenstance that during his adolescence Gus Tyler's mother, who "worshipped learning," moved her family into a house directly across from the Pratt Library. All through high school he "lived" in that library. There he found

. . . one of those little old ladies. She brought the whole library to me, she ran around like crazy; she was delighted. I got a bigger education preparing for debates in the Pratt Library than I got from all my schooling. . . . They used to have stacks of books worn from overuse, and truly dedicated librarians took care of you.

No school, not even City College, which struck him as mediocre, made Alfred Kazin a voracious reader. Rather it was the street and the family: "My sister Pearl and I used to carry three or four forged library cards so we'd be sure of enough reading." And yet neither father nor mother particularly encouraged the bookishness of their children: "They just took it for granted."

The library was a prime agency of socialization for these youngsters inside and outside New York City. It meant a great deal to Joseph Bensman as a boy in Two Rivers, Wisconsin, as it did to Diane Ravitch in Houston, Texas. It means even more to them in their adulthood. Now they need books in order to write books. New York offers them unequaled resources for research in sociological theory and American history. And the Lincoln Center Music Library is of immense value to Barry Brook as he and his students tap its resources in building a first-rate department of musicology. Museums and libraries literally hold Percival Goodman in the city:

What keeps me and many of my friends in New York? Well, there's the Natural History Museum, the Museum of Modern Art; you can include Columbia as a piece of territory and you've nearly got it. Maybe the Brooklyn Museum if you're interested in its Egyptian collection. . . .

I used to go to the 42nd Street library after work. I'd have dinner at the Automat and spend the evening in the fine arts section of the Public Library. Now that I know more, Avery Library at Columbia strikes me as better. Avery's the best architectural library in the country, maybe in the world. . . . To anyone with a passion for architectural scholarship, Avery is indispensable.

And if your passion happens to be Jewish scholarship, then the available riches are without parallel. As a student first of the French Revolution and of French literature, then of rabbinics and Hebraism, Gerson Cohen had the Seminary Library "where you could get all the Jewish books you might want" and the New York Public Library which "was a whole world" where "you could get everything!" The eccentric chief librarian of its Jewish division and his assistant are men he remembers with the greatest respect. But there was more: Columbia, "with its great Semitics collection"; Union Theological Seminary, "with its great theological collection" and its comparative religions collection; more recently, the Leo Baeck Institute, "with the greatest collection of German Judaica"; and as a special treat, the Lubavitcher Rebbe's library, containing "a vast collection of Jewish Sovietica," to which only the elect had access, "And I was one of them!"

High on the resource list of intellectuals interested in Jewish studies is the Yiddish Institute, known as YIVO, to which several respondents allude. Cohen refers to YIVO's remarkable anti-Semitic files as well as "portraits and pictures and archives of East European life." But no one is in a better position to appreciate the marvels of YIVO than Isaiah Trunk. Is it too much to say, as Trunk does, that "YIVO now has the world's most extensive documentation of our vanished East European culture"? We think not. Indeed, one might argue that although most of its bearers were exterminated, that culture will not wholly vanish as long as the archives in YIVO (and those in Yad Vashem, an Israeli center of documentation) still exist. For scholars who wish to keep the Jewish past, and not only the tragic past, alive in books and articles, YIVO is a treasure house. No wonder Trunk's attachment to New York is virtually identified with the one institution in which he spends all his days. Or that scholars come from many parts of the world to reconstruct the remains of a civilization that Hitler never completely obliterated.

But he did obliterate six million Jews, including one million children. This is the Holocaust that no one involved in our dialogue is about to forget or let others forget. And to all of them except Singer, who long ago began to take a grim view of human nature, and possibly Morgenthau for similar reasons, it came as a profound shock. Only a vision of human depravity like that of Isaac Bashevis Singer proved to be shock-proof. Even so, readers may be taken aback by Singer's misanthropy. The marvelous stories Singer has written, for all their implicit diabolism, still leave us unprepared to hear an explicit declaration like this one: "To me the Holocaust did not begin in 1939. To me the Holocaust began from the moment man was created." To a great writer who believed even before Hitler that "human life is one big slaughter," and who felt it not just as a Jew but as a human being, the Holocaust was intelligible as one "link in a chain of holocausts." Singer, the vegetarian who abominates any kind of slaughter, mentions human slaughter over and over: "I am convinced that although men are so jittery about their health and about prolonging their lives, you can always get them to slaughter other people, thereby endangering or losing their own lives." If Singer's imagination is fully equal to the horror that befell a whole people whose way of life is his subject matter, the same can hardly be said for anyone else. The more predictable liberalism or radicalism and humanitarianism of Jewish intellectuals, with their antecedents in the Enlightenment, barred them from anticipating Hitler's handiwork.

As a religious boy and afterwards as an advanced student, Irving Greenberg experienced several crises, but their upshot made him "more humanistic, more liberal." The Holocaust was different: "It challenged the whole idea of God. . . . The shock kept deepening. It didn't go away. I think one ordinarily overcomes shock or develops protective numbness to it. But this shock drove me into looking for new categories."

Gus Tyler discovered that, on account of Hitler, his revolutionary politics had to be reassessed: barbaric Nazism opened his eyes to the danger of any dictatorship. The Holocaust deepened his growing anxiety about the possible triumph of Leninism. Years before the massacre of six million Jews was known to him, Gerson Cohen paid a visit to the Hyde Park Library. Learning there of FDR's refusal to help save any of those victims, Cohen, like most of his informed coreligionists, was disenchanted with a president who had seemed to be their great friend. As a twenty-three-year-old he already knew the passive role Roosevelt had played. But "the trauma of his life" occurred at a YIVO exhibit of concentration camp materials, for there he saw "a bar of soap made of Jews." And the Holocaust reduced him to "a state of despair for the world."

Alfred Kazin, after having read "enormously in the literature of Nazism," is not sure even now that he understands that phenomenon. In his view a word like *tragedy* does not adequately convey the meaning of Auschwitz.

> . . . the Holocaust made me believe more and more in certain ideas of human nature which I had been loath to accept. . . . Over the years I became . . . concerned about the Holocaust and later made a visit to Belsen. . . . The Holocaust was a political fact for me. More than anything else, it meant Marxism—even my little bit of Marxism, or the socialism I did embrace—could never explain the Holocaust. . . . It made me feel there was some unconscious drive in politics which, in my naïve youth, I hadn't grasped.

Speaking of the early editors of *Commentary*, a Jewish magazine launched in 1945, Midge Decter recalls that as youthful radicals they had been more or less internationalist in their ideological commitment. Then came World War II and the Holocaust: "To put it much too crudely, Hitler taught them that they were Jews. . . . They had fought in the war or worked for it. They were Jews and they were antitotalitarian. Those two feelings were very much related—how after Hitler could they not be?" And while some wondered about an all-good and all-powerful God who allowed babies to burn (for these thinkers were unarmed with Singer's conviction that God has no mercy), others paradoxically turned to God. For a while supernaturalism, even mysticism attracted the New York intellectuals about whom Decter reminisces.

Shlomo Katz, a secularist and Labor Zionist, went through an even deeper revulsion when news of the Holocaust reached him. In 1944, he was on military duty at an army air force base near Fairbanks, Alaska. During the summer in that area the sun never sets. Katz felt strange sensations while on assignment in a control tower with no traffic in the air or on the ground: "But the impact of the news about the Holocaust in that midnight, sunlit and empty—seemingly abandoned—world started working on me. I became subject to some very powerful religious moods— moods of retreat from the world, from life, moods similar to those expressed in Joseph Glatstein's poem 'Goodby World.' Total renunciation and resignation. They still come over me occasionally."

Because, as Justine Polier remarks, "It is hard for young people today to grasp the situation of those days," let alone to have "Buchenwald burned into their consciousness" (as it was into Victor Gotbaum's when his outfit helped liberate that death factory), we have largely limited ourselves to people who remember the ferocity of Hitler's Final Solution. Revisionist historians too young to qualify as witnesses have placed a heavy load of blame not only on President Roosevelt but on American Jewish leaders, above all Stephen Wise, for their failure to rescue those who were about to be slaughtered. No one who pays attention to Justine Polier's remarks can sustain the case against her father. To be sure, Wise and his associates knew better than anyone except the authorities who were joined in a conspiracy of silence, what lay in store for European Jewry. He was not indifferent to the fate of his fellow Jews or indifferent about seeking action on their behalf. Justine Polier remembers "the hostility and the duplicity of the State Department" as well as the open, organized anti-Semitism of Father Coughlin and other rabble-rousers. She and her father had early intimations of the Holocaust:

The full horror of what was going on reached me just before the war. My father went to Paris to meet the first Jews who had escaped. When he returned he was charged with exaggerating. To his warning that there would be a world war if the abominations were allowed to continue, the response was that he was histrionic, an exaggerator, a demagogue.

Not even the president's Jewish advisors, mainly of German background, favored intervention. They no doubt agreed with those influential Jews in Germany who felt that Hitler was not so sinister after all. The Wises knew better. Stephen Wise helped to organize a U.S. committee to admit Jewish children from Germany. Despite the aid of Clarence Pickett, Marion Kenworthy, Marshall Field, Eleanor Roosevelt, Bishop Sheil of Chicago, and "some wonderful bishops in the South"—a true roll of honor!—the Congressional bill to save ten thousand Jewish children was defeated. "Father pleaded with the tongue of angels before the Senate Committee" but to no avail. The American Legion Auxiliary opposed this effort and Cardinal Spellman "refused to associate himself" with it. Such an episode is but one of several that Justine Polier chronicles. Together they account for the "sense of impotence" that was so pervasive. "Walls of loneliness surrounded the few Jews who spoke and tried to act. . . . The antagonism was unbelievable." Who, after reading these sorrowful recollections, will hold Stephen Wise responsible for the indifference of others? And who in the light of that indifference can doubt Morgenthau's judgment that "man in society is bad" or fault him for invoking the ancient wisdom that came to his lips: *homo homine lupus?*

In one way or another, but chiefly as a direct consequence of anti-Semitism, the Jewish intellectuals now in New York were always made to feel their marginality. That there might be a recrudescence of Judaeophobia strong enough to allow for another Holocaust, in the Middle East or even in America, is far from unthinkable to them. Given the peculiar history and general dispersion of Jewry over almost twenty centuries, it is probably true that "any sensitive Jew always remains a kind of 'lost tribe' in his own self," as Shlomo Katz put it to us. But a part of the ageless exile should have ended more than three decades ago when Israel came into being as a state presumably very much like other states. Zionists of every stripe expected some kind of normalization to ensue. None in our group, which includes at least one vehement anti-Zionist in the person of Henry Pachter, is so blind as to claim that it did ensue.

As Max Weber repeatedly pointed out, Jews in the Diaspora are a pariah people. In their homeland, which the great powers granted them after the Holocaust and partly in compensation for it, they were to have become simply a nation among the nations. Instead, they became a pariah nation. And the destiny of that nation is generically no different from Jewish destiny in the Diaspora. Never was the interdependence of fate that links all Jews more marked than it is in this situation.

Henry Pachter, who considers the creation of Israel to have been a calamity, nonetheless recognizes that he too is implicated in the Jewish state, that accursed "outcome of world history." Thus:

I have to be responsible for Begin's mistakes. My daughter may have to die because of people she has never known. . . . What happens to Israel will have an enormous influence on my own life, but not because I have an *attachment* to Israel. The community of destiny has been imposed on me by *others*.

Is a Jew anybody defined as a Jew? Apparently. And this formulation of Jean Paul Sartre's is all the more galling to Pachter, who sees himself as a lifelong opponent of the existentialists. But, "Sartre's absurd theory is right: I am tied to a people with whom originally I was not by choice associated." Choice is the operative word in Sartre's system. By its exercise the human species is "condemned to freedom." Not the Jews—of whom Sartre wrote, "Ils ne peuvent pas choisir de ne pas être Juifs." Not even Henry Pachter can choose not to be a Jew or not to be "implicated" in the Jewish state.

Jewish identity, Jewish ethnicity, if not Judaism itself, is inescapable. Imbued with this idea, Hans Morgenthau finds it laughable that a contemporary New York Jew might try to escape from himself, say, by changing his name. Stein, who is the son of Finkelstein, will no longer be able to cover his tracks. Finkelstein by any other name remains Finkelstein.

Joseph Bensman is a defiant Jew and a habitual iconoclast. In his early youth he was taunted by gang boys, some of whom simultaneously accepted him as "their" intellectual. Respected for his brains, he never ceased to be the "Christ-Killer" they dubbed him. That humiliation prepared him for more of the same. It came in the army, as it did to Solotaroff and Gotbaum and nearly every other Jew who saw military service during the forties and fifties. The army (or the navy) was a crucible in which every impulse to assimilate was burned out of them. Through these and other means the move from shame to pride, inaugurated by American black intellectuals, became a constitutive feature of American Jewish intellectuals—and of Jews in general. Here is Bensman, still more the universalist than the particularist, discussing a trip to Israel, which sharpened his ethnic pride and reactivated his old fears:

The pride is in what the Israelis have accomplished. . . . I've been in other arid areas, southern Yugoslavia, Egypt, and North Africa, and seen forbidding physical environments. I can well imagine what the Israeli pioneers did with their own work, their massive effort. . . . Even their will to survive makes me proud.

And what is his fear? "The fear I share with all Jews that Israel may not survive."

No one articulates this fear more poignantly than Midge Decter who grew up in a Zionist culture that totally enveloped the girl as it did her parents, friends, and schoolmates. Upon reaching Israel as a mature woman, she was less than "enchanted" by it. But that personal response she took to be "absolutely irrelevant": "I went to Israel and I thought, 'It doesn't matter whether I like this place or not. It is mine. And everything that happens here happens to me as well as to these people.'" Moreover, because Jews everywhere are so close to those in Israel, if the state goes down, "it's the whole ball game. . . . I can't logically justify this feeling. I just have it. If Israel goes that's the end of the Jews." She is filled with outrage that the world should permit or contrive the annihilation of Israel: "It just outrages me beyond the point where I am a Jew. And as a Jew I think the destruction of Israel would be the end of the whole thing. It's not *supposed* to come to an end." And then spurning mystical ethnicity, she yet evinces it up to a point in this *cri de coeur*: "There can't have been that much accumulated suffering over so many centuries just to wipe us out at the end."

Kazin is somewhat less apocalyptic, but apprehensive all the same:

What happens to Jews in one country affects them in other countries. It's contagious. It's like the bloody assassins of the president. One takes up after another. There's no question about it. Anti-Semitism has increased everywhere as a result of the attacks on Israel.

Morgenthau, who lived long enough to declare that his concern for Israel and his involvement in being a Jew were directly related, went on in this vein: "If Israel were destroyed tomorrow it would demonstrate the monumental failure of Judaism." His frame of reference was social and political. Whether or not he felt personally imperiled, a debacle in Israel would result in the diminution of his "consciousness as a Jew." That consciousness had grown with the years from 1967 until his death in 1980. Earlier he thought of Israel as "a nation of schnorrers," a people who survived on handouts. The war of 1967 changed all that. It proved the Israelis could stand on their own two feet: "I remember vividly being in a cab here (in New York) immediately after the war. I started talking to the driver. I didn't know that he was Jewish until he turned back to me and said, 'I am a Hebrew and I'm proud of it.' It was this transformation that also took place in me." Morgenthau was proud of the triumphant way in which Israel overcame its enemies. For him it was a kind of biblical victory: "You could imagine the cohorts of God fighting the battle of the Jew." And yet he knew the underside of this victory, that it "created a deeper contempt for the Arabs." For, more than anything, certain Jewish values, above all justice, appeared finally to have made his ancestral faith attractive to him. Starting out as a "German who by accident went to church on Saturday rather than Sunday," Morgenthau became a reader of the Yiddish press (all but incredible for a German Jew) and a man who patiently sought out an audience with the learned and pious Lubavitcher Rebbe (absolutely incredible). That he came to terms with his Jewishness on a positive basis meant much more than abstract admiration for a people possessed of martial virtues.

To Percival Goodman, those virtues are repugnant. A frequent visitor to Israel, he regards it not as a homeland but ideally as a spiritual center, a place that should not specialize in making commodities but in "manufacturing peace." Asked by "a group of nutty Orthodox men" to rebuild the Temple in Jerusalem,

Goodman told them that he would do it when the Messiah comes (mindful perhaps of Franz Kafka's observation that the Messiah will come on the day after the day after). As soon as he first landed at Lod Airport, Goodman began to doubt that Israel was on the right track. "There was a busybody stamping passports," a procedure that seemed to him to be un-Jewish. "Hadn't Jews had problems enough with this sort of thing? Documents! I felt that Israel should be open, that the UN ought to be in Jerusalem, that the big Israeli export should not be refrigerators, turnips, or oranges. It should be peace. . . . If they had gone into the peace business, Israelis wouldn't have the problems that bedevil them." In Goodman's opinion William Blake had a better understanding of Zion than many Jews. Blake saw Zion as "an image, a utopia, something we aspire to." Furthermore, "The Jew is *not* somebody from Judea, not any more. Two thousand years have made the Jew an international being."

Such a Jew is paradigmatic. If Goodman thinks that the UN should be located in Jerusalem, Yip Harburg is convinced that New York *is* the United Nations. Among its inhabitants, there are "more Jews than in Jerusalem, more Italians than in Rome," and it is "Puerto Rico's home away from home." All this

. . . gives the city a unique vibration, a feeling of constant renewal—evolution—rebirth. The ridiculousness of racial barriers is emphasized, and national enmity reduced to absurdity. It is still practical to see the possibility of a world united—if not in Gucci's, at least in Macy's basement.

Walter Mehring, the German Jewish poet, wrote of Berlin before Hitler that it was a Weltstadt, a city open to the world. Intellectuals need such a city. All intellectuals, whether Jews or gentiles, but Jews more so since for them nothing less than individualism, pluralism, and ecumenicism will do. A closing of cultural ranks is the deadliest possibility. It flies in the face of Jefferson's dictum, "United we fall. *Divided* we stand": so long as no single group can lord it over the others, all are free. Such a balance does obtain in New York City. Jews, particularly those who devoted themselves to reading, writing, studying, and creating, were long thought to be equally homeless everywhere. For the present at least they are much more at home in the city that harbors a great many of them. But Jewish intellectuals of today are disenthralled. They have been at home for a while in Berlin and Warsaw—and in Kutno, the birthplace of Isaiah Trunk, who miraculously survived and returned only to discover that Polish Jews were not admitted to their own former homes. Can there ever again be scales on the eyes of a man who learns that, "After all the Polish people had been through, we Jews were still the enemy"? Did it matter that a country once populous with Jews was suddenly "Judenfrei"? Not at all: "We've learned that Jew-hatred does not require the presence of a single Jew! Polish anti-Semites made war against ghosts; there were no Jews." Evidently there is more than one way to be "a haunted Jew."

The last word can never be said on this subject. We do, however, rather like the comment of Soma Morgenstern, a twice-displaced man of letters, as the next-to-last word: "I'm an un-hyphenated Jew, with my roots in my shoes, and I feel most comfortable in New York because there are more Jews here than in Israel." Or could Ernst Toller, the German Jewish playwright who made it to New York too late, have come closer to the mark when he noted in his memoirs that ". . . if I were asked where I belonged I should answer that a Jewish mother had borne me, that Germany had nourished me, that Europe had formed me, that my home was the earth, and the world my fatherland"? *Pari passu*, with the necessary American adjustments this statement speaks for most—no statement speaks for all—of us New York Jewish intellectuals, the interviewers as well as the interviewed.

Or would it be more appropriate to end with a joke? After all, Jews *invented* gallows humor. And wit may be found on every other page of this book. It is a strand in our mosaic that, for lack of space, we have had to omit from this introduction. We have also not discussed the Jewish intellectuals' special affinity for blacks—brilliantly elucidated by the jazz historian Dan Morgenstern and the great wordsmith Yip Harburg; and the black–Jewish friction, of which few people have a better grasp than Diane Ravitch; and many more plots in every narrative, each with its subtle subplots.

We happened to have heard the joke in a public address by our friend Shlomo Katz, who raised the question: Why are American Jews concentrated on the East Coast and the West Coast? Answer: for the same reason that phobic people insist on aisle seats. There may be a fire.

He became a disturber of the intellectual peace, but only at the cost of becoming an intellectual wayfaring man, a wanderer in the intellectual no-man's-land, seeking another place to rest, farther along the road, somewhere over the horizon.

Thorstein Veblen, "The Intellectual Pre-Eminence of Jews in Modern Europe"

PART ONE

THE EUROPEAN IMMIGRANTS

THE YIDDISH WRITER
AND HIS AUDIENCE

Isaac B. Singer

I CAME to this country from Poland in 1935. My brother, I. J. Singer, was here and, like any other Jew who foresaw what would happen in Europe, I wanted to leave Poland. I did not know exactly what to expect, but I had read a few books and articles about America. One of them was a book called *OK* by the Russian writer Pilnyak whom Stalin later liquidated. He made fun of America and of New York, but I was still left with a great desire to go there. He said it was full of cars and full of money; I decided that cars and money were not such a terrible thing.

I arrived on May 1, 1935. My name was little known in Poland and even less here, although I was not totally unknown. The writers here read the magazines from Poland, just as we read their magazines. Most of the best Yiddish writers were here, and names like Levick, Opatoshu, Leyeless, and Hirschbein were not unfamiliar to me.

From *OK*, I imagined that every house was a skyscraper and that the streets were full of people. But it so happened that when I came I was taken downtown, straight to the *Jewish Daily Forward*, and then to Seagate, and it was kind of an anticlimax. It looked too idyllic. I stayed at first in Seagate which was, so to speak, a village, near Coney Island. When I finally saw Coney Island, I

Isaac Bashevis Singer was born in Poland in 1904. He came to the United States in 1935 and worked as a journalist on the *Jewish Daily Forward* in New York City. He is a prolific novelist and writer of short stories in Yiddish. His books include *The Spinoza of Market Street and Other Stories* (1961) and *Enemies: A Love Story* (1972). Singer won the Nobel Prize for literature in 1978.

said, "Yes, this is New York." It was noisy, it was colorful—
mostly noisy. To a degree it corresponded to the images in my
mind from *OK*. But reality never corresponds to writing or to
painting or to anything else. I went to work for the *Forward*
immediately, but only as a freelancer. It wasn't a regular job. I
just published one article at a time, and they paid me for each one.

When I got here, it was still Depression time, Everyone I met
told me about losing great sums of money in the stock market—
fifty or a hundred thousand dollars—fantastic sums of money to
me. I could not believe that these simple people were so rich.
Later I understood that they did lose a great deal: the stocks went
up and then went down. So there was the Depression and everybody talked about his losses. But just the same, people were
dressed well and they ate well.

Personally, you might say I had a hard time. I needed at least
fifteen dollars a week to live. This was not a lot of money but I
couldn't earn it. I sent a story to the *Jewish Daily Forward*. They
kept it for four weeks. Then they called me up: the editor wanted
to discuss the story with me. Meanwhile, I had to pay rent, which
wasn't easy, but somehow it did not really depress me. Although
there was an economic depression, *I* did not feel depressed. I
managed. How? Well, everything was cheap. You could go into
a cafeteria and eat a dinner for thirty-five cents, or even less. I
brought clothes with me from Poland. Books I could get for
nothing in the libraries. Paper and ink were also cheap.

I wandered about in various New York neighborhoods. I
lived in Brooklyn for a time. I lived in Williamsburg. But I didn't
explore that part of the city in order to be able to write. I lived
there and naturally I saw and heard things. Now I live in Manhattan.

New York has changed. When I arrived in this city you could
walk on the Boardwalk or through Central Park at night and
nobody bothered you. I saw people sleeping on benches. Now
it is a different society. As far as security is concerned the change
is just terrible. In my time people were not afraid to go out in the
evening. That they can't go out now is to me the greatest misfortune in New York. Of course, it has affected my life. I'm afraid
to go out even to buy a newspaper in the evening. And yet I love

New York, and I like the West Side. It's a big city and you have more privacy here than anywhere else in the world. Even when my picture appears in many newspapers and magazines and I have a play on Broadway, no one knows me. I walk in the streets and I'm just nobody. I like that. I wouldn't enjoy working in a little town where everybody said hello to me and knew me and all about me. Privacy is a wonderful thing. It's good to walk in the streets, to be with yourself, not meeting others all the time. Lately, I do meet people who say "hello" to me and "I read your book." But two steps away no one knows me.

I never seriously considered living anywhere else but New York. Why? First, because the *Jewish Daily Forward* where I was working then, and am still working, is here. My publisher is here. Also, it is a big city, and I'm a big city boy. I was born in Warsaw which was a noisy, dusty city just like New York. Also, I do not drive a car, so for me to live in the country is to live in prison. I have to live in New York. To a degree, it reminds me of Warsaw, mainly, I suppose, on account of the many Jews. I see my people here. Here there are still Jews who speak my language and even if they don't speak it, their parents did, and thus they know a little. To me, Jewishness is not only a religion; it's a way of life. And even though that way of life has been distorted, there are still remnants left. What Americans call Orthodox we would have called assimilated or Reformed. Today the difference is not so great. In the thirties there were very few Orthodox American Jews. And there were many Socialists. But I saw Yiddish newspapers on the street, I saw Jewish people. Since I wrote and still write only about Jewish life, many of my readers were here in New York. Recently I began to write about Jewish life in New York. In the first thirty years I didn't because I felt that I understood too little about the city or its way of life. Now I have lived in New York more years than I did in Poland. I finally feel that I know New York quite well. But still I only write about Yiddish-speaking people from Poland, never about people whose only language is English.

I did not associate much with the writers when I first came here. In Poland I did, but here they looked like strangers to me. Some of them were considered to be great writers. I did not think they were so great, and they might have know about it. So I kept away.

I was not involved in politics. Naturally, I was concerned about it. I wanted Hitler to be defeated. But I am not a man of politics. I wasn't then and I'm still not today. I always knew that politics is a waste of time for a writer. I had enough freedom here. In Poland there was less freedom, but even there I could write what I wanted. Here Roosevelt was president and he spoke about the Four Freedoms. There were plenty of fighters for freedom without me. I felt that it was most important for me to do my work.

After a number of years they made me a member of the *Forward's* staff, on a weekly salary, which I still get today. For many, many years I needed them; now I may say they need me. I feel that since I needed them for so many years it would not be right to abandon them now, although it is time for me to have a little rest. But every time I decide to stop I suddenly get an idea for a novel or a story and it starts all over again. The readership of the *Forward* is shrinking, but it still has about forty-thousand readers and I assure you that they read me. If I make a mistake, I get forty-thousand letters (which is an exaggeration), but they really write! Once I wrote by mistake that the worshippers recited Yizkor (a memorial service for the dead) on Rosh Hashana. I got a million letters. "Yizkor on Rosh Hashana!"

To write about New York, you have to know the streets and you have to know how people speak. Although people speak Yiddish in this city, it is different from the Yiddish they spoke in Poland. I had to know just how Jews spoke Yiddish *here*. As a matter of fact, in Poland I only wrote about a small part of that country, the part where I lived, around Lublin and Warsaw. I would never have written about Białystok or Vilna because I didn't know their language as well. And without knowing all the nuances of the language, I couldn't know the people's way of thinking well enough, especially their emotions which are deeply connected with language.

There is so much correspondence between a language and a way of thinking. Yiddish here has many English idioms and I had to learn them all before I dared to write. In Poland I was satisfied

The old *Forward* building on the East Side.   YIVO INSTITUTE FOR JEWISH RESEARCH.

to be limited to my region, to my few towns, and now if I write about people speaking Yiddish I mostly write about people in New York; although the people in New York and Chicago speak approximately the same Yiddish, so many of their idioms are borrowed from the English. For example, here people say for "making a living," "Ich mach a leben." In Poland they say, "Ich hob parnoosoh."* It's a different word and a different notion altogether. There are thousands of idioms used in American Yiddish taken from the English and because they use these idioms I have to know them.

Yet I have no great desire to write in English except now and then an essay or a review. Fiction I would only write in Yiddish. But in time I began to translate my work, always with a collaborator. So I've got quite a good idea of the English language. My audience in English is certainly bigger than in Yiddish. And not only in English but also in Italian, in German, in Japanese. Everything I write gets quickly translated into Japanese. I don't consider all this as such a success; neither am I particularly surprised by it. I read Japanese writers or Italian writers. There's no reason why they shouldn't read me.

A number of Yiddish critics have claimed that I broke with the tradition of Yiddish writing, and they are right. I did not go their way because the Yiddish writers were both sentimental and social, very sentimental and very social. They constantly fought for what they thought was a just world. They scolded the rich and praised the poor. I never felt that this was my function in literature. I was interested in specific stories and individual, exceptional people.

I am besieged on the telephone. It rings all day long. But I like to be in contact with people because they tell me stories. Instead of interviewing me, I interview them. People are so willing to tell their life stories that it's really astonishing to me. I have a talent whereby after speaking with people for ten minutes they tell me their life stories. Some of them probably come to me with that intention. Just as I like to write stories, I like to hear stories.

* Special attention has been given to the faithful transliteration of Yiddish terms. In this case, the editors tried to retain the sound of Singer's "parnoosoh" instead of the accepted "parnasah."

I'm convinced that every human being has at least twenty stories to tell—his or her stories. Mostly I'm interested in people's sex life, or call it love life. I write about this. It changes all the time but the more it changes the more it is the same. I would say, nevertheless, that modern man has become so free in sexual matters that it is perhaps something new in history. In Poland the problem was always how to make a living. People were poor and undernourished and sick. They spoke about jobs, particularly about how to get them. Here people are not so poor; they eat and dress well; most of them have good homes. Their sex and love life has become very important. They're not embarrassed about discussing it.

I feel that there is no literature without love. There has never been a good novel about anything except love. Try to write a novel about how a bank was founded, how a factory was organized, how a government changed—it will bore you stiff. You must have a love story. Of course, you can put many things into it. The reason we call a novel (*roman*) a "romance" is because it's a love story.

In olden times people felt that sin was connected with sex. Today's people do not think there is such a thing as sin or crime in sex as long as they don't kill anybody. There is a great curiosity about sex and love today, more than in earlier times. This attitude is an outcome of the present situation. It is also an outcome of beliefs. It is an outcome of many things. Actually, everything is an outcome of many things: if you say that this ashtray stays here, you may then ask, "Why does it stay here and not in the air?" Your answer would be: "Because of gravity." And why there is gravity you don't know. Since the ashtray is attracted to all the bodies in the universe, this ashtray is connected to all of creation. And so is the brain, the human spirit.

Yes, the critics were right: I broke with tradition. To me, even Peretz was sentimental, less so than Sholom Aleichem, but sentimental all the same. I departed from that tradition without especially planning to do so. My first book was *Satan in Goray* which is a book about demons, sexual orgies at the time of the false Messiah, Sabbatai Tzevi, about the supernatural, and psychic phenomena. Such subjects were never touched before in Yiddish literature. A Yiddish story was often about a poor young man in a little *shtetl* (small Jewish town in Eastern Europe) who fell in love with the daughter of a rich man who didn't want him for a son-in-law. This type of stuff did not speak to me. It was provincial, silly.

I am very much rooted in Jewishness but not in modern Yiddishness. I write about Jewish people. I write about epochs in Jewish life even hundreds of years ago. I know the Talmud and studied the cabala (Jewish mystical movement). I'm more versed in Jewishness than many of the Yiddish writers who were brought up by ignorant parents. Jewishness, yes. But Yiddishism was connected very much with socialism and with making a better world. There was all this business with Marxism. It was not, as they say, my cup of tea. The critics said that I don't write in the *tradition* of the Yiddish writers and I said, "Yes, you're right. I don't and I don't need to."

I would say I was more influenced by non-Yiddish writers, because as a child I read Tolstoy, Dostoyevsky, and Flaubert. Of course, I read some of them in Yiddish, but they gave me another type of perspective. I got acquainted with world literature when I was very young (fifteen, sixteen) and I discovered a different approach. There was a library in town where I could read novelists like Knut Hamsun. I was delighted with Hamsun. I read Strindberg and Ibsen, all in Yiddish. Later on I learned Polish and began to read writers in Polish. Then I read them in German and became interested in philosophy. I was fifteen years old when I got to Spinoza's *Ethics* translated into German. I would say spiritually I did not remain in the environment of those who read only Yiddish.

And I read Americans like Edgar Allan Poe and I was delighted. I read Jack London's *The Call of the Wild* and liked it very much. I read Mark Twain translated into Yiddish or Polish. I even heard of Sinclair Lewis and Upton Sinclair in Poland. I met the English novelist, Galsworthy, once when I was in Warsaw where he came on a visit. I couldn't speak to him but at least I saw him.

My father complained bitterly about my reading secular works. He didn't let me do it, so I had to hide and do it behind his back. However, my father thought that reading books written by gentiles was less a sin than reading certain books by Jews because the godless Jews, in his opinion, made fun of Jewishness while the gentiles ignored it altogether. I wouldn't get scathed so much by Hamsun as by Peretz.

Looking at the Jewish writers today, I agree with my father. I think that Mendele really made fun of Jewishness. He criticized the Jews severely while Hamsun or Strindberg left them in peace altogether. Today there are so few Jewish writers left, there is really no one to talk about. Of Jews who write in English, well, they are like American writers. But I will tell you, when I read a book it has to be very good. If I'm not delighted by the first three pages I stop. Therefore, I read very few books written in the twentieth century. When I want to read fiction I go back to the nineteenth century, to the Russian, to the French, sometimes the English novelists.

I still think that Hamsun's first few books, *Pan, Victoria,* and *Hunger,* were masterpieces. Later he became a bad writer and a Nazi. When *Hunger* was published in an American edition, I wrote a preface. There I told about Hamsun's role in Europe, how deep his influence was, and I mentioned that it was a bad day for his admirers when he became a Nazi. (He was a man of spite and he became a Nazi to spite the Norwegians. He wasn't recognized in Norway; he was in Germany.) Hamsun did not resemble, say, someone like Maurice Chevalier. Chevalier was an opportunist who would even have become a Jew if there had been any money in it. Hamsun was in his own way a serious writer but he was spiteful and bitter.

When I came to this country, and during the war years, I felt like everyone else that we had to get rid of Hitler or the whole world would fall to pieces. This affected my work, and for the first seven or eight years in this country I wrote very little apart from my articles as a journalist. I stopped writing fiction. I felt there was no future for Yiddish. I never expected to be translated. (Besides I had personal problems.) But then in the early forties I began to write again and since then I've never stopped.

The formation of Israel had an effect on me. I have written a number of stories about Israel. The existence of that state is much more than a political phenomenon, and I was delighted when it became an independent country. But since I write in Yiddish and Hebrew is the language there, I never contemplated settling down in Israel. I knew that my readers were here and later on when I began to be translated into English I had readers here who read me in English. I still feel that, after Poland, this is my country. I love Israel; I've been there often; I have a son and four grandchildren in Israel, but I never think about living there. I would have given my son a very Jewish education but his mother became a Communist and took him with her to Russia. They remained for two years, and then they were kicked out. My first wife was one of those who always would wave the red flag. When they kicked her out of Russia she went to Israel and my boy was brought up in a kibbutz. So, after all, he got a Jewish education. He speaks Hebrew, writes in Hebrew, and is an editor for a Hebrew magazine. He is also a farmer and a schoolteacher. He knows a little Yiddish, not as much as he should, but he understands it. He has just translated my book *Enemies: A Love Story* into Hebrew and I'm going to edit it.

In this atmosphere, I'm stimulated enough to be able to write. For years I wrote without any success; now I have a little recognition. I go out lecturing and speak to thousands of people (a few weeks ago I spoke to almost four thousand people). People come over to me and make me sign my books. Scores of them say to me, "You've given us so much pleasure." I don't know what kind of pleasure I've given them, but since they say so I'm ready to believe them.

One of my lectures is called "My Philosophy as A Jewish Writer." It's connected with the cabala, with mysticism. Another one is "The Cabala and Modern Man." Yet another is "The Autobiography of Yiddish." I am for Yiddish. I think people who want to call themselves Jews should be interested in Yiddish because it contains a culture of the Ashkenazi Jews (Jews from Central or Eastern Europe) that covers seven or eight hundred years. Zionism was made in Yiddish and so was the Jewish version of socialism and Hasidism. You cannot be a Jewish writer and not know about these things. You must know Hebrew, too. However, if you only know Hebrew, write about Jews who speak Hebrew; if you write about Jews who speak Yiddish your Hebrew will not help you: you will write like a stranger. I don't write about Jews who speak Hebrew, although I know Hebrew very well. I do the editing of my Hebrew translations. I could sit down and write a story in Hebrew, but I don't write about Jews who speak Hebrew, just as I didn't write about Jews who lived in Vilna: their language is not my mother tongue. I don't know it as thoroughly as I know the language of people from Lublin or Warsaw.

How do I feel about the revival of religion here? I think it's nice that people do go back to religion because, with all my many doubts, I'm a believer. I believe in God! I once said that whenever I'm troubled I pray and since I'm always in trouble I always pray. I'm religious but at the same time I don't flatter the Almighty. I say He has created a murderous world and I have moments when I hate Him for creating it and for doing so much wrong to the animals. To me the Holocaust did not begin in 1939. To me the Holocaust began from the moment man was created. From reading I know very well that the whole history of humanity is one big holocaust, with some short interruptions. One hundred thousand people, or at least sixty thousand people, perished in one day around Verdun. Wasn't that a holocaust? Naturally, I suffered more when I heard that Jews had suffered. But the whole history of humanity is one big holocaust. I have a kind of imagination that makes things that happened ten thousand years ago seem as present as things that happened yesterday. Even before the Hitler destruction I had the feeling that human life is one big slaughter. That was my feeling. Not just as a Jew. As a human being.

The Holocaust was a link in a chain of holocausts. I am convinced that although men are so jittery about their health and about prolonging their lives, you can always get them to slaughter other people, thereby endangering or losing their own lives. If, today, politicians made propaganda saying let's go and conquer Mexico or Canada, we need a million people, there would immediately be a million people ready for the adventure. I can never reconcile myself to this. Although I am a religious man I know that it's actually God's fault. It's how He created people. What Malthus said is true. There is not enough food for all creatures. Consequently they have to fight. God has made it so. He may have a good reason for it, but I'm full of protest about it. I don't consider God good. I consider Him mighty, I respect His wisdom, but I don't see His mercy. When I read about little children carried on points of bayonets I say there is no mercy in a God who sees this and remains silent, no matter what the motivation may be. And how about the animals? I'm a vegetarian. When I see how much the animals suffer, how they are mistreated and slaughtered. . . . To me, our treatment of animals is proof that there is not much to hope for from human morality.

Also, when I see how murderers walk about free to kill people and how eager the lawyers, judges, and do-gooders are to help the murderers and ignore their victims, I have no hope for any system. I do not believe that a socialistic system would help. The Russians and the Chinese are both Communist, but give the Chinese a chance and they will attack Russia and kill millions of people in the name of communism—just as Stalin killed twenty million Russians because he suspected them of being Trotskyists or anarchists.

Some of God's commands I do obey. Not all. I am not sure that God revealed Himself and told us exactly what to do. So I have my own way of thinking what is right and what is wrong. That the Ten Commandments are basically right—about this there is no question in my mind. I have my doubts about God's goodness, as you know. Although God may be good, I don't see it. I believe in free choice, but by that I do not mean you can do anything you want. You can't walk on the ceiling like a fly. You have to walk on the ground. But we are all free to choose between lesser evil and greater evil. Just to control yourself partially is a big achievement.

There is not much goodness, but I don't deny there is some. The Almighty shows His wisdom in having created the sun and the moon and the grass, the earth, and the flowers. But then He destroys His creatures as mercilessly as He created them. God has created us so that what a man builds in a year another man can destroy in a second. You just light a match and the house burns. Because the power of destruction works so much more effectively than the power of construction, the bad ones really control the world.

Israel may be a new thing in history. That so many people should go back to a country which they left two thousand years ago and go back to their ancestral language is a unique case. But again, it is connected with so much suffering. They went back to Israel because they were persecuted. The gentiles had always said to the Jews, "Go back to Palestine." Now that they have gone back to Palestine, they're being told, "Go back to Poland, go back to Russia." Persecution is in the nature of human beings. Take one who is persecuted today, give him a little rest, and he will persecute others.

My roots are in Jewish life, but my way of thinking needn't be Jewish. Jews don't think that the whole of life is one big holocaust. Some of them are highly optimistic. They are sure that sooner or later, something will bring redemption. A leader will do it! I don't believe this. They have tried the League of Nations and the United Nations. I have no real hope that humanity will ever be redeemed.

I'm not upset about Jewish life of our time. As long as the Jewish people live and they are left in peace, I'm satisfied. I don't criticize *them*. They're not as pious as they were, but let them be what they want. As long as they let me be what I am, they can be what they are. I try to describe them as I see them. I'm not a writer with a message. I don't preach anything. I don't write about *the* Jews. I write about a particular person. If I say that a man named so-and-so is *meshugah* (crazy), it doesn't mean that all men are *meshugah*, or if another man is a swindler, I don't mean that all men are swindlers. I am not a sociologizer. I don't even say "such men" are like that. I refer only to this particular person. For me it's enough to write about an individual. I don't need him to be a symbol. I say that just like one's fingerprints, every human being is different. If I write about one man, I mean one man. Not all men, not all Jews.

I think that a person who really wants to be a Jew should know everything about Jewishness: the Bible and the Talmud, Hasidism and the cabala if he wants to be a one hundred percent

Jew. But Jewishness is not an either/or. There are grades. You can be a Jew simply by birth. You can be a Jew because you belong to the synagogue. You can be a Jew like my father for whom Jewishness was the very air he breathed. I am not so much like my father. He saw the world through the Holy Books. My father never knew about Newton, Darwin, Malthus. I read that the earth is older than six thousand years. I could not have been as hypnotized by the old books as my father was because I heard the other side. Even the Lubavitcher (head of a Hasidic sect) is not the same kind of Jew as my father; the Lubavitcher went to college and he may have his doubts. I'm not sure about that. I know that although Jews are a people for themselves, just the same they're part of humanity and they have all the good sides and the bad sides of humanity.

Yet I do think that the Jew is intellectual. Even an ignorant Jew is a *potential* intellectual. Jews are born intellectuals—which doesn't mean that they are born good. They are thinking people. I don't know why. Jews think, they like books, they go to colleges and to universities. You see a tailor and ask what his son is doing. He says, "My son is an astronomer. He is a professor." There are many reasons for it, which I won't go into because I'm not a sociologist. Perhaps because Judaism was persecuted, sooner or later the ignorant, the anti-intellectual, had no reason to stay. They left. Who stayed with the Jews? Generation after generation of believers, scholars, and because they did not intermarry, we have a great reservoir of intelligence among the Jews.

About the survival of Yiddish—I don't think many people will speak Yiddish one hundred years from now, but I'm sure they will investigate the language. There'll be a lot of research on Yiddish. Many people get Ph.D.s in Yiddish studies, and they will get thousands of them in the future. In fact, some have already got their Ph.D.s writing about me.

I speak Yiddish and I love it as my mother tongue, but I'm not so hot that others should know it. If people ask me about a book, I will answer them, or write a review, but I don't go out in the streets and scream, "Here is a good book. You should all read it." I'm not by nature a propagandist. It's hard to explain.

If Yiddish disappeared it would be my personal tragedy, but I wouldn't call it a world tragedy. When human beings suffer hunger and sickness and when they are afflicted by crime, this bothers me. I'm bothered when I think how many innocent people die from all kinds of causes, suffer from cancer, heart trouble, whatnot. I always see before my eyes the hospitals, the invalids, the innocent victims. I felt this when I was eight years old. Here I see violence on the streets with my very eyes. In Warsaw I read about it in the newspapers which also bothered me terribly, but here you look out the window and you see it. My compassion has always been not only for mankind, but for the animals. The idea of a slaughterhouse makes me miserable.

This is a very grim view, but even so, at the same time I have written very funny stories. It is well known that humorists are pessimists and vice versa. The only philosopher who was somewhat of a humorist was Schopenhauer—and he was a great pessimist. The pessimist sees also the ridiculous side of the coin. The humorist sees mostly how easy it is to hypnotize people, to make fools of them, and how many fools God has created who don't even need to be hypnotized. They are born fools!

The intensity of suffering does not have to be always the same. It's sometimes more, but if there were never any repose humanity would not exist and the animals would not exist either. There's no hope, no universal hope. There may be hope for some people, let's say young men who make their careers, become professors or bankers. But if you think about creation generally, there is no hope. There will never be any real justice, never any prolonged repose. The strong will always rule the weak and step on them. . . .

Art cannot make me forget the tragedy of the world. I write for my own gratification and also for the gratification of my readers. They come to me and they say, "You saved my life, you made me happy." I don't think I can do that, they say so . . . I don't really believe it—a novel can't do that.

I think that basically Malthus was the greatest sociologist and thinker. He saw the real misfortune. All the others had a remedy: they said, "Do this, do that." Malthus said there's nothing we can do. Birth control might help, but if ten nations use birth control and the eleventh doesn't, it will become the strongest and conquer the other ten. So if the Chinese refuse to have birth control, the Russians must refuse, and the Americans must refuse, and so on. The net result is that we can't do anything.

What's most important for the remainder of my life? I would like peace in New York and to be able to live out my years in New York, but I'm not hopeful. I wouldn't like New York to go bankrupt, but there is very little I can do about it. It's possible they'll do something about it. The quality of life matters to me, but since I have given up hope of creating what they call a better world, nothing is of great importance. Now (1975) I have a play on Broadway called *Yentl*; it's an entertaining play, not pretentious, not full of aphorisms. It has changed somewhat from what I wrote. I wrote the story about Yentl who wanted to be a scholar. I had a collaborator who tried to generalize it and give *Yentl* a sociological tint. I take it tongue-in-cheek. I think there are very few great plays in the world! A good play is really as rare as a pink elephant.

After I arrived in New York I went once in a while to the Yiddish theater. I liked it because the actors spoke my language and they always entertained me. The plays were bad but somehow the actors managed to entertain the audience. Lately they write plays that don't entertain. They write plays for the *feinschmeckers*, for the elite, for people who like allusions to Joyce and Kafka. When I go to the theater I want to see a love story with humor and a little joy, not to convince myself how erudite I am. I don't give a hoot for all these allusions to Joyce. As a matter of fact, I don't read Joyce. A theater is not made so you can sit there and recognize a passage from Joyce. A theater is made to entertain. No entertainment—no theater!

Strindberg wrote a few good plays; however, he is such a great writer that you cannot really put him on the stage—his work is literature. Strindberg's theater isn't really a war between the sexes; it is his personal war, his truth. For me, however, the truth about one man is just as important as the truth about ten million. Strindberg was a completely jealous man who could not stand the idea that if he were not here his woman might have married another. That kind of jealousy is an obsession. Nowadays people are not so obsessed by it. The hippies and others tried unsuccessfully to root out jealousy. It's a human feeling and it can be intensified to a very high degree. If we concentrate on one feeling it becomes a neurosis or a madness. There is a thing that Spinoza said which I consider great. It's not philosophy but psychology. He said everything can become a passion. And when Spinoza says "everything" he means everything. This is absolutely true. Concentrate on anything and it becomes very big. Passion exaggerated cannot be a good thing. Again Spinoza, "If any emotion becomes too intense, there will be great suffering." Even a passion for justice becomes a cruelty. A man with a passion for justice would like to kill all the people who are not just, and after a while he will create an Inquisition. It is true that Jews have a stronger sense of justice than non-Jews. But even so, if the Jews have a chance, they may also persecute. At present they are better than the others, a little better, but far from good. My passion for justice to animals is good only as long as I have no power. If I had great power I would kill the whole lot of hunters. I would do bad things.

I started writing for children when an old friend of mine, whom I have known for thirty years, became an editor at Harper and Row. She had been after me to write children's stories; she bothered me until eight or nine years ago I sat down and wrote "Zlateh the Goat." Since then I have been a writer for children. I think children are the best readers. A child does not read because there is a message. He will not read because the book was advertised or got good reviews. For him to read a book it must be interesting. He will not read a boring book like students who do it because the professor tells them to. So to me a child is the best reader.

Am I a New York Jew? I have lived in New York for forty years. You cannot run away from the environment. There are three million Jews in New York, but I always deal in my work with one particular Jew. I'll tell you why to me the story of one man is enough. Men are created in the image of God and therefore they have very little mercy! They create stereotypes to be able to persecute other people, to spit on them, to say bad things. If you ask a Frenchman from Brittany about other Frenchmen of, say, Provence, he will declare that they are pigs and should be killed. As a matter of fact, the German states, until the latter half of the nineteenth century, used to wage wars with one another. All they need are a few politicians and a little propaganda and they will fight again.

I see us all as miserable creatures who did not ask to be born. We fight for things, we are fooled, we are disappointed, I don't deny sociology, I don't deny environment. I say that this concern is not really my occupation. I look for the spiritual fingerprints, for that which makes people different one from the other. I know we have millions of qualities in common with one another, but I look for what it is that makes each one of us different. For what is common let others look. To me, individuality is the very essence of art. The moment an artist tries to generalize he is lost to art. I do generalize, but only in conversation. When I sit down to write, my subject is every man's ability to be a little different from the others. I deal not with what unites people but with what separates them and makes everyone unhappy and misunderstood in his or her own way.

2.

FROM A RUSSIAN *SHTETL* TO THE FOUNDING OF *MIDSTREAM*

Shlomo Katz

I RECENTLY rediscovered my birth certificate. The date, 1909, is fairly clear. It's an ancient, faded little document signed by a Russian "government" rabbi: "so-and-so was born to so-and-so and his name was entered in the Jewish registry of births." This event took place in a very small town in the southwestern Ukraine. To give people some idea of its location, I tell them that it was twenty miles from a larger city named Balta, famous for its pogroms. That's one way to establish geographical coordinates.

The pogroms I remember vividly. When the Tsarist army disintegrated, officers of various political complexions organized loose bands which, lacking a central authority, terrorized entire districts. There were also outrages perpetrated by the Ukrainian and White armies. It was a huge thing, this business of creating fear and insecurity. It began when I was very small. Even before 1917 the Russian army wasn't doing very well; recruits passing on their way to the front or soldiers coming from the front had considerable liberty. The boys had to rest up, and this meant heavy drinking, beating up Jews, sometimes killing them. Memories and tales of the pogroms of 1905 were still fresh, and were

Shlomo Katz was born in Russia in 1909. He came to America with his family as a child and grew up in Minnesota. In the thirties he came to New York City where he worked as an editor on the *Jewish Frontier*. He was the founding editor of *Midstream* magazine, and a writer of short stories and articles as well as a translator from the Yiddish. Katz died in 1979.

absorbed by youngsters who hadn't themselves experienced them. In relation to what became a permanent sense of insecurity, all these were major factors.

When the Bolsheviks took over our town in 1921 there were no pogroms. We also had no newspapers or mail service. Hearsay and rumors were our sources of information, and the countryside was still infested with marauders. So when an opportunity presented itself, we fled. But at first, for Jewish kids in towns like ours, the term Bolshevik was something to revere. There was a popular Yiddish song. A mother asks her daughter, "*Wu bist du geschlufen, tochter meine getrie?*" (Where did you sleep, my dear daughter?) And the daughter answers, "*Unter a brik, mit a Bolshevik, momme s'iz gevezen a mechayeh.*" (Under a bridge, with a Bolshevik, Mother it was a pleasure.) This is just cute stuff, but many young people became deeply involved.

We didn't know then that the Bolsheviks practiced their terror from the very beginning in larger cities. But in a little town like ours—they came in, set up a revolutionary committee, and that was that. So if we were sympathetic to them, it was largely because they imparted a sense of physical security to us.

They also confiscated many belongings and levied "contributions" on the more affluent. Well, we knew that worse things could happen. They organized a free public library. Their acquisitions method was simple. Committees went from house to house and took whatever books they liked. Two Red Army men came to our house. We had a lot of books. They examined them, and their attention was caught by a two-volume edition of Friedrich Nietzsche. A difficult and unfamiliar name. And they were not too literate. They read it as "Nischchiy." *Nischchiy* means "poor" in Russian. The writings of "Frederick the Poor" seemed suitable fare for a public library in a Soviet-ruled town.

Apart from all this, the main influence in my early years was Zionism. One could almost say that I was born a Zionist. Aside from the religious home environment and learning the Bible in *cheder* (Hebrew school), Zionism was in the air. I remember discussing with other kids—at the age of five or so—which is the bigger country, Palestine (we invariably called it Eretz Yisrael) or Russia? We concluded that Palestine was bigger. The proof was self-evident. There is the Bible and on every page it talks about Canaan and Judah and Israel, while Russia isn't mentioned once. We thought like the ancient Egyptian muralists. Pharaoh is tallest, his minister a little shorter, the conquered princes bearing tribute are just little midgets. But mainly, I suppose, it was the overall mood that influenced us. Events of the preceding years upset whatever old equilibrium had existed. Young people dreamed of a socialist Jewish homeland in—where else?—Eretz Yisrael.

My secular education ran parallel to my *cheder* education and this was a heavy burden. You went to *cheder* all day, and then you came home and had to work on arithmetic, geography, and Russian declensions. The last year that we were in town there was no more *cheder*. The new regime disapproved. But there was a modern Talmud Torah (Hebrew school) with some fine teachers, but it lasted only one season. The number of pupils decreased as families emigrated. One of the last teachers to leave organized the still remaining kids into a Hebrew-speaking club that met weekly. One member of the club had an older brother who was a big wheel in the local Revolutionary Committee and he sent us a message: "Disband! Hebrew-speaking groups are not wanted under the new regime." We staged a demonstration before the Revcom headquarters. Someone ran out with a broom and chased us away. That spring of 1921 we left.

Zionism pervaded many aspects of life. We were in *golus* (exile), of course. The pogroms and persecutions proved it. The language testified to it. Anything that was protracted was "long as the *golus* . . ."

In the mind of a child the idea of the return to Palestine sometimes took on weird forms. One day it was "unquiet" in town—this means that nothing had happened yet but there were rumors of an impending pogrom. My mother, who was a very nervous and imaginative woman, ordered us: "Stay indoors." It was a beautiful spring day. We lived on the edge of town in a mixed neighborhood of Jews, Ukrainians, and Russians. Some of the gentile kids were playing outside. Rolling a hoop was our favorite game. And here I was indoors, looking through a crack in the door, watching them, and I decided then and there, "When I grow up, I'll be in Jerusalem, in our own Jewish country. And there I'll make a pogrom on them." You think I meant to hurt them? Lord, no! But there *they* would have a stay indoors and I would be running around outside.

We had relatives in Minnesota. Around 1920 we received a little note from them by messenger, "Let us know who of you is still alive and we'll try to bring you over." We smuggled across the border to Rumania and spent on entire year presenting affidavits to American consulates. But they finally gave us our papers. And so one beautiful cold January day we got off the train in St. Paul, and the relatives were there to meet us. We boarded a couple of taxis and there was St. Paul: two-storied wooden houses, snow-covered lawns with some trees on them, overarching elms covered with rime, and hardly a soul to be seen—an enchanted winter scene. And, outwardly at least, unbelievably peaceful.

When I finished high school I went to Chicago where I worked for a while, returned to St. Paul, then went to New York. Going to New York was, in a way, taken for granted all along. There were the boyhood dreams of growing up and taking off. But it was also a retracing of one's steps. In New York I automatically linked up with the Labor Zionist crowd—and yet I no longer quite belonged among them either. They were mostly Yiddish speaking. I knew Yiddish, but one doesn't live in the Midwest from age twelve to eighteen without being stamped by it in more ways than language. True, I was in many ways an alien in the Midwest, but it had also become a part of me.

Let me explain. Have you ever heard of Oelewein? It is, or was a railway junction of sorts in Iowa. During the Depression, in the course of my peregrinations, I often rode in the cabooses of freight trains. Often for many hours they stopped at Oelewein, probably waiting for shipments from farther west. Did you ever hear corn growing? Oelewein is a place where one can hear it grow. I heard it. Lying around waiting for the train to get ready. In the summer, in Iowa, cornfields all around, and each time a leaf unfolds, there is a little rustle. You take them all together and there is a kind of whispering . . .

In my early twenties I went to Palestine. I lived there for two years and worked in kibbutzim. Come to think of it, I am still basically a kibbutznik at heart to this day.

A while back I cited a ditty which glorified the early Bolsheviks. In another version of that song, when asked by her mother where she had slept, the daughter answers, *"Oif a boidem hay, mit chalutzim zwei.* (In a hayloft, with two *chalutzim.*) The *chalutz*—the pioneer—personified the heroic essence of Socialist Zionism. In my teens I felt that I must be a *chalutz.* It may seem strange that cultural and ideological seeds planted during childhood in Russia should mature years later in Minnesota. But it is not too strange. For instance, Golda Meir underwent a similar development—Russia, Milwaukee, Kibbutz Merchaviah. Why didn't I stay? Most of the people who at that time went from America to Palestine returned. I was too young, too romantic, not of an age for permanence. But I felt I mustn't miss out on being a *chalutz.* That's the way of young people—ready to lay down their lives for a cause, but not ready to settle down.

In addition to my youth, there was also the matter of generational difference. I worked in Kibbutz Ein Harod for a year. Wonderful people. But on the average they were ten to twelve years older than I. They came directly from Russia. They started from scratch in a wilderness. So, although I knew Hebrew I felt somewhat like a stranger there. In other, younger kibbutzim, the *chalutzim* were mostly from impoverished small towns in post–World War I Eastern Europe, Lithuania, Poland, Rumania. They were dedicated boys and girls. But in that case there was a cultural gap between us. I had grown up in a minor American metropolis. Part of their motivation was economic. For them kibbutz meant not only a social and national ideal, but also work and bread. Someone from America seeks what is called fulfillment. I liked them, they liked me, and still there was a certain strangeness between us. I was actually a product of a mixture of several cultures—the Russian Jewish, the final gasp of Jewish immigrant life in St. Paul, where, because of the smallness of the community, it ended sooner than elsewhere, and the midwestern. This mixture produced a great restlessness. A friend of mine in St. Paul once said to me, "Why are you always rushing to meet your fate? Stay put, it will catch up with you."

What was driving me? Tensions resulting from living in "different worlds," a foot in each of two cultures. Not like the kids born in St. Paul, living on their peaceful snow-covered streets. Children of twelve or thirteen were still babies. We, the handful of Jewish immigrant children, already knew many other things . . . revolutions, migrations; we cut our teeth in a manner of speaking on the differences between socialism and communism, Zionism and assimilation—ideas that were meaningless to the native-born at that time. Obviously, there was a thick wall of alienation between us.

I will say this: that I, and many like me, were born at the wrong time. There is a thing called "unfinished revolutions." If a person experiences an entire revolution, a whole sequence of events, he has in a sense settled his scores. In my case there were the beginnings of both a Jewish and a social revolution. But by age thirteen I was already out of all that and in the culturally remote Midwest. When years later in 1930 I came to Kibbutz Ein Harod, which was founded in 1922, its members were not only a decade or so older than I, their development during these years had been a natural continuation of their past. I too knew Hebrew. Now and then someone would say: "Come on, you're one of us (*echad mishelnau*); don't tell us you are an American." But the gap was there nevertheless. They went to Ein Harod directly from the turmoil of Russia.

My family also went—but to America. They had logically fulfilled their revolution in accordance with their convictions. I was still dashing around. In New York one could at least drift with the tides, without basically finding rest here either. Even my army service was a kind of unfinished revolution. I spent nearly four years in the army in World War II, the first part in the infantry, yet I was never in combat; I never fired a gun in anger. So that my score with Nazism remains somehow unfinished too.

Detailed information about the Holocaust didn't come through to me till late, in Jewish periodicals I was receiving. When the news started reaching me I was way up in Alaska as a Russian interpreter at an army air force base near Fairbanks. It was during the summer of 1944. Summer in Fairbanks means there is no night, and there I'd be on duty in the control tower at night. No traffic of any kind either in the air or on the ground. It's hard for me to reconstruct that situation. But the impact of the news about the Holocaust in that midnight, sunlit and empty—seemingly abandoned—world started working on me. I became subject to some very powerful religious moods—moods of retreat from the world, from life, moods similar to those expressed in Jacob Glatstein's poem "Goodby World." Total renunciation and resignation. They still come over me occasionally.

In 1938 I came to New York, permanently this time, except for the army service and a stay in Israel in 1946–47. There was a vacancy as managing editor at the *Jewish Frontier*, the Labor Zionist monthly which Hayim Greenberg edited, and it was offered to me, at twenty-one dollars a week, a princely sum at the time. I was only too happy to have it.

In New York I naturally gravitated to Labor Zionist circles and met many fine people to whom I responded almost as one does to blood relatives—they were *haimish* (warm, homelike). But I was already also imprinted with other knowledge. For instance, in the fall I could get homesick for the smell of burning leaves. In St. Paul, come autumn, people raked the fallen leaves together and burned them and one could see towering columns of smoke ascending in the calm Indian summer air as if from so many altars. There were also other images that exerted their call. In New York the mind could be very busy along half a dozen different channels; of course, this is more conducive to daydreaming than to productive work.

At one time I used to say that I loved New York, and it was true. But now I am in a state of estrangement from the city. To a person with my background New York had much to offer. Merely sitting on a park bench and sensing a kind of kinship with other people was important. For one knew that they would respond to a tune, or to an idea, the way you did. It was this atmosphere that gave me a feeling of "at-homeness." In the thirties, during the Depression, it would happen that I'd get off a freight train someplace under Riverside Drive, and by a sort of gravity I'd be drawn to the Village, and I'd feel at home there. Yet in the autumn I was homesick for the Midwest. Torn allegiances. In America I'd hanker for Emek Jezrael, but when I was there, in the midst of the sunny landscape I'd sometimes long for a grey, suicidally depressing December day in Chicago and the moods associated with it.

Much of one summer during the Depression I spent in Union Square in New York. All night there would be radical groups talking, arguing, singing. There comes to my mind one old song about the capitalist system which "is good enough for Norman Thomas, good enough for the Jewish *shammes* (sexton) but not good enough for me." At dawn we'd exchange information about which were good places to swipe a bottle of milk or some rolls. Those places—coffee shops and such—which during the day gave you a handout, them you left alone. From the mean ones, who turned you away, you'd try to grab something. Then all of a sudden a summer shower, a downpour, and everybody disappears. Half an hour later it's over and everybody is back—new meetings, new arguments, new songs. I was pretty much out of place there too. I guess I was the only Zionist on Union Square. But then I suppose that any sensitive Jew always remains a kind of a "lost tribe" in his own self, experiencing lostness in all its varieties.

In 1955 I started the magazine *Midstream*. The publisher was the Theodor Herzl Foundation. The people who sponsored it, some Zionist personages in the U.S., weren't quite sure what they wanted. What did I want? I wanted to produce a Jewish magazine, a Zionist magazine that would differ from the existing ones which were primarily devoted to stimulating donations or serving narrow organizational interests. No young Jewish man or woman with intellectual proclivities or reasonably good literary taste paid any attention to them. I wanted a magazine that would deal with issues and avoid pieties. I also wanted a magazine that would publish good fiction. I believed that one good story tells a lot more than several good articles. But though I had much editorial freedom, especially at first, I did not have as much as I would have liked. The thinking of those responsible for the magazine's financial existence was cast in the conventional and organizational mold. I wanted a more open-minded audience. At this point I was subjected to pressure, sometimes mild and sometimes not so mild.

I published some outstanding pieces of fiction, many of which were later anthologized and reprinted. My experience with a story by Herbert Gold is an example of what I mean by pressure. "Encounter in Haiti" appeared in the second issue of *Midstream*. It dealt with an Old French fascist living in Haiti and the way he abused the natives, using Haitian women and refusing to pay them for their services. The "moral" of it was that even a defeated, old, impotent fascist could still soil whatever he touched. The story caused some grumbling and I was called in for a chat with one of the big shots. "What's this I hear? That you are publishing pornography?" This man hadn't troubled to read the story himself, but he had been told that one of its characters was a prostitute. I said, "If you are going to approach it this way, you'll have to throw out a good part of the Bible."

Another example. I published an English translation of a story by the Soviet Yiddish writer, David Bergelson, who was shot by Stalin. A couple of days after it appeared one of the bosses meets me in the hall: "Shlomo, you know, in the last issue there is a story . . . and the language. . . ."

"What's the matter with the language?"

"Well, you know, a four-letter word. . . . We shouldn't. . . ."

It was a story dealing with the period of the Russian Revolution, about a Jewish surgeon working with the Red Army who gets news from his home town that there had been a pogrom and his wife and children were killed. So he goes to his commander, a tough front line colonel, and he says, "Look, since I got the news I can't go on working. I must return to my town to see what happened. I am a surgeon, but when I now come to operate on an injured soldier, I feel that I am not cutting a human being, I'm cutting shit." And the colonel says: "Well, and what did you think you were cutting before? It's shit you are cutting." This was the offending word. I said, "Bergelson is a major Yiddish writer and a martyr. I am not going to bowdlerize what he wrote."

An editor is always to a certain extent at the mercy of his bosses. One could be brave and say, okay, I quit. But one doesn't do that easily. The magazine meant much to me. I felt that I was

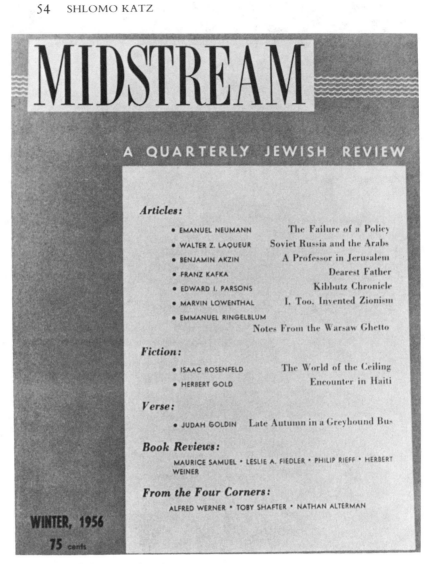

MIDSTREAM

A QUARTERLY JEWISH REVIEW

Articles:

- EMANUEL NEUMANN   The Failure of a Policy
- WALTER Z. LAQUEUR   Soviet Russia and the Arabs
- BENJAMIN AKZIN   A Professor in Jerusalem
- FRANZ KAFKA   Dearest Father
- EDWARD I. PARSONS   Kibbutz Chronicle
- MARVIN LOWENTHAL   I, Too, Invented Zionism
- EMMANUEL RINGELBLUM
       Notes From the Warsaw Ghetto

Fiction:

- ISAAC ROSENFELD   The World of the Ceiling
- HERBERT GOLD   Encounter in Haiti

Verse:

- JUDAH GOLDIN   Late Autumn in a Greyhound Bus

Book Reviews:

MAURICE SAMUEL • LESLIE A. FIEDLER • PHILIP RIEFF • HERBERT WEINER

From the Four Corners:

ALFRED WERNER • TOBY SHAFTER • NATHAN ALTERMAN

WINTER, 1956

75 cents

The cover of *Midstream*, Winter 1956.   DANIEL ROSENBERG.

publishing good stuff, and that it was worth tolerating while not submitting to the pressures.

This did not mean that the contents of a Zionist magazine could be just anything. Obviously, many subjects are too remote to be relevant. But Jews throughout the world are one people who have experiences of many different kinds. A certain kind of experience in Israel with Arabs, another kind in Russia with anti-Semitism, still other kinds in the United States with assimilation. Here we enjoy political and civil rights and even economic affluence, but at the same time there are grave problems. We are affected by cultural and national problems about us, as in the case of blacks—and what is happening to the blacks I felt was very much a part of the subject matter that should be handled by *Midstream*.

There comes to my mind the recollection of Claude McKay, the very gifted black poet I met in the thirties. We got to be friendly and we talked a lot. His situation was intolerable. He was anti-Stalinist, which meant that the black intelligentsia in Harlem (then mostly Stalinist) boycotted him. We met usually in Harlem. He was very sensitive about coming downtown. "Why should I come downtown? Why don't you come up to Harlem?" I was only too glad to do so, but with him it was a matter of ethnic self-assertion. I used to argue with him: "Of course there is Senator Bilbo and all the rest of that gang." Please remember, this was 1938, 1939. "But Bilbo will die, or be kicked out. The direction for your people is forward, and while the Negroes in the United States are now in a terrible situation, they have a future. If it isn't now, it's ten years from now, twenty years from now. But look at our Jewish situation. We are well off, you say, and enjoy most of the rights of whites. Only we are up for extermination while you are just being oppressed and you have a tomorrow." Now, how did I know about extermination? It was long before the Nazi extermination, but the Hitler program was pretty clear and anybody who knew Central and Eastern Europe could very well guess that if it came to war Jews were going to be killed. We didn't think of six million, but we visualized great bloodshed. He couldn't see my point of view. That is, he could see it rationally but he couldn't share it because he felt his own hurt, the hurt of a black man, and his own personal hurt. So we talked to each other across a table, yet with a million miles between us.

Well, a sort of postscript to Claude McKay. As I was being discharged from the army, I sat around some air base rec hall sweating my last days. I happened to pick up *Catholic Digest*, and

I read that Claude McKay spent the last couple of years of his life in a Catholic refuge of a sort, and there he died, lonely, ill, and broke. And though this has no bearing on our subject, it has a bearing on the total isolation of that man. At that time, if you weren't in with the Stalinists, then the intellectual establishment boycotted you. He was a black man living in Harlem. And he lived in Harlem because he was a black nationalist and identified with his people.

I got close to the problem of this kind of isolation and Americanization during the Depression. I used to stay often in St. Paul because I couldn't get a job anywhere. I briefly attended a college a couple of times for a few semesters. Well, I had to take a streetcar two blocks away from where I lived in a very rundown old Jewish neighborhood that was already being infiltrated by Mexicans and blacks to some extent. At the streetcar stop, shivering in the Minnesota winter, there was usually a black girl also coming from the same neighborhood. After a while, we'd begin to nod a greeting to each other, and then on the way home, we walked together. "What courses are you taking?" "What are *you* taking?" That sort of thing. And the old Jewish women, in the spring when it was warm and they sat on the porches, started gossiping. It was a small neighborhood and "news" got around. "Have you noticed? Katz's boy is going around with a *schvartze* (black person)?" In this sense, I was obviously closer to the problem by virtue of the fact that I had lived in St. Paul, a small city, even though the high school I went to had only one black student in my class. We were exposed to the black situation and were sensitive to national issues and discrimination. We responded. I continued to publish material in *Midstream* on blacks and by blacks despite some static. Our circulation was never big, and it was aimed at intelligent people whom you couldn't scandalize.

The New York City teachers' strike of 1968 was a different story. There, of course, we were caught betwixt and between, so to speak. The vital interests of the mass of Jewish teachers were threatened by blacks seeking to occupy this economically important position. That created a difficult and ambiguous situation. It was easy for some self-styled radicals: "Oh, boy, let's go and break the lock off the school which is on strike. . . ." Jews were polarized: "They are threatening our bread and butter, therefore they are our enemies." And there were nasty things said and done by blacks, threats of violence with heavy anti-Semitic overtones.

Individuals felt torn by the issue. I will say to the credit of *Midstream* that so far as I know it was the only Jewish magazine which tried to see both sides. A couple of articles, notably by Ben Halpern, showed this dichotomy. And a few Labor Zionists even argued in defense of the black aims. They pointed out that when pioneering Jewish immigration first started in Palestine, the intellectual or middle-class Jews who came there were not used to hard labor and couldn't compete in the open market with Arab workers. Whether it was digging holes to plant orange trees or digging ditches, the Arab worker, who'd been doing that ever since he was a child, could do it with less effort and cheaper. It was then that settlers coined the slogan *kibbush avoda*, which means "conquest of labor;" and it had two connotations. One was that the Jewish intellectual or student should break himself, in a sense, and become a laborer. And let me tell you, many of them did break themselves. There used to be a song in the late 1920s, a song of the *chalutzim*. I remember a couple of lines in which the *chalutz* boasts, "I am not a clerk, nor am I bourgeois. I work in a stone quarry." It became romantic to do the heaviest labor. But to produce, you first had to work for a couple of years until you became accustomed to it. The second meaning was simply "conquest of economic employment positions." For instance, in '31 I worked by the Dead Sea. We had a temporary kibbutz of about one hundred people there and the climate was intolerable. The British government was constructing a highway from Jericho to the Dead Sea where a company began to extract potash. The government provided work on a competitive basis. The Histadrut, the Jewish Labor Federation, said, "We want to do every possible kind of work. That includes building a road at the Dead Sea." So it put in a competitive bid for a section of the road. And there we were, working just for our food, so that we could hold out in that terrible climate.

The parallel to the New York City teachers' strike is quite obvious: here were the blacks coming up with ambitions to occupy economic positions which they felt were theirs by right. Granted,

many of them were not qualified. Well, *chalutzim* weren't qualified, to begin with, to work in quarries and to dig the run-off
ditches along the road, but they were motivated by the idea of
"conquest of labor." It was they who built the kibbutzim and the
moshavim (larger, less socialistic collectives) and the cities. Such
were the youngsters who built that section of the Jericho Dead
Sea road. So have a few Labor Zionists refused to be blinded by
what was going on in Brooklyn. They saw the tragedy of con-
flicting rights. Yes, they said, "meritocracy" is a wonderful thing.
But on the basis of "meritocracy" any Arab youngster of fifteen
or sixteen could last twice as long at hard physical labor as a *chalutz*
who had recently been a university student. That strike was part
of a constant shuffling and reshuffling in this country, and we
Jews, because of our social and economic position, will be caught
betwixt and between again and again.

The school situation led to a cooling off of relations between
two groups that in the past tended to line up on the same side.
There's talk now about a rapprochement. At any rate, the edge
has worn off the conflict as it was in 1969. Even Eldridge Cleaver
has finally seen the light. I am waiting for James Baldwin and
LeRoi Jones to do the same. The basic threat to Jews in America
doesn't come from blacks anyhow. The threat is implicit in the
Jewish situation. That, after all, is elementary Zionism.

Most of my adult life has been spent in New York City. I
used to be a tremendous walker, and wherever I went I would
meet faces that were familiar even though I had never seen them
before. I felt more at home in New York than I did in Chicago,
and certainly more than in St. Paul. Also in New York I found
an economic niche. In the Midwest I felt "unemployed" even
when I had work. But within the past ten years this feeling of at-
homeness in New York has dissipated somewhat.

In New York there is now the question of violence, and how
one perceives it. I live in a mixed neighborhood. Frequently I stay
up late. Suddenly, late at night, I hear screams. I run to the window
and look out, but all I see are a few people quietly standing at the
bus stop. Where the screams came from I don't know. Judging

by their intensity one might think somebody was being murdered. For people like me, violence means only the ultimate—murder—not simply a fight or a heated argument. And screams mean violence. Any unexpected movement means danger. Let me give you an example of how vividly this comes back to my mind. It happened one summer day in 1918. I was about nine years old. You know the way they build clay houses in the Ukraine? Outside, along the front wall there is a whitewashed clay step, like a bench against the wall. And on sunny Saturdays old women sit and gossip. One such Saturday I got into a game of hide-and-seek. I came galloping down the street toward my house where these women sat on the stoop. They jumped up. "What's the matter?"

"Nothing. We're playing hide-and-seek," I said.

"Shame on you," they cried. "A big boy like you, don't you know enough not to run, that when you run people get scared?" For if you run, somebody's pursuing you, and if he's pursuing you, it's in order to do you violence. Such was the logic. So I (and others) learned the lesson; and if now in New York, many decades later, we often react with panic, who is to say where its roots lead to?

The city has changed and I have changed. We grew away from each other but it is not because of the changing ethnic situation. I can say with a clear conscience that so far as anybody is antiracist, I am. Yet somehow, I now feel "out." If I had a place to hang my hat; if I could drop in some evening on *haimische menschen* (kind men) who "know" what I "know," my attitude might be different. But there is no such hangout any more. The nearest thing to a community is Zabar's, a shopping center—thank you very much! I miss the central dining room of a kibbutz— or the Stewart and Waldorf cafeterias of a former day, or even the Village, impersonal havens that provided a measure of social and cultural shelter without infringing on individuality. I miss them just as my old father missed *shul* (an Orthodox synagogue) when he came to St. Paul.

One day, if personal circumstances allowed it, I'd like to retreat to a desert, somewhere in the Southwest. (Remember Jeremiah? *Mi yeten li m'lon orchim bamidbar*—who will give me a wayfarers' hostel in the desert?) Other times I think I'd like to spend my remaining days in Jerusalem. It is a strange, magnetic city where one doesn't really die but somehow merges into history.

Obviously I'm not as optimistic as I was in my youth. I may not have been very optimistic then either—it was rather a kind of desperate eagerness. . . . I remember a statement somewhere in the Talmud that goes like this: "No man dies with half his desires fulfilled." A tantalizing statement, for it does not indicate whether no man dies with *only* half his desires fulfilled, or with *even* half attained. I opt for *even*. It appears more likely.

3.

THE HISTORIAN OF THE
HOLOCAUST AT YIVO

Isaiah Trunk

KUTNO IS a town between Lodz and Warsaw famous, not because of me, but because of the great Jewish writer, Sholom Asch, whose birthplace it was. I was born there in 1905. My father was the local rabbi. He belonged to the third generation of Kutno rabbis. Although in Poland there were no formal Jewish differentiations or any denominations other than Orthodox, our home was relatively liberal. My father was among the founders of the Mizrachi Orthodox Zionist movement in Poland. I was a Zionist at an early age.

I got a traditional Jewish education until I was fourteen or fifteen years old. Then I moved to Lodz and attended the Jewish high school. Such a school was bilingual—Hebrew and Polish were the languages of instruction. There was a whole network of such institutions called Braude Schools, named after their founder, Zev Braude. He was a senator and an activist in the field of Jewish education who organized such schools. I attended one of them for two years. Then in Warsaw I enrolled in the faculty of humanities and wrote a dissertation on medieval Jewish history in Poland.

Of course I was aware of anti-Semitism, but as a student I didn't personally suffer from any of its direct manifestations. I did witness anti-Semitic outbursts by right-wing Polish students. And

Isaiah Trunk was born in Poland in 1905. After World War II he came to the Yiddish Institute in New York (YIVO) where he worked as a scholar and historian of the Holocaust. He received the National Book Award for his *The Judenrat* (1977). Trunk died in 1980.

we all knew of the *numerus clausus* or quota system: Jewish students had great difficulty in gaining admission to the School of Medicine or the so-called Polytechnical School. You had to be very, very lucky and have pull, so to speak, to be registered in such a school. Also, for years before the outbreak of World War II, when the anti-Semitic trend was ascendant, Jews were increasingly excluded from academic pursuits.

That process, unfortunately, had only "ups," no "downs." But I graduated in 1929, before it got very bad. Still, I saw the beginning of a great anti-Semitic trend in the universities and colleges of Poland which really reached a peak in the second half of the thirties.

I think it is not too much to say that Warsaw in my time was the intellectual center, the "brain" of the Jewish Diaspora. First of all, there was in that city the greatest concentration of Jewish cultural activities. The press and the publishing houses are a major case in point. For instance, in Warsaw you had during the thirties at least six dailies in Yiddish. Apart from the very many publishing houses and associations, there were Hebrew and Yiddish educational organizations of which TSYSO is an outstanding example (TSYSO is an acronym for Tsentrale Yiddishe Shul Organization). In these secular Jewish schools the language of instruction was Yiddish, as against Tarbut schools where the language was Hebrew. All in all there was tremendous cultural endeavor, a great eruption of energy, of intellectuality, and creativity in the Jewish population.

I was drawn to the Bund (Jewish Workers Party), and belonged to a club of Bundist intelligentsia in Warsaw. Also, I joined a circle of young Jewish historians while we were all still students. It was founded by Immanuel Ringelblum. The late Dr. Raphael Mahler belonged to the group of over thirty students who came from various colleges and universities inside and outside of Warsaw, Dr. Philip Friedman among them. Our purpose was to study problems of Jewish history, especially those of Poland. My awareness of research in Jewish history was cultivated and sharpened in that circle. I was a member for several years. We published the results of our research in Yiddish.

The Institute for Jewish Research (YIVO) was also sympathetic to our views on secular, rather than religious, Jewish scholarship. We did not direct our efforts toward narrow groups of scholars, but to the Jewish *volkintelligentsia* (lay intellectuals). We accumulated primary source material with a view to understanding our own past.

I spent several years in the archives; this was necessary for my thesis on Jews in the central Polish province called Mazovia (where Warsaw is located) during the fifteenth century. For years I had to sit and read the archival material which was mostly written in medieval Latin. This experience gives you some idea of the direction we took. Other students were not interested in ancient or Jewish medieval history, but in modern Jewish history—in new trends, new philosophies. The Polish archive where I studied, the Central Archive of Ancient Documents, was, to a large extent, destroyed in the siege of Warsaw. But fortunately, a great deal was hidden in the cellars of the local and regional archives, and almost all were saved.

After finishing my graduate work, I taught for a year or two in a TSYSO school. Then I became a teacher of history in Jewish secondary schools, mostly speaking Polish, but also Yiddish and Hebrew. The Polish authorities were not very happy with these schools; there were harassments and acts of discrimination. Jewish schools were never subsidized by the Polish government. Mainly parents supported them. The Jewish communities were not very rich. They were always struggling with deficits, but the whole burden of financing the education of Jewish children was theirs.

I continued to teach until the outbreak of war in 1939. That was a time of chaos. The Soviet army came from the east while Germans pushed us from the west. Finally, I reached the Soviet Zone of Occupation where I resumed my old career as a teacher in the Jewish schools of Białystok which the Soviets supported. Their policy in the occupied areas was not to antagonize, not to impose their system right away, but to inflict it gradually.

On the third or fourth day of the war an order was issued over Polish radio calling on all males of a certain age to go east in order to organize the Polish army of resistance. Of course it was a bluff. The army was disorganized and demoralized. My stay in Białystok was brief.

In June 1940, I was already exiled by the Soviets to the Far East because I refused to become a Soviet citizen. My place of exile was Komi, ASSR, short for Autonomous Soviet Socialist Republic. For those like me it was a great hardship to be there. I became a woodcutter—it was my new profession. After a while, my brother reached Białystok and we were exiles together. I had family. I was with my wife. My brother ran away as a single man, although he also had a wife and even a child, but the child was only a baby. The mother couldn't go with him. For a certain period my brother and I were together. Then he was sent to a labor camp. We were, you might say, half free. Families were not sent to labor camps, but they were limited in their movement. We had to remain in the woods and work there. They wouldn't let us out. But still, my brother's situation was worse than mine— he returned from the camp with heart trouble and died a few months later.

From Israel we got some information about what was happening. There were letters; they took a long time but some news filtered through to us. Not that we were aware of the Holocaust. Later, after Stalingrad, we were sent to the Ukraine where Soviet victories had taken place. The last years of the war, '44 and '45, I spent in Chercon, a big Ukrainian city.

Since we were so close to Poland, some news of what had happened to Polish Jews was leaked to us. But as late as 1943, I knew about only a fraction of the horror. The Soviet press did not help. As long as the alliance between Soviet Russia and Nazi Germany lasted, Russian newspapers were silent about the Jews. Afterwards, they wrote not about Jews, but about Soviet citizens: "The Fascists have murdered Soviet citizens"—and so on in that vein. The first more or less complete news about the scope of the Holocaust and the extent of German murder came to us late in 1944 when we read the communiqué of the Soviet commission which investigated Maidanek. It provided us with the first inkling we had of gas chambers, ovens, and crematoria.

In February of '46, those Jewish refugees from Poland who spent years of the war in Soviet Russia were sent in organized echelons to Poland. Fortunately, or I should say miraculously, in Lodz I found two of my cousins who had survived the Warsaw ghetto. They provided me with a roof, which was very difficult to secure because Lodz was experiencing a great influx of repatriated refugees from Soviet Russia. They were returning from concentration camps and DP camps. But I was fortunate; one cousin had a room for me.

Unlike much of Poland, Lodz was almost intact. But Warsaw in January of 1945 was entirely in ruins. When I spent a few months there, I couldn't find my old street, let alone the house we once lived in. I stayed in Praga, a suburb of Warsaw. We lived in barracks. Jews were not even admitted to their former homes. When I came back to Kutno, I went looking for our old house. People seemed to be asking themselves, "Is he a Jew? How did he survive? What's he doing here?" Only with the help of a Jew in the Polish militia was I permitted to enter that building. I just wanted to look at the house in which I was born and where I had lived for many years. But I got so—not just disgusted—but frustrated with feeling, "This was my home, and now I am not only a stranger but an *intruder*."

After all the Polish people had been through, we Jews were still the enemy. War had to be waged against us. We've learned that Jew-hatred does not require the presence of a single Jew! Polish anti-Semites made war against ghosts; there were no Jews. Sometimes animosity is so inbred that we see such irrationalities.

My wife had left pieces of furniture with an ostensible Polish friend. This "friend" greeted her, not with skepticism but with ice cold irony. "How did you save yourself" was her question. It did not convey satisfaction about a friend who was saved; rather, the tone expressed disappointment. And she had difficulties getting the furniture back. Such was the attitude of the Polish population except within certain liberal circles, and among some of the clergy who were at best indifferent.

Lublin was the nucleus of a Jewish revival in postwar Poland. There had already been a Jewish central committee and an organized historical commission to do research into the Holocaust. Later the commission moved to Lodz and from there to Warsaw where it has remained the Jewish Historical Institute.

In the beginning Zionists, Socialists, and Orthodox Jews also participated; it was all part of the system. At first they let the tiny remnant of the Jewish organizations participate in building the new order. Finally, when these people were not needed any more, they were thrown out. This happened in Lublin, then in Lodz, and finally in Warsaw. The Central Jewish Committee wandered from one city to the other.

I soon realized that a basic change in the methods and the policy of the Historical Commission had occurred. I knew that it was no place for me to do objective research, so I got a visa from France. But the Polish government, and not only the Polish government but the Jewish Communists in the Institute wouldn't let me out so easily. For several years, I struggled for permission to leave Poland. Fortunately, in 1949 there was an agreement between the Israeli and Polish governments allowing Jews to migrate if—and only if—their destination was Israel. Soviet Jews are technically in the same position today.

Well, we left for Israel . . . got there in January 1950. I joined the Kibbutz Lo'hamei ha ghettaot, the ghetto fighters' kibbutz. Two friends with whom I had worked at the Jewish Historical Institute in Warsaw, Nachman Blumenthal and Dr. Joseph Kermish, and I started to organize the Warsaw Ghetto Fighters' "Research Institution." That sounds pretentious; actually, we occupied only one barrack. But in this Kibbutz Lo'hamei ha ghettaot, there were Yitzhak Zuckerman, Ziviah Lubetkin, his wife, plus Tsvi Schner, a major force behind this effort, who is still secretary of the Beth Lo'hamei ha ghettaot, where there is now a very great museum on the Holocaust. Yad Vashem came later, in '53.

Most of the documents then on hand consisted of eyewitness accounts. We were in contact with the Paris Centre de Documentation, but German documents were the prime source. The Nazis kept records. In Lodz they left whole archives of their administration of the Ghetto. We had thousands upon thousands of files. My early work about Jewish labor camps in Poland came out of Nazi records.

Also, we started to receive important documents from various parts of the world, for instance from the Jewish Agency in

Istanbul, and then from different rescue agencies in many parts of the world. Now, Kibbutz Lo'hamei ha ghettaot has a very large archive with hundreds of thousands of pieces. I would say they have more about the Holocaust than we do at YIVO. Our research interest is centered only in part on the Holocaust; Kibbutz Lo'hamei ha ghettaot and Yad Vashem are exclusively devoted to it.

How was YIVO transferred to New York? First of all, the Germans occupied Vilna in June of '41 (this was the second time); it was learned that they had removed the archives, the library, and everything else. YIVO was made into an assembly center for the Einstatzstab Rosenberg, a German agency whose task was to plunder art and archives and libraries in the whole of Europe. They made YIVO a center for gathering all this plunder. By '39–'40 there was already an established branch of YIVO in the United States. Actually, it was founded in 1925, almost at the same time as YIVO in Vilna. Jacob Schatsky was one of the organizers. Max Weinreich may have been in Denmark. Anyway the war caught him elsewhere in Europe, not in Vilna. So he was able to emigrate to the United States, as were Elias Tstcherikover and other scholars. With this nucleus, the branch became the headquarters of the Vilna YIVO. Now, the Nazis, scholars among them, were interested in organizing or founding research institutes about the Jews. Alfred Rosenberg was one who organized such an institute, Rosenberg in Frankfurt, Goebbels in Berlin. They didn't destroy this material. There was a commission whose head, Dr. Pohl, decided what material they "needed" and what could be sold to paper mills. A large quantity of documents that they found in YIVO was sent to Germany in order to be integrated in this Institut der Judenfrage. They even employed a group of Jews to sort out the material, much of which was in Yiddish and Hebrew. It was a part of their system to use Jewish labor. (But then, even in the crematoria they used Jewish labor.) Here they used it to destroy Jewish culture. But, fortunately, they didn't fully succeed.

Among them was the famous Jewish poet, Abraham Sutzkover. And one of the YIVO scholars who didn't run away, Zelig Kalmanovich, kept a very interesting diary which was published recently by his son who had escaped to Israel. And, so, when the

Germans shifted this material along their retreat from the east, all of it got to Germany. Finally, the treasury of Jewish cultural creativity, not only from Vilna but from some other European countries that had been plundered by Alfred Rosenberg was found in Offenbach, a Bavarian city in the American Occupation zone! Among the officials of the American Occupation we had friends of YIVO. One of them, Seymour Pomerantz, now retired, was a major archivist in the National Archives in Washington. Also, Dr. Koppel Pinson was one of the American officials. And there were others, who when they realized what was at stake, started— of course, with General Eisenhower's permission—to separate material belonging to YIVO. Lucy Dawidowicz was also there, working in this group and the late Zosa Szajkowski sent us very important material which he found in the Nazi Archives in Berlin, for example, from Goebbels' Nazi Propaganda Ministry.

In 1947 more than four hundred crates of material plundered by the Nazis were sent to New York and we have it all here. I am just now working on archives which were in the YIVO Institute of Vilna. We have millions of pieces on Jewish linguistics, Jewish folklore, the Jewish way of life, Jewish literature. We have the archives of the rabbinical school in Vilna which was established by Tsar Nicholas I. We have archives of the Teachers Institute which was also founded in tsarist Russia. The school records of the Society for the Promotion of Enlightenment Among the Jews are very important. Indeed, YIVO now has the world's most extensive documentation of our vanished East European culture. It begins with the last decade of the eighteenth century, covering the nineteenth and twentieth centuries until the Nazis wiped nearly everyone out. Material I work on now concerns Jewish life in Poland between the wars. It's varied and invaluable material pertaining to many activities of the Jewish community: material produced by political parties concerning elections to municipalities, to Jewish communities, to the parliament in Poland; material relating to libraries—very illuminating material. Also about trade unions, other economic organizations, cultural groups, scientific organizations. These resources were indispensable to those who wrote memorial books on Jewish communities. We have between 350 and 400 memorial books, each devoted to a community de-

The Yiddish poet Shmerke Katcherginsky, an inmate in the Vilna ghetto, working at the collection of Jewish books and documents which the Nazis were selecting for the museum (circa 1942).   YIVO INSTITUTE FOR JEWISH RESEARCH.

YIVO scholars studying the books brought in crates from the Offenbach Department to YIVO.   YIVO INSTITUTE FOR JEWISH RESEARCH.

stroyed by the Nazis. The authors drew heavily on our resources. We have unique documents, originals for which there are no substitutes.

Scholars come to us from Israel, from France, and many other countries. *We* have the archives of the French Judenrat (the Jewish Council created by the Nazis). A young scholar from Israel sat here and wrote his doctoral thesis about the French Judenrat. It took him almost a year; there was no other place to study that subject. Or let's take the problem of immigration to the United States. Nobody can write a dissertation about Jewish immigration to the United States, from the 1860s on, without our material because we have the documents of HIAS (Hebrew Immigrant Aid Society); we have the materials of the HIAS in Lisbon; of the American Joint Distribution Committee; and much more that has not even been sifted. Our immigration materials concerning Jews are the richest in the United States.

From the Vilna YIVO we have our very rich rabbinical library which consists of thousands of volumes. Very few people are aware of this, but the yeshiva bochers (seminary students) from Lubavitch Yeshiva got the hint; and now groups of them come looking for the books.

Lucy Dawidowicz worked at YIVO to prepare her excellent study of the Holocaust. She still comes because we have primary sources, archival material that you can find nowhere else. And it's not mainly in Yiddish. For example, YIVO has very rich Nazi documentation which we call the Berlin Collection. It consists in part of original Nazi documents of Goebbels' Propaganda Ministry, of the Ministry for the Eastern Territories which was headed by Rosenberg. Hannah Arendt's conception of the Judenrat is one side of the coin whose other side comes out of YIVO archives.

One reviewer of my book, *The Judenrat* (which won a National Book Award), wrote: "A shocking and horrifying book; one that should make you ashamed of the human race for its humanity. Readers who are convinced that they knew everything that went on in Hitler's death program should read this book if they want to rearrange their thinking." Of course, no one will ever know everything, but I learned a lot because I worked on

The Judenrat for six years using our archives. Then I read a great deal more in Hebrew.

There was a joint Holocaust project of YIVO and Yad Vashem that published *fourteen volumes of bibliography* on the Holocaust. My book on the Lodz ghetto was also published by the Yad Vashem Martyrs and Heroes Memorial Authority in Jerusalem, and the YIVO Institute for Jewish Reseach. It has not yet been translated.

As I said, I learned a lot about the Judenrat: how it was established, how it worked, the relationship between German authorities and the Jewish population. It came to me not only from reflecting on this topic for six years. I went to the Yad Vashem archives in Jerusalem, to London and the Wiener Library Archives, and to our own archives. I wanted to visit Poland, too, but I was refused a visa. Apparently, they still blacklist me there. Their refusal, however, came before the Six Day War and the interruption of relations with Israel. But I brought a good deal with me from Poland, so I didn't absolutely need to make that trip.

Hannah Arendt's conception of the Judenrat was, in my opinion, one-sided. And a half-truth is sometimes worse than a lie. Of course the Judenräte were forced to collaborate, or I would say, to cooperate. You *have to distinguish* between collaboration and cooperation. Not that there was no collaboration—of course there was. What Hannah Arendt omitted, in my opinion, is that without the Judenrat the situation would have been worse. She believed, contrariwise, that without the Judenrat it would have been better. Look, they gained time. The Judenräte were active for three, in some ghettos, for four years. They managed to forestall, to alleviate the worst for a while, to save people. Much depended on who represented the Nazis. The Nazi bureaucratic system was permeable. *Individuals* made policy on the spot. There was no system of laws for the Jews. They were outcasts, beyond the civilized world, beyond the law. For this reason, every German official assumed the right to decide the fate of the Jews—to do with them as he pleased. So, there was an opportunity for contact between a Judenrat and officials who, for one thing, were not immune to bribes. *Almost all of them were corrupt.* Thus the

Judenräte were able, not everywhere but in many cases, to post-pone the final calamity which was deportation to the death camps. They were able to organize some relief through the Joint Distribution Committee. There were channels in neutral countries, in Portugal, Switzerland, Sweden. The idea that without the Judenräte a good many Jews would have been better off is entirely false.

I was immersed in these matters when we left Israel, and we left not for ideological reasons but because it was a very hard time. My wife and son were sick. Israel itself had gone to the extreme limits of austerity. We went to Canada, reaching Montreal too late for me to start as a teacher because the school year had already begun. But I was asked to be principal of the Peretz School in Calgary. We were Canadian residents for a year. Then a member of the Hebrew Institute in New York came to Calgary as a fund-raiser and we met. Through him I received an invitation from YIVO, arriving in this country as a tourist, eventually becoming a U.S. citizen.

I was overwhelmed by New York. First of all, I found my cousin, J. J. Trunk, who was a rather famous Jewish writer; he had published, among other works in prewar Poland, a seven-volume epic on Polish Jewry which is now a classic. He was the only male member of my family still alive. Soon I met many people I'd known in Warsaw: I discovered a group of Jewish writers, historians, novelists, poets, and they have been most important to me.

I don't need all of New York. For me, New York was YIVO; it still is. Oh, there are conferences and performances in the city, but fundamentally, there is YIVO. Bookstores are valuable. However, I brought a whole library with me from Israel, and that library never stops expanding. Almost every week there's a new book in my mailbox or a package of books awaiting me at the post office. I divide my library, this part in my office, the rest all over my home—in closets, in the basement, everywhere I have books spilling all over the place. Nevertheless, I make extensive use of the Public Library, which has a good Jewish collection, although with regard to the Holocaust, it is only fair consisting mostly of popular books. But on Jewish life before the Holocaust the Public Library has rare and significant books that can be matched perhaps only in the Jewish Theological Seminary.

These days, apart from writing, I have taught and lectured in various universities. This past year, I taught the Holocaust at Haifa University for a whole semester. What do I think about courses in this country on the Holocaust? I don't remember who said it but this is a very fine epigram and much to the point: "Jewish life in the United States is a mile wide and an inch deep." There are good Holocaust studies in Hebrew and Yiddish. The trouble is that too many people consider themselves capable of writing about the Holocaust, a fact that has diminished and cheapened the whole thing. I am against this proliferation. Every month another book! Because there's great demand, there are suppliers, too many suppliers.

The demand is understandable. You have a general awakening of Jewish consciousness in this generation. For young people the Holocaust comes as a terrific shock. They want to know more about it. That all of European Jewry walked like sheep into the ovens is a myth which is receding in their minds. To have believed that myth was simply a matter of ignorance. As long ago as 1968, at Yad Vashem I took part in a conference devoted to Jewish resistance. In a recent book of mine I have a chapter on Jewish resistance. The stereotype about Jews going to the slaughter like sheep is false from beginning to end. The world knows about the Warsaw ghetto uprising. There were many, many other instances where Jews went to the slaughter not at all like sheep. *There were more than twenty ghettos in active resistance when the last dark moment descended on them.* Not that it mattered much in the long run. What defenseless unarmed population could resist the Nazi war machine?

I am not opposed to the teaching of courses devoted to this subject. I just have reservations about their quality. At YIVO, we established a center for advanced Jewish studies. Over a period of several years YIVO has offered courses dealing with the Holocaust, but on a scholarly level, not as superficially recorded by freelance writers. We have tried to educate teachers of the Holocaust. For myself, I was involved in the creation of a textbook published by the American Association for Jewish Education. It's meant for secondary schools. I wrote a few chapters. Holocaust courses are a good idea, but everything depends on how they are realized. Too often this good idea is badly realized, which is not to deny that here and there you have excellent teachers of the Holocaust.

I am not very familiar with the status of Jewish studies in the whole country. Their growth, however, on one side, is clearly a positive phenomenon. It shows that interest in the Jewish heritage, Jewish civilization, Jewish culture, is very strong and apparently getting stronger from year to year. But, on the other side, I must repeat, *we are lacking first-rate teachers*, not only for the colleges but for the high schools. Even the yeshivas and the day schools complain about a shortage of real teachers. For institutions such as YIVO there is also the severe problem of inadequately trained archivists. All in all, it is fortunate that we are not a wholly negative exception.

4.

THE TRAGEDY OF THE GERMAN JEWISH INTELLECTUAL

Hans Morgenthau

I AM often asked about the late awakening of my Jewishness. Where does it come from? Why? I suppose it is the accumulation of a lifelong experience of anti-Semitism. At some point one cannot allow being treated this way without taking a stand. The awakening didn't happen late or yesterday. I'll try to explain.

The fundamental difference between American and German Jewish society is open German anti-Semitism. That fact molded one's whole life. At the age of eighteen I wrote an essay, which I still have, for my school on "What Do I Hope To Gain From Life?" Primarily, the answer was "to feel that the burden of anti-Semitism be lifted from my shoulders." But if you want prime examples of anti-Semitism in America, I also experienced them aplenty. For instance, trying to find a sublet for the summer around Columbia University, or trying to find a place to sleep, or to be served at the Dartmouth Inn in New Hampshire. I had a number of experiences as an émigré in which deans or heads of departments said to me, "We've never had a Jew before, and we are not going to start now." Since I was well conditioned, I wouldn't say that this surprised me, but I thought, "Oh, it's the same old story."

Hans Morgenthau was born in Germany in 1904. He was a distinguished lawyer, educator, political scientist, diplomat, and adviser on foreign policy. He wrote numerous books on American politics and social science. Morgenthau died in 1980.

And yet there was a difference. Here the prejudice was covered up by Anglo-American cant. Nobody put a fist under your nose and shouted, "Why don't you disappear from the face of the earth, you dirty Jew." I knew Jews who totally identified with German history and culture. At the same time they were told by the German gentiles that Jews didn't really belong. But since most Jews didn't see any alternative, they made a superhuman effort to prove to themselves and to the rest of the world that they were as good Germans as anybody else. Even with Hitler, the majority felt: "Why should we get out? We are Germans. We haven't done anything wrong."

They tell the story of a German Jewish organization (called the Nationale Deutschenjuden) composed of people who were Nazis in everything except their origins. The joke goes that they demonstrated with the slogan, "Raus mit Uns": Out with us; out with ourselves. That epitomizes the irony that a Jew's consciousness made him a German while his environment denied it.

Here's another example. My father was the son of a rabbi. We went to *shul* on the holidays, Rosh Hashana and Yom Kippur, wearing our high hats. But we walked on side streets so nobody would notice that we were Jewish. Now, out of the 2,400 inhabitants of our small town, 2,399 knew that we were Jewish. But somehow we attempted to conceal from ourselves and from our neighbors that we were Jewish. The grotesque, completely irrational practice was so striking—on the one hand you honored the highest holy days, and on the other hand you wanted as few gentiles as possible to know that you honored them. I was told over and over not to do this or that. "Don't do it. People will see you are a Jew. They will criticize you. Especially don't dissent." My father would have turned in his grave if he had known what I did over Vietnam. A Jew opposing the official point of view? You don't *do* that if you know what's good for you.

Hitler did not come as a great shock to me personally. It did to my parents. I heard Hitler speak in 1922 in Munich when I was relatively young and got an enormous impression of him. It was obvious to me that "This man means business." I was then eighteen. Most Germans I knew simply dismissed Hitler as a clod. I took him very seriously. It was immediately after Lord Northcliff had died. He had been the great British press magnate and bitterly anti-German. Nazis spread the rumor that he was a German Jew by the name of Stern. Hitler said, "This German Jew did such and such. . . ." A woman turned around to me and exclaimed, "All Jews ought to die like that. If not, they should be killed." I certainly was frightened and decided to emigrate in 1932.

In my case it wasn't a question of emigration pure and simple. There was an opening at the University of Geneva. And I took it even though I might have waited for something better because I thought it was not a moment too early to leave. A small minority agreed with me. When I heard all sorts of stories in Geneva, I called my father: "Get the hell out of there!" He was calm for a couple of days or weeks. Then my father got an anonymous telephone call telling him that he was on the Gestapo list. He jumped in his car, went to the frontier and never came back.

I remained in Switzerland until 1935, when I got an offer from the Spanish government to teach diplomats. I trained the present foreign minister, and his predecessor, and this work I did until a week before the Civil War broke out. I went on a vacation to Italy, and never returned.

Given my background, I was clearly an assimilationist. Even after the advent of Hitler, when you were stamped as a Jew, you still didn't accept it. You waited. . . . I remember when I called my father: he insisted, "It's one of those things. It will take a couple of weeks until the revolution settles down. Then everything will be all right." You see, the German Jews were patriots. My father fought in the First World War. He possessed a Russian rifle. And when the Nazis came to power my mother hid it under her coat and then threw it into the river.

I guess that toward the end of the Second World War, probably in 1944, I first knew about the Holocaust. If that sounds early, it was not due to any inside information. My grandmother had disappeared in Theresienstadt, others disappeared, so many that they couldn't all have died natural deaths. The terrible truth began to dawn on me. When I talked about it in those days, American Jews tended to think that I was unconscionably exaggerating.

Early on, as a refugee I felt alone in the sense that most American Jews with whom I came into contact made no bones about the fact that this whole business was a big embarrassment to them. After all, they were well on their way to assimilation. All of a sudden another set of Jews descended on them with a common plea, "My God, we need jobs!" When I came to this country in '37 I went to the Jewish Appeal or whatever it was called, and I approached a social worker who reacted this way: "Teachers! We've got thousands of unemployed teachers. This is the Depression. You want to teach here? We don't need you." How often I said to myself, "If I were to take this talk literally, I would go to the George Washington Bridge and jump into the Hudson." "Why don't you open a chicken farm in New Jersey?" some professional helpers seriously asked me.

Stephen Wise perhaps strengthened my morale because he always gave me a sermon, but he didn't help much. Oh, if I went looking through my correspondence I would probably find that he wrote a letter to somebody and that this guy then wrote another letter to some third person, and so forth. At least, he got the ball rolling. I had a second cousin who was employed at Hunter College as a vocational adviser. She was a friend of one of the collaborators of Stephen Wise. It was anything but a religious or Zionist connection that brought me to Rabbi Wise.

When I slept in bedbug hotels and ate at Horn and Hardart, New York seemed repulsive to me. Fifth Avenue, but not in the surrounding districts, was attractive enough. It still is. But my first question was, "How do I keep myself from starving?" Whether the city or the sunset was beautiful really did not interest me. I needed a job. Would I have settled for anywhere? Sure. I did settle for anywhere. I went to Kansas City.

People have asked me why, in the last several years, I have become much more sympathetic to Israel and more Jewish. I really don't know. When I first went to Israel in 1955 I thought and said that it was a nation of schnorrers (freeloaders), a people who had no real sense of their own identity. They lived on handouts from the United States and the world Jewish community. And they could only make it as long as those handouts continued. I was not mistaken at that time. Even now there is some truth to it. But the war of 1967 proved Israel was a nation, that its people could fight and stand on their own feet. I remember vividly being in a cab here immediately after the war. I started talking to the driver. I didn't know that he was Jewish until he turned back to me and said, "I am a Hebrew and I'm proud of it." It was this transformation which also took place in me. That war, in relation to experiences of four thousand years, worked its magic. The experiences alone obviously didn't do it. You know what tricks memory can play. As I said, I have no clear recollection of what brought about the change. I can only guess that it was this.

I was certainly not affected by Hannah Arendt's book on Eichmann. In fact I told her time and again, "You have raised monumental questions and have disposed of them in subordinate phrases. It just doesn't work. It's not that simple. For instance, that Jews didn't resist." It's a much more profound question. As for the German Jews, they were prevented from resisting by their whole complex moral attitude toward Germany. What was the name of the organization of German Jews? "The Society of German Citizens of Jewish Religion." You were a German who by accident went to church on Saturday rather than on Sunday. Hannah had once been a Zionist and afterwards became an anti-Zionist. Her case was extraordinary. If there is any similar development in my case, it's the opposite. Usually in Germany, you were either anti-Zionist or non-Zionist. It was not an issue. In my home town, I couldn't even tell you that there was a single Zionist. In my family, I mean among uncles and aunts and cousins, to be a Zionist was unthinkable. Why should a German Jew be a Zionist?

My concern with Israel and my involvement in being a Jew are connected. If Israel were to be destroyed tomorrow it would demonstrate the monumental failure of Judaism. It would prove that Judaism could not survive as a political and social entity. More particularly, with the reduction of Russian Jewry to a minor factor in world Jewry, the situation would prove Judaism's weakness. I might not feel personally imperilled but I would feel a diminution of my own social consciousness as a Jew. As I was proud in '67 so would I be ashamed in '80 or '81. The pride of '67 was based in part on a military victory, but also upon the *type* of military victory. I mean the triumphant way in which Israel overcame all its surrounding enemies. It was a kind of biblical victory. You could imagine the cohorts of God fighting the battle of the Jews. Unfortunately, Israeli pride in victory created deeper contempt for the Arabs, and a gross underestimation of their power, which I found amazing even before '73. I remember a discussion at a dinner party with Dayan in '71 or so. He spoke of the Egyptians as a bunch of nitwits.

Kissinger? In substantive terms, he is right. Why? For military and political reasons. The accumulation of nuclear weapons per se is not a rational military objective. You can reduce it by ninety per cent and still be capable of destroying the enemy a couple of times over. The unlimited steamroller is a remnant of the past, and James Schlesinger bought it. Kissinger did not. Kissinger wants a slow but perceptible reduction in nuclear weapons. In the Middle East, he wants to remove the Russian influence. I think he overdoes his own Jewish identification. Probably, he does more with it than is there. But there *is* something there. It's not just a fake. The other day I was at the home of Thomas Finletter. Also present was the widow of Marshall Field, a very intelligent and charming lady. We talked about Kissinger. I said, "He has a very strong Jewish consciousness." And Mrs. Field replied, "That's exactly what I'm afraid of." As long as that view prevails, and as long as Kissinger has his way, American support of Israel is secure. The support is broad but thin. Even the Jewish reaction to Kissinger is part pride and part anxiety. I can still anticipate an absolutely friendless Israel, especially if the Russians play their cards right.

Nobody knows what would happen to world Jewry if Israel should disappear. It certainly would mean a great deal but exactly what it would mean goes back to the question: Why have the Jews survived to this day? Let me say there is something empirically inexplicable in the survival of the Jews as a people. Obviously, there are lots of sociological explanations if you look for them. But similar explanations could have been given for, let's say, the Armenians if they had survived, but they didn't. Under the aspect of eternity, I see something special about the Jews: their insistence upon the law, upon compliance with certain divine commandments, is something which I find inordinately impressive.

With respect to 1967, it came to me that I belong to this formerly despised race, which had all of a sudden proven that it was as good as any other ethnic group, and in a particular field which required virile qualities. But the historical mission Jews have embraced implies that there is a moral fiber, a moral power in the Jewish character which has contributed to, if it isn't responsible for, Jewish survival under sociologically unacceptable conditions.

I'm always reminded of this when I go back to Europe. For instance, to Munich. I adore Munich as a city. But I would never live there because I would not want to be with people of whose vile convictions I have no doubt and of whose deeds I have very little doubt. Or Berlin either! I was a student in Berlin and I went back for the first time in 1950. I went to the street where I had lived and the only house left standing was one in which I had lived. And there was still the name of the aristocratic lady with whom I had lived for one year. The maid opened the door and I asked to speak to the lady. "Are you Mrs. so and so?" and she said, "Yes. You left Germany in the thirties, didn't you?" She walked out of the room and never came back.

I recall certain types sitting in a Munich restaurant who caused me to think, "I'm certainly lucky that I can get out of Germany tomorrow morning." To give you one example which I wrote up and which the Germans disliked greatly: in Germany it's common usage if you enter a cafe in which somebody is seated at a table where there are two extra chairs to say, "Would you mind my sitting down?" You do sit down and frequently you start a conversation. I sat in a cafe where there was light music, very much like the Plaza (Hotel) in New York. Along came an elderly businessman and a younger fellow who sat next to him. We went through the formalities: "Will you allow me to sit down?" and they exchanged stories. The younger man said, "When I was a student at Heidelberg six of us once went on a train to have some beer. There was only one compartment free: it had four places, so we couldn't sit together. But there were two Jews sitting in the first two places. We said, 'Get off your behinds,' and they refused. We opened the doors and threw the first Jew out of one window of the racing express train, and the second Jew out of the other." And he added, "Only Jews could be so stubborn." I say this to report what kind of people surround you in Germany. And they are "perfectly civilized."

The Holocaust could not happen again in Germany only because there are not enough Jews left. . . . It might happen here under certain conditions. I couldn't give you a scenario, but human nature being what it is, a concentration of popular discontents and of physical fears in a particular group make it possible anywhere. Man is both good and bad and in society he's bad. *Homo homine lupus.*

A man like Theodore Adorno could go back to Germany. It was his country. Also, I understand a certain attraction in returning to the old predicament. I lost it completely after revisiting my home town a few years ago. I used to dream of the landscape and miss it terribly. When I saw it I knew every tree, I knew every turn in the road and it was just another small town. I looked at it as a complete stranger. How someone from Kalamazoo would look at it I haven't the slightest idea. But I looked on as somebody from the outside. I had nothing in common with those people. I knew that I was born up there, in that apartment, and I remembered certain incidents, but I had no emotional attachment. That surprised me. By now all my emotional attachments are in this country. Which didn't prevent John Roche, for a while President Johnson's intellectual-in-residence, from writing that I was one of those Europeans who simply didn't understand what America was all about.

Surely I am comfortable in my part of Manhattan. Jewishness has something to do with it in certain respects, especially in speech. In talking to gentiles you don't hesitate to use Jewish words: *meshugah*, kosher. There is so much that is specifically Jewish here. You expect to run into Jews continuously: you always expect to be touched by the emanations of Jewish life. How else could it be in a city one of whose main ethnic characteristics is Jewishness? If you go to certain parts of Yonkers you'll find a German influence. Or to certain parts of Michigan where you'll find a strong Dutch influence. You'll inevitably be greeted by a Vanderhooven and see tulips everywhere. Just so, you expect a lot of Jewish expressiveness in New York. I'm a great deal more at ease in New York City than I would be in Grand Rapids. The Spanish poet

García Lorca was aware of the Jewishness of New York. In his poem "Nueva York" he refers to the ugliness of street life in New York due to Jewish influence. He talks about "the unpleasant mixture of races." Perhaps that impression registered naturally on someone from Granada. I find my neighborhood the only civilized part of an American city. This part of Madison Avenue reminds me of the beautiful Rue St. Honoré in Paris. I love to walk around both areas. It's important to me to move among civilized-looking and well-dressed people. You go in a restaurant and you are surrounded by men and women of culture, however superficial the culture may be. Obviously the Jews have made a heavy contribution to that culture.

To some extent that's true wherever they are. Aside from the formal aesthetic impact, look at the influence of Jewish scenes in American literature. I read them in Malamud, in Saul Bellow (at the University of Chicago I knew Bellow quite well). I read Roth. I read Podhoretz. If you want to go a little farther down, I read, let's see . . . the *Daily Forward* in Yiddish and, in English, the *Jewish Press*. Mailer falls in between somewhere. I find him a marvelous writer but only when he's very good. Otherwise I find him an infantile showoff. Undisciplined. Without real structure of mind. He really doesn't know where he wants to go. What I used to admire in Mailer's political analysis was his gift for language. I remember, for instance, his remarking about Hubert Humphrey, "When Humphrey hears himself say, 'Democracy exists in Vietnam,' he believes it to be true because he has heard himself say it." Now that is very profound. A man who can hit on such a formula deserves my respect. I don't think I ever would have discovered it independently.

In Germany we had German Jewish anti-Semitism directed at Eastern Jews. To say of a man, "He is an *Ostjude*," was as bad in our eyes as we were in the eyes of real gentiles. But we were on our way, and those guys, just by walking around, reminded us that we were not on our way and that in the minds of the gentiles we had no right to be on our way. As for the so-called Jewish establishment in this country, what I find interesting is that most leaders have come to organizational power not because they are politically able but because they spend a lot of money for

Jewish causes. A rich man who is perfectly willing to give two million dollars every year to the United Jewish Appeal will assuredly be heeded no matter how shallow his mind may be.

It also interests me that in this country assimilation has taken on certain aspects of pluralism. Assimilation doesn't mean that you merge your own entire ethnic or cultural being into one big melting pot out of which something entirely different emerges. Today in America assimilation means the coexistence and interpenetration of different cultures. Assimilation presupposes two things: something to be assimilated to—a given culture, in this case America—and someone who wants to be assimilated into it. For us, a culture was something to be assimilated to. Mr. Schoenberg became Mr. Belmont. This is no longer true. The incentive for such assimilation, which really means a full flight from your own ethnic identity, has been enormously diminished. What prominent Jew in this day and age would be taken seriously if he allowed himself to be baptized? James Schlesinger is already converted. But, let's say, if Judge Rifkind tomorrow were to become an Episcopalian, everyone would say that he must have taken leave of his senses. Remembering that fifty years ago Mr. Schoenberg became Mr. Belmont makes us smile. Fifty years ago name-changing was an important step in assimilation. Today it would be a senseless, debasing, and useless gesture. Isn't that right? Take the New York City politicians Finkelstein and Stein. The father is Finkelstein. The son is Stein. There's hardly a Jew in the city who doesn't find this amusing. And, in effect, it is. Because the son of Mr. Finkelstein, whatever he calls himself, is still the son of Mr. Finkelstein. And will be so until the end of time.

Certain intellectual influences have left their mark on my Jewish consciousness. I am a member of the Jewish seminar at Columbia, which was originally organized by Frank Tannenbaum. Now Salo Baron is head of the project. He's a great historian, a great Jew. So is the Lubavitcher Rebbe. My son goes to *shul* (orthodox synagogue) every Friday evening and is very much interested in the Hasidic movement. The Lubavitcher Rebbe has a secular education. He matriculated at the Sorbonne as a nautical engineer. He constructed ships. His family name is Schneerson. He is most interesting to me. I had an audience with him at two o'clock in the morning. I could not help being impressed that here was a man who had made it the mission of his life to preserve the Jewish heritage, something I could not do both because I wasn't sufficiently educated and because I was psychologically unprepared. But this man did it and he continues doing it.

The Lubavitcher's presence is an example of why I find New York so amusing, fascinating, and stimulating. Generally, that means the great variety of people you meet, the great variety of physical and architectural environments that exist. From here I can see the sun rise, from the other window I can see the sun set, and from the third window I see Central Park. My friends are important to me. They're part of the environment. Another part is made up of the intellectual and aesthetic surroundings. If not for them, who would want to live in this accumulation of cement?

Of course human contacts are an essential part of the environment. Personal relations make it impossible for me to live elsewhere. I am certainly in New York because I choose to be. Take a place like Antioch College, or a place like Oberlin, where the *Kenyon Review* is published. They are not overwhelmingly important, but there you do find intelligent people who have intellectual concerns. I was not uncomfortable for short periods in such a milieu. I even taught a couple of summers at the University of Wyoming and at Santa Barbara. They were pleasant enough. But the variety of people in New York is matchless. Consider today. I have not been well, so I have not been out very much. Yet this morning I had a visit from a publisher who's an old friend of mine, then a visit with you, and tonight I go out to Hannah Arendt for dinner. There's a variety of worthwhile contacts I couldn't have at Oberlin or in Atlanta.

For me, Chicago meant Hyde Park, a village which happens to be legally under the jurisdiction of Chicago. And within its boundaries a great university happened to be located. I retired from that university at age sixty-five. After that you can imagine what a trauma City College was to me. Teaching at City College is terrible, first of all, because the students are completely incompetent. I was unprepared for that. You could only teach on an extremely elementary level, and even then it was difficult because they mostly weren't interested. Why should a kid in need of total remediation care about the balance of power in the eighteenth century?

The college notwithstanding, New York is my city now. Nevertheless, if you'd get the Bavarians out of Munich, I could live in Munich.

5.

THE JEWISH NOVELIST IN NEW YORK—AN ÉMIGRÉ

Soma Morgenstern

I LANDED in 1941 in Hoboken in a small coast guard boat meant to hold three hundred people; there were six hundred on it. The captain told us that the boat had never sailed across the Atlantic—this was its first time and it was thirty years old. The trip cost me five hundred dollars and I didn't even have a bed.

Nobody expected me, but a journalist who knew me, a Social Democrat, took me over to New York in a ferry and called a taxi. I had an address—the Hotel Park Plaza. The taxi was my first confrontation with American technique. The door of the taxi was broken and would not close. I had to hold it with a shoe string!

Along the way I was astonished to see houses of three to six stories. I had thought that every building in Manhattan was a skyscraper. To reach the Park Plaza, we had to drive on Broadway, and my driver pointed to the trees. I knew Broadway and 42nd Street very well from the movies, but finding trees there was a great surprise to me. It was then that I realized I could stay here.

I went to Hollywood and after two years I came back to New York. The prospect frightened me. The city overwhelmed me. Nevertheless, I soon started to love (not like) New York. I discovered how charming it can be. It is a city that never goes to sleep. I once forgot a raincoat in a Greek coffee shop. A week later

Soma Morgenstern was born in East Galicia (the Soviet Ukraine) in 1890 and lived in Vienna until 1938. He was a cultural correspondent for the *Frankfurter Zeitung* and a novelist. He came to New York City in 1941 and remained there until his death in 1976. Among his works are the trilogy *In My Father's Pastures* and a novel of the Holocaust, *The Third Pillar*.

when it started to rain, I realized I had no raincoat. I went back
to the shop and there was the raincoat hanging in the same place
I had left it. I didn't ask the owners; I just took the coat and left—
something that could never happen in Europe. This shop never
closed. At that time there were many such coffee shops in the
city. Gradually, I came to understand what was going on here—
music, art, theater. . . . This is a real metropolis with a big public
for everything—the worst and the best. In Europe—in Vienna—
there is a small public for good things—for Schoenberg, for example. In New York, for everything—good or bad—there is a
big public.

When I reached Vienna I thought it was the greatest city in
the world. After all, I was born in a hamlet, a little *shtetl* (small
Jewish town in Eastern Europe). I had a love affair with Vienna
until the Nazis came. When I arrived in Paris I realized that it was
five times Vienna. But when I came to New York I knew this
was a higher—not a way of life—but a higher degree of commotion, which I like. I lived near the park and I loved to watch
all the commotion.

A metropolis is something which gives style to every layer
of life. New York was the only metropolis and it still is, despite
those murders that are going on. It, not Paris, is the center for
painters and for *haute couture*—you know, women's fashion,
something which has always interested me. In Paris you see old
women dressed for the cemetery. In New York you see seventy-
year-old women dressed like girls, not like dead bodies. Why?
Because Jews made the textile industry in New York. When I was
in Europe I thought that America was savage, but later I found
that in every regard—in entertainment, industry, and other
areas—it surpasses Europe.

They used to say Vienna is not Austria, and it was true; that
Berlin is not Germany, and it was true. But Paris is France, only
on a higher level. And it's the same with New York: New York
is America, only a little better because, like the restaurants, it's
mixed with European influence. I go to the park every day, as if
I were in a small town. Oh, I know New York is not a collection
of *shtetls*; it's a massive mixture. I see no essential difference between Manhattan and Brooklyn; although there's more wealth in

The "commotion" in Central Park.   THE N.Y.C. PARK DEPARTMENT.

Manhattan, they have the same character. Vienna was a metropolis that went down. It *became* a provincial city. When I went back to Europe I found that it is no longer Europe. I thought I'd stay because my bread and butter is not in America, but only Paris had survived. Vienna was provincial shit. It was dirty and occupied by the Russians (which I admit I liked very much because it had been occupied by the Nazis).

On account of my upbringing I like small towns, but I don't like the people who inhabit them. You are not a free man living with people in provincial cities. You lose your freedom: everybody knows who controls everybody else. Personal freedom was invented in big cities. In New York I have the freedom *and* the privacy that I need. In Europe, Ferenc Molnár once described New York City to me. He said, "I like New York for many reasons. The main reason is that in New York you can go to a hotel and live as if you were alone in the only house on top of a high mountain in Europe. You can disappear for three or four months, holed up in your hotel, writing away. Nobody cares about you and you don't care about anybody. You are a solitary man in the midst of all that brouhaha—alone!" He was absolutely right.

I have a friend here, Leonhard Frank, who was well known in Europe. He was a Bavarian; he looked like a handsome, clean-faced Englishman—before he opened his mouth. He was a very good writer. We became friends in the concentration camp. He came here from France where he didn't dare open his mouth and say good morning. He just kept quiet. But here he started to open up because English is closer to German than French is: you know, a fish is a fish. . . . So he liked it better in New York. But I was really happy here and that made him angry. So he said, "What I don't like about you, Soma, is that here you are a happy man. You were miserable in France, but here you are happy."

I answered, "In France you must report to the police every two weeks. Here I went only once to the police and that was just to check in."

Again, he asked, "But why are you so happy?"

So I told him, "You are a Bavarian. Suppose you came to a city where out of eight million people there were three million Bavarians. Now, I am a Jew and I always was. I didn't wait for Hitler to tell me. I knew very well how many Jews there were in New York, but to know is one thing—to live it is something else. How would you feel if there were three million Bavarians in this city? Would you be happy or not? Imagine . . . all that sauerkraut!! Here I have the Jews, so here I am at home, and I never was at home before. I was only a statistic along with two and a half million other Jews. Here I am a reality. Why should I be unhappy?"

I find Jews in New York appealing and disappointing in about the same measures as in Europe. In New York I met a charming man, a real American, not one like the majority of them who came here when they were six years old. He was born here and his father was born here. His name's Al Hirschfeld. He is an American Jew who sometimes doesn't understand what I say, and not merely because of the language barrier. I told him what I don't like even now is that on Saturday and Sunday theater prices go up. In Europe—even in old Vienna under an absolute monarchy—

on Friday, Saturday, and Sunday there were lower prices so that poor people who work all week could go to the theater. When I said that to Al in 1943, he looked at me the way you look at a fool. He told me, "But, Soma, these are the best days for business." So I told him that that is just what I don't like about it! That aspect of business! In Europe where there was a monarchy, there was respect for poor people and students. High school boys could go to the theater cheap on Saturday and Sunday. I assure you that if I see Al—who is a very dear friend of mine—tomorrow, and I tell him this again, he will give me the same answer. Here, people take for granted that what's good for business is good for everybody.

I also don't like a certain type called the "allrightnik," someone who throws everything away and loses himself. We had that type in Vienna. Here, to be sure, assimilation is not so dirty as it was in Germany, although it's starting here too. Too many college boys who cared about Vietnam didn't care about Israel. That's really German assimilationist thinking. It's also what communism means everywhere. Finding it here is what disappointed me most about America. American Jews hadn't absorbed the lesson of Jewish martyrdom in Europe. They had learned nothing. The people who argued that socialism meant Jewish redemption still believe it. Those who claimed that communism would liberate the Jews still believe it, and the new generation falls into their mistakes. Let me say again—they didn't learn a thing! When Israel came into existence, something positive happened. It happened again after the war of '67. But since the Yom Kippur War, things have gone bad. The Yom Kippur War exerted a negative influence because American Jews are like most Americans—they like a winner! Remember, American Jews are American just as German Jews are German. I reproach the German Jews more than I do the French Jews who are *French* Jews; German Jews are *German* Jews too. The difference is that French Jews are French Jews; the German Jews, except for the Zionists and Orthodox, were and are (even here) *Jewish Germans*. Kissinger is a Jewish German. I'm an unhyphenated Jew, with my roots in my shoes, and I feel most comfortable in New York because there are more Jews here than in Israel.

I still like New York, but I don't use it anymore. I don't go out in the evening because I'm afraid. I got mugged one time—this is not a pleasure. But still, I'm sure New York is more interesting and even more comfortable than London.

What enchants me is the intensity of life in New York, its business, arts, everything. On the other hand, when I came here I said to Ludwig Lewisohn, "You know the influence of the Jews here and in Europe. Tell me, how many works in literature are there written by American Jews that will survive?" He said, "None!" And I found out that he was right. You can't expect Ben Hecht to survive; even better talents get lost. Later I was astonished by one exception: Mailer's *The Naked and the Dead*, a book that will survive. In my opinion, it is the best antiwar book ever written. Even when I first read *War and Peace* I wanted to go immediately into an army. I don't like Mailer and what he's doing; he's crazy with the American craziness about money, millions of dollars, etc. But Mailer wrote one book, and it will survive.

I don't see supposed Jewish dominance of the arts as particularly dangerous. It will not provoke the charge that Jews run everything. If we Jews exaggerate, I take it as a natural thing to do; however, I have something against self-hating—like Philip Roth. I have nothing against Kafka who wrote in German; he is still a Jew. Kafka is a dangerous writer. Dangerous, not dangerous? He is the most dangerous. But this is a question for philosophers. It is not dangerous for the Jews to be in control of TV networks, the media, and the arts—if they do good things. I don't like it when they help to ruin America. In reality, everything is dangerous to the Jews, the good and the bad. There is no treatment for it. There could be a holocaust here or anywhere, but like a pogrom it would have to be well organized. There never was a spontaneous pogrom; without planning, it would not succeed. Even such a thing as the Germans did had to be programmed like a war.

The New York Mets are my personal vice. I like baseball because compared to other sports it is less brutal. As a matter of fact, it is not brutal at all. In Europe my interest was like that of my brother Jew, Kissinger, who likes soccer. In Vienna there was better soccer than you have ever seen. Tops! There was even a Jewish team that could beat the British in London. In Vienna, I went every Sunday with Alban Berg to the matches. When I came here I didn't realize what baseball was. I read the *New York Times*. A friend of mine who came here a year before me said, "Soma, if you read the *Times* you do not know New York. You have to read the *Daily News*." So I thought that since my friend had been here longer, he must know. And he did. For a stranger the *Daily News* has better news about New York because the *Times* is on a higher literary level. So I read the *News*, and one day I saw an item: In a bar there were two people sitting. One said to the other, "The Dodgers are bums."

The other said, "Would you repeat that if I went home and came back with a gun?"

The other man said, "I will."

So he comes back with a gun and says, "Now, repeat it."

And the other said, "I'll repeat it—the Dodgers are bums!" So he shot him in the stomach!

This was my first exposure to baseball. I didn't even understand this type of reportage or what baseball could be. Then I started to understand that it's a sport. At first I was biased against baseball; those uniforms reminded me of the chimney sweepers in Vienna. So I didn't like baseball, but my best friends—Brooks Atkinson, Gus Goetz (the playwright), and Al Hirschfeld—were all baseball fans and connoisseurs. I asked them to explain baseball to me. They all tried, but there was something wrong with me, I just couldn't understand. It was awful.

One evening at Al Hirschfeld's, sitting in the garden after dinner, there was a gentleman I had just met. He ran the book review column in the *Times*. I forget his name. He died a few years ago; he was a very charming man. I told him that three friends were teaching me baseball but I couldn't follow it. In fifteen minutes in the dark, he explained to me the sense of baseball, and the rest was just watching and learning because there are ninety rules. I will never forget this man for what he did because it was such a big part of my being Americanized. I don't think you can be Americanized if you don't understand baseball. All the other sports are not American. It would be a bad sign if football replaced baseball because there is a relation between baseball and the national character, and football is a brutal sport.

When I first came to New York, there were four kiosks on the corner of 72nd Street and Broadway where you could buy all the foreign papers. I was still very interested and read all the papers; one day I would buy a Polish paper, one day a French paper, and others. The kiosk nearest to me was run by a Jewish fellow. One day, when I bought a Yiddish paper, he looked at me strangely. A week later he said, "May I ask you a personal question? You are buying newspapers in so many languages. Of course, you are European but you are not the type who reads Yiddish papers." This astonished me. And yet, what he meant was that he could tell my type by my dress—the way I can recognize a German Jew here in New York from behind, by the way he wears his hat. This man was not a photographer selling pictures by profession, but he was right—I'm not the type who buys Yiddish newspapers. I explained to him that in Vienna for thirty years I never read a Yiddish newspaper; there was never one to get. I still read the Yiddish papers once a week in order to retain my Yiddish. But now, there is no man at a paper stand so interested in people who buy papers, no man with such an eye. All that's gone.

6.

JAZZ—THE JEWISH-BLACK CONNECTION

Dan Morgenstern

WHAT HAPPENED when I first hit 52nd Street? It hit me right back! Thereby hangs a tale. Let me begin at the beginning.

I was born in Munich, but only by coincidence: my grandmother had a country place not far from that city and my mother spent the last part of her pregnancy there. So I was born in Munich, but I spent my early years in Vienna, which was my home until 1938. By then I was eight years old. I moved to Denmark and remained there until 1943. Then my mother and I escaped to Sweden, where we spent eighteen months. We returned to Denmark and reached America in April 1947. My father had already been here for six years—and as a U.S. citizen he could bring us in on a preferential visa.

Before our arrival I was obsessed with America. The United States had always been a dream to me. My father wanted to come here before the war. He was born in Poland and the Polish quota never came through in time. I was terribly interested in American life. I read voraciously about the United States, my image formed partly by Faulkner, and then on a slightly lower level by James M. Cain and such. Each of these writers had a tremendous ear for American speech and an eye for certain details of life in America. I learned American English from books, including hardboiled mysteries by Dashiell Hammett, Raymond Chandler, and a good

Dan Morgenstern was born in Germany in 1929. He is a jazz historian and critic. He is director of the Institute of Jazz Studies at Rutgers University and has edited several jazz journals and produced many jazz concert series and television programs.

novelist named Jonathan Latimer who did scripts in Hollywood but also wrote mysteries that were funny, slangy and very atmospheric.

I knew that I wanted to come here and that some day I would. Although I loved Denmark and Copenhagen and I'd have had no problems in staying there, America was the great magnet. That was the place. And it still is! Particularly if by America you mean New York City. But I got a real feeling for New York less from books than from movies. During the war, in Sweden, American movies were the principal fare. In 1942 the Nazis had put a stop to them in Denmark. For me, one of the best things about Sweden (first of all, there were *lights!*) was that you could go to American films. I had seen the New York skyline in films, so reaching the port of New York was a case of déjà vu. But this city is so tremendously impressive that you really must be here to take it in. I was something of an expert on the history of New York. And I knew about Manhattan, particularly 52nd Street, which was just about the first place I wanted to go—because it was "Jazz Street."

I'm a child of the Swing era, and the Swing era was an international phenomenon. Swing was popular in Europe, especially in Denmark which was always very Anglo-American in its cultural orientation. So I grew up with those sounds. . . . Actually, my background was also classical because of my father's interest in music. He knew many musicians who often visited our house, people like Alban Berg and Otto Klemperer, the conductor. Alban Berg, as a close friend of my father's, paid us frequent visits. My father was a cultural correspondent who wrote about all the arts, including music, which he understood exceptionally well. I remember that on my fourth or fifth birthday, Berg gave me records of "Eine Kleine Nachtmusik." My parents took me to concerts for young people in Vienna on Sunday afternoons. They were originated by the Social Democrats and continued under Dolfuss and Schussnig. But records were my passion. I loved them. My mother had a wind-up phonograph and popular music records, among them several that were borderline jazz. I now know that some of them were jazz-flavored, mostly from the late twenties and early thirties.

The first time I was exposed to the real thing? Probably when Jack Hylton's orchestra came to Vienna. Jack Hylton was the English Paul Whiteman and the man who brought Coleman Hawkins to Europe. It was like a stage show. They did an Ellington medley and during "Mood Indigo" the lights went down; the trombone and the trumpet players had sparkling mutes in their horns which produced an interesting visual effect. But it was the very beautiful melody that got to me. I had this experience in 1935, so I must have been five going on six. A little later someone gave me a record of Fletcher Henderson's, a great jazz record with Roy Eldridge, Chu Berry, and Buster Bailey. I can see in retrospect that it was the one *real* jazz record I heard as a child in Vienna.

But my interest didn't really develop until I came to Denmark, when my mother took me to see Fats Waller, who performed in Copenhagen late in 1938. Fats came out in a white suit of tails and a silver top hat. He started to play and sing. Now, I had not seen very many black people at all, and certainly not very many who were so huge. He was over six feet tall, a big man who had a tremendous personality. Fats got through to me although I couldn't understand what he said—he was speaking English, of course. His facial expressions and body language were thoroughly infectious. At about the same time, my mother took me to see the Mills Brothers and the Quintet of the Hot Club of France, with Django Reinhardt and Stephan Grappelli.

By the time I got here, I was seventeen, and I wanted to go to 52nd Street. New York was the jazz center of the world, and 52nd Street was still vital, although no longer at its peak. In fact, 1947 turned out to be one of the final years on the Street. Jazz continued to be played there in a club or two well into the 1950s, and Jimmy Ryan's stayed on for a very long time, but then it still had at least seven or eight places where jazz was played. The Street always had its share of non-jazz places, but in one city block (and a bit beyond that a few clubs across Sixth Avenue and on the other block towards Seventh, Hickory House and so on), you could listen to dozens of great musicians. And they had their own hangouts. The White Rose Bar was where most of the guys went. There you had whiskey for a quarter and beer at fifteen cents or a dime. It was there that you could rub shoulders with all these incredible people. Nobody stayed in the club during intermission, except perhaps very late at night, because the clubs were small and you couldn't move around comfortably in them; every available space was taken and the management didn't particularly like to have you there. Well, we'd go to the White Rose or we'd hang out in front of the club. If you just walked down the street, you'd quite frequently see someone like Coleman Hawkins grabbing a smoke. It was an intimate place and, as such, it was unique.

Fifty-second Street in its glory had most of the action. But there was always the Village, where jazz started way back. I guess Nick's in the 1930s was the first well-known jazz club. The Village also had Condon's and the Riviera, which was on Seventh Avenue South. On the East Side you found piano places, and there was also music in Brooklyn. As always, as there is today, there was jazz in dozens of places all over the city and in the suburbs. Even in the worst days for jazz, which would be the sixties (they were the worst days for me, and in historical terms too I think jazz was at a low ebb), even then there was plenty going. We had lofts in the Village and at least a few midtown clubs and little places with piano players. There's never been a New York wipe-out since the advent of jazz in this city—which supposedly dates from the Original Dixieland Jazz Band coming into Reisenweber's in 1917, but actually goes farther back than that.

There were other cities that went through stages, but if you take Los Angeles with its own concentration of musicians, well, it's so spread out that, although there are many fine musicians around, you may have to drive fifty miles from one place to another. On 52nd Street you walked across the street and that was it. You could spend a whole week there and still not reach every band you wanted to hear in depth. It was my starting point.

But Harlem may have been more exciting; after hours, it certainly was. And there was the Apollo! There in early '48 I saw Dizzy Gillespie's big band with Chano Pozo. The Apollo was a scene unto itself. The interaction between performers and the audience was extraordinary. The Apollo audience responded to

Fifty-second Street in its heyday.   WILLIAM P. GOTTLEIB.

the music in an entirely different way from people in a club on
52nd Street, where, although blacks were not excluded, they were
not exactly welcome. They were there and they were served, but
it wasn't the same. I had been to concerts where the audience was
mixed. But the Apollo was an institution, one of the last remaining
black theaters of a great circuit where the bands would play and
the singers and dancers would perform. I can't say this too em-
phatically: the rapport between audience and performers was
unique. It has not been seen before or since. The audience was
aware of every nuance of the performers' art. People didn't disrupt
the performances, but they responded by calling out enthusias-
tically. There was real give-and-take.

The first time I went uptown in style I was in the company
of Lips Page. Lips' real name was Oran, which, by no accident,
is my first son's middle name. Oran's a beautiful name and Lips
was a beautiful man, one of the warmest, most generous, and
vibrant human beings I've ever known. He was starstruck, as they
say. Nothing worked right for him. He knocked at that door but

99

never got in and then, of course, he died much too soon at forty-six. But Lips was a fantastic performer who loved people as they loved him. I realize these are all clichés and do not hesitate to add one more: he was in touch with everything and everybody. That's why with Lips you could walk into the Lotus Club, a bar in Harlem that had a turnstile so no one could leave without paying. Beer was served in bottles; nobody bothered with a glass; beer was a quarter and whiskey thirty cents. It was a "bucket of blood," as they used to call a rough place like that one. You'd walk in with Lips and you were welcome. He could make the place jump. Everybody's attention riveted upon him, And he could do that just as effortlessly at the Stork Club.

Through Lips, I first got a taste of the Harlem scene. It's difficult for this generation to understand Harlem in those days because there are so many barriers now to normal human contact. The situation of blacks in this country hasn't improved so much. Certainly blacks today have gained a tentative toehold in many areas of American life, and in those days, of course, that wasn't the case. But in jazz there was a genuine feeling of brotherhood. We should not forget that jazz was the first publicly integrated sector of American life. Jackie Robinson went to the Dodgers in 1946-47, and that was a big deal. But in the jazz world, Teddy Wilson and Lionel Hampton had been performing publicly with Benny Goodman—Teddy since 1936 and Hamp from late '36 or '37. Bands after that were not thoroughly integrated, but the Street was. Mixed groups played there as a matter of course. Joe Marsala's band at the Hickory House with Red Allen is a good example. In Harlem there was a feeling of acceptance among musicians and those around them. If a white male came up nobody would judge him right off the bat, but unless he was accompanied by a female he was suspected of being there to get some action—and that was too often the case. But if you were with musicians, you were there either because you were a musician or you were a friend of a musician, and you were accepted. I never felt any overt hostility in Harlem. Occasionally in a bar you'd get an elbow, a tangible cold shoulder. But with Lips you had entry. Those who call Harlem nothing but a ghetto or think of it only as a giant slum are wrong. There are nice places to live in Harlem even today. Certainly there were then. Parts of Harlem were fancy and parts were very down home and there was music in a lot of them and Lips was welcome everywhere.

One place we went was a social club. There I saw Art Tatum and Billie Holiday. Billie was just relaxing and eating. They had decent food, too. Usually in Harlem the two things you could eat anywhere were good chicken in the basket and barbecued ribs with delicious potato salad. Plus, I was introduced to chitlins by a friend of mine on a New Year's Eve in 1948 or '49. My friend said, "Try some." I did, and they were delicious. Then he told me what I was eating. Now, I hadn't been raised on kosher food, but still, pigs' intestines! I told him it really tasted good. And I ate some more because it *did* taste good. Later, I also discovered such delicacies as pigs' ears and tails, which are very tasty. Black people learned to make do with what they could afford, things that were practically given away by slaughterhouses in the South and Chicago. Chitlins—you could get a bucketful of them for a few cents. They learned how to prepare such scorned edibles and to make them taste delicious.

Initially most of the American whites I was exposed to were my father's friends, fairly recent immigrants, mostly Middle European Jews. Ironically my main interest in those days was film. I was crazy about it, and hoped to go to Hollywood. But I was also taken up with jazz. I would go with my parents to somebody's house. I was an eighteen-year-old boy; I rarely saw anyone there around my age. It wasn't easy to find common ground. Then, if jazz came up, it seemed like something very exotic to them. Since jazz was a minority phenomenon, culturally, I sought respect and recognition for it. Sometimes we'd quarrel about that, but not my father and I, because he was musical enough to take jazz seriously. My father knew many musicians. Karol Rathaus was one of his closest friends, and Rathaus *was* interested in jazz. He'd ask me about it. In general, these immigrants were not prejudiced against blacks but some began to take on white American attitudes. I soon found out that going to Harlem was considered dangerous. You wouldn't necessarily be robbed or mugged but it was a place to avoid.

Now the jazz world consisted of whites and blacks. I was sometimes one of maybe two or three whites among several hundred blacks. Seldom did I think self-consciously about that ratio because it felt perfectly normal and very warm. I began to meet other blacks. Through involvement with jazz in Harlem and elsewhere I came to know a whole range of jazz fans: hustlers, longshoremen, laborers, postal clerks. Doctors and lawyers too. So I learned something that should be obvious to anyone with an iota of human sensitivity, that the term black, or Negro, as one then said, covered a lot of territory. All the stereotypes were idiotic. Okay, but there was also a marvelous ambience in the Harlem of my youth, a certain style, a panache, a resilience in dealing with a world which, without humor and insouciance, would have been intolerable.

You could go down to the Central Plaza in downtown New York where they had weekend sessions and most of the audience would be white college *age*, but not college kids. They drank beer and loved "When the Saints Go Marching In"; they'd bang on the tables and even stand on them. By then it would be midnight and they'd have downed several pitchers of beer. This was also a very real response to the music, but it was different music, although mainly performed by blacks down there, too. Jazz, of course, always has permeated every level of society. The Duke of Windsor sat in on drums with Duke Ellington's band; the Duke of Kent collected Ellington records; in France there were enthusiasts among intellectuals or artists and also among society people who went to see those "charming" and "fantastic" Negro performers in Paris between the wars. The music cut across everything. That's why it also cut across racial barriers.

I didn't realize until later how privileged I had been in the entrée I received. The things I learned on a musical level *and* on a human level equipped me to make jazz my profession. And I realized I knew something that a lot of American whites didn't know, and that too many of them didn't want to know. I had had an inkling of the so-called Negro problem which concerned and interested me very much even before I came to the U.S., partly because of the experiences I had as a Jew in Hitler's Europe. It didn't, therefore, completely surprise me that some Americans preferred not to know that blacks were oppressed. But that's a truism. I discovered it in various ways. Anyone could do the same by reading daily papers. The situation of blacks turned me leftward politically, where I was inclined to go anyway because the Danish underground, which after all saved my life, was so largely Communist. Although many others participated in it, Communists were the organizers and the Communist party in Denmark had a pretty strong moral position after the end of the war, which naturally they threw away. Those Communists were as incapable of dealing honestly with the Danish political system as they were with democracy everywhere else. With a black friend, I almost joined the Communist party. He did and I didn't.

Direct association was primary. And yet I scoured the literature for anything it could teach me. I was a great reader of Faulkner and Caldwell and Richard Wright, and anything I could get my hands on by black writers, of whom there were not as many then as now. But there was Claude McKay. And there was James Baldwin, whom I had the good fortune to meet in the Village. Erskine Caldwell wrote a powerful novel on the "race" issue called *Trouble in July*, and I was impressed by it. I met Ralph Ellison much later. *Invisible Man* was *the* key novel. I loved that book in 1952. I read it in the army. It was a marvel to me. Ellison's thinking was so close to my own. *Invisible Man* won the National Book Award, but I don't think it was really understood. On the contrary, it was generally misunderstood. I suspect Ellison's withdrawal from the public arena is a symptom of that fact. Fiction and poetry haven't made much difference. Neither have social and psychological studies. God knows, they were available. I read *An American Dilemma* and everything else I could find to help me master the available data.

I don't believe black friends cared very much that I was Jewish. They usually knew that I was European and it was important, but some white Americans were also accepted. If you were straight, you were okay, and a European was considered more likely to be straight.

Ethnic pluralism, which so far works better in this country than anywhere else, is particularly important in the jazz world. For better and for worse, Jews have dominated cultural management. I don't think it's any accident that Irving Mills, Joe Glaser, Norman Granz, and George Wein have all been Jews. As with the movies two kinds of Jews got involved; the Louis B. Mayer types who had the business sense to see that there was something to this strange new gimmick, and the others, who grasped it on a higher level. Some combined both. All these people, although they were very different in many ways, had one trait in common: they accepted and promoted black talent for what it is, the greatest talent in jazz music. Non-Jews like John Hammond (who is a patrician and that's no accident either) have done the same thing. There is a black man named Stanley Crouch who, if he can get himself to sit down and do it, has a great book about jazz in him. So far he only has a title, which is *Outlaws and Gladiators*. It's a great title because, in a sense, jazz has always been an outlaw music. It was eventually presented at court, but still has that outlaw strain in it. It's a minority music, black in origin, and by and large attractive to minority people. In New Orleans they were Italian and Jewish and Irish. And it was like that everywhere, notably in Chicago, where white jazz was predominantly Irish and Scottish and Jewish. Of course, the Italians and the Irish have great musical traditions of their own. So that was all part of it. Perhaps those people, being members of minorities themselves, were able to take a couple of jumps over the others. Responding to music which they knew to be black in origin was easier for them.

Many Jews contributed to jazz by becoming excellent musicians. Some of them were successful like Benny Goodman and Artie Shaw, and some were not but made very good music—like Davie Schildkraut. If you break it down, there have been some splendid musicians. Benny Goodman, for instance. Goodman's success and his image as the King of Swing created certain problems. People ask: How could a white man be a King of Swing when Swing was black music? But given the context, America in the 1930s, it was almost inevitable that if you had a King of Swing, and it was kind of nice to have one, he would be white. He turned out to be a Jew, which is also pretty good, if you look at it from a certain point of view. Due to the not-so-hidden anti-Semitism of some Jewish writers on jazz, Goodman has come in for a lot of lumps. And their theme has also been picked up by black commentators. They accept the myth, and it *is* a myth, that white jazz musicians were exploiters who copped somebody else's music. That's about as silly as you can get. A wonderful thing about jazz is that it communicates—it's a great musical language. Naturally, inevitably, other people had to pick it up. If jazz had been exclusively black, it would not have become a world music.

From an idealistic standpoint, black musicians did not receive the recognition or the profit that they deserved. But how often does talent reap its own reward? You've got a mixture of elements which are sometimes erroneously lumped together under the heading of race and racism. It is not true in other areas of American cultural life that the most talented are the most successful. But on the matter of public success for a black person, jazz created unmatched opportunities. It was simply not possible in any other field for a black person in America to achieve the kind of recognition that went to Duke Ellington and Louis Armstrong forty or fifty years ago. And this wouldn't have been possible if a white audience had not accepted the music. The black audience alone could support it only to a limited extent. But in prewar America when it came to the highest level of popular success, the greatest visibility, the biggest monetary rewards would ipso facto go to whites.

So back to Benny Goodman. A Jewish jazz critic in the *Village Voice* once said that Benny Goodman was a man of limited talent who knew how to exploit blacks. That's disingenuous and dishonest and wrong. Benny Goodman was a very gifted musician who also happened to be an ambitious man with certain skills. He had the intelligence to get himself good management and the good taste and the courage to use black artists as part of his performing team. To call that exploitation is to turn things around and distort them. It wasn't just exploitation; it was also a calculated risk that paid off. And after that you might say it was a sure thing. Benny Goodman did not sit down and decide, "I'm going to take Fletcher Henderson and have him write arrangements for me and exploit him." Benny Goodman was fond of Fletcher Henderson and respected him greatly. He paid Henderson just as much as and sometimes more than he paid white musicians who worked for him. Fletcher Henderson was very happy about the Goodman band assignment at a time when he was broke. Later, when Henderson again fell on evil times, Goodman hired him to play piano in his band. Maybe that was just another version of the old plantation system. But within the realm of jazz, as a music and as a social phenomenon, I don't think that it was. Even if I put myself into the "victim's" shoes, I still say that "self-serving white exploitation" is a simplistic, smug label for what happened.

Men like George Gershwin teach us something else about the interethnic quality of jazz. Gershwin was a very gifted musician who had the ears and the sensibility to hear things. He appeared on the scene coincidentally with an outpouring of musical creativity in this country. That rich period started in the teens and really soared in the twenties. It was tremendous. I would accept American popular songwriting—the Broadway musical show— as an art in itself. If you agree, then you have to say that we produced some great artists, and that a large number of them happened to be Jewish. Arlen, Berlin, Gershwin, Rodgers, Kern— all Jewish. Cole Porter wasn't, but he loved Jewish music. We also had some fine black songwriters who were ripped off; other people were ripped off, too. It was a rip-off business. But the inspiration that Gershwin found in black American music and which ultimately led him to create his masterpiece (*Porgy and Bess*)—I don't think that was accidental either. Musically there are links that might have predisposed Gershwin to hear that music in a certain way and find empathy with it. But that music was in the air by then and Gershwin started out as a very young man who played demonstration for song publishers. He had colleagues like James P. Johnson. He knew who Fats Waller was and who Art Tatum was. After all, Gershwin was a piano player too. And there was ragtime and there was jazz. It was only natural that he developed more of a feeling for the blues than for black church music, which also influenced his work. The blues isn't really melancholy music. Neither is cantorial music really melancholy. They have something in common because the melody, the scales they use, are non–Western European. In regard to emotional content there are parallels; cantorial melisma and the melisma of a great gospel singer are quite closely related. But Gershwin was exposed to a black strain in American popular music which was already there, which had been there from Stephen Foster and probably even before, but certainly from then on. And he knew what to do with it. He heard it more deeply and more truly than most people. Not that I would want to shortchange Harold Arlen, the son of a cantor, who wrote wonderful tunes that lend themselves marvelously to jazz exploration.

Some very great jazz musicians have been Jews. I wouldn't overemphasize that point; it applied perhaps equally to the Irish. And a lot of great white jazz musicians have borne the Indian heritage with them. Pee Wee Russell was part Indian and the rest English stock. Big Chief Russell Moore is a full-blooded Indian. (Many great black musicians have Indian in them.) Many Jews have *written* about jazz. Jazz journalists and jazz critics are quite often Jewish. In New York, the white audience for jazz has always been heavily Jewish. But that's inevitable. There'd be no cultural life in this city if you took the Jews out of it. When I started making friends and meeting jazz fans, I soon realized that people like me were crazy about the music. It would be hard to overlook the fact that a large percentage of them were Jews, including Jewish girls, who like not only the music but also the musicians.

It seems self-evident that there should be a bond between people who have suffered oppression. I strongly believe this even though the black-Jewish relationship has often been awkward. Many clumsy mistakes have been made and American Jews as a group have not been entirely successful in linking arms with the blacks, for which, of course, there are a number of reasons. An affinity is present even among Jews who harbor social and cultural prejudices against blacks. *They* feel the affinity whenever racist crimes or awful indignities afflict black people—which is why the civil rights movement drew so many Jews into its orbit.

More recently we witnessed some ridiculous business with Andrew Young—a minor uproar for a while. The New York *Post* fostered a big lie about Jews demanding Andrew Young's resignation from the UN. There was an uproar on TV. Blacks were being televised from a church in Harlem at a political meeting. One guy got up and said he was a minister and that some blacks were talking nonsense. And he added, "If they knock on the door to get Jews tonight, they'll be coming to get you and me in the morning." It's true, and the sooner both parties realize that, the better.

As for myself, in some sense I identify with blacks but trying to do so completely is a kind of pathetic fallacy. I can't identify with an American black ultimately to the deepest level, just as he can't totally identify with what I've gone through. But there *is* a link. One is constantly reminded of differences, but our common humanity is all that matters.

I am not a survivor like those émigrés who came here and had to rediscover that there was some good in human beings. I didn't need that lesson because the Danes had taught it to me. The question of human nature, in light of the Holocaust, deeply interests me. A large part of my life has been governed by what happened in Europe under Hitler. I saw our neighbors welcome the Nazis to Vienna, full of joy, cheering and waving swastikas. I had scarlet fever, which was one reason my mother and I stayed and my father, who was on the blacklist, split right away. He took the last train out to Switzerland. But we saw the transformation of everyday associates into Nazis who forced us to leave our home. But being in Denmark was a lifesaver for my psyche. Denmark is a wonderful country and the Danes were marvelous people. The Holocaust meant for me, among other things, that for quite a few months after Denmark was occupied by the Germans we had no contact with my father. (In time, we found out that he had made his way to Marseilles and we heard from him before he came to America in '41.) Then communication was cut off again until we got to Sweden. We eventually discovered that my grandmother, my aunt, several of my uncles and cousins were all murdered.

I'm still very conscious of the whole horror. It doesn't take much to set me off. Reading about the trial of a war criminal or hearing Hannah Arendt's name mentioned is provocation enough. But in trying to come to terms with all this I was fortunate to have my father and his faith for support. The Holocaust, he felt, proved that Western History had moved from humanism to nationalism to bestiality. On the other hand his Jewishness had become unshakable, even universal. Jewishness was his pride; the pride in the sanctity of all human life as arrived at in Deuteronomic law. He often reminded me of the biblical obligations of man to *all* men, an idea he found lacking in Plato's Greeks who blithely accepted slavery. Now I guess I can see a tragic aspect to his life. Here was a Jewish novelist writing in the German language in the thirties. Hermann Hesse had compared the earlier novels favorably with the Russian masters. Suddenly his audience is removed and then literally wiped out! When he sat down to write *The Third Pillar* his intention was to look at the Holocaust through the eyes of the man who knew the world only through God's Torah. But the Good Samaritan was also there. My father cherished and loved this Good Samaritan, the decent Christian Witness who daily risked his life for unknown Jewish victims. This idea had been my experience because of Danes who, in the most ordinary and matter-of-fact way, although I did not know and never saw them again, risked their lives to save mine. At least I could begin to see that all humanity was not depraved. Not even all Germans. When I first came back to Germany as an American soldier stationed at Dachau, I was resentful. I must say that in the abstract, I hated Germans and wanted nothing to do with them. And yet I came to understand that not all Germans were bastards or murderers, that many Germans, like people everywhere, were just human beings caught in a process which was beyond their control, and that some individuals managed to retain some decency.

Much of the best in our culture is the creation of black Americans. I fully agree with Albert Murray's thesis in *The OmniAmericans* that blacks, in a sense, *are* the OmniAmericans because so many characteristics that we tend to think of as typically American are typically black American. That's not African—it's black American, which is a unique phenomenon. That contribution is much larger and deeper than students of American civilization generally recognize. It transcends the sizable contribution to our language, the x number of expressions deriving from that subculture. Attitude, style, and pacing are all involved. White

Americans don't walk like Europeans. We have a rolling gait that some people think comes from the cowboys, from sitting on horses. Ain't that many people who sat on horses! It comes from watching black Americans walk and dance. Now Harlem was the center of that subculture. As Duke Ellington said, "Harlem is it," you know, like the *Arabian Nights*.

Harlem at one time *was* it. I'm not sure it still is, but there are men and women striving to regenerate Harlem, and people who, much to their credit, have never left Harlem. Al Murray is one. Things never end abruptly. They peter out. Some beautiful things ended in Harlem when the urban crisis hit New York as it did every other big city. There's still a vibrant cultural life in Harlem even though "things ain't what they used to be." With the decline of their old neighborhood, blacks began to have an enormous influence on life in Greenwich Village, which also changed drastically and continues on its own dynamic path. And now we have Soho.

New York is like a living organism that constantly regenerates and reconstitutes itself. The city is very much alive today. New York City is still the world center of jazz. You can't hear Cecil Taylor with an eight-piece band in a club, which just happened the other week, or see the Newport Jazz Festival, or go to the performance of multifarious music in so many places anywhere else in the world. You don't have such a concentration of musicians, and you don't have that special New York "thing." There's a vital musical scene in this town. Jazz is still very strong. I think it's more than proven that all these premonitions of its impending death that you used to hear in the fifties and sixties were really way off the mark. But on the other hand, so much of the music now exists on recordings and in other transmittable forms and there'll be more of that, what with the coming of various video formats and even better sound reproduction. It may no longer be necessary to be in immediate touching distance of all this. But I wouldn't think that I would have to raise my children in New York City because it's a great town for jazz. There are people who were raised in Perth Amboy who became great human beings; it'll come out regardless. But I think given the stimulating environment that you can find here, certainly I would prefer to raise my children in the city.

Because New York is the center, it is no wonder that Louis Armstrong moved here early. Louis, of course, was the incarnation of jazz. I met Louis for the first time in 1948, backstage at the Roxy, and I followed him until he died. (My second son Joshua's middle name is Louis.) There were always many other people around when I saw Louis. Although I traveled on the band bus a few times, was backstage often, and visited Louis' house a few times, reasonably intimate moments were rare occasions, because there was no way of "hanging out" with Louis. Louis couldn't hang out; Louis was celebrity—a world-famous celebrity—and, as he said very poignantly in an interview I did with him just before his sixty-fifth birthday, he literally couldn't go anywhere to relax or enjoy himself. He couldn't go the movies. When he went to see the Liston-Clay fight in a movie house—the one that ended after half a minute with Liston sitting on his ass— he never even got to see that, because when people recognized him they all started asking for autographs and shaking his hand. He couldn't go to the beach, couldn't even go to his dentist. He said he once went to his doctor and then to his dentist, which was a three-block walk. On the way some kids, two nuns, and other people began to gather—"Hey, there's Satchmo!" It took him an hour to go those three blocks. He said, "Of course, in one sense, it's wonderful and I wouldn't want them to stop asking for them autographs because then you know that you're through, but on the other hand . . . "

Louis lived in Corona in the same house he bought in the forties. He could have had a lot more, but Louis didn't want that. He wasn't home that much anyway. He had a nice home and felt very comfortable there. It was a lot better than the shack where he was born. This man grew up in what was extreme poverty even for a black child in 1900.

But his Jewish connection in New Orleans was recently restated. I was very moved when after his death I saw the film George

Wein made at the seventieth birthday tribute to Louis at Newport. At one point Louis talked about the Russian-Jewish family he worked for as a very young boy in New Orleans, and how moved he was by the "Yiddishe Mama's" lullabies. Louis wore a Mogen David around his neck and when asked about his religion he replied that he was raised a Baptist, always wore the Star of David, and had an audience with the Pope. But he *lived* in New York!

7.

THE RADICAL ÉMIGRÉ
IN THE METROPOLIS

Henry Pachter

A COLLEAGUE recently reminded me of my half-facetious answer to his question about why I became a radical. Apparently I said, "Because I was Jewish." What did I mean? I might simply have been in such a mood. But more likely something was on my mind: If you look at the authors of the *Weltbühne*, or those who were connected with the expressionist movement, the psychoanalysts, the Marxist writers, the Frankfurt Institute of Social Research, you'll see that 90 percent of them were Jews. Everybody who was a little different, or sensitive, was somehow an outsider. Jews I think in some way reflect their position as outsiders. An outsider may become an aesthete or a radical, or a cynic and a ruthless profiteer.

Being Jewish need not have predetermined my politics. Other Jews of my age and in my class were not radicals. Yet I'm quite sure that being Jewish and feeling some kind of alienation contributed to radicalization. Gentiles had more alternatives in expressing their dissent. They could be Nazis, or they could be members of the Youth Movement *and* Nazis. I had high-class Nazis in my school: intelligent, cultivated people who thought of themselves as radicals. They could rationalize the mixture by defining it as the German revolution against the West and against

Henry Pachter was born in Germany in 1907. He was professor of Renaissance studies and the sociology of ideas at City College. He is author of several books and articles, including *The Fall and Rise of Europe* (1975) and *Paracelsus: Magic into Science* (1951). Pachter died in 1980.

Western pseudo-civilization. May I elaborate? The first thing I wrote consciously as a radical was inspired by *The Persian Letters*. I had read Max Paasche, an anarchist who wrote an imitation of Montesquieu, and I in turn imitated his style. Paasche and Hermann Hesse were favorites of the Youth Movement. Also, my father, who had a print shop, published Bellamy's *Looking Backward*—a translation, of course—and another utopia by one Jagoda, I forget the title. All this fascinated me. When I was about fourteen, I read Rousseau's *Emile*. I have been addicted to Rousseau ever since. These were the influences in my thinking. From the Youth Movement I graduated to political revolution.

Every radical in Europe has two countries, his own and France. To be radical means you follow the great French revolution—"liberty, equality, fraternity." The French brought enlightenment into the world. The Youth Movement also had a romantic Rousseau cult: going back to nature, living a natural, nonbourgeois life. We were anti-Western, anticivilization. This was perhaps not political radicalism but I would call it a cultural revolution. At that time it seemed to us to be a radical secession from the world of our parents.

As to the generational revolt, America has had a time lag. Sixty-eight here looked to me like 1923 in Germany, with the same social base in both youth movements, the same dissatisfaction with adult society, the self-hate of the middle class, of bourgeois culture. You have some of the same symbols like letting one's hair grow; then we wore short pants, the equivalent of jeans. We also cultivated a dirty or neglected appearance. This was part of our protest against "Kultur." We didn't occupy any buildings, but we sang bloody mercenary songs of the Thirty Years War, pirate songs compared to which Pete Seeger is a piker.

I was born in Berlin. My father was Jewish, but my bar mitzvah and his wedding were the only occasions for which he entered the synagogue. He had been a Social Democrat since 1890; my grandfather was liberal. There was a current joke among Berlin Jews: What do you keep of the Jewish religion? Answer: the *Berliner Tageblatt* (equivalent of the *New York Times*), the liberal Jewish press. I supposed my mother's cooking was a little more Jewish . . . but, actually, we had very little Jewish life.

There were a few Jews in my class. One was really not very likeable. Another was much respected as a sports character. And then some were converted. I never found out whether they had one or two Jewish parents but each was known to have come from a Jewish family. They overcompensated by voicing their patriotism strongly. In my school Jews mixed well with others. My experience may not be typical; I had some friends but none really close. (I've never been very gregarious.) I personally had no difficulty. However, a few things happened that reminded me of the reactionary and anti-Semitic mentality of our teachers. Some openly attacked the Republic. Shortly before graduation our history class approached the present era. So the teacher asked who was a member of the Youth Movement. Six hands were raised, and he said to me: "You too? I thought you were a member of a different group." Most clubs of the Youth Movement indeed were anti-Semitic. Not the boys in my class, or else they wouldn't have had those baptized Jews in their group. If they had reservations against Jews in the abstract, they made no direct application of anti-Semitism. This same teacher introduced us to socialism with the following words (also at that time): "Socialism was founded by F. Lassalle, a Jew, and K. Marx, also a Jew. There you see that this is nothing for Germans."

In our class we also had the son of the editor of a vicious anti-Semitic newspaper, a certain Sedlatzek. His Polish name did not prevent him from being very German. We had political conversations in which he clearly expressed his dislike of Jewish judges, doctors, writers, etc., and he favored laws to curb them, but he said he meant nothing personal.

On the other hand, you could get into trouble with people you didn't know. If you met groups like Bismarck Youth and they felt compelled to show off, a Jew in their midst had to be careful. The amount of violence changed from year to year. It was worst during the inflation years, '21, '22, '23, especially in Bavaria. In the later twenties one did not hear of incidents. Then in the Depression it started up again, but this time it was organized. Nazis did not act spontaneously, but on command; their purpose was to terrorize the suburbs. Beating up "commies" or Jews was a means to achieve hegemony in the streets. This terror was by design. Therefore I distinguish (spontaneous) social anti-Semitism from political (organized) anti-Semitism. The terror in the thirties was definitely political.

A story about anti-Semitism. I had a great teacher in Freiburg, Georg von Below—very conservative, a real Prussian Junker so reactionary that he addressed every lady in his class as "mister." He didn't recognize the Republic. But he was a great teacher. And when he died, I had the honor of sorting out his books. He had an enormous library. His wife asked me to help her sell it, but she wished to keep some items. When I came across half a dozen books on race science (not really bad anti-Semitic books, but basic race science) I asked Mrs. von Below, "What shall I do with these?" She said, somewhat angrily, "Put them away in a corner. These books are important, I know, but one doesn't want to see them or touch them." Well, that's the attitude of these aristocratic people.

In the thirties you had organized political anti-Semitism, but I think that at all times there was less spontaneous anti-Semitism in Germany than in the United States. There were no restricted beaches, no restricted hotels except for one island in the Northern Sea, Borkum, where Jews just didn't go. The Nazis were there, so you stayed away. Only when I came to this country did I find out about restricted beaches . . .

As for Germany, however, you would find no Jews in the steel industry, and in the chemical industry, Jews were in research but not in management. After receiving my Ph.D., my professor of medieval history advised me not to seek a career in his field (there were very few Jewish medievalists) but to go into modern history.

But we did not experience social discrimination. For instance, in our house we lived on the ground floor and on the second floor lived an editor of the Nazi newspaper *Angriff*. My mother looked very Jewish. She couldn't be mistaken for an Aryan. Whenever he met her in the hall, he opened the door for her, doffed his hat. He was extremely polite. We never had problems with neighbors and my parents lived in that house until 1939.

My father never understood what happened in Germany. Here is a characteristic story. I published the first underground paper in Berlin, on the day after the Reichstag fire. Soon we received information that people had been taken to secret dens and severely beaten by the Nazis. When I brought the paper home with this information, my father looked at it, gave it back to me with a gesture of disgust, and said, "This cannot be true. Such things do not happen in Germany. Here we have a government of laws." He could not believe it. His attitude was a common one. If you were in jail, people assumed that you must have done something bad. "The police don't make mistakes." Once men or women were in concentration camps, you could not persuade others that their detention was arbitrary. They said, "If they're in concentration camps they must have done something. You can't arrest just anyone. That doesn't happen in Germany." People refused to believe that in a civilized state power could be abused or that the Nazis could not be controlled. Well-to-do people would look down on the plebeian Nazis: "Let them talk. The bankers in New York will tell Hitler to be reasonable." As a Marxist of course I too had to believe that the banks were powerful enough to tell Hitler to let the Jews alone.

Some German bankers in Berlin thought that this was indeed possible. They even paid him money. They did not anticipate Nazi fanaticism. Few of us had any sociological or psychological insight into the structure of the Nazi movement. Hitler mobilized people who had never been in politics before, for whom politics was really an emotional reaction. Nazi marches were a manifestation of their impotent rage. I got my first inkling that this movement was different from other political parties shortly after they had come to power in February of 1933. When they were handing out jobs, everyone wanted to be prison warden or bailiff—the "little man" taking the role of his tormentor. Nazis, of course, were busy beating up people. There I saw violence for its own sake. Later, violence was sanctioned by the Nazi state, but this state no longer had the mentality of the German civil service and of government by law. Those who see the Nazi state as an overblown bureaucracy are mistaken. My late friend Franz Borkenau published in Emil Lederer's magazine an essay *proving* that fascism was impossible in Germany because the structure of the German civil service was unable to produce or maintain a terrorist regime.

Unfortunately that article appeared in March 1933, when the Nazis had achieved power. Most of us assumed that if the Nazis were really to follow their program, they would be out of power within four weeks. "Hindenburg will not tolerate it. Neither will the army or the banks." Many even thought in April 1933 that Hitler himself didn't want it. An orderly dictatorship is one thing, and as Marxists we thought the bourgeoisie would be happy with it. The Brüning-Hindenburg dictatorship, even the military dictatorship of Schleicher, was thought possible. But an anarchist dictatorship on the right was not held possible. Hence Hitler gave them something to do, which was the Jewish boycott of April first.

Anti-Semitism in the beginning had to be promoted. As I said before, there was little spontaneous anti-Semitism. The thugs were ordered out: "Tomorrow at eight o'clock in the morning you picket a Jewish shop." It was the most orderly pogrom in history. People did not of themselves go out and help them. Even in '38 when they organized the "crystal night"—smashing thousands of windows—it was strictly a party action. On their own, the people did nothing. On the boycott day, April 1, 1933, I insisted on entering a Jewish store, being Jewish myself, and the crowd told me, "Be reasonable, go home. Don't ask for trouble."

Yet another story, this one about my father-in-law, the father of my future wife. I was going with her at the time. It must have been 1930. Her father was a Protestant minister in a village. One day, she invited me to stay in their house. When I appeared there, I was not only Jewish, I was unkempt and I was sporting a "Russian shirt." In other words, I was a Communist and a Jew. The old man looked at me and didn't like what he saw. He was unable to preach his sermon while I was in the house, and I was asked to leave.

Three years later, on the day of the boycott, in April 1933, I got a letter from him. He was having an eye operation, after which he would be blind, and this was his last chance to write a letter. He wanted to use this opportunity to apologize to me. He explained that it had been just too much for him. The villagers were conservative, and he couldn't have a boy in the house who was Jewish and a Communist. He apologized to me on the day of the boycott! Now, the man was outstanding in some ways and I couldn't say that this was typical, but his attitude would become characteristic of the "church bearing witness."

Some people say that I should write a big book on what really happened. But no one knows what *really* happened. I don't think Hannah Arendt's book, *The Origins of Totalitarianism*, describes the Nazi ideology or how it came about. We had a long conversation about it. I asked her, "How do your three sources jell into one? Anti-Semitism, imperialism, the new masses?" Some Jews were imperialists, too. Anti-Semitism and other forms of racism have different roots. Anti-Semitism had originally been a leftist movement, but more recently it had been connected with anti-republicanism. Conservatives called the Weimar state a "Jew republic." Republicanism also was "French" and Western. Moreover, Jews had become prominent in a number of ways, some of which were not so beautiful. Many had come from Poland with a different kind of business morality, and we were ashamed of them. They gave Jews a bad name. In the farm areas, there were districts where anti-Semitism was economic, where "every cattle dealer was a Jew and every Jew was a cattle dealer." And peasants don't like cattle dealers!

Not now, but at that time I felt some hostility toward East European Jews. They "made anti-Semitism." Our family had a certain way of talking about them, as of misbegotten relatives. You kept aloof from such Jews. If you were inclined to help them, you gave money to an institution. . . . The problem was that they refused to be acclimatized. They refused to be German. It was embarrassing to see them talk with their hands and to hear their pidgin German. Here, in the U.S., it's different. Yiddish is not a derivation of English; non-Jews don't understand what Yiddish speakers say. In Germany they talked a German dialect which was despised and ridiculed. And some of them were speculators, confidence men, scandal-mongers. You had to see this in the context of German society. When such Jews got rich they showed it. In the old German class structure, titles counted, but conspicuous consumption rather declassed a person.

Well, I started an underground paper. My wife got arrested along with certain other comrades. It was impossible to continue publishing. So I decided after half a year of Hitler that he would last for some time, I thought five years, which was no longer a brief interlude. The dangers now were of a different order. My Jewish nose was a warrant of arrest. I became a danger to the people in my underground group. Then someone who didn't know me asked, "Have you heard about Pachter? He's supposed to be very good at underground work." Fortunately, my informant lived in another district, But I got scared. That was quite enough for me. I decided to leave.

Luckily, I could emigrate with a passport. It was not necessary to cross the frontier illegally. When I reached Paris in January 1934, I gave a speech to socialist groups. I said, "Hitler's going to last five years"—and they almost lynched me. My pessimism was treason, defeatism. German socialists expected to be back in Berlin the following year. As it turned out, I had been too optimistic.

I stayed in France seven years and when war broke out we were interned. I won't say much about France, but I must tell you that the Popular Front was one of the best experiences of my life, even if it was also a disappointment.

After the defeat of France someone in the U.S. put my name on a list. Who made it to America and who didn't was a lottery. I received an emergency visa, not as a Jew in danger of being exterminated but as a political refugee worthy of being admitted.

My parents emigrated from Berlin in time, shortly before the outbreak of the war. My father had been sent to a concentration camp, and was released on condition that he and my mother would emigrate. When he emerged, he was a frightened man, even in Paris. I took him to my apartment and the first thing he did was close the windows. When I objected that it was hot, he insisted that we could not talk with the windows open. I told him that in France he need not be afraid of the police, but he remained skeptical and subdued. The next day we went for a walk and he decided to test democracy. He approached a policeman and asked for directions. The policeman answered politely, and the old man came back smiling. Later he and my mother went to Palestine. The joke they heard there was, "Do you come out of conviction or out of Germany?" The British, as mandatory power, were hostile to Jewish imigration, but a relative who happened to be a celebrity interceded with the authorities. Without him, we would not have obtained visas. Hundreds of thousands did not get out. A very small group did not want to get out. Another uncle, a very rich man, insisted that he had to stay where his money was. He ended in the gas chamber.

For many of us the United States was our only salvation. We had to like it. Of course there was culture shock. Imagine what it was like to encounter educated and civilized people speaking a European language who nevertheless thought and acted so differently. If all Americans had looked green in the face, I would have understood them better. West European intellectuals fail to understand that this is a civilization *sui generis*, not a derivation from theirs. They arrive with a preconceived image of what an intellectual should be, and then they discover that American intellectuals are a different, and from our point of view, a lesser breed. Those social scientists at the Frankfurt Institute had this attitude to the enth degree. They thought they were standing high above everything in America—read Adorno on jazz or on education, and you will understand what I mean.

I had a tenuous connection with the Frankfurt Institute. I had written reviews for them. By the time I arrived, they had a house on West 117th Street and their telephone went through the Columbia switchboard. But the Institute was not part of the university. I thought they might have some kind of employment for me, but they wouldn't even give Siegfried Kracauer a job even though they had obligations to him. To me they had no obligations. I was just a friend who had been to Frankfurt a couple times. Kracauer belonged to the crowd, so to speak. I knew that he looked forward to a position at the Institute. But it was his great fortune that they refused him because then he was forced to become an American expert on film. At the Institute he might have been lost.

Then I too was lucky. Someone paid me to attend a Quaker seminar at Dartmouth. The Quakers ran a summer school for refugees. It provided an excellent opportunity to learn about America, including middle America, its small towns and so on. That experience was one reason I didn't try to get a small-town college job. Instead, I stayed in New York. We still weren't sure how the war would end. I considered myself a political animal who had to go back to Germany to help, no matter what kind of regime would follow the Nazis. So, let's say I didn't rush into American life. In a small town I would have had to become American, adjusted to the academic rat race.

But soon we were to be integrated into America in an unexpected way. The New Deal–Popular Front idea of an antifascist populist crusade opened the vista of a different kind of democracy, a different kind of freedom. After the twenty-second of June, 1941, the left joined America under the Popular Front ideology. Paul Robeson forgot that he was black and sang about "all the people." I was a German Jew, and yet part of this democracy. We happened to live in a house full of Communists constantly preaching "democracy" to me. After the twenty-second of June in '41 they were very sincere democrats, and could not do enough to win "this war for democracy."

During the war I worked for the OSS (Office of Strategic Services), but not in any cloak-and-dagger operation. I scrutinized German newspapers, trying to find out how much butter or oil they had, whether their morale was holding up, and such information as you can get by reading between the lines. This office had been organized by an Austrian Socialist named Kotzlik, and the staff consisted of Socialists and Communists, many of them Jews—all by cooptation. Most of these fellows were interested only in politics and German morale.

I also worked for Ernst Kris and Hans Speier at the New School for Social Research. We produced a book on German propaganda during the war, using transcripts of Nazi radio broadcasts. Why these files were kept secret I never understood. My job was to determine what insight we might get out of this material on German morale and on Goebbels' intentions. However, the job was secret. No one was supposed to know that these speeches existed, although they had been transcribed from the German radio. I had to lock them up every night. Once I used the wrong key and within ten minutes the police were there. Another time Ernst Kris came with terrible information. He'd been at a meeting with top BBC and Voice of America executives. They had documents showing that people were wantonly killed in Auschwitz. As a specialist in propaganda analysis he was asked whether it would be advisable to publicize the Holocaust, to let it be known that people were being burned in gas ovens. They decided not to publicize it because BBC had a record of credibility which it didn't want to risk. We were convinced that no one would believe such a horrible story. People had bad memories of World War I atrocity stories which turned out to be false. They had become propaganda-wise. Therefore it was decided not to use the story. So in this roundabout way I knew about the Holocaust, but I am convinced that most Germans knew nothing about it—except those involved and the few who were sufficiently alarmed and bothered to find out.

The existence of concentration camps and the fact that people were beaten and killed by Nazis—this was supposed to be known, for the regime depended on terror. But extermination as a "solution" was the Nazis' secret plan which they did not dare to advertise. We knew about the so-called mercy killings, euthanasia of idiots, etc. We also understood that the Nazis were capable of anything. Yet "anything" did not include genocide. The word did not then exist. Louis Adamic had drawn my attention to the Nazi policy of deliberately separating Slavonic workers from their wives. He said, "Hitler is going to win the demographic war." But that people would just be exterminated, that was something so barbarous that we did not expect it.

By '44 everybody knew a little more. BBC had spread the information piecemeal on a confidential basis. It got around and the public was not so astonished when they finally heard of gas chambers on the radio. By that time we also knew about Nazi atrocities in Russia, for instance how they had dealt with the Ukrainians. In a qualified sense I was prepared for it. After the extermination was confirmed, I would have thought, "Knowing the Nazis I'm no longer surprised." Another afterthought: our Marxist training—the theory that anti-Semitism is just a front for political manipulation—prevented us from seeing that the top Nazis *believed* in their mythology. Even Hermann Rauschning (in *The Revolution of Nihilism*) wrote that Hitler had told him not to take anti-Semitism seriously.

When I'm asked about the Allies not bombing, say, the road to Buchenwald, I have to answer: we never expected that. It's very easy to be wise after the fact. At the time, we did not feel that it was possible to do anything. It did not occur to me that airplanes should be diverted from war-essential missions to disrupt traffic to the extermination camps (a similar observation is made by Kissinger in his excellent memoir); the gassing method was used after the Nazis had simply shot Jews over mass graves; there did not seem to be any virtue in forcing them to return to the first method.

Among those who perished were members of my family. Close friends, too. So in a personal way, the Holocaust does concern me more than it might other people. But I have to say that atrocities shocked me wherever and to whomever they happened. In fact, by the time we learned about Auschwitz I also got information from the Pacific, and I was just as shocked when people told me that American soldiers didn't take Japanese prisoners. . . . Once you accept that this country is democratic, that it is humanistic, and we want to be different, then it's hard to digest such stories. People reacted to the atrocities in Vietnam when they saw them on TV. Many had not realized that war dehumanizes all people of all races.

On the question of Hannah Arendt's Eichmann book, I'm afraid that it does make some sense, because I know that some Jews were cowards, or were seeking an accommodation with the Nazis. You'll find an involuntary admission in the memoir of Ken Baumann on the Jewish Cultural League (manuscript printed at the Leo Baeck Institute)—a nobly intended enterprise which could function, however, only as long as it was useful to the Nazis. What Hannah did not get at is this: a situation in which you have to decide who goes to the gas oven, and if you don't decide, someone else will. I've known people who had to make this kind of decision, even before the Holocaust, in concentration camps. It was a struggle for survival. The political prisoners were better organized than the nonpolitical types. They could give each other jobs, send each other to the hospital, and so on. Naturally, they did what they could for their friends. Why should I save people I don't know? I save those whom I do know. Many of the inmates had no other motives. Some took money. And some took the money even though they would have rendered the same service anyway. Hannah Arendt, who was comparatively safe, took potshots at others who were in a tragic situation. There could be no heroes in the concentration camps, and she wanted heroes. If I thought that all her information was correct, which it wasn't, I would still have hesitated to publish it in the righteous way she did. Here's a quote from Melville's *Billy Budd*: "Forty years after the battle it is easy for a noncombatant to reason about how it should have been fought."

After the war, I had to think of my future, and the way it was decided fits the catch phrase, "only in America." My neighbor, Ernst Cassirer, died the day after Roosevelt died. His widow asked me to read galleys that were still floating around, which is how I came to know the publisher, Schuman. Schuman wondered if Cassirer had left any manuscripts. He wanted to publish a series on the "lives of scientists." Could I find an interesting life? I answered that few scientists had really interesting lives. In the case of Galileo, to be sure, something happened. But Copernicus, for instance, just looked at the stars. He had no struggles. Little did I know then about American publishing. Schuman did get a sensational life of Copernicus, where we are told that in Copernicus' time Cracow was ruled by the beautiful Bianca (follows a chapter on Bianca—and did she have a life!). Then I mentioned that perhaps Paracelsus, a Renaissance doctor, could be written up dramatically. Schuman jumped: "What do you know about Paracelsus?" I did know a little, for I had studied the Anabaptist movement in which he was involved. Whereupon Schuman opened his desk drawer and gave me a contract! But I didn't know how to write a book in America. I thought I had to justify the great honor and include a hundred footnotes. Also, I had not yet learned to write a sentence shorter than half a page. When Schuman saw the finished manuscript he almost fainted. He gave me a good copy editor, and together we wrote a book that sold 20,000 copies. This book gave me an entrée to the New School.

I had no other credentials. On the other hand, I could not

get any grant on the ground that I had to finish my studies. I was in between. When the war ended and the OSS office closed I took a job in public relations and market research. This too is certainly something that could not have happened elsewhere.

I answered an ad. A man was looking for an economist. I had read Marx, so I could be an economist. I don't know why he liked me. I was really a phony. He had started a public relations firm. It was a one-man shop but, first of all, he wanted to hide his profits, and secondly he wanted to have an organization. If a client came to him he had to show that someone was sitting there. My job was epitomized in this kind of experience: a man wants to set up an outfit to sell washing machines in Venezuela. My boss is asked to get him a bank loan. So he summons me and tells the client: "Here's a German doctor. He knows everything. Henry, how much would it cost to do research on washing machines in Venezuela?"

"Well," I reply, "Latin American statistics are very poor, and we will have difficulty getting them." When the client leaves, I turn to my employer: "Mack, look here. In Venezuela you are either so rich that you have servants to do the washing for you, or so poor that you can't afford a washing machine. What do we do the research for?"

Says the boss, "It doesn't matter. You write a memorandum. We will bind it in gold strings because what does matter is that a bank executive sees the memorandum. . . ." And I kept this job for seven years.

The boss had, as a client, one big ladies' wear chain that opened a new store somewhere in the South every week. I had to find out which side of Main Street was the best location, what the neighborhood was like, whether any significant population movement was occurring. About this I always wrote memos. I also published a weekly dope sheet for the garment industry. I was in a constant race with *Business Week*. I wrote my copy on Friday and at the end of the day *Business Week* came out with the yellow sheet they have up front in the inside. My boss would always check to see whether we were in agreement. We were, and he didn't know how I did it.

One day, I got a call from the *Journal of Commerce*. It was the lady whose job was to do what I did, to forecast trends in the garment industry. She wanted to meet me. She was very charming, we had a good luncheon, and she informed me that my sheet was extremely useful for her column. Her secretary cut it out for her. I said, "My secretary cuts *your* column out for me, and I find it very useful because I write the sheet on the basis of your column." Between just the two of us, we made trends in the fashion industry and set the prices!

There is another German exile, a former business editor of the Berlin CP paper, who did that on a much larger scale. He published a sheet, to which banks subscribed, that noted exchange rates. He knew how much the peso was worth in Saigon. I asked him, "How is it that the banks need you? Don't you use the information which the banks provide? Why do they subscribe to your paper?" His answer was, "They don't know how to use their information. As Marxists, we have the right conclusions."

Old Marx would never have dreamed that his method could be used to make money. But to some extent it is true that my reputation and his were based on our Marxist training. For instance, Senator Taft had said that if you removed price controls, prices would go down. This friend and I said prices would go up even more. During those seven years I had a good record of prediction, thanks to my Marxist training.

How I became a foreign correspondent is also very interesting. At Berlin University I had met Jurgen Tern. We were both in a graduate history class, where I also had met my wife. Later, she and I used to play a game: Which of the people we had known in Berlin became Nazis? I always said of Tern, "I'm sure he was never a Nazi." Then, after the war, I received a German paper. At the top on its masthead was Tern's name. He was the editor, which meant he had been cleared by the occupation authorities. I was so happy, I sent him a postcard and a pound of coffee, for I knew they had nothing at the time. He wrote back: "What are you doing?" I sent him some memos I'd written about economic conditions in the U.S. He answered, "This is funny. They tell us here that in America there are no problems. Can't you write something for me?" That's how I became the first German correspondent in New York after the war. They couldn't transfer money at that time, but my wife's family in Germany was really hungry, so I asked that he send my honorarium to my father-in-law.

I did my newspaper writing on the side, for I was still doing market research. A lot of information crossed my desk that interested German readers. Suddenly I found myself in a very good position. German industrialists who visited New York had read my articles. Since they did not know how independent the press is here, they admired my courage. I criticized Truman. I also told the Germans that their two countries would not be united again—and *this* took courage, since Dulles told them all the time that he was thinking of nothing but German reunification. Everyone came to see me on account of my articles. I was well situated.

So when my firm finally folded, I asked Tern if he could give me a permanent job. Of course he was glad to do that. I became a foreign correspondent and went to Washington very often. I knew many State Department officials in the Truman and Eisenhower administrations. I also had close friends in the German embassy. Later I concentrated on the United Nations. From about '48 to '68, for almost twenty years, I had an office in the United Nations.

And there I saw the same situation as in the garment industry. In the morning foreign correspondents got together and decided what was going to happen that day. If they wouldn't report it, it couldn't happen. When Dulles came, he got nowhere because all the foreign correspondents were Democrats. Lodge had the same trouble until he hired a Stevenson Democrat as his press officer.

I still say the UN is judged unfairly. Obviously, it cannot solve any problems which the powers don't want to solve. But, if the powers want to solve their problems, it is much easier for one to bow to 127 nations than to bow to another nation. If you have a constructive solution, the United Nations will help—even though sometimes you might solve your problem bilaterally. At one time we solved the locust problem. Locusts were breeding in one Arab country and eating in another, but the two governments had never been able to get together. The United Nations got them together, but later political hostilities brought the locusts back.

After you've been at the United Nations for five years you can usually write all the speeches. If not, you ought to be condemned to hear them. I'd rather watch who was going to lunch with whom, who sits in whose seat, because delegates wander around in the Assembly. They visit each other. The pattern tells you something. And there are times when even as a newspaperman, you may be used. For example, I had become friendly with a Polish delegate and he had told me things, always in his house, which certainly the Russians would not have liked to hear. He said, "Don't write about our chat. It's confidential." But one day he proposed that we have lunch in the delegates' dining room. So we had lunch at the UN, where of course we were seen, and he steered the conversation to certain economic problems of interest to Poland and Germany. As soon as we rose from lunch—well, it hardly took two minutes for the whole German delegation to surround me. "What did he say?" The Pole had expected that. And the Germans knew exactly what to ask. Many times also delegations will use newspapermen to tell their side of a story, and it takes both experience and courage to resist their blandishments. Newspapermen cannot be bought with money, but with "confidential information."

At the UN the Israelis, too, often use blunderbuss tactics. They don't consider other peoples' concerns; they only talk about their wrongs, and that's poor psychology. I am afraid most people don't like to hear about the Holocaust again and again. It is just too much. Anyhow, the Holocaust doesn't justify settlements in the Sinai. In the UN you have to show that you can be useful to others. For a while, the Israelis were doing very well, not in the United States so much, but indirectly. Like development aid in Africa, where they were excellent, putting top experts in the field and doing a lot of good. Abba Eban was the only Israeli who knew how to enlist other delegates. He had more of a global outlook. Delegates who liked him said he was no Israeli—he was a South African.

But it didn't last long enough. In the eyes of those who speak

Press facilities at the United Nations. UNITED NATIONS/X. NAGATA.

for Third World solidarity, Zionism is an ally of imperialism. The oil sheiks sent money and the Russians brought more pressure. Recently delegates have come forward and denounced Zionism. You know these processions of delegates with accusations when everybody has to be there to condemn Israel. Sometimes ambassadors later explained, "That was just rhetoric for home consumption, but we are still your friends." And they didn't mean it.

I am an anti-Zionist, but I have always held that when a government is actually in power you have to recognize it. I knew that Israel was here to stay as early as 1949 when my father, who was seventy-five, wished to leave Israel and come here so that I could take care of him. The Israeli government didn't want to let him out because he hadn't done his military service! I thought, "If its bureaucracy has developed to this point, the state of Israel has to survive." But I do not believe that Israel is a solution to the Jewish question.

Now the Arabs have not been able to reconcile themselves

to the creation of Israel. Were they to recognize Israel it would benefit them. It also would benefit the Israelis if they were to give up their fighting stance. They could have been masters of the Near East, engineers, counselors, industrialists, scientists, if only they had decided from the word go to develop a Middle Eastern state. As things stand, there no doubt are Arabs who think in terms of the destruction of Israel. I don't know whether this means they would do it or they have plans to do it or that they could prevail. There may be Arab leaders now who would like to compromise, but they're not in power. If I were an insurance broker, I would not try to sell Sadat life insurance.

Frankly, I am frightened. I'm critical of Israel because Begin's policies invite catastrophe. I have never been as scared about the Jewish fate as I am now. What worries me is, number one, the notable erosion of support for Israel in the United States; second, the deterioration of international relations in the Mideast and in Africa; and third, the Israeli blindness to these developments. American Jews overwhelmingly feel that if Israel goes down so will they. That's the big difference as against our situation in Germany. Then there were Jews all over the world. They fought for the right to be here. Now the Jewish faith is identified with or closely tied to the state of Israel, and I don't think in the United States people would wait for Goebbels to tell them when to fire at the Jews.

In this country there's much more native anti-Semitism and native violence. Of course, I am implicated in all this. And it's a personal defeat in many ways because, for instance, I have fought the existentialists all my life, but history may have proven them right: I have to be tied to a people with whom originally I was not by choice associated. Sartre's absurd theory is right: I am not the person I am but the character which others attribute to me. I have to be responsible for Begin's mistakes. My daughter may have to die because of people she has never known. If this is the outcome of world history—damn it!

What happens to Israel will have an enormous influence on my own life, but not because I have an *attachment* to Israel. The community of destiny has been imposed on me by *others*. The accident that I was born in Germany could not make me a German nationalist; the accident that I found a most appropriate asylum in the USA has not made me an American nationalist.

After the Second World War, I had a conception of the United Nations as a vehicle for organizing peace and political security, and of spreading democracy. There were a number of good things, particularly the idea of collective security, in the first ten or twenty years after World War II. Recently, the trend has been steeply downward on most issues about which I feel some concern. I guess that as I age in this city I am losing my idealism.

I have been in New York City now for about thirty years. Not only is my work here, but I am a city guy. I was born in Berlin and I lived in Paris, in London, and then in New York. I'm lost in a small town. From my West Side apartment it's twelve minutes' walk to Columbia. I go the the library, check magazines in the academic bookstores . . . do just as I please. In a small college town, life gets too personal. You have to know everybody. You have to go to every party. If not, you are defined as an enemy. In New York you can lose yourself. I can do everything I want to be stimulated, or I can leave it alone. In a small place, I couldn't do that. Friends tell me that even Princeton is not good from this point of view. Social life, organized around the university, is too close.

New York is a city of three million Jews, of whom I know relatively few. Obviously in New York I'm not really in middle America. I'm in a Jewish-Irish enclave or exclave. It's part of the attraction. This city is not confined, it's not clannish, or rather, I could join any clan, but I don't have to.

And I'm ten minutes from Times Square . . . I go to the ballet once or twice a month. Today I go to Martha Graham. In two weeks I go to the Berlin Ensemble. When I crave ballet in the summer, there's Saratoga. Music is important to me, even WQXR, lousy as it is. I fought for WNCN. So there are a number of things here. I walk to Columbia and I meet someone who interests me and often we repair to the Straus Park Cafe. Between 107th and 108th there are three cafes and the new one in the middle is called Straus Park. And then on the other side of Broadway is the Balcony, which is also a good place. They're mostly filled with students or young faculty, and my building is full of Columbia people.

I have not deliberately presented a picture of the European intellectual, but it probably came out that way. In my classes I sometimes do it deliberately to show them the difference. We have many friends who are refugees, but I don't frequent any particular cafe because of them. I'd rather go to the Figaro and my favorite place used to be the Peacock on 8th Street.

My fellow editors of *Dissent* are friends. The magazine strikes me as being too "Jewish," but that is probably just my mistake. Still, I think Irving Howe should have gone out of his way to find more people who were not Jewish. Socialism should have an appeal to non-Jews and non–New Yorkers. I probably like the outsider's position. I've lived with it. I mean I am a cosmopolitan, rootless Jew and I rather like the situation. Consequently, I have a certain detachment. I can judge American policy without being emotionally involved in it. I can also judge Israeli policy, even though I may be emotionally involved in it.

I accept marginality. Okay, Jewishness contributes to it. You take that for granted as part of the background. But I'm not only a Jew; I'm an intellectual. They're not synonymous, although I must confess I'm always very disappointed when I meet a stupid Jew.

Simmel's remark, that being a stranger helps to make some people interesting, is a socio-psychological piece of analysis that does not imply a value judgment. In fact a person who feels like a stranger can become unhappy, obnoxious, a tyrant. Weininger and Hitler are types I have in mind. It's simply the case that our marginality *may* be advantageous. I hope that mine has been.

In the New York environment I found all my old German Jewish prejudices against Eastern Jews confirmed. They are provincial, with few exceptions narrow and self-righteous, and have generally more chutzpah than most other tribes. They cannot see three inches beyond their Jewishness, and are unhappy if other Jews don't share their provincialisms. I am being forced, by Jews as well as anti-Semites, into the position of having to defend a cause which is not my cause. People who feel Jewish also feel good when they defend the Jews. I have to defend the Jews, and occasionally even Israel (which I still consider the greatest misfortune that ever befell Jewry), but this prevents me from doing what I really want to do. I have a political investment in "the Jewish question," which unfortunately does not make the question any less burning or any more manageable. Maybe this typifies the overall tragedy of politics.

PART TWO

THE NEW YORK
NATIVES

8.

FROM THE LOWER EAST SIDE TO "OVER THE RAINBOW"

Yip Harburg

I'M A New Yorker down to the last capillary. I grew up around Hester and Allen Streets, in the heart of the Lower East Side, which was also the pushcart center of the world. When I was about seven, we moved to 11th Street and Avenue C, a sort of borderline between the Irish and the Italians that was just becoming Jewish.

Among the kids there was plenty of friction. The enmity was supposedly residential—block by block—but we Jews were always aware that the goyim were after us. Since they came in gangs we formed gangs too. We fought the 14th Streeters who were Italian, we fought the Irish—and both of them fought the Jews. They had big gangs. Battles fought with vegetables and rocks were frequent. I remember using my mother's washtub boiler top—huge, oval, tin-plated—as a shield; it looked like a replica of Greek armament. We all had shields to guard against the rocks and battles.

Our folks didn't know much about all this. A kid was automatically independent at the age of eight, surely by the time he was ten. The street, not the home, was your life. Your parents spoke Yiddish. That alone made you a displaced kid. The older generation of men and women brought their Russian and Jewish culture with them. They spoke no English. Down on the street

Edgar "Yip" Harburg, a librettist, lyricist, and author, was born in New York City in 1896. He contributed to many Broadway productions, such as *Finian's Rainbow*, and films, including *The Wizard of Oz*. He wrote such famous songs as "Over the Rainbow" and "Brother Can You Spare a Dime?" Harburg died in 1980.

you were being Americanized, but in a special ghetto way. Parents were very proud of children who spoke English and could interpret for them. This put the parents in an inferior position.

The drama of life was enacted within a context of poverty. You lived from month to month. But youngsters didn't feel the sting of it because everyone else was poor too. We knew no other way of life, and it didn't mean much to a kid who turned the street into an exciting playgound. You could swipe your sweet potatoes from the grocer, light a bonfire, and eat 'em right there at midnight. The potatoes tasted a hell of a lot better than those your parents bought, baked, and forced you to eat at a table, on top of having to wash your hands. What adventure! We'd have lookouts on different streets to warn us that the cops were coming; then we'd squash out the bonfire and beat it.

My parents were Orthodox Jews, though not as strict as the Hasidim. To some extent they were tongue-in-cheek Orthodox. My father did go to *shul* (Orthodox synagogue) regularly and I usually went with him. Whatever religious feeling I had evaporated when I was about fifteen in the face of a devastating personal crisis. I had an elder brother, Max, twelve years my senior—my hero—my inspiration. He was the first born. Max and my sister Ann survived nine others who died before I, number ten, was born. Max became a famous scientist. At the age of twenty he got a B.S. from City College. We never knew exactly how he did it. He was a quiet, taciturn youth, tiptoeing in and out of the house like a mysterious stranger. A superb physicist and mathematician, with a law degree and a master of science degree from NYU and a Ph.D. from Columbia. I remember his having written a thesis on the weight of the earth, news of which was all over the papers. We were too naïve to encompass all this but we had the feeling something important was happening. My parents were mystified. I was a kid; he was my god. Wonderful people started coming to the house—scientists, mathematicians, physicists. It was a world apart. And then, at twenty-eight, he died of cancer. My mother, broken by the shock, died soon after. The tragedy left me an agnostic. I threw over my religion. I began seeing the world in a whole new light. My father was shaken, but something in him had to carry on. He had a great sense of humor. He was a little Santa Claus of a man, with a darling, loving disposition. I told him I was not going to *shul* anymore, *"Papa, Ich gehe nicht."* We talked in Yiddish. He said, "Well, sonele, I don't blame you, I can understand. But I'm an old man. I need insurance."

The House of God never had much appeal for me. Anyhow, I found a substitute temple—the theater. Poor as we were, on many a Saturday, after services, my father packed me up and told my mother that we were going to *shul* to hear a *magid* (itinerant preacher). A *magid* was a super rabbi who usually came over from Smolna or Slutsk or some unpronounceable place. But somehow, instead of getting to the *magid* from Slutsk we always arrived at the Thalia Theater where the great Madame Lipsik or Tomashevsky was performing. These excursions were an adventure not only in art but in mischief, for we never told the mamma. As far as she knew, it was the holy Sabbath; we were out soaking up the divine wisdom of a *magid*.

Do I remember Tomashevsky? I remember every bit of him. Everything in the Yiddish theater set me afire. The funny plays had me guffawing; they were broad and boisterous. And the tragedies were devastating. When Tomashevsky paced up and down at the end of the second act, and his daughter came into the room pleading with him to come back to mamma, to cease living with that whore, his mistress, his exit was exquisitely dramatic, followed by his Jovian outrage of guilt. There he was pacing up and down. Beating his chest, until the moment he uttered his mighty last words: *"Mir Kennen Leben, Aber Mir Lasst Nicht!"* ("One can live, but they won't let you!") Such scenes stay with you forever. I look back on them with great delight.

The Yiddish theater was my first break into the entertainment world, and it was a powerful influence. Jews are born dramatists, and I think born humorists too. Yiddish has more onomatopoetic, satiric, and metaphoric nuances ready-made for comedy than any other language I know of. Jewish humor was the basis for so much great vaudeville, my next passion. Whenever I could rake up a quarter, I would spend weekends in the gallery of the Palace Theatre watching these most wonderful performers: Al Jolson, Fanny Brice, Willie Howard, Ed Wynn, Bert Lahr. Memorable times! Saving up the quarter, walking maybe five miles to the theater, going up to the "pit" in the third gallery, reveling in the great artists. I was hooked.

As for myself, my passion to be an actor was consuming. Luckily, the public school I attended, P. S. 64, had a lovely stage. When the teachers found that I was a talented reciter and actor, they had me on all the time. I experienced the whole gamut of roles, from the high tragedy of the death of Cromwell to the whimsy of Jack Frost and Peter Pan. There wasn't a play I didn't get the lead in. I won prize after prize for acting and reciting.

I liked school because of the acting, the drama, and the recitation. Basically, I loved the English language, the poetry. We had inspiring teachers. I was a whiz at "The Village Blacksmith" and "The Wreck of the Hesperus." Once I invited my folks to a recitation contest. I won a prize that evening with "Spartacus and the Gladiators." They wept at my "Gunga Din," and Tennyson's "Lady Claire." Those were the beginnings, the roots of my passion for rhymes.

This continued at Townsend Harris, a special place which combined high school and college (CCNY) for seven years, cutting off a year. There were tough competitive entrance exams— you had to be a masochist to attempt to get in—and those admitted were an elite group, real studious kids from the Lower East Side. Grind or not, I *had* to get in, to finish school as fast as possible, and get to work full time. As it was, I worked at odd jobs all the way through. Most of my fellow students were also the sons of immigrants, all of us pursuing an education as though our salvation depended on it. "Get that degree!" was the aim of life. We were driven. At the same time, the education was terrific.

There was no place to study at home, a cold water apartment with no steam heat; the stove was in the kitchen and it was always cold. So my study was the library on 10th Street, right opposite Tompkins Square Park between Avenues A and B. It was a fine, warm, clean place, and there were lovely librarians, with blond hair and blue eyes and elegant accents. The attraction was magnetic. And they put me on to some great books. I devoured the contents of Carolyn Wells' *Vers de Société* and gravitated towards light verse of all kinds. When I came across O. Henry, I gobbled up every one of his stories. He made a dramatic impression on me; to this day, I can't write a poem without an O. Henry twist in the last line.

My passion for humorous verse and stories goes all the way back to Mother Goose. My father, too, delighted in good satire. It was one of his great joys to sit at night and read me funny articles by great Yiddish writers from the columns of the Jewish press—stories by Sholom Aleichem and others that tickled and delighted us both.

Perhaps my first great literary idol was W.S. Gilbert. I adored his light verse. One day at school I pulled out a book of his Bab Ballads and other poems, and the kid sitting next to me showed great and excited interest. His name was Ira Gershwin (we always sat side by side—he was "G," I was "H"). Ira took a look at the book and said, "Do you know that a lot of this is set to music?"

I was incredulous. "There's music to it?"

"Sure is. I'll show you." He invited me up to his house, a "swank" apartment on Second Avenue and 5th Street, with a Victrola! Compared to most of us, the Gershwins were affluent; Ira had an allowance, and money to buy magazines, books, and records. He was great about sharing them with me. That first afternoon he played *H.M.S. Pinafore* for me. There were all the lines I knew by heart, put to music! I was dumbfounded, staggered.

Gilbert and Sullivan tied Ira to me for life. Gilbert's satirical quality entranced us both—his use of rhyme and meter, his light touch, the marvelous way his words blended with Sullivan's music. A revelation!

We had something special in common, Ira and I. Among other things, we both hated algebra, he more than I, so one day in class we started a little paper called *The Daily Pass-It*. We wrote verse and he did some cartoons, which we passed around the room, giving our classmates a real chuckle. Our rag was "printed" on Townsend Harris toilet paper to make it real establishment stuff. Soon we wrote for the official high school paper; our column was called "Much Ado." It was an imitation of "The Conning Tower," Franklin P. Adams' column in the *Daily World*. We were living in a time of literate revelry in the New York daily press—F.P.A., Russell Crouse, Don Marquis, Alexander Woollcott, Dorothy Parker, Bob Benchley. We wanted to be part of it. In college, at CCNY, we started a column called "Gargoyle Gargles" in the campus paper, and I ran another column called "Silver Lining," in the *Mercury*, a monthly.

When Ira left college, I suffered on with the goddamn trig-onometry and differential calculus. But I did take some very good courses in Shakespeare with a professor named Coleman. Another teacher who influenced me greatly was Professor Otis. He rec-ognized something in me and made me wait after school one day, saying, "I want you to continue writing, especially humorous pieces." I once wrote a parody of Marc Antony's speech at the burial of *Julius Caesar*: "Friends, Romans, countrymen. . . ." It was a satire on the teachers in which I had them kill each one of the students after an exam. Otis loved it, and I became his pet pupil. He strongly encouraged me to write.

I began submitting little poems for publication. A magazine called *The Parisian* was the first to buy a poem from me, for ten dollars. After that came *Judge* and *Puck*, ten dollars, fifteen dollars here and there. It was evident that you couldn't make a living this way. At that point I never thought of writing poems as a career. As for songs, I had no idea how they were written, let alone that they could mean anything to me. I thought words and melodies sprang more or less full-blown like Athena from Zeus' head. In the meantime Ira's brother George had become a pianist, then a composer. When Ira began writing words to George's music in the twenties, I became aware of lyric writing as a possible profes-sion.

But by then I was established in business, the electrical ap-pliance business, with a colleague of mine, Harry Lifton, Professor Robert Jay Lifton's father. Harry got the capital. He liked me; my verses in the college papers gave me a following and a popularity which Lifton confused with genius in every department of life. So when Harry Lifton, a go-getter extraordinaire, said "Come on, let's go into business," I went along with him.

It was the boom period of the twenties and we started to make a terrific amount of money in appliances. For seven years we went up and up, and were worth about a quarter of a million by 1929.

Business or no business, my first love in those heady days was still the theater. I went to all the musical shows and all the straight shows—and devoured them. The variety was staggering. There were something like sixty or seventy shows a season. You didn't know which to go to first. The New York theater was proliferating and explosive. There was a burst of enthusiasm, freshness, and new writers experimenting with new things. Rodgers and Hart, the Gershwins, Cole Porter, Kern and Hammerstein came on the scene with a whole new kind of song and show, far removed from Tin Pan Alley, more literate, more sparkling. As for straight theater, suddenly you became aware of all the exceptional imports—Ibsen, Shaw, Chekhov, Molnár. Plus Americans like O'Neill and, later, Tennessee Williams. I depended on the theater for my spiritual life. I attended every show I could get into; balcony seats were $1.50, standing room was $1.00. For me business was a side show. The theater was the main event.

The crash came and I found myself broke and personally in debt for about $50,000, my name on all sorts of contracts that I had never read or cared to. All I had left was my pencil. So I went to Ira for some money and some advice. He put me in touch with a composer . . . and a $500 check, enough to see me through for three or four months. I sent my wife and two kids off to California, assuring them, "I'll break into this new business somehow." I rented a little back room four flights up in a house on 85th Street, from a Russian friend living with her mother. Her name was LaLa—not a show girl, but a sober secretary with a literary bent.

One day LaLa told me, "I have a good friend who's married to a composer. Maybe I can get you two together." "Fine. I'll phone him." Meanwhile Ira had called Jay Gorney, recommending a fellow classmate. Luckily, Jay's lyricist, Howard Dietz, had just teamed up with a new composer, Arthur Schwartz, and Jay needed a new collaborator. He asked who I was. Ira answered, "Well, he hasn't written song lyrics, but you'll know him from "The Conning Tower." He signs himself "Yip." To which Jay responded, "Oh, Yip from 'The Conning Tower'!" Ira made a date for me. LaLa also made a date for me with her friend who was married to a composer, and *he* turned out to be the same Jay Gorney!

We clicked. I worked at the Sterling Watch Company in the daytime and wrote with Jay at night. We wrote a dozen or so songs together, right off the bat. Just then, Earl Carroll had a new theater with a turkey in it called *Fiorito*, which flopped. Jay and I caught him on the rebound and played him our songs. "Great," he said, "These'll make my new revue." The show was called *Sketchbook*—an immediate hit. Around that time, J.P. McEvoy, the satirist, was writing another show, *Americana*. He was looking for a lyric writer, and we happened to meet at Gorney's house. He'd seen our revue and thought the songs were cute. Did I want to write his new show for him? "Sure." So the Shuberts hired me on his say-so and I went to work with Vincent Youmans, the composer they'd hired. But after we wrote the opening song, Youmans took his $5,000 advance, got drunk, and disappeared. The show had to open in a couple of months. Catastrophe! What to do? The only way to do it is to call in several composers and let them all feed me. When good tunes set me off I work fast. That was okay with the Shuberts: "You select the composers you want to work with." So I grabbed a few tunes from Jay and a few from a then little-known guy named Harold Arlen, and one from a complete unknown named Burton Lane. That's how the show was written.

The whole revue took a satiric point of view on the forgotten man. It was the first such show with social comment. "Brother Can You Spare a Dime?" flowed naturally out of it. We cut out all the usual tap dancing and hired the Humphrey and Weidman dancers and José Limon. The first show to have ballet. Mucho advance for Broadway.

It was clear to me from the start how much skill goes into writing a whole show. Much more complicated than writing single songs for Tin Pan Alley, where a good titillating jingle does the trick. But in good musicals, each song is a whole scene; you need to soak yourself in character, motivation, mood, tempo, everything. You're advancing plot, you're extending dialogue, using music and lyrics to make the statement explosive and emotional. Each song has a different problem, or many problems. Each one has to be fitted, guided, placed.

"Brother Can You Spare a Dime?" called for a lyric to identify the fellow in the breadline, just back from the wars. A bewildered hero with a medal on his chest ignominiously dumped into a breadline. I wanted a song that would express his indignation over having worked hard in the system only to be discarded when the system had no use for him. The lyric required political, economic, and sociological knowledge to prevent maudlinity. I wanted to avoid, "Please mister—I've fought your country's war, I did my part—can't you spare a dime?" This is sentimental, tear-jerking, on the surface—second-rate.

My analysis started with an awareness of the injustice of a society in which the man who produces, who builds towers, makes railroads, farms the land, is left empty-handed. Why doesn't he share in the wealth his sweat and skill have produced? So much for analysis. How to say all that poetically, dramatically, and with lasting emotional impact, to make the song neither pitiful nor sentimental but an intelligent dramatic statement?

Well, it was a situation many were going through, so the title, the central phrase, had to be popular. Wherever you went you heard "Brother can you spare a dime—Brother can you spare a dime?" The people who pleaded weren't begging. They had dignity as human beings; they'd accomplished things in their lives and were proud of it. Thus: "Once I built a railroad, made it run, made it race against time. . . ." He's not sighing about it—he's feeling his strength, and brings that strength into the song. But suddenly he looks at himself and stops short, puzzled: "How the hell did I get into this position, where I find myself saying, 'Brother can you spare a dime?'" The dramatic juxtaposition of this phrase with the upbeat of what went before—"I *built* that railroad"—makes a powerful rhetorical statement, put in a lyrical way for greater impact.

The reaction was tremendous. After that song, I had no trouble getting jobs, one show after another: *Walk a Little Faster*, with music by Vernon Duke, which had a lovely score, including "April in Paris," and charming performers—Bea Lillie, Clark and McCullough; Sid Perelman did the skits; all in all another smart show. An edition of the *Ziegfeld Follies*, *Life Begins at 8:40*, with Ira and Harold Arlen, starring Bert Lahr, Ray Bolger, Luella Gear—we had nothing but fun.

Each composer affects a lyric writer in a different way. Being a very eclectic guy, I always liked trying a new style, whether it was a sad social comment like the Dime Song or something like "Lydia the Tattooed Lady" for a zany fellow like Groucho Marx. I'm a chameleon—I love putting myself into everyone's shoes—and each composer lends me a pair.

A great song requires a great melody that comes right out of the heart and brain of the composer without any constrictions imposed by a lyric. Feeding him an idea, a title, is fine, but usually if you give him a complete, immutable lyric first he'll start underscoring and usually a banal melody results.

My longest and happiest songwriting association was with Harold Arlen. From my first contact with him, on *Americana*, I knew his music had a special quality, an originality that is hard to describe. It's a challenge writing lyrics to Harold's tunes. They're complex and sophisticated and touch me deeply. Harold's melodies have a depth and often a sorrow that always made me strive for wit and profundity. He's an eclectic too—his songs range from "Blues in the Night" to "Over the Rainbow" to "Paper Moon." Working with him is a perpetual fascination and challenge.

Arlen's hallmark is his synthesis of Negro rhythms and Hebraic melodies. They make a terrific combination, a fresh chemical reaction. George Gershwin did this too, in his own brilliant way. Gershwin and Arlen created a new sound in American theater music by combining black and Jewish elements. So many Jewish themes creep into Harold's tunes. It was in his blood; his father was a cantor in Buffalo, and Harold always spoke of him as a great theme-and-variations man. Just hum "Stormy Weather" to yourself, for instance, without words, keeping the rhythm free:

Nobody could have written that but a fellow who had been influenced by Jewish liturgical music. Or try Harold's happiest tune, "Get Happy," and clap along with it:

La la la la la   la la   la   la la

"Clap hands, *mach kichelach* (make cakes)." Very Jewish. I was raised on that music.

Maybe that's why I gravitated so strongly to Arlen and Gershwin. Going to synagogue with father, hearing the music of the cantors was ingrained in me—still is. Cantorial music moves me more than any other. It was a big influence. When I first heard "Summertime," I felt as if I had known it all my life. And "My One and Only"! Talk about a song starting out Jewish and turning black.

Da   da   da   da   da____

Don't forget, both the blacks and the Jews are Semites. There's a great kinship between them. And the Jews are great assimilators. They take something from here, something from there; they've been en route for centuries. Along the way they picked up North African and Moroccan influences; when they got to Spain it was Flamenco; in Russia a romantic, Rimsky-Korsakov/Prokofiev element that influenced George especially. The Jews brought this musical melange to America, where the Negro beat was added to create a grand composite, a real melting pot

sound. No coincidence that the musical theater is preponderantly
Jewish. Look at the roster of names: Berlin, Kern, Gershwin,
Arlen, Hart, Sondheim, Hammerstein—all Jews. The main exception is Cole Porter. Even he took Jewish tunes and adapted
them to his fancy patrician language; think of "Begin the Beguine"
or "What Is This Thing Called Love?":

Porter was fascinated by Jewish music. He loved it.

All the songwriters got together regularly at the Gershwins
in the twenties and thirties. Something like Fleet Street in Samuel
Johnson's time—an artistic community where people took fire
from each other. We'd hang around George's piano, playing our
latest songs to see how they went over with the boys. We were
all interested in what the other fellas were up to; we criticized and
helped each other. There was great respect for each others' work,
and the integrity of our own music and lyrics. Sometimes we
would hear a whole great score before a show opened, a new
Gershwin show, or Rodgers and Hart. We ate it up, analyzed it,
played it over and over. You wouldn't dare write a bad rhyme
or a clichéd phrase, or an unoriginal or remotely plagiarized tune,
because you were afraid of being ripped apart by your peers. This
continuous give-and-take added to the creative impulse. It worked
as incentive, opened up new ideas, made it necessary to keep
working and evolving.

Everyone you could imagine came to the Gershwin parties
on weekends, not only songwriters, but all kinds of people—
performers, critics, actors, novelists, choreographers—the likes
of Moss Hart, Oscar Levant, Harpo Marx. Wherever the Gershwins happened to be living, whether on Riverside Drive or in
Beverly Hills, when we were all out West writing for the movies,
their home was always crammed with creative people.

There was a huge migration to Hollywood in the thirties. When I first went west on the Santa Fe, George S. Kaufman and Harold Arlen were on the same train. Everybody was being shipped out. At that time movie musicals were bursting onto the American scene. A songwriter needed hits to get his degree in ASCAP (American Society of Composers, Authors, and Publishers). For that, chances were much better in films. The New York critics looked down on them. Broadway was the snob literary Park Avenue and Hollywood skid row. But for a while, especially during the Astaire/Rogers period, Hollywood was making some great pictures with a wealth of good songs. Kern, Berlin, DeSylva, Brown, and Henderson were out West. So was the money.

Socially we were a refugee colony of New Yorkers. We were doing well—life was luxurious. I had never lived in a house with a garden around me. Sunshine, sunshine every day, everywhere. Shorts, tennis, golf, swimming, kumquats. Refugees? Like hell.

I shuttled to New York at least every two years to do a show. My heart, my big heart, was where the real tinsel blazed—Broadway. The cynosure, the center of all sophistication was still New York. The goal, the dream, was the Broadway show. Those of us who came back periodically to the stage were always honored, envied, and rewarded. In the movies the target was the mentality of a twelve-year-old.

Economics and politics imposed other restrictions. Institutions like Metro-Goldwyn-Mayer or Warner Brothers had to be on ass-kissing terms with the IRS and Washington. Also, movie money came and still comes from the big banks. Film companies can't afford to jeopardize their credit and profits. These are necessary for the completion of every picture.

On top of this already restrictive situation, I had trouble with incipient and then full-blown McCarthyism. Ever since the "Dime Song," popular though it was, I had my imprimature—a "Red," a Socialist, a radical. Never left me. Even in the forties, picture producers worried about "radical" innuendos in movies. Practically all of them were right-wing Republicans. They believed that Roosevelt was a Red, and his supporters, of whom I was one, were suspect. The moguls, like most big businessmen, were frightened—that FDR was about to turn the United States into a United Socialist State. Unemployment insurance! Welfare! My God, old age pensions! The whole New Deal scared the moguls to death. Movies with "messages" were the death rattles of tumbrels on the cobbles. *Verboten*: businessmen and banker jokes. The writer was stymied. He bristled. He was shaken to the marrow of his First Amendment. Writing was examined and censored. A picture I did called *Meet the People* produced a panic. The producers kept shouting, "Messages are for Western Union."

On Broadway there were no questions. The theater was still free; you could say anything as long as you weren't dirty. Not that Hollywood was a total loss. Far from it. Somehow *The Wizard of Oz* did happen in Hollywood. Serendipity of course. And fairy tale.

Once upon a time, in 1937, two little girls with beautiful voices were kept captive in a castle by an ogre named Sam the Goldwyn. Their names were Judy and Deanna. For several years they were kept silent—given high salaries but no songs. So they became a liability to Sam the G. Louis B., of the castle across the lane, who fancied himself a knight in shining armor, mounted his National City Bank Horse and rescued Judy from a fate worse than death—silence. A picture was designed for her based on the beautiful classic, *The Wizard of Oz*. The rest as they say, is history.

Everyone agreed that *Oz* would be great for Judy. Harold Arlen and I were in New York doing *Hooray For What?* starring Ed Wynn. In it was a song that hit the air waves called "In the Shade of the New Apple Tree." Arthur Fried, the producer of *Oz*, loved it; he thought it had just the charm and mood for the *Wizard of Oz*. Before us, many teams of writers had tried to get a musical version out of the delightful tale, without success. Finally Arthur agreed with me that we needed a new concept, to experiment, and let the lyrics and music wag the plot.

So we put aside the six or seven existing scripts and started from scratch. We let the songs tell the story, and wrote the scenes around the songs, saving as much of the existing scripts as we were able to cue into the songs. There was no rainbow mentioned in the original story. We created "Somewhere Over the Rainbow" to express the situation of a little girl who wanted to fly away from home, to go somewhere with more life and color than drab Kansas. The song gave birth to stunning visual effects and a new bit of plot.

Whatever weakness existed in the original story we replaced with new ideas. For example, my satiric sense rebelled when the Wizard gave the Tin Man a red pill for a heart and the scarecrow a white pill for a brain. It was pat—and meaningless. My humorous spirit said, "Put a little bit into this. Why not show up some of the follies we live by?" When a guy goes to college, he doesn't emerge with any more wisdom than when he went in. All he's got is his diploma. So let's be realistic: give the scarecrow a diploma—and ipso facto, a brain. In like manner, the do-gooders of the world never achieve hearts, but testimonials. Ergo, a watch for the Tin Man—that ticks like a heart. Plus an inscription for good deeds done. And last of all, the coward who survives a war never achieves courage. But he does get a medal. And forever after, that medal terrifies the community.

I wrote this scene for W.C. Fields, not Frank Morgan, who ended up with the part of the Wizard. Can't you just hear Fields saying his lines with that inimitable delivery? "Little girl, in my country where I come from. . . ." I wrote it in that style because I was still used to writing for Broadway. I demonstrated all the parts to Louis B. Mayer and others with all the passion of my schoolboy experience. Thank you, P.S. 64!

When I'd had enough of this, I returned to New York for good to collaborate on *Finian's Rainbow* with Fred Saidy, to Burton Lane's music. Then came *Jamaica* with Harold Arlen. The New York ambiance was tonic. Working in Hollywood meant living in a celluloid world. Much as I enjoyed the sun, the swimming, the open car, and the writing, the songs ended up in the mouths of two-dimensional people, singing to a one-dimensional audience. In Hollywood, people are isolated. If you're going to dinner at a friend's, it's probably a fifty mile drive. The car, the tennis court, and the swimming pool symbolize human existence out there.

In New York you think differently. It matters to be in contact with people who respond to world events as they do to the four

Sheet music for *Finian's Rainbow*. DANIEL ROSENBERG.

seasons, with vitality and action. New York City is vibrant, vigorous. And because it is so compact, it is the energy center of the world. Take a walk down Fifth Avenue from 59th Street to 42nd. Friends you haven't seen since Buenos Aires, Paris, Glocca Morra—you name it—pop up in front of Rockefeller Center. That can't happen in Hollywood where walking is taboo. To post a letter, buy a cornflake, you take a limousine. Your car is your salon. There's no rubbing shoulders with humanity. It's reflected in your writing.

New York is *the* United Nations: more Jews than in Jerusalem, more Italians than in Rome, Puerto Rico's home away from home. This gives the city a unique vibration, a feeling of constant renewal—evolution—rebirth. The ridiculousness of racial barriers is emphasized, and national enmity reduced to absurdity. It is still practical to see the possibility of a world united—if not in Gucci's, at least in Macy's basement. Truly. The great melting pot.

New York is New York, but times of course have changed. Kids today are born old; they and their city survive on hi-fis, electronics, porno, and plastic surgery. There's none of the joy and wonder of youth. Between television and fast foods everything is on the same treadmill; the whole culture reflects this. Their music, their lyrics—even their lovemaking—are instant like the coffee. Science is king; God is astrology.

The world is pretty grim for them. I grew up with a different attitude. The world had its problems then, many drab and terrible terrors—but none like the atom bomb and overpopulation. There was always a certain hope. A dream. A goal. Manners and grace that go with hope. Every immigrant family that came to this country knew that education would improve their lives. I was aware. I empathized with my father in his sweatshop, my mother at her washing and making hair nets for a living on the Lower East Side. I always had hope that someday they would be liberated. It became part of my chemistry, my nervous system. To get somewhere, to move forward—to freedom from drudgery.

Most of all, our sense of humor was a survival trait handed down from father to son. New York became the vaudeville capital of America, inventing laughter that only the tears of persecuted peoples like the Jews and the blacks could produce. And songs. "It's only a paper moon, sailing over a cardboard sea. . . ." New York, the mecca of the downtrodden, became the song and dance city of the world by jesting at its scars.

To thrive in it as a lyricist, one has to be on Mount Olympus, looking down, like Puck surveying the scene below and singing, "It's only a paper moon." But, "Look to the rainbow" over Times Square.

9.

THE INTELLECTUAL
AND THE ILGWU

Gus Tyler

THE BIG question attendant upon my birth was what to name me. The revered person in our family was my grandmother whom I never knew, and her name was Gittel. If you're to be named after Gittel and you're a boy, obviously your name has to begin with a *gimmel* (letter in the Hebrew alphabet). So, as far as my mother was concerned, I would become Gedaliah. My father left all this, along with the whole world of ideas and agitation and everything else, to my mother. She was the mouthpiece. But then my Uncle Elias said, "He's gonna run around the streets and kids will call him Gedaliah? It doesn't go." My learned uncle made a literal translation: "Godol" is "big"; Gedaliah means "great," so my name became Augustus.

Only a few years ago, I saw my birth certificate for the first time. And I discovered that some Protestant, probably a Swede, at the Board of Health wrote me down as Gustav. My father's name was an abbreviated Tilovitsch. They knocked off the "itsch," of course. It came out Tilove, which was pronounced Till-ovey or Tie-love by most of the teachers. What else would T-I-L-O-V-E be? Anything but a Jewish name.

In the family drama, my mother was a central character. She came from Lithuania, near Białystok, a very small town known as Sopovskin, after a prince whose name was Sopovski. She came

Gus Tyler was born in New York in 1910. For most of his professional life he has been a theoretician and educator for the International Ladies Garment Workers Union. He has served as a close adviser to David Dubinsky. Tyler has written extensively on labor in America and is now Vice President of the ILGWU.

here at ten or eleven with her father. The rest of the family was still over there. She had sisters—Lilly, Bertha, and Rosie—and a brother. Not yet a teenager, she went to work almost immediately in a white goods shop owned by Dudley Sicher. It was one of the better shops, or at least you could say it was a *shop*, meaning you didn't do your work at home. You went to a factory; that was class already. She was there long enough to teach her sisters, one by one, what the trade was, and they joined her. By the time she was sixteen, she was a mother and sort of surrogate wife to her father, who had left *his* wife over there. So my mother raised everybody. She was a matriarch at the age of sixteen! She raised her sisters and her brother and took care of my grandfather because basically he didn't believe in work. He was a good-looking man who used to hang around the synagogue and kibitz. He didn't even think of himself as a learned man, but he came from a line of people all of whom were *magidim* (itinerant preachers). His name was Magid, Simon Magid, and he was a self-appointed *magid* where nobody needed one because in Brooklyn you had plenty of establishments for troubled people. But he, nevertheless, would go around and kibitz. My grandfather was terribly earthy, even vulgar, with a liking to play with children and spoof them.

Actually, the active *magid* was my mother. Her name also was Magid, of course, and she played the role of a *magid*. I was an infant when we moved from Sumner Avenue to our long-time residence just a couple of blocks from where I was born, Hart Street between Tompkins and Marcy, now in Bedford-Stuyvesant. That wasn't a good neighborhood, but it was adequate and upwardly mobile. We lived in a tenement house and had a railroad flat; there were no elevators: we walked up four flights to reach our place. We shared a dumbwaiter with seven other families. If you had a heavy load of groceries and you didn't want to carry it up four flights, you put it in the dumbwaiter, went upstairs and pulled a rope to hoist the bags. The dumbwaiter served another purpose: it was a corridor of conversation within the building. The real purpose of the contraption, of course, was to enable the janitor to gather garbage. My mother must have established her authority very early. Regularly, through the dumbwaiter, voices sounded: "Mrs. Tilove."

My mother would stick her head into the dumbwaiter shaft. "Yeah, what is it?"

"I think my child has the whooping cough. What should I do?" Or, close to election day: "How should I vote?"

She'd give advice; she didn't consult anybody, she just assumed she knew the answers. My mother came out of the *magidic* tradition which prescribes that if you don't know, invent. What difference does it make? The spirit of God is within you and you can only speak the truth. You command an awful lot of respect that way.

There were eight families in that building which was our *shtetl* and she set every one of them straight. There was a woman downstairs who called up in the morning, "I have heartburn."

My mother would ask, "What did you have for breakfast?"

Well, she had had strawberries with cream and "a lot of sugar."

My *magid* of a mother would tell her, "My advice to you is that tomorrow you have a little bit of strawberries, but don't put on the rich cream, and *no sugar*."

The woman says, "I love the sugar."

My mother says, "You love the sugar, you better learn to love the heartburn." She made herself a kind of rabbi to the *shtetl*.

She was a peasant girl with no education, yet she was able to read Yiddish and English. Don't ask me how. She loved reading and worshipped learning. But she was a peasant. She'd say to me, "You know the reason people have so many colds in this country? It's because they run around in shoes. If they went barefoot the way I did all winter on the ice and in the snow, they wouldn't have colds." She was a "back to nature" person. God did not intend for us to mess with His works, including His decision that nobody should be too poor or too rich.

She had two marriages, the first to an actor named Lieberman, whose family came from St. Petersburg—they were Court Jews who had fled to this country, Court Jews from St. Petersburg. I think they met through a *shadchan* (marriage broker). Otherwise I don't know how the hell she could have come to him. He was a very well-educated European Jew who performed on Second Avenue in the Jewish theater. I've seen pictures of him as a handsome young man and my mother as a good-looking vivacious woman. He couldn't make a living as an actor, so in between roles he was a silversmith who made lovely things. You know how they used to make silver stick in those days? They licked it with their tongues. Well, he died at an early age of the poison in that stuff, and she was left with their daughter Anna. For a while grandparents looked after Anna, and my mother opened up a little candy store. Then the *shadchan* went to work again, and she met my father. His wife had died in childbirth, leaving him with a daughter of his own, Hannah. They got married, each bringing a child from an earlier marriage. My father knew how to run a sewing machine and how to put a garment together. For many years he was a children's dress contractor. I guess he went bankrupt twenty times. Each time he'd come back again and be a worker for one season and a boss for one season, but he was never a successful entrepreneur, he lacked the killer instinct. A contractor was a guy without capital who didn't invent a style, didn't need a large plant, didn't have to reach out to sell. All he had to do was organize a group of workers to produce a garment from goods which were given to him. The dress contractor is a whole story that ties into the ways of New York Jewry. That occupation provided an avenue to upward mobility. My father never made it, but he was an interesting man. My mother, the *magid*, talked all the time. By contrast, my father would have been a silent man even if he had spoken *any* language fluently. But, as he explained it to me, he was born in Russian Lithuania and he never had a chance to learn Yiddish properly in school. He started in a Russian language school, came to this country, went to night school and studied a little bit of English but never learned to speak it. The girls in the shop were Italian; he picked up some Italian from them but he never really learned that language either. On one famous occasion, he said to me, "I cannot read or write *in four languages.*"

That was my father; he did not quarrel with life or with fate. During one very difficult period, broke and unemployed, he went to Scranton to help run a plant out there while our family remained in Brooklyn. It was a very bitter moment, and I actually heard him say "Demnit." This was the pinnacle of his protest. Otherwise, he continued to be accepting: "That's life." My father was

Buntsche Shweig incarnate, satisfied to demand no more from *Gan Eden* (the Garden of Eden) than a warm roll with butter.

There was an interesting relationship between our family and the family of my mother's first husband, the Liebermans. Her husband had two brothers. Both were well educated. One was Elias Lieberman. He went on to become New York's first Jewish high school principal. That was a big moment for New York Jewry because the educational system was then controlled by Catholics. If you weren't a Catholic you were nothin'; it used to be Protestant, then Catholic, then Elias Lieberman became the first Jewish high school principal, and he was my uncle. Later he became Assistant Superintendent of Schools. His brother Max was chairman of the English department at Bushwick High School. That was also a tremendous thing. Elias also published poetry. So I had in my family a poet and a high school principal who used to visit us, maintaining contact, though their culture was entirely different from ours.

There was still another culture for me outside the home: the street. The street was our playground (one of New York's most famous heart surgeons recently told me that he has fond recollections of me going back about fifty-five years to the time when I was the celebrated "two-sewer" hitter). The street was our social center where we exchanged stories about ghosts and girls; it was also a battleground—especially when we were invaded by the Sanford Street gang. They were Irish, rough, and tough. When they came we ran.

Then, one day, Big Mick—that's what we called him— moved on to our block. "You don't run," he said. "You fight."

"But they can kill us."

"Yeah, but if you hurt just one of them once, they won't come around so much."

We got ready for the next invasion. We gathered milk bottles from the local groceries—empty ones. We stored them at the back of the dark alleys that ran from the front to the back of the building, a walkway that led to the janitor's apartment. We added some rocks and sticks and metal objects to the bottles.

When the Sanford Street gang came, we ran—as if in flight and fright. They chased us down the narrow alleys. We were ready with shrapnel made of broken glass and every other imaginable bit of ad hoc ammunition. We did serious damage—more serious than I care to account for. I liked the experience. I liked the gang life—for now we were a gang, too.

On the street, you were judged by how you hit the ball, how you made out with the girls, how you stood up in a rhubarb, how much punishment you could take and how much you could dish out. In the process, I learned that man does not live by words alone—even if he is Jewish.

In a sense, I always had two lives: the gentility of my home, as fostered by my mother and father in their different ways and as embellished by the Liebermans and, on the other hand, the gangsterism of the street. These were two separate worlds appropriate for two separate personalities. I somehow survived as a well-integrated schizophrenic.

In the house there was a bookcase, with an early *Book of Knowledge* or its equivalent. I used to look at the pictures even before I could read. However, once I became a little more interested in books there was a library not far away, the Tompkins Square Library, and we moved right across the street from it. In high school, I lived in the Pratt Library because in my freshman year I joined the debating team and I was assigned a subject, maybe "child labor." I went to the coach: "How do you go about this?" "You go to a library. Not Tompkins Square. You won't find much there. Try Pratt." So I went to the Pratt Library and found one of those little old ladies. I remember her very well. She brought the whole library to me, she ran around like crazy, she was delighted. I got a bigger education preparing for debates in the Pratt Library than I got from all my schooling. I found out that if I applied myself conscientiously for one week to any subject, I could master it. At least that was my illusion. I'm not sure, by the way, that that's wrong. Pratt was and, I think, still is a superb resource center—although it's right in the middle of an endangered area these days. Pratt's a great place, especially as a reference library. They used to have stacks of books worn from overuse, and truly dedicated librarians took care of you.

After graduation from Boy's High, an excellent school, I got a scholarship to NYU, and we moved to the Bronx, where I was within walking distance of the school on University Avenue. By then my sister was a piano teacher, and my father was a contractor once again and had an income. We were able to manage. I had become a committed socialist. I had been teaching socialist Sunday school in 1928 while still a junior in high school! I gave a course at 167 Tompkins Avenue on "Value, Price, and Profit." You've got to be a *chutzpadik* Litvak (Lithuanian Jew) to do that. The Socialists in Williamsburg had elected an assemblyman by the name of Shiplacoff. He represented a solidly socialist neighborhood, and some time in the early twenties, maybe earlier, they bought a three story building at 167 Tompkins Avenue. I was the guru of that building, in a way. I didn't know anything about finances. (They were taken care of by Sam Helphund, who was a hunchbacked little man and a dedicated Socialist.) It was one of those buildings with a basement, parlor floor, and more stories. In the basement Helphund ran a pool parlor and paid the mortgage with the proceeds. But in the other stories, we made revolutions. We had our meetings, we turned out our literature, we had our own mimeograph machines, we were all on fire. We had little stands out on the corner of our own street. We were making revolution!

In 1934 I left NYU as an active young Socialist. Louis Schaffer was then labor head of the *Jewish Daily Forward*. He had a staff, but wanted me too, so I became an assistant editor. Pretty exalted, right? For fourteen dollars a week, I was given a title. I wrote in Yiddish, sort of. I said, "Louis, I'm not really very fluent in this language. I write it, but I write it phonetically."

He said, "That's the way the language is written."

"Well, I'm not much good at it."

"Listen, you're a smart young Jewish Socialist. It'll work out."

I used to write *mittung notitzen*, notices for meetings. It's that kind of language: you don't have a *zamlung* (Yiddish), you have a *mittung* (Americanized Yiddish). We used to publish *notitzen* for a *mittung*. "This society meets on such and such a day." I'd write the notice by hand in Yiddish and read it the next day. The very first time I was printed in Yiddish in the *Jewish Daily Forward* my contribution wasn't signed, but I didn't give a damn. It came out all different: the spelling, the wording. I was horrified. I found a columnist for the *Forward*. His pen name was Tsivian. He had been an engineer in Russia, belonged to the old Russian Social Democratic movement. As an intellectual, he wrote a column for the *Forward* over a period of years. I came to him: "Tsivian, what goes on on this paper? Here is what I wrote and this is the way it appears." "Eh," he says, "you're lucky. By you, they only change the spelling. By me, they change what I say."

My favorite story about Tsivian goes back to the time when some of us first heard talk about the A-bomb. This was prior to the Second World War. Tsivian wrote an article on nuclear energy in which he explained that out of something or other that weighed one gram, you could get enough energy to run this, and this, and this, and if you had to pay the electric bill on it, what that would cost—something like a billion dollars. I came in that morning and said, "Tsivian, I read your piece. Very interesting." But you know how snotty young people can be. I said, "Aren't you vulgarizing the question in saying 'if you had to pay for it on your electric bill here's how much it would cost'?"

Tsivian looked at me like the presumptuous youth I was. "You'll learn, you'll learn. That's how the masses think."

Later the same morning, when a learned editor and old Socialist came in, I told him all about Tsivian's article, that it dealt with atomic energy which could generate tremendous amounts of electric power. "How much would it cost me going on the bill?" was his question. I have never forgotten that experience.

David Dubinsky (later president of the International Ladies Garment Workers Union) paid a visit to Vienna. There he saw young Socialists dance and jump and parade and act and sing. He got hold of Louis Schaffer who was then labor editor of the *Forward*. Louis was an entrepreneur. He managed Eugene Victor Debs' East Coast campaign when Debs was in jail in that famous year he ran for president. He organized the labor stage and produced *Pins and Needles*. Dubinsky summoned him and announced, "I was just in Vienna. They're doing a lot of things there that should happen here." Stimulated by the New Deal, ILG (International Ladies Garment Workers Union) membership was growing; Dubinsky had money; he wanted what the Austrian Socialists had. Louis went over to the ILG and took me with him. I stayed for about a year and then I said that although I enjoyed my work at the International—I was writing booklets and pamphlets, putting programs together—I wasn't meeting any workers. Louis claimed I was better off. But I objected: "No, I must meet workers. I have to get in there with the masses." So he looked at me: "Young romantics, you're all crazy." However, I made arrangements with Local 91, Children's Dress Makers, and I did get down there with the masses. It was important. I trained a lot of guys for top posts in the ILG. I have done that for many years. Part of the training is to send them where the masses are and let them roll around in the gutter for two or three years.

As I look back at it, 1933 or 1934 was a traumatic year for me. I came out of college and Hitler rose to power. Ideologically, I was in a terrible fix because, as a Social Democrat, Hitler's coming to power convinced me that social democracy was useless. In Germany where you had the largest, most powerful Social Democratic party in the world, Adolph Hitler was now in office! That knocked everything into a cocked hat. I began to reorganize my life. For a while I thought of writing poetry, but my literary period didn't last very long. That's because I have no capacity at all to stay out of the action. I cannot live in an ivory tower. I've written and lectured a lot; I've lived in the academic world more than many academicians, but I can't bear the absence from the trenches.

On account of Hitler my politics had to be reassessed. I favored a revolution, but I was afraid of Lenin's concept of party structure because within it lay not only the threat of dictatorship, but of one-man dictatorship. I became a Luxembourgist. Then I encountered James Cannon, the grand old man of American Trotskyism. He put it to me: "You have to make up your mind. Are you going to be a professional revolutionary or aren't you?" I was "going to be a professional revolutionary, period!" Well, when you're a professional revolutionary, that's it. You find yourself your own little pad, and work out of it for just one cause. The move meant a sharp break with my family. Not a war. There was no anger. We didn't disagree. I just went my way. It must have caused them considerable pain and grief, not because they objected to my being a dedicated revolutionary, and not because I wasn't bringing in any money, but because they didn't know where I was sleeping, whether I was sick or dying.

I had a theory that since Karl Marx intended the working class to be united, it followed that there should be one working class party. If disagreements existed within the working class on how you achieve socialism, then argue them out within one party. I was an *organic unitist* who believed that the Communist party, the Socialist party, and the Trotskyists should coalesce in one political organization. So far as I was concerned we could pick up a bunch of guys in Chicago who created the Proletarian party, as we did, along with a few others. Even the De Leonists—although I didn't think anyone could assimilate them because their whole goddam movement revolved around the fact that somebody left them a building! But, all right. Theoretically, I was for unity *and* I was against the United Front. Figure that one for logic. The United Front, created by the Kremlin, was just a way for one party to wage war against another party by infiltration and stealing its members.

Now James Burnham, a philosopher, had come out of the American Workers party with Sidney Hook. In fact, Sidney Hook, Jim Burnham, A. J. Muste, and a couple of other intelligentsia *were* the American Workers party—a perfect name for a party that probably did not have a single "worker" in it. The AWP merged with the Trotskyists, and they joined us at a Socialist party convention which must have been about 1936. I wrote a resolution on war, saying that in the event of war we'd use whatever means were available for turning it into a proletarian war for power.

By this time I had left the ILGWU and was editor of the *Socialist Call*. I wrote my resolution, representing a left wing caucus headed by a former Lovestonite, Herbert Lam, and myself, which in our moment of self-congratulation, we called the Clarity Caucus. Burnham objected to my resolution. He insisted that it read something like this: "In the event of war, we will turn the imperialist war into a civil war, and Soviets will be our instrument to power." I pointed out that "Soviet" was not an English word.

So he countered with " 'Workers and Soldiers Councils.' That's English." I wouldn't have it. I didn't know whether we wanted Workers and Soldiers Councils. "Why have them just because they emerged in one proletarian revolution? Who says it's got to be that way in all other revolutions?" Professor Burnham is a logician. Consequently, we debated first on philosophical, then on practical grounds. Philosophically, he argued from the Russian experience. To me, the philosophic reply was illustrated by some elementary algebra. In a simple equation: $x - 1 = 0$, if $x = 1$. Give me $x^2 - 4 = 0$, $x = -2$ and $x = +2$; there are two possible correct answers. If you go to several unknowns, you will get even more correct answers. Raise the powers and you get more correct answers. My case was that the social equation is complicated and that philosophically and mathematically it is wrong to say there's only one answer. Burnham now shifted the ground from pure logic to pure politics: ". . . From a practical point of view . . . if you want to have a following, you must take a definite position whether or not you are absolutely sure of the answer."

I said, "I can't do that."

He replied, "Then you'll never be a leader."

I agreed. "I'll probably never make a revolution, but that's the way I see it." This exchange was a turning point in my life.

This conversation took place about a half-century ago. It probably did not happen as neatly as I now recall it. I have undoubtedly polished it unwittingly over the years with the kind of fantasies that one reads back into turning points in one's life. I am probably oversimplifying Burnham and over-rationalizing my own thoughts. But the incident, transformed by time and the pressure to fit the pieces of life into a meaningful mosaic, has repeatedly served as a pivotal point in my thinking and doing. I fear sectarians; I fear their certainty; I fear—above all—their self-righteousness, their presumed monopoly on morality.

It was only years later that I concluded that my reluctance to accept absolute answers in political life was "geo-congenital," my *misnagdic* (traditionally Orthodox) tradition. To me the *misnagdic* Jew, like other Jews, believes in the Messiah but insists that although his *shtetl* is Sopovskin, he comes from Missouri. He believes in words and wisdom—but they must work. If not, words and wisdom are just talk; what works is *tachlis* (the nitty-gritty).

I have followed Burnham over the years and have been repeatedly impressed by his brilliance and his brittleness. He could easily have been a Jesuit in an earlier century or a Hasid in Williamsburg today. We stood for two irreconcilable views of what life is all about. I felt that inherent in his argument was the essence of dictatorship—which he would have denied. For him there was only one correct answer to which he clung without mercy. All doubts about any alternative were to be dispelled. That's not my view, not the way I live, not the way I've *ever* lived—entrapped as I am in the categorical interrogative.

I had another political crisis in 1938 after being editor of the *Socialist Call* for a few years. We had dumped the right wing of the Socialist party; the old guard was out; its members reorganized as the Social Democrats. We were the Socialist party and I was editor of its official publication. We pursued a left line rather consistently and, I then thought, very rationally. We had a position on war. It was the traditional one: "We support no capitalist government in any war."

To be sure, the SP supported Loyalist Spain. What's more, we looked upon the democratic government of Spain not really as a *capitalist* government, but it made no difference: we were sending our people over. The Communists organized their Lincoln Brigade, and I organized the Debs Brigade. We didn't recruit too many soldiers, but we sent enough. I remember writing fiery front page editorials calling for enlistments. I was praying to God that the United States government would crack down and tell me I was in violation of the law, which I was. I hoped they'd at least send me to prison. We needed a few martyrs of our own. But they paid no attention to me at all. Our belief then was that we were building a *workers'* army, and that was okay. But to support the *United States* government in a war was impossible.

Now, some time in 1938, while going along with this idea, I reached an ugly conclusion: namely, that I was talking nonsense. Here was Hitler well on his way. Why, the son of a bitch would sweep the world. What to do? You had to kill him. And you couldn't kill him by going over to Spain with a workers' brigade.

(This was the Litvak coming out.) So what do you do? You go to war. The United States was the only country that could stop him and he had to be stopped. So, I came before the editorial board of the *Socialist Call*. I proposed that we do an about-face. They looked at me as if I'd gone mad. I sat down and wrote an absolutely brilliant historical analysis, with quotations from Marx and Engels and Lenin to justify my position. The upshot was we had to go to war, but the party said no. So I resigned.

When I broke from the Socialist party, I gravitated back to the ILGWU. I had been organizing workers ever since 1932. If you're a Socialist, that's what you are supposed to do. Whenever anything was up, several of us offered our talents. We could cause a few riots, agitate some people, write and distribute leaflets, man picket lines, sing songs. Youth is energetic. The garment industry represented a real challenge. Certain trades are inherently hard to organize. They're small and competitive, labor-intensive, and relatively unskilled. In an area that requires high skill, like the building trades, you have a limited number of people who go through an apprenticeship and form old school ties. It's not hard to organize them. They have striking power. Owners can't move the building or run away with railroad tracks, let alone a highway. In small manufacture, you distribute a leaflet and on Monday morning there's a response to it. By Tuesday morning the shop is gone. Your people are semiskilled or unskilled; they have no faith in themselves. They're not ready to make war. They're glad to be working—jobs aren't so easy to come by—and all of them know they're replaceable. A measure of how tough it is to organize certain industries is the pitiably small percentage of unionism in textiles. Let's not forget that textiles were the first manufacturing trade in the United States. There were textile factories in the 1820s, with strikes and unions developing very early. Today the textile industry is still almost totally unorganized. It's a big industry, by the way, with probably a million employees—unorganized. The needle trades—that's men's and women's clothing and apparel— are more unstable than textiles. In textiles, you have thousands of competing producers, but the textile plant has a couple hundred people in it. There aren't many textile plants employing only twenty or thirty workers. The average shop in women's apparel has forty people. Men's clothing may be bigger, fifty, but not in the shirt factories. They're small and competing and they fold up and there's low capitalization, they're marginal producers, they run here and there. How do you organize the damn thing?

Historically, the apparel trades had an advantage, which was *ethnic cohesion*. They were overwhelmingly Jewish. Or Jewish and Italian. It's a curious phenomenon. Organization of the apparel trades in New York was as much an outgrowth of the mood in the Jewish community as it was a collective bargaining effort. The *Jewish Daily Forward* was the voice of the Jewish community; in addition, there were at least three other Yiddish dailies, and they were like one when it came to this kind of a question. If Jewish workers went out on strike, the whole goddam Jewish community stood behind them. Also, many of the employers were Jewish, and they were not aliens. They fought, and made trouble. I mean, a class brother is a class brother. Nevertheless, these were their people—fellow Jews.

Jewish ethnic identity was always a factor. Louis Brandeis once stepped in. Who was he? A German Jew, a respected man, who happened to represent the Jewish manufacturers of Boston. He said, "Let's settle this thing," and they did. There was one famous situation in the early 1930s, when the ILG didn't have a pot to piss in. The union couldn't function; it was bankrupt. The union was thinking of a general strike which David Dubinsky didn't know how to finance. He went to his brother unions. They were broke. And who the hell said you could organize garment workers anyhow? David Dubinsky went to two people, *both bankers*, Felix Warburg and Herbert Lehman. They gave him the money, with words like: "Here, it's a loan. Pay us back when you can." Dubinsky took it. And he did pay it back, 100 percent, no interest, but 100 percent. *They* gave him the money. That's quite a story. But it's how Dubinsky operated.

He was a totally integrated man, which doesn't mean that he never felt internal anguish or a measure of doubt, but there simply was no rift within him. He knew he was Jewish, working class, a Socialist, an anticommunist, and a democrat. In his life work he knew that an organization had to have a strong leader. Dubinsky knew he was not the Messiah, but he also felt that, for the moment, he was not a bad substitute.

I find a measure of the man in one memorable give-and-take we had. It was about a compromise he was forced to make. Even though he was my boss, I chided him: "It was a mistake; we didn't do the right thing."

Dubinsky: "You should've told me not to do it."

That left me flabbergasted: "I should have told *you* not to do it?" You don't tell that man not to do anything. Why should I have told him?

"Because you're a Socialist. Sometimes I forget I'm a Socialist, and you should've reminded me what a Socialist would have done." What *would* Dubinsky have done? "I would've screamed and yelled at you and told you you're crazy. You should've done it!"

He fought the Communists like crazy. He was the ultimate Communist-hater in the labor movement. But Dubinsky would come to the personal rescue of Communist after Communist. If they got in trouble and needed a few bucks, he'd find ways to help them out—while hating and fighting their politics to the death—without publicity. That's the man.

Dubinsky was very Jewish, but there is little in the needle trades that's Jewish anymore. I guess Italians are the second largest group in the industry today. It's 80 percent white and 20–25 percent black and Hispanic across the country. But I don't think there's a black and Hispanic majority, even in New York, where we have 25,000 Chinese and a large number of Greeks. And there are still waves of Italian migration. If there's a resentment of Jewish leadership, we get no active expression of it. The trade's overwhelmingly female—85 percent of the membership. Women come and go. They're certainly not like electrical workers who make a life of their trade. These are poor working-class women. Which means the average worker is in the factory four or five years, has a kid, is out four or five years, comes back, and stays another four or five years. They work in many branches of the needle trades: in millinery shops, in fur shops, in stores. With a transient population like that, you're not likely to get organized

David Dubinsky addressing a rally at Madison Square Garden on June 13, 1957, marking his twenty-fifth anniversary as President of the ILGWU.   ILGWU.

opposition easily. In relation to the union, the workers are in a kind of alienated situation that we try very hard to overcome. To the members, there tends to be a thing called the union, and guys who run the union. As they see it, some guys run a butcher shop, others a grocery store and still others run a union. The member pays a certain amount and expects to be taken care of. That's the relationship as they see it. Our problem is involving and activating the membership.

But what does that mean? In 1915 our people discussed Marx and Engels, Feuerbach or Bakunin. The cloakmakers would sit and make like they were philosophers. We don't dare touch those subjects now when it's necessary to explain what a union is. You could say we've had to revise our program. These days we organize all kinds of activities to "unionize" the member. Everyone has to join because we have a union shop. They pay dues but have no idea what the union is. So we have programs to unionize the union member.

In conducting educational work among members in urban areas, the single largest obstacle we face is crime. I don't mean the criminal element in unions, a subject that stirred my interest when Rudolph Halley came along as prosecutor in the Kefauver hearings. I got involved in the Halley phenomenon and helped run his mayoral campaign in the fifties. I began then to think about organized crime. Although corruption is universal (you find it in philanthropies, in universities), I was more perturbed by the penetration of organized labor by organized crime. Organized crime is a power machine with economic and political connections. Also, it's like the Communist party. When Communists come into a union, they're not just an opposition faction. They come in to take over. And they take over for an economic and political purpose. The same thing is true of the underworld. When organized crime enters the labor movement, it's there to take over. I wasn't too worried about corruption per se. I was worried that the American labor movement would end up in the pocket of organized crime. I felt it was a huge problem about which workers could do something on their own, but in the end it would require all the resources of our society to solve. Organized crime hasn't just penetrated unions; it has penetrated corporations, local, state, and Federal government. That's why my book on organized crime touches every facet of the system.

We still haven't come to grips with that colossal problem, but the immediate trouble now in attempts to activate our urban members is street crime. You cannot do very much while union members are at work in the shop, although we are now developing programs for education in the shop. We say: "Tonight there will be an English class for Spanish-speaking members. It's a good course." Many want to come after work; some arrive early at five or six o'clock. But when it's dark they're afraid to go home on the subway. They're even afraid to come to the office. So, street crime badly injures our lines of communication within the union. And there's a second problem: the bootleg factory. Often it's in somebody's house or in a little store with a dozen machines. The employees are illegal aliens and are paid below the minimum wage, in shops like those back in 1890. When you find one, you're afraid to enter the neighborhood. If you want to approach workers one by one, you have to go knocking on their doors. Who the hell wants to walk in those strange dark halls? . . . It's your life!

These are far more serious problems than relating to the member once she's in the shop. There are problems of relating there, too, but they are language problems. We've got to have a Chinese staff, a Hispanic staff, we have to look for someone who speaks Vietnamese, we have people who speak Greek. We can relate and communicate once they're in the union, but sustaining a program that carries them beyond work hours is terribly difficult, and reaching them in their neighborhoods is almost impossible. But we're working on that, too, trying to organize through the community. We take people right out of the shops and off the streets. And they are good people at a certain level, but if you begin to talk about the causes of inflation, or "How do you overcome unemployment?" or "What was the New Deal?" they're lost. How do you educate them? You devise a program. And we have programs. They're relatively successful, too. There's nothing ineducable about our workers. It's just that no one's ever taught them very much.

I came to Local 91 in 1934, and I began to study Italian because Italians predominated. We didn't have the crime problem. We used to have meetings; we used to have drama groups; we used to run late at night. No more. I guess the big change came after World War II.

When black women came into the shops, they didn't earn a lot of money but they made a living. They were and are very hard workers and super-respectable in every way, church-goers with conservative and traditional values. But their kids were in serious trouble all the time. They didn't learn bad habits from their parents; a whole generational thing was happening.

Black-Jewish tension troubles and shocks me. I still have not been directly exposed to it, but I read *Commentary* and the daily papers. I'm aware of what's happening. I followed details of the teachers' strike in 1968, and tended to go with the union, but it brought out basic tensions. I wrote an essay on this aspect of the situation for Shlomo Katz who was editing *Midstream* at that time. The piece I wrote was about Herbert Hill and Paul Jacobs, two personal friends of mine over many, many years. I felt that they were *meshuga*, but I understood the nature of their *meshugas*. My title was "The Politics of Self-Hate." The manuscript contained chapter and verse and Shlomo loved it, but I finally had to disappoint him. The article was set up in type when Dubinsky got wind of it. He asked me not to publish it because it would exacerbate a bad situation between the ILGWU and the NAACP. Herb, who was labor secretary of the NAACP, was a close friend of Adam Clayton Powell. Adam had asked David Dubinsky for a political contribution. Well, the ILGWU had never endorsed Adam Clayton Powell; we were attached to the Liberal party, which was running its own candidate for the House. We had no use for Adam, none at all. Anyhow, Dubinsky refused. Word came back through an intermediary that if David Dubinsky did not support Adam, he'd be in trouble. That's all you have to tell David Dubinsky. He reacted in typical fashion: "The Tsar of Russia couldn't frighten me. What do I care about a Tammany politician?" Within a few days, an apprentice cutter—a "spreader"— was charging the ILGWU with discrimination. This spreader had made application to be a cutter, and the union told him he hadn't served his apprenticeship long enough. Herbie Hill and Adam Clayton Powell "investigated" and reported that the ILGWU excluded blacks from Local 10, which is the Cutters' local, a choice local. We had 275 black members in that local, out of 7,000—not so many, but certainly no exclusion. That spreader's case became a cause célèbre. Adam Clayton Powell figured he would get Dubinsky. He was also riding a little wave of anti-Semitism, which was always there. This was in the early sixties or late fifties. We went down to Congress and argued. Adam Clayton Powell was embarrassed by the whole thing and the committee decided that it was ridiculous. There was no case. There was nothing. At one point they said, "This isn't even worth entering in our records."

And Powell ran out on it; he took a tour of another country. We won the round. We won the war. That didn't stop Herbie, who went on with his *shtick* ("thing").

Meanwhile, Paul Jacobs wrote an article for *Harper's* in which Dubinsky was equated with the establishment. It was a strong attack on the ILGWU and its leader. Of these, my old friends, Paul and Herbie, what could I say? Surely, the ILGWU is not beyond criticism. What the hell, it's just another institution. But to single out David Dubinsky and the ILGWU for an assault made no sense when there were reactionaries, even Fascists, all around us. Go to war with the Klan. But why pick on David Dubinsky? You're not going to find anyone much more liberal than he is. Don't let's make him a god or a saint but why make him out to be a Jewish racist? Anyhow, that's what inspired my essay called "The Politics of Self-Hate." I'm sorry it wasn't published because it diagnoses a disease as typically Jewish as diabetes.

All of us old Marxists had a unilinear and universal concept of history. We presupposed that all societies evolve and progress in the same manner. Feudalism breaks down and you get capitalism; capitalism, before it breaks down, creates a working class; and the working class takes over. That's the theory—with refinements along the way. It was a global concept by means of which you saw nothing but the class struggle. Now, if you were to ask me whether I still hold to this view, I'd say yes, there *is* always a class struggle. People who earn their living in different ways struggle against one another. However, if you were to ask me, "What is the single most dynamic force in the world in 1979?" I would not say it's the clash of classes. I would say it's nationalism, or tribalism, which is a force that I came to recognize very late in my life. I went through the whole Second World War without recognizing it as a major factor. Nowadays, when I look at a political situation, I think "class," because that's imbedded in my head. But right away I also go ethnic.

I do not look upon my Jewishness as tribalism. I look upon it as a manifestation of universalism. I became a Zionist after World War II, thinking that Jews, with their lives in jeopardy, must have a haven somewhere on this planet. I didn't think Israel was going to last very long. I didn't think it was going to last *this* long. How could a Jewish island survive in an alien world? I was some futurologist, wasn't I?

The question remains—what kind of Socialist am I? About that it's very difficult for me to be objective. As the years go by, I redefine what I am. First, I said, "I'm a universalist and a Socialist." Then, someplace along the line, I said, "Well, there is a Jewish breed and I belong to it." Then I came to the conclusion that Sephardim (Jews of Spanish or Portugese origin) lived in another world. So I was really an Ashkenazi Jew. Then when I met the Hasidim, I decided they also lived in another world. So I'm a Misnagdic Ashkenazic Jewish Socialist rooted in the working class—who's still a universalist.

Yet there's another strain. I didn't learn very much from my grandfather, aside from the fact that when things get bad you should smile and say "I hope God knows what the hell He's doing." Make a joke and admit, "Okay, I can't control everything. I'll do the best I can." But one thing I did learn from him. I must have been an infant when he began giving me lessons in social insecurity that prepared me for the Holocaust. The Spanish Inquisition was a daily event in my household. I don't know who the hell made him an authority on the Spanish Inquisition. He probably invented most of it. But my grandfather imagined such horrors and such tortures! The phrase that stuck in my head was that they would beat the Jews *mit eisener ritter* (with iron whips). At a given point somebody would descend upon the Jews and wipe them all out. That made a deep impression. I also must tell you, it still does. That little piece of insecurity I will never be able to remove from my existence. No matter how sophisticated I am, no matter how knowledgeable, that sticks.

10.

THE YIDDISH INFLUENCE ON AMERICAN THEATER

Harold Clurman

I LOVE three European cities: London, Paris, and Rome. I wouldn't want to live in any of them because my friends and my work are here in New York. I love London as well as New York. But I'm an American. My fight is with America, not with England.

I used to prowl the streets of New York, but not any more! I prowl more in Europe than I do here; they have safer streets. I've always felt that this country is much more violent than most. I've always been a little bit scared in New York. I had the feeling, even years ago, that when I was walking in the street a drunk might come over and punch me for no reason at all. There are drunks (and murderers) in England and France, but somehow they seem to be less threatening. D. H. Lawrence said there's something violent in America, there always has been, and Arthur Schlesinger recently remarked that there's a tradition of violence here, of ordinary violence.

My attachment to New York is simply based on the fact that I have worked here. Also, it's a theater city. If I had started in Chicago or San Francisco I'd have moved to New York. Ballet dancers don't stay in Texas; they come here. All this is going to change somewhat, I suppose, because New York is getting weaker. The whole situation is becoming difficult, financially and

Harold Clurman was born in New York in 1901. He was a drama critic, film producer, and author of several books on the stage. He directed numerous plays on Broadway and was cofounder of the Group Theatre in New York. He died in 1979.

otherwise. By now, there are aspects of life in this city that I've come to hate—the dirt, the constant noise, the rudeness.

(INTERVIEWER: But here you are a young seventy-five and you're living in New York.) I'm seventy-four! Don't make me an old man. I'm a young fella of seventy-four. As I said, my work is here. I'm a critic here. I'm a director here. I'm a lecturer here. Yet I go away every time I get a chance. This year I was in India— Calcutta, Bombay, and New Delhi. I was in Berlin, Warsaw, and London. Every chance I get, I go away. I love to travel away from New York and come back to it.

Right now New York City is a shambles. As for the Jews, they're getting rubbed out by Americanism. But still, consider Clive Barnes, who's half Jewish, observing that if the Jews didn't go to plays in New York, there'd be Yom Kippur every night in the theater. Why all the theaters would have to be closed. He's absolutely right. Also Jews are the greater part of the audience at concerts.

All this makes New York rather special. There are not many cities like New York. First of all, most cities are pretty dull. Vienna's a dead town. Why? Because it has no Jews any more. Because who were their Jews? They were Freud, they were Schnitzler, von Hofmannsthal, Mahler (who converted!), Bruno Walter—all Jews. That's one of the reasons New York is still a great town. Most of the conductors are Jewish. Most of the violinists are Jewish. When they asked Dimitri Mitropoulos after the war, when he'd been in Berlin, "How are the orchestras?" he said, "Everything was fine, except they don't have many good violinists in the orchestra." They said, "What's the matter?" He said, "No Jews."

I've had this kind of Jewish consciousness now for about fifteen years, although in a way it was always there. Over time it grew and grew. Nothing dramatic happened to me. It was just my reading, my observation mainly that there was anti-Semitism in the world.

I didn't have the experience of life enough when I was a kid to know what it was all about. I didn't understand Jewish history until later. Then I had to find out my past. In another sense it started when my father talked to me. He had the greatest influence on me. He took me to the synagogue to introduce me to the fact that there was a Jewish ritual, and he would explain it. He felt very Jewish and he was proud of being Jewish. He always spent time with me. He was a doctor who never learned to drive, and though I was under age he asked me to drive the car. So I used to drive him to his calls. I used to go along with him to operations and God knows what. And he talked to me and taught me so many things.

He took me to the Yiddish theater when I was six, and took me there constantly. He read Jewish poetry and stories to me in order that, since he wasn't religious, I'd at least know what it was to be Jewish. He was not Orthodox, although his father had been fanatically Orthodox.

In my house we read Yiddish literature, and he would lecture on Peretz. Although a doctor, he was deeply interested in literature and was a very good critic. As far as I know he was the first man to write an article in Yiddish about Mark Twain. He was the first man to write a review of the *Kreutzer Sonata*, which he read in Russian before it was translated into English. He wrote for *Der Tag*, a Yiddish daily, and he was very good at it. Later on he was known mostly as a writer of popular articles on medicine, but he was essentially a literary critic. One of the reasons he didn't pursue that calling, apart from its not being very remunerative, was that he abused everybody. He was very arrogant. For instance, he used to deride Abraham Cahan as a socialist. He said not only was Cahan's socialism very superficial but so was his literary criticism.

When they were young my parents struggled for a while on the East Side. My mother finally told my father, "You know, you should be a doctor."

"Well, maybe, but it's impossible."

"It's possible. I'll open a candy store and run it 'till you graduate."

So we moved to New Haven. Mother ran the candy store and Father completed his studies at Yale Medical School. Then he came back to the East Side to practice.

During the first ten years of my life I lived on the Lower East Side on Rivington Street. I was born on Rivington and Essex in a building that no longer exists. We moved to a building at Rivington and Suffolk, a building that does still exist, which was at that time occupied on its lower floor by a dentist and on its upper floor by my father and the family. My father wanted me to know Yiddish. First he asked me to study Hebrew, which I did up to about my twelfth year. But then he realized that it was a mistake: "I should have taught you *Yiddish* instead." Why? He thought that there was no currency for Hebrew. I wasn't going out in the street to talk Hebrew; on the other hand, I was going to the East Side theater, where I learned most of my Yiddish. Much of the rest came by listening to his patients who spoke Yiddish, and to him chatting with certain Orthodox people who spoke Yiddish. So that was a living thing. And Hebrew wasn't. Nor was it going to be. He doubted that the Arabs would ever relinquish Palestine.

Politically, from the beginning he was very anti-Soviet, in the sense that I *am*, but not in the sense that I *was*. And later on he knew better than I did that Stalin was a monster. He had early experience with the Russian revolutionary movement and had read Russian, whereas I took it for granted that since almost everybody in the United States was against socialism of any kind, they lied terribly about the Soviet Union. Therefore I didn't credit the things that were said about it. My father knew better.

Until Irving Howe's book, *World of Our Fathers*, the pictures painted of the lower East Side placed too much emphasis on the poverty, the vulgarity, the crudity. They forget the great idealism there, and also, even more especially, how very friendly it was to artistic endeavor. People studying, growing, aspiring, people reading together. I had some of the most wonderful discussions— I never could get to bed. To this day, I go to bed at three in the morning because when I was a kid all I used to hear in my home, starting at nine o'clock, after dinner, were these violent (they seemed violent, but they were really very friendly) discussions about American politics, about Russia, about literature, about art. I didn't understand them all—how could a seven, eight, ten-year-old boy understand those abstruse subjects—but I was fascinated by the passion and the heat of it. And though I saw terrible things—my father as a doctor was sewing up gangsters—and people falling from fire escapes—I found also that there was a good deal of sincere Orthodoxy.

Many of my father's friends were Orthodox; he had had a good friend who was a very Orthodox Jew, a sweet man who naturally wore his hat in the house. His daughter, a lovely girl, his only daughter, died when she was engaged to be married, at the age of twenty. She was the queenly kind of Jewish virgin of the old ghettos, the kind you read about in books. A year or so after this girl died, my father, the atheist, asked this old man—and I never forgot it—"Do you still believe in God?" And he said, "I believe in Him but I don't understand Him." This was very touching. I was then eight or nine years old. All that has an influence. To discuss whether you believe in Him, or don't understand Him, and so on. But I felt that was not only *my* home, even though my home was special. It was aristocratic, in a certain sense, since my father had gone to Yale and was a doctor. And he was constantly reading. We had German books and Russian books in the house, and pictures of Shelley, Disraeli, and others. All of that made a big difference.

My brothers didn't take quite so much to his intellectual, spiritual, and you might even say "religious" side. They all wanted to be Americans. This made my father bitter. He once found my oldest brother reading a sports book and asked him, "Why don't you read this?"—a book he had given him. My brother said, "This interests me more, the sports." Well, it cut my father to the quick! He mentioned it to me very often! What a dreadful answer he'd gotten. Probably he really devoted himself to me since I was the youngest, and also by then he was established. He earned a good living as a doctor.

I may have a more favorable memory than others because I was in a more privileged position than most. But I also went into homes of people who were crude. I also went to *cheder* (Hebrew school). But the *cheder* was such an awful place I didn't want to study there. My father took me out immediately and gave me modern teachers. For a while I could read the Bible. But it's like

Latin, which I also studied. I've forgotten most of it. When I was
in Israel and directing there, words came back to me just as they
do when I read a quotation in Latin. Whereas the Yiddish I've
never forgotten because I kept going to the theater. I was fascinated
with it. I heard Yiddish on the stage and my father read to me
and so forth. I absorbed it.

I was six years old when I first saw Jacob Adler. That was
in 1907. I remember it very well. I've written about it. I didn't
understand the Yiddish, particularly, but I understood the acting.
The first play was *Uriel Acosta*, a romantic German piece written
in 1840 or so. Uriel Acosta was Spinoza's heretical student who
went through the whole anathema pronounced against Spinoza,
and he recanted too. Many years later somebody told me that I
imitated what I had seen, specifically the scene in which he recants
in the synagogue. The ritual required that they step on him, and
when they stepped on him he got up and revolted. The girl asked
him, please, to recant. She said, "Please, don't do this," and he
threw her down the steps. Later on, a girl I knew reminded me:
"Remember what you did to me? Years ago, when you were
about eight? You threw me down the steps because you were so
impressed by this gesture." After a while I was an absolute fanatic.
I wanted to go to the theater all the time. And slowly I began not
to understand the plays so much as the words. I mean after all
there were plays about illegitimate affairs which I couldn't understand. I was quite an innocent. Nowadays, kids know all the
erotic verses when they're eleven years old. I got more sophisticated at about age fifteen.

Jacob Adler was a great actor, an extraordinary personality.
There are very few actors of that kind. Actors today are shrimps.
It has to do also with the fact that most of the population is
composed of shrimps. And there's a reason why. It's true of the
American theater, too. You see, they had to be tough. Not in the
lowest sense, but to withstand the difficulties—in the Jewish case,
the villages they came from, the prejudice against them, the pro-
hibitions aimed at Jews in the towns. In order to be an actor under
those conditions you've got to have real power that provides you

with the ability to survive. That was true also of the American theater where conditions were very bad. Actors were big, hefty pioneer men. Men who built the theater were like the pioneers who built the rails. Those who set the standards were great personalities. Adler also had enormous sex appeal. He was six feet one or two, with beautiful white hair at a very early age. He had a splendid figure, like a Chaliapin, with a wonderful voice, and authority. They called him the King. He wore a high hat and he made a fortune. They used to pay him a thousand dollars a performance. You know what it meant in those days to have a thousand dollars a performance? The same as today without taxes. Adler was a terrific actor! There was also David Kessler, who was his colleague and rival, a man whom Jed Harris (the American director/producer) described as the best actor he ever saw in his life.

Program / **פּראָגראם**

Saturday Evening, November 26, 1910.

SHYLOCK.
Comedy in 4 acts, by Wm. Shakespeare.
CAST OF CHARACTERS

Duke of Venice	Mr. Goldstein
Prince of Morocco	Mr. Schacht
Antonio, a merchant of Venice	Mr. J. Kessler
Bassanio	Mr. Schrage
Salarino	Mr. A. Schorr
Gratiano	Mr. Shoengold
Lorenzo	Mr. Ginsburg
Shylock, a rich Jew	Mr. J. P. Adler
Jessica, daughter to Shylock	Mrs. R. Prager
Launcelot Gobbo	Mr. Rubin
Gobbo	Mr. Goldstein
Portia, a rich heiress	Miss F. Adler
Nerissa, her waiting-maid	Miss Goldstein
Tubal, a Jew, Shylock's friend	Mr. Rubin

Senators, Officers of the Court of Justice,

ATTENTION ! ! The ladies are kindly requested to remove their hats when the curtain rises for the accommodation of the visitors on the rear seats. It is strictly forbidden to speak or whisper one to another while the performance is going on. The audience is kindly requested to applaud only with their hands. The ladies' lavatory is to the left on the inside lobby. Gents' lavatory is to the right in the lobby. Kindly report any inattention on the part of the employees to the Manager, Mr. I. Abramson.
BOX OFFICE TELEPHONE, FRANKLIN 920

After the Performance Visit Ph. ZEITLEN'S Cafe and Restaurant, 231 GRAND STREET, Opp. Bowery Bank Building, NEW YORK

SPECTORS PIANOS
USED IN THIS THEATRE
EXCLUSIVELY
SALESROOMS
Grand Street   cor. Orchard St.
NEW YORK

Program for J. P. Adler's *Shylock*, 1910.   YIVO INSTITUTE FOR JEWISH RESEARCH.

The Jewish histrionic tradition was created largely by these serious actors who did the better plays, mostly by the models of Russian actors and visiting German actors whom they used to see passing through certain towns in Russia. The Russian school was the best school, really. "Best" is perhaps too strong a word. But they were very fine actors and in many respects theirs *was* the best school.

The Russian-German influence was given a particular Yiddish flavor especially in character roles. What were the character roles? There were Jewish parts. Adler played Shylock and Uriel Acosta, and men of the world. He was always larger than life. Also, the Jewish people, just those people who were pushcart peddlers and salesmen, the "vulgar" people, looked up to him. He was their hero. He represented a Jew who was clean, who was strong, who was proud, who was not a schnorrer (freeloader) or a schlemiel (jerk), but capable, powerful, dignified, and effective. That was their ideal. (Now our ideals are downward instead of upward. Kids want to be like the great gangsters or the great dope fiends or the great killers.) Even religious Jews did not object to the idea of making a hero out of an actor. After all, he was a *"shayner* Yid" (beautiful Jew). I suppose the *extremely* religious wouldn't go to the theater. But after all there were relatively few of those.

In this respect the theater was much more vital on the East Side than the American theater is today. That little world produced conditions for what I would call *true theater*. A true theater can only exist where the community is homogeneous. Even in a heterogeneous society there are homogeneous communities. For example, if we had enough socialists in this country to be a group that was identifiable, whose members shared certain values, you could have a socialist theater. In what sense did the Jews have a true theater? In the sense that the fairly religious, the semireligious, the ignorant, the quasi-ignorant, the aspiring—all could gather in one place, in the theater. They couldn't get together in the *shul* because there were the "Apikorsim"—apostates, the heretics, the unbelievers who didn't go to *shul*. But they did go to the theater. And so did many men who went to *shul* go to the theater. They had a common bond and a common memory of the old country. That's why it was very fine theater—and its's what I have meant by the theater as a social center.

There's no such thing as "only aesthetic" in community art. You can have the "only aesthetic" experience if you lock yourself in your room and want to read Greek tragedy in the original. Then you can be quite alone. But if you go to the theater you've got actors who come from the community. You have audience, you have workers; you need a collective memory, a social base.

The Yiddish theater fed the Broadway theater; it fed me in the sense that I saw my first plays there. Paul Muni was from the Yiddish theater, and the Adlers: Luther was a very fine actor, Stella is perhaps the *best* teacher of acting. And there were quite a number of others. Also the musicians—Irving Berlin and Gershwin. They heard the Yiddish theater, its music, and they got that feeling. The old East Side was full of singing. In and out of the synagogues!

In those days I was only slightly aware of anti-Semitism. If you walked down to the Bowery you could get to see anti-Semitic gangs who wanted to beat you up. And you said you were Polish or you'd get somebody who was with you to say you were. But the schools were full of Jews. When I went to DeWitt Clinton there was a large proportion of Jewish students. The schools were not good. For me they were too crowded, especially high school. Too crowded, too dirty, too indiscriminate. I preferred to go to the theater and to read books. I skipped classes. I played hookey, as they said, and went to the library to read . . . *Jean Christophe* or Frank Norris or Theodore Dreiser.

When I was seventeen I asked to go to the opera and I got to go two or three times a week. I also went to art galleries. In the arts, my father may just have acted as the springboard for me. He didn't know much about painting or music. I'd say "Look, I'm reading a book by Romain Rolland in which some man gets very angry and says he doesn't like the philosophy of Brahms." I asked myself, "What? Brahms has a philosophy? *Music* has a philosophy?" So I began to listen to music and read *more*. Then somebody says, "This painting shows decadence." Paintings showed decadence? What? So I started looking at pictures. By the age of twenty I had already seen all the moderns including Matisse and Picasso. Also I had heard all those discussions. In other words, my father gave me the literary beginning, and from it, from reading, making references and cross-references, I took off. I went on.

So by the time I met Aaron Copland when I was twenty and we were both about to to to Paris, he was astonished that I knew not only about George Jean Nathan, who was then the leading critic, in my view, of the theater, but also about Paul Rosenfeld, who was one of the leading critics of music. He was astonished that he'd met a person who knew something about music (because I got to go to concerts). So, long before I met Copland I was something of a connoisseur, a very young connoisseur. Then I met Copland and my musical education was completed through him.

I had a lust for everything I could *feel*. Consequently, I was never very good at science. My father was a doctor and my brothers were good at science. Not me. But I still want to know. Only when I read Bronowski or some other popularizer I find that I know less than when I began. Because, perhaps, scientific books are badly written. And, second, I'm a layman.

Speaking of my book, *The Fervent Years*, I've been fervent since I was old enough to yell. (There is some New York quality about that. You know, I shout.) The first play I ever did, independently, was *Awake and Sing*. People asked me, "Why did you have three characters talking at the same time?" And I explained it to them: "Because in my family everybody was a disputer. I was the youngest. In order to be heard I had to yell louder than anybody else. As a result I have never stopped shouting."

The others were also fervent in their arguments. My father was a Socialist. He'd say, "You, you're among Americans, you don't know anything, you're not cultured." We fought like hell. He'd say, "Don't say that about Balzac. You haven't read enough about Balzac." I'd say, "You're old-fashioned." America was no good and that made me the patriot in the family. They used to say in the Group Theater that I was the most patriotic American. Look, when certain critics—like Brustein at Yale—say, "Oh, you want to do contemporary American plays," I say, "What's wrong with that?" We are here, we live here. I don't care if we're not as cultured as ancient Greeks. We're in the United States, our cultural work has to be created *here*, for *here*, and if it's good for here it will have an influence through the rest of the world.

I worked very closely as a young man with Lee Strasberg. He had an influence on me. Strasberg is more of a Talmudist than I am. There's something slightly pedantic about him. But he has a very good mind, and he's a very special person. Well, I am too. But he's special in certain strange respects. He certainly had an influence on me. He introduced me to the Stanislavsky system. I was more literary at the beginning. He was more theatrical. But he was born in Europe, in Galicia. That makes a difference, too. He's a Galitzianer (a Jew from Galicia)!

Clifford Odets was important, too. I had an influence on *him*. He was also influenced by the environment and that was a Jewish environment. But he had hardly any Yiddish and he didn't know much Jewish lore. But there was authenticity in his characters. He didn't have to know much. After all, you walk into a kosher delicatessen and you learn something about Jewish life. Maybe you get a horrible picture but you get something. His Jewish upbringing was scattered. He was a very divided man—even before the Hollywood period. Here in New York he was divided. He wanted to be a revolutionary, but he also wanted to drive a Rolls Royce and tell "the truth" to the world. He was a revolutionary who didn't want to work in a small theater. He wanted to work on Broadway. When I said, "Go into such and such a theater with the play because it's small," he said, "What do you want with those old theaters—you've got to go big—Broadway." He wanted to be Lenin and King George. That's the division. He wanted to be the special, intellectual leader and to hobnob with stars—Joan Crawford or whoever. He wanted to be the world's greatest baseball player. He used to claim, "If I had studied music I would be like Beethoven." He wanted to be everything. He was a child in that respect, but a real playwright. I've been asked, "Why don't you write plays? You write well, you understand people. And you understand theater."

Answer: "Because I'm not a playwright."

"Well, you write . . ."

"You don't understand what I'm talking about. I know more about art than ten painters but I can't draw lines. You have to know your limitations." Odets couldn't see that.

Now, on Jewishness and Americanism: If you're Neil Simon, then you're contributing your Jewishness to America and America has contributed to what you are. But if you're an intellectual you have a different problem. It's as though Irving Howe all of a sudden decided, "I can make a million dollars if I write editorials for *Time* magazine." But he knows he's not going to do that. Or, if he writes them, they'll be *his* editorials and *Time* will throw him out. After all, there's no such thing as the complete American.

But, if you ask me, "What are you first?" I say, "First I'm an American." The origin, the root came from my Jewishness which, insofar as it is that, has contributed to making me a better American, a fuller American, a broader American. There's no conflict.

One day in Hollywood, a man asked me, "How do you like my picture?"

Now I had to offer criticism of pictures that were being made. I said to him, "In the scene where the strike begins you have a fellow saying, 'Let's strike!' A troublemaker. And he has a Jewish accent." I asked the dopey gentile, "Why did you give him a Jewish accent?"

"I wanted to show he comes from outside."

"But why a *Jewish* accent? Aren't there any outsiders who don't have Jewish accents?"

"Well, I wanted him to be somebody who was not quite American."

I said, "Look here, you, I'm ten times more American than you are. What the hell do you know about America?"

He got absolutely livid and said: "I'm glad you feel that way."

I kept yelling, "Don't you pull any of that stuff. You're no more American than I. You're far less. Talk about American history, let's talk about American politics, let's talk about American economics. You don't know a goddam thing except making your lousy pictures. So don't pull that stuff. Just shut up about being un-American. Because I'm Jewish."

Who the hell is American? Roosevelt said, "The whole country is made up of immigrants. My family is one of the oldest. We're Dutch." A Catholic never says he's not American. Why should a Jew?

The real shock of anti-Semitism did not come with Hitler. It was a long-developing thing. I remember in 1924 I went to see Isadora Duncan. She mentioned a certain dance critic and she was going to answer his criticism of her. He didn't like her dancing because he was against modern dance. And as she said that, a man in the box cried out, "He's a dirty Jew!" And she looked up and said, "But I like the Jews." At which the audience applauded. He got frightened because the audience applauded her, so he said, "Well, not the dirty ones." All this happened in Paris in 1924.

You begin to read history and you get to see it, and after a while you get to know it. I was in Moscow one day and there was a very nice interpreter, most respectful. She said everybody held me in esteem when I delivered lectures. Then she looked at my papers. She came to the part about if I die or something happens to me who shall they notify, which read "Samuel Clurman." She said, "Are you Jewish?" She didn't say anything else, but the sound of it made it clear to me that she was—what?—programmed in anti-Semitism.

Once in London I went to a big, swank party. I was a hero at the time because I had produced a play called *Golden Boy*, which was a great success, and one day I said, "You people had better get wise to yourselves (meaning the English) and make a common front with the French against Hitler." And one women responded, "You are only angry at Hitler because he's bad to your people." I knew what she meant but, well, I'd like to meet her some time so that I could ask, "Whose people was he against? Hitler dropped bombs on England. Did only Jews get killed?" You don't need any excuse for anti-Semitism. You can say, "I don't like you because I don't like the way you tie your shoelaces." When you don't like somebody you find reasons for not liking him. Do you remember about the guy who exclaimed just before Hitler, "Oh, those Jews, those Jews, those Jews. They're ruining Germany."

And the guy next to him countered with, "It's not the Jews, it's the bicycle riders."

"Why the bicycle riders?"

"Why the Jews?"

I've been connected with *The Nation* since 1956. Before that, I wrote in *The New Republic* and another magazine called *Tomorrow*. When I came to *The Nation* there were very reactionary critics—politically and otherwise. Ben Haggin in music was very reactionary, and Joseph Krutch was very reactionary—nice fellow, but reactionary. The politics didn't concern me. I would write for a fascist paper if it had enough readers and let me say what I had to say. I wouldn't write for papers that censored me. My nephew Dick Clurman called me up one day with a message, which was: "Don't work for *The Nation*."

"Why not?"

"Well, I wouldn't say it's red. It's in-between. It's grey."

"I'm sorry, they offered me a job and I'm going to write what I have to say, and if that's a black mark against me I guess I'll have to accept it." And I've been writing there without restriction for twenty years.

A lot of my friends were caught up in the McCarthy era. They were sweet people. I liked it that they were Communists. I didn't agree with them but I liked it because they wanted to do something. They were politically naïve, but it came from a very good source so I could never be angry at them. They used to call me a counter-revolutionary. When Odets told me, "I'm going to be a Communist," I said, "I think that's silly because you won't stay with them and then they'll hate you. Actually both sides will hate you. They will try to tell you about the theater. You should tell *them* about the theater. They're ignoramuses. You know about theater. They know all about Marx. I do not recall that Marx ever put on a show."

There's a wonderful story about Lenin during the time when

many of the Bolsheviks were in Geneva. One of the comrades got sick. Lenin said, "Go get him a doctor."

"He's already had a doctor."

"He's not getting better."

"The doctor was a good comrade, a good Marxist."

"I said, 'Get him a good doctor.' I don't care if he's a good Marxist or not. All I want is a good *doctor*."

If I could, I helped people when they got blacklisted. I gave them jobs. Morris Carnovsky, an old friend and a sweet man, said, "Hey, you're giving me a job in a play . . ." (a play called *Tiger at the Gates*, which had an English cast). He said, "You're giving me a job." "You know," I said, "that's our business."

The FBI questioned me, but not officially. I didn't give them any names. First of all, they began to pull cards out: signed, radical documents. They said (this was 1932, 1931) I signed these things. They took out about ten. I stopped them. "Wait a minute, wait a minute. Don't take any more out. If you've got fifty papers, I want to tell you I signed two hundred, and I'll tell you why. Because in those days I was for the Soviet Union. After the war I was not for the Soviet Union any more. Now if you want to do something about it, do something about it."

The agent wanted to know, "If you had fascists in the company would you denounce them?"

I answered, "I had a person who wasn't a fascist because he wouldn't even know what that word meant, but he had all the fascist opinions."

"Why did you use him?"

"Good actor."

He said, "Well, *did* you have Communists?"

I said, "If they were Communists, would they have told me?"

So then finally he asked me, "Can we have tickets to the theater?" It was very funny.

Another day they came and asked me about John Garfield. "We have word from a girl that he asked to join the Communist party. What do you think of that?"

I said, "Was he in bed with her?" Then he asked me something else, and I said, "He was naïve. He was a naïve person."

"Was he politically naïve?"

"Yes, of course, politically naïve. Otherwise he wouldn't have been in the theater. Jimmy Cagney—anybody—we're all naïve."

Oh, there was one other thing. "Well, it's all right about your signing in 1931 or 1932, but we have something here in 1937, when you sent a wire to the Moscow Art Theater congratulating them on their fiftieth anniversary." I said, "Tell you what, if they were to ask me again today to send them a letter of congratulations, I would."

"What do you mean by that?"

"I mean it's a great theater, that's what."

"You signed for Hans Eisler. Why?"

"Because he was a damned good musician and I wanted him to have a successful concert." They finally just gave up.

Looking back now, it was a wonderful period—terrible, wonderful, silly, great. The thirties. The Group Theater was a marvelous experience. Full of pain, full of disappointment, full of anguish. Marvelous. In New York we struggled for something, for an ideal. We were fighting to establish something good in the middle of a very difficult economic, political, and social situation. When we went to Hollywood we went just to stuff our gut. In Hollywood, you don't see anybody. When I go to the theater in Hollywood, I'm always surprised: "Oh, they have people here?" You could take a walk in Hollywood. . . . One day I took a walk with Elia Kazan. We had to visit the deathbed of Clifford Odets and we decided to walk. It was a Sunday. We walked for thirty blocks and were all alone on the street. People looked at us out of cars. At night time we might have been arrested. What kind of crazy people were walking in the street? They must be nutty wastrels or gangsters who lost their car.

What I fundamentally believed in the Group Theater I still believe. That I made a mistake about not producing this or that play, those are things that we all do all the time. I would not direct again unless a very good play came along, one that I was very enthusiastic about. There was always fun and there was always pain in directing. But the Group Theater, as such, had to come to an end at that particular moment. It couldn't recur in its original form because the situation is such that if anybody wants to make a theater today, the kind we had, he would have to raise half the money himself and the government would need to give him the other half. You can't make our kind of theater group any more without complete subsidy.

In the sixties we had a rebellion that was silly, but it showed there was a big ache. All that stuff with the heroin and psychedelic drugs made it look like a crazy man's rebellion. Anger had a reason but no very rational outlet. The worst thing right now is this: I don't see any real anger. Even though we're only a few years away from that furious indignation, '68, '69. It all died. There is now a lack of culture. When you start being a revolutionary and you don't know what the hell you're talking about, that's due to a lack of culture.

Intelligent youth are getting more mature, but I teach at Hunter and it's bad. There is among the young a mindless activism alternating with a mindless apathy. You have to have a mind to begin with. You have to be a *mensch* (a real man). They're not *menschen*. I give courses in theater, one in criticism. They ask me, "What do you think of Clive Barnes?"

What do I think of him? "I'm talking about criticism, my friends, I'm not talking about Clive Barnes."

"Yes, but what do you think of him?"

"I think he's a very fine typist." Then I said, "Look, you're taking a course in criticism, you're university students" (these are M.A. candidates). "Do you think I'm a good critic?"

"Oh, one of the greatest."

"Do you read me every week?"

"No."

"Do you read Barnes every day?"

"Yes."

"What are you doing here? What *are* you doing here?"

A number of years ago at Harvard I lectured to two hundred students in one class (which I don't approve of) taking a course in drama. I look at the class before I start. "How many people here go to the theater once a month?" Twenty-five people raised their hands—in two hundred. I don't say anything. "How many people here read Walter Winchell?" A hundred and seventy-five people raised their hands. "I'll tell you what, I think you're a bunch of crooks. You're stealing money from your parents. You're not educated people and you never will be. If you're taking a course in drama, it's just a snap course. If you're really serious I'll tell you how you should start getting interested in the theater. There's a burlesque house down on Howard Street, the Old Howard. I suggest you go there, because first of all you'll see people in three dimensions. You'll see that there actually are people there. That's the first step. Then after you get used to seeing the girls naked, or half-naked, then you might go on to a little musical comedy. And after that, after a little while, you might even go to another theater to see some plays, and later on, you'll read the books that you're reading here. Otherwise, this is all shit!"

That was in the late fifties and it's worse now. Now *I'm* the indignant one. I'm the fighter. People ask me, "As New York goes down, do you expect 'the fabulous invalid' to expire?" Nowhere will the theater die completely. We'll have bad years. The English theater was in terrible shape in the mid-nineteenth century, until Shaw and Wilde came along. It's in bad shape now, but it's still there. Everything expires and everything gets reborn. I'm a pessimist. I think the world will go on.

II

"NEW YORK JEW"
Alfred Kazin

YOU MIGHT say I was born into two Jewish orthodoxies. My mother was an Orthodox Jew, and my father was an orthodox Socialist. I grew up in an entirely Jewish section of Brownsville. The neighborhood was more Orthodox than my family, but we observed all the Jewish customs and holidays. I went to Talmud Torah and had a lot of Hebrew training and was bar mitzvahed. In my childhood, it never occurred to me that there was any other way of life.

And our way was very primitive. Grand-uncles wouldn't eat with us because, Orthodox or not, we couldn't help but contaminate them. There was a constant sense of much holier people. Still, Jewish traditions in our world were incredibly diverse. One grand-uncle was pious; his brother, who didn't wear a beard, was a big businessman, a Tammany type; another had fought with the Jewish Legion in 1918. I was aware of a great many simultaneous traditions, but Orthodoxy remained the heart and soul of it all.

Brownsville was then the largest Jewish neighborhood in the Western world, a community situated at the other end of the subway line near the ocean and the Queens border. Originally it had been a series of "new lots," out where the subway ends, called East New York. When the subway crossed the river and came out to Brooklyn, many Jews saw a chance to escape the Lower East Side ghetto and move there. Brownsville was so Jewish that the name itself became as familiar a Jewish word as the Lower

Alfred Kazin was born in New York in 1915. He is a writer and critic of European and American literature. Among his writings are *On Native Grounds* (1942), *Walker in the City* (1951), and *New York Jew* (1979).

East Side. But, even more than the Lower East Side, it was distinctively Jewish. Even in the heyday of its Jewishness, the Lower East Side kept remnants of older Manhattan settlers, whereas Brownsville was peculiarly and overwhelmingly Jewish. Living there was like living in a Polish or Russian *shtetl*. A rumor I remember hearing as a kid concerned a certain delicatessen that did not have really kosher meat; whereupon, a real boycott went into effect.

Brownsville was remarkable sociologically because it seemed that everyone of a certain generation went through it. Even those who soon moved on, like the family of Meyer Schapiro, lived there. At its height, there were about 100,000 Jews in Brownsville. The area, say from 1900 or 1912 to World War II, was composed entirely of immigrant Jews. Then blacks began to replace Jews, who finally departed. They left mostly as new members of the middle class. My parents lived there longer than most because they were never very adroit economically and managed only in the last years of their lives to move out.

I considered my neighborhood as part of an extended family—and I felt all the ambivalence that goes with such an association. I never overestimated the education I got. I always thought it was quite bad. Even City College lacked a well-rounded program. It wasn't school that made me a ravenous reader. It was the neighborhood and the family. My father and mother neither encouraged me nor discouraged me. They just took my voracious reading for granted. My sister, Pearl, and I used to carry three or four forged library cards so we'd be sure of enough reading. I've always been able to go quickly through a lot of material and, of course, the Jewish tradition has much to do with my desire "to know everything." And I *am* very Jewish. My passion for knowledge makes me very much of a type. A great many traits that once struck me as being wholly personal I now see as the marks of a distinct culture.

Our intellectual voraciousness was really a feeling for history. Why don't my students nowadays know many facts? I suspect it comes from their sense that history is meaningless. And perhaps it is. I certainly wonder more and more about the meaning of history. When I was young nothing seemed clearer in its progress.

I *was* an Hegelian, even though I wasn't a Marxist. History was like the Mountain of Peace in Dante. It was solidly there, you walked up and around it. Even now, when I rearrange my books, the Greeks always come first—and so on up to contemporary American fiction. It bothers me not to have a book in its proper chronological place.

My father was a house painter; my mother was a dressmaker; I grew up in a rough, working-class environment. Of course, there was another side. There were always books in the house. My father didn't work for years during the Depression, and yet we were always given money for music lessons. I was a fiddler, starting at age six—like most Jewish kids of my age. What a pity I didn't have the genius of Jascha Heifetz. My parents did everything to bring it out. Just imagine, I used to get five bucks every Sunday morning for my violin lesson.

The one stretch of freedom, or of good luck, my father had came at an early age. He was a painter on the Union Pacific Railroad and that took him out West. Having fallen in love with the whole populist spirit, he was offered a homestead in Wyoming. He heard Eugene Victor Debs debate in the 1912 election. A large part of my early feeling for the West came from his stories, or stories he read to me in English. He spoke to me in English, as he spoke to my mother in Yiddish and we never knew whether he was speaking English or Yiddish. For various personal reasons I preferred speaking English to my mother. She couldn't speak English. I didn't realize until later on that she was speaking Yiddish and I was speaking English. I know it sounds strange, but our bilingualism was so complete. And it's not strange at all. It's very often that way.

In the normal course of events I fell in love with other forms of modern Western culture, especially with American culture. A great many of my feelings are extremely ambivalent in the sense that I feel both an enormous fascination with Jewish culture and a great dislike of certain features of it. That didn't mean conflict. I was simply part of two civilizations. I lived in both at the same time and there were two pulls. Then, because of the Holocaust, and some wreckage in my personal life during the war, I became much more consciously Jewish. It amuses me now to read pieces

I wrote when I was still living in Brooklyn which are much more critical and sardonic about Jewish life than anything I did later on.

I went to City College at a time when its student body was mainly Jewish. My problem there was the presence of many very brilliant guys, mostly super-Leninists. I regarded Leninism as poison. My father after all, and my mother, had been born in Russia. I knew about the Revolution and about the history of radicalism. Quarrels were constant and so was my antipathy to Bolshevism. This didn't endear me to many of my classmates, quite a few of whom are now far to my right.

I became self-consciously Jewish when I began to write and to publish in the thirties. I started young, at a time when there was still a lot of open anti-Semitism. I knew as a matter of course that it wouldn't be easy to get certain jobs. I naturally didn't try to become a professor. Later I became one but almost by accident. I don't have a doctorate. I began to publish while in college and because of my books I was asked to teach. Then I became a professor. As a writer and critic I felt freer than many academic men.

However, even in the literary world of New York, anti-Semitism was obvious. As it happened, I fell in love with American literature and the native Protestant tradition. I began to work in that field when it was still relatively unsystematic. I seem to have written the only historical book on the whole modern period of American literature. I say that not as a matter of pride but as a source of wonder. To be sure, I had an historical sense, which is probably the strongest feature of my writing. As a young reviewer and writer, a freelancer in New York, I was invited everywhere. I had experiences which made me realize that I was regarded as a Jew. It had to do with a phenomenon Henry James touched upon in *The American Scene*. Coming back to New York, James noted the obvious "lowness" of people. It's something you can observe everywhere in this city. I was being watched, and judged. It struck me as being a question of *manners*. I did a lot of my writing for the old *Herald Tribune* book section. Lewis Gannett was the daily book reviewer and very friendly. Nevertheless, he once asked me if I thought that Jews walked differently from other people. I didn't realize that he was being hostile. On the other hand, it's typical that Gannett, who was a great liberal and who was a descendant of the famous Yale president and Hebraist, Ezra Stiles, had actually been a correspondent for the *Jewish Daily Forward* at the Versailles peace conference. He was not an anti–Semite, but he seemed to share the general view that Jews were *low*. Only after the Second World War, when Jewish intellectuals and writers began to appear in large numbers and the Jews became a distinct and acceptable middle-class group, did a new respect come about. In the thirties, it was very different.

I don't think people today realize quite how much the situation has changed toward and about Jews. New York in the thirties was hard on blacks and Jews. Jews then were substantially a lower class. They were workers, they were artisans, they were shopkeepers. As Henry Kissinger's patron said when he made him go to Harvard, "Gentlemen do not go to the City College of New York."

I began to teach evenings at City College and then I was fired—mostly, I think, because they were jealous of my writing and publishing. No doubt, they also had it in for me because I was a maverick. For the record, they claimed that I could get a job anywhere else because I was a good teacher. I did teach at the New School and elsewhere. Then, when *On Native Grounds* came out in '42, when I was twenty-seven, everything suddenly worked out for me—and all at once.

At twenty-seven, I became an editor of *The New Republic*. My first wife and I moved to Manhattan—a big thing for me. I began my recent book, *New York Jew*, with a bit out of *The Great Gatsby*. Approximately: "Once we slide over this bridge, anything can happen." And that was my feeling. The city directly represented an important historical and literary tradition. Melville and Whitman, James, and Edith Wharton had been New Yorkers. They all meant a lot to me. I could trace their lives in the city. I felt close to them. In addition, going from Brownsville to Brooklyn Heights, which was my favorite neighborhood for a long time, and then going from Brooklyn Heights downtown to Gramercy Park, symbolized a kind of journey in history. In 1942 when *On Native Grounds* appeared and I was living on 24th and Lexington, right across the street you could see one of the most famous Whitman collectors in New York. He kept a bookshop. Down the street was the Regiment Armory where the famous Armory Show had been exhibited. Muriel Draper lived three blocks away. I had a thing about Brooklyn Heights and the Brooklyn Bridge, and the Roeblings,* about Whitman, who always seemed to me to be the greatest figure in American poetry, except for Emily Dickinson. It pleased me to live right across the street from where Whitman himself had put *Leaves of Grass* to press.

And, of course, New York was the center of magazines and publishing, with a very genial and exhilarating kind of social life. When a publisher took you to lunch and talked about other authors, there was a great sense of being close to them. Writers were my heroes; I knew a lot of writers. Delmore Schwartz, the poet, seemed to me, as to many other people, the most gifted writer of my group. He was *it*; and we all knew it. He meant more to me than any other writer produced by American Jewish life. And *Partisan Review*, even though it was run by ex-Communists like Philip Rahv and William Phillips, was nonetheless a wide open magazine. There were so many parties; there was so much freedom and openness.

I didn't start traveling until '43 when I became an editor of *Fortune* after leaving *The New Republic*. I came on when Archibald MacLeish had just left, but Jim Agee and John Galbraith were there. New York City seemed absolutely glamorous. It *was* glamorous. I would go down from my office in *The New Republic* on 49th Street to my publisher's office which was then 383 Fourth Avenue. I can't describe the exhilaration of getting out of the office at four or five o'clock and riding down in a taxi. I remember one particular incident. You know the circular ramp that goes around Grand Central? Every time my taxi would careen around there, especially if I'd had one or two drinks, I reached a state of high ecstasy. I was only twenty-seven and some good reviews were coming in. It was a wonderful time. After teaching at City College and suddenly getting fired, I was making fifty dollars a week as an editor. When the book came out they made me literary

---

* John Augustus Roebling and his son, Washington Augustus, were chief engineers in the construction of the Brooklyn Bridge.

editor and gave me a raise. Then *Fortune* asked me to work for a hundred and fifty dollars a week, which in 1943 was easily thirty or forty thousand dollars per year in today's money.

New York was the center of the action. It was close to everything. The feeling I have now, which is that a lot of people I respect don't like New York, bothers me. But at that time, just the opposite was true. Everybody you cared for and everything you needed was here, the publishing houses, the magazines, many more newspapers than there are today. *The New Republic*, in many ways the most important magazine to me, was still published in New York. The magazine didn't go to Washington until Henry Wallace took it over, an act typical of that provincial man.

But when you did work in New York on *The New Republic* or later on across the street in Rockefeller Center for Luce, you had lunch with Jim Agee and Dwight Macdonald and Delmore Schwartz and Robert Fitzgerald and Louis Kronenberger. The Luce magazines were full of wonderful writers. And although I didn't care for him, there was Paul Goodman. I always thought he was his own greatest fantasy. Even so, Goodman was a very exciting person, with his air of being the Diderot, the young Marx, of our time. And Saul Bellow had just arrived. I met all these people in New York—Saul Bellow through Isaac Rosenfeld, whose wife was my secretary on *The New Republic*. I met everybody at one fell swoop.

Isaac Rosenfeld and Saul Bellow were both from Chicago. I, the New Yorker, the Brooklynite, felt that they were more metropolitan, partly because of the University of Chicago, which had a certain *brio* all its own in those days. And also because as young Chicagoans they were in the center of their city. I think that New York writers were by definition provincial because this city is too big and Jews occupy too small a part of it, too far from the center. Jews did not write in those days about the center. They wrote about the Bronx and Brooklyn. And, as Mailer says, "Brooklyn is not the center of anything." Personally, it took me a long, long time to get to the other place, to the center or the heart of activity.

Some fabulous exiles were here. Nicolo Chiaromonte, Hannah Arendt, Marc Chagall. Early on, I was very much taken with

Italy and Italian culture. My friend Paolo Milano, an Italian who had emigrated because he was a Jew, taught French and Italian at Queens College. I worked for Max Ascoli later on when he ran *The Reporter*. Ascoli was a member of the famous Action party and had come over as a refugee from fascism, not from the Nuremberg laws.

Anyhow, New York was remarkably open. But now it's a great sorrow to me in many ways. I feel cheated by my old girlfriend, New York. This has to do with two things. One is that when New York is not opulent, when it's not roaring, when it's not proud, there's something intrinsically wrong. And right now it is in a badly battered, sadly depressed state. And yet, I have to admit that the very thing which made New York so glamorous for me when I was young, namely being close to certain magazines and publishing houses, bothers me about a city which is now so much the center of the so-called media. I used to cherish *The New Republic* and the writers around *Fortune*. I don't like many magazines now at all. I write for them, occasionally. But I don't think much of them. There's too much writing down and too many synthetic celebrities. What it comes down to is the lack of any real point to our culture. Money drives us more than ever. As far as I can see, the "media" are dominated by a limitless hunger for money and publicity. Even Norman Mailer always gets caught. The whole career of Mailer, with all of its triumph and instability, is a good example of what's happening to New York. He wouldn't have gone out so hungrily for money and for fame if New York itself hadn't changed. Nothing bad happened to Mailer, but his gift, which is considerable, was colored and surrounded by the new America that came in during the Second World War.

I did a piece for the *New York Review of Books* on the "New York Jew," based on my journals. It describes a good many things and has portraits of Isaac Bashevis Singer and others. I mention an experience my wife and I had when we were crossing the street and an enormous Mack truck driven by a black man came down the street. I held out my hand because he was coming so fast and he started cursing me as a Jew. I wrote, "How did he know?" I was trying to be funny, but there is no question that Jews may be dislodged from the position they now occupy in American intellectual life. There is suddenly a great deal of malicious, sometimes quite hysterical anti-Semitism.

And of course, the term "New York Jew" is a phrase that's always about to be uttered. I want to tell you two stories in this connection. I had a very painful experience at the Midwest Modern Language Association some years ago. I was one of three speakers along with Paul Goodman and Louis Kampf, a professor of literature at MIT who is super-super-left and was then president of the Modern Language Association. I was reading a paper called "Whatever Happened to Criticism?" on the differences between criticism in a cultural context and the kind of criticism that had replaced it. When Kampf began as the first speaker, he said to this audience in the Middle West, "Did you have to invite three New York Jews? You had nobody else?" He made fun of memories I'd put into *Starting Out In The Thirties*, and I heard him with incredulity. I had never met him before. The super-leftist was insanely aggressive. Kampf said that he wanted to besmear Lincoln Center with shit to show his contempt for bourgeois culture. Perhaps we're at the end of a period. When I began in the thirties there was a certain suspicion of Jewishness and now we're right back to a certain *hostile* awareness of it which comes, very obviously, from the whole super-left spirit again. In my time it came from the establishment.

Another story: in Cape Cod this past summer I had an extraordinary conversation at a party with a lady who lives in Wellfleet. She didn't like Bellow's writing: his English rhythms weren't very good. Bit by bit, this lady, whom I've known for many years, began to get on my nerves, "Why don't you say that you don't like him because in your eyes he's too Jewish?" "Well, I guess that's true," she admitted. Then I asked her, "Do you have any idea what it's like for me as a Jew and a professor of English literature to have to read and teach people . . . ?" I gave her a quotation from Henry Adams' letters: "There are 500,000 Jews in 1899 in New York eating kosher and all of them deserving to drown." This is pretty standard for Adams, who is violent on the subject. And he happened to be one of my intellectual heroes. Her face fell: "My God, I never realized that."

Truman Capote, whom I used to know very well, wrote a piece for *Rolling Stone*. He complained there were too many Jews in New York publishing circles. I wrote him a very strong letter. I wanted to say, "The too many are not Jews, they're homosexuals." In certain areas Jews are dominant, but we're certainly at the end of a period. Some of the best writers in America, like John Berryman, were absolutely captured by their Jewish friends. Berryman wrote a beautiful story called "The Imaginary Jew" for *Kenyon Review*. And again and again in his work he expressed his belief in a kind of sacramental worth among his Jewish friends. He was mad about Delmore (Schwartz), as we all were because Delmore was such an extraordinary poet. On the other hand, the newer and the younger writers are much less involved. Writers too young to remember the Holocaust inevitably breathe a different spirit. In the thirties, people like Michael Gold and Sam Ornitz, and even Clifford Odets, who I thought was marvelously talented, were still talking about the trouble of being Jews and nothing else. They were Stalinists, so there was always this bloody propaganda. Yet, *Jews Without Money*, Gold's one novel, is a very good book. And there was one masterpiece in that period, Henry Roth's *Call It Sleep*, a very beautiful book, ignored at the time, and still ignored. It's a difficult book. Admiring readers don't always admit how difficult it is.

As for myself, I was never truly part of a *group*. I was part of a generation. And that generation was not exclusively Jewish. There's no question that at first I was running away from my Jewish past. Let's put it this way: I was still enough of a socialist to believe that a lot of Jewish things would somehow be absorbed into a larger whole. It was an aspect of that old-fashioned sentimentality which I now abhor—you know, the idea that Jews and Judaism would all be incorporated into a seamless web, which I now regard as a ridiculous cultural abstraction. The very fact that I entered into an American literary world meant there were certain features of my own background that I didn't tolerate as happily as others. I don't think it was shame. I had intense personal problems at home connected with the crippling weakness of my father.

I had from the very beginning written as a Jew; I never felt the way Lionel Trilling did. Trilling's manner amused me. By contrast, I admired Harold Rosenberg. Harold was a professional intellectual whose ideal was total freedom of mind. And even though he was a bit of a *flâneur*, I loved it. I used to call him "the Maccabean" because I loved his pride. He enjoyed being Jewish so much. That's it very simply.

Toward the end of his life my father had a stroke and developed aphasia. There's an Orthodox institution in Brooklyn called the Menorah Jewish Home, run by Max Weisman, who used to write for *Partisan Review*. By a fluke I got hold of him. He knew my writing and was willing to admit my father. Thus, my father, the Socialist, spent his last year and a half in an Orthodox Jewish home. They were very sweet to him. And this is part of the allegory. My father had always thought he was superior to religion. In the home something happened that moved me very much. He began to speak most peculiarly. He could only say a few words, but one that he kept saying was the Hebrew word *l'fo'necha*: "Behold I am standing before Thy face," the first prayer a devout Jew says in the morning. I realized that my father's early years of *cheder* had left a deposit in the bottom of his mind. He would say, "How are you? *L'fo'necha*. How's the family? *L'fo'necha*." At first this irritated me, but the trauma soon moved me. Jewishness is a *world*, one that's increasingly important to me.

I wrote a memoir, 1940 to 1970, that touches on all this. When you're writing a book you pursue an object night and day until you've got it. But I wrote the book also because in the last few years I've discovered—and this is the simple fact—that nothing has as much emotional and spiritual value for me as the Jewish experience. I can't explain why. If anyone would say to me, "Well, what is your position on the following?" I would have to answer: "I do not go to synagogue. I have not sat up all night reading Hebrew. My body will be cremated. Yet, I have and have always had some kind of religious impulse." I'm very much like my father in many ways. And I'm very much like my mother. I'm also aware that the emotional life can be quite primitive and the intellectual life quite refined. The two have nothing to do with each other. It's a terrible thing.

As a student of literature over the years I've always been most intensely concerned with transcendental figures, poets like Blake. It moves me very much that my daughter at Smith has fallen in love with George Herbert, the Anglican poet. She's doing her honors' thesis on Herbert and is planning to take a Ph.D. immediately and write her thesis on him. Well, he was the poet whom I worked on when I was in college, too, and to explain to her that in 1934 or '35 on the 137th Street subway I was immersed in George Herbert would seem very funny. Our backgrounds are so different. But nevertheless I do have a tremendous *nostalgie*, if you like, for religious things. I'm not an Orthodox Jew. But on the other hand I would not be interested in religion without being Jewish. And being Jewish doesn't mean a thing to me without continual awareness of my religious condition.

I don't think that Israel would have any meaning whatever except in final reference to the religious experience. Why is Israel so crucial to us? I understood why Israel had to be established, because it is the country of the Bible and why originally American Protestantism supported Israel. I also understand why, with the decay of Christianity, Christians are so hostile to Israel. For me, all these factors are basic. I never had any trouble understanding the Zionist argument, but it came to me in non-Zionist terms, in terms of the return promised in the liturgy. The fact is, one never gets away from it. I was glad to see, in one of my visits to Israel, that this point was recognized by certain Labor party theoreticians who, on the one hand, knew that ultra-Orthodox Jews had been anti-Israel for a long time, and apart from the extreme fanatics, there were Hasidic Jews who made life difficult. These Jews are embarrassing from the Western, hygienic, super-sophisticated point of view, which the Israelis have. Nevertheless, said my contacts in the Israeli bureaucracy, *they're the ones who explain why we're here.* That's the point. I feel precisely the same way.

Yet, I have a very deep quarrel with Orthodox Jews. The quarrel has to do with their idea of themselves as the "elect."

Whenever I see an Orthodox Jew I recognize the face that secretly burns up Christians. I've seen it again and again in many parts of the world. I saw it in Russia when I was there, among Jews. This is not psychological. It's related to the fundamental problem of epistemology. Either you have the "truth" or you don't have it. I envy Orthodoxy, but I shy away from Orthodox Jews.

Jewishness is something else. It is, in various forms, like Yiddishkeit (Yiddish culture), a sentimental tradition that developed as an American Jewish product. It's a derivative of the Enlightenment, of the enormous secularism of the Jews who wanted to keep their "heritage" or their "identity" and therefore adopted something called "Jewishness." To me, Jewishness means something about which I have a rather critical, even a scornful understanding. Like the word "Yiddishkeit," Jewishness means something specifically American. It evolved in this country in places like the Workman's Circle schools, which taught Yiddish, and in the Yiddishist movement. It grew up among a great many radical Jews who originally tried to keep something Jewish as part of their makeup. When the radical component went, which it often did, they held on to Jewishness. I think also, frankly, that it was a ploy by immigrant fathers against native sons, a way of saying, "You are shallow. You lack an understanding of the deeper spiritual meaning that I acquired."

I've never gone in for theologians like Abraham Heschel who seem to me to be essentially literary figures. I knew Heschel. I thought he was charming, fluent, essentially a literary fellow like myself, a man who could write about anything and wrote about Jesus as a Jewish rebel against the ancient establishment, as I was a Jewish rebel against the modern Jewish establishment. I'm still vastly interested in Christianity, or what I call *Jewish* Christianity. There are a great many remarks in the New Testament that seem to me to be more Jewish than parts of the Old Testament. Like "What good can come out of Nazareth?" which appears to me to be one of the most Jewish remarks ever made. Jesus belonged to a cultural period which now doesn't seem meaningful to people. But in the twenties and thirties, in Brownsville, a lot of my friends and I had all sorts of ideas about Jesus the rebel and Jesus the prophet. It was a sticky romanticism which I haven't kept at all.

As for the Jewish establishment, I dislike it more than ever. Then again, there's not much of an establishment because it doesn't have much power. I don't think *the Jews* have much power in America. There's an ominous symbol, our being six million. Many Jews have money today, but even so their position hasn't changed much. As to their intellectual preeminence, something like one-fifth of the university professors in America are supposed to be Jewish. That figure I heard in Israel, not in America. (The Israelis know all about American Jews.) Much of the hostility directed at New York in the current crisis signifies resentment over that preeminence.

Do I share that hostility? No, no, no. I've lost a lot of my romanticism about New York. It's been beaten out of me very, very slowly. I've lived all over the country, have taught at Smith, Amherst, Harvard, Berkeley, and in several midwestern universities. My long love affair with New York turned on the memory of growing up, the excitement of thinking of myself as a self-creator. When I wrote *On Native Grounds* I had a daily sense of excitement, of cultural roaming. I'm tired of the subway, I'm tired of the crowds, I'm tired of the violence, but when Kansas and Indiana say "New York" they also mean New York Jews. We can't distinguish between the two things. I'm tired of paying the rent I pay here. I'm tired of fighting with my stupid Jewish landlord about every leaky pipe. But *I* am what Kansas and Indiana mean when they talk about New York Jews. They mean all the City College professors and the Columbia professors, and now the Harvard professors.

I am not an organization man. Every organization makes me nervous. There's not a single group I wouldn't feel nervous belonging to. Even in the Zionist and the organizational world there are a lot of Jewish *machers* (big shots). Also, whatever I can tell about official Jewish religion still reflects all the things I didn't like about it when I was young. It's very narrow, very defensive, and intellectually fourth-rate. But then that's true of all churches.

The question then is, "Where would I go for Jewish self-defense?" And the answer is: "To my family! To the cause of my misfortunes!" Look, Jewish self-defense in America, if and when it comes, will not be a problem. Ever since the '73 war it's been very clear that Jews are in a much shakier position than we previously assumed. There is the constant irony of Jewish existence, that Israel, which was formed to normalize Jewish life, is now a pariah nation, exactly the way in which individual Jews have been pariahs throughout Western history.

Being Jewish is a mystery, a divine mystery, in which I'm very happy to be included. But I don't understand it in the sense that I don't understand why there is a perpetual struggle just to keep alive. It's one thing to appraise someone who's about to kill you. It's something else to tolerate him. There isn't time!

I suppose the big political question in my life has always been Hitler. When I was young, the radicals contended that Hitler was the product of German capitalism. Although that sort of thinking was not germane to me, I knew perfectly well that it was false. But I'm still not sure I understand what Hitler was all about or that anyone else does. I've read enormously in the literature about Nazism. I still don't understand it. On the other hand, as so often happens in Greek tragedy, what counts is not the *why* but the *action per se*. And what happened to the Jews was an action, too much of an action, that has to be appraised on its own terms.

I want to say one more thing about the Holocaust which is quite important, apart from the obvious word "tragedy," which doesn't seem really to convey it adequately. I grew up as a Socialist, that is, as a believer in the Enlightenment, as a believer in our democratic system. My father was a Bundist. I was a member of the Young People's Socialist League. And the Holocaust made me believe more and more in certain ideas of human nature which I had been loath to accept. I was thirty when the war ended, and in England as a correspondent. Over the years I became more and more concerned about the Holocaust and later made a visit to Belsen. Clearly, there was no economic or military purpose for the Holocaust. The destruction of European Jewry was a horror which cried out for explanation in its own terms. The Holocaust was a political fact for me. More than anything else, it meant Marxism—even my little bit of Marxism, or the socialism I did embrace—could never explain the Holocaust, or why the Nazis went out of their way, even to their military disadvantage, to capture and destroy Jews. It made me feel there was some unconscious drive in politics which, in my more naïve youth, I hadn't grasped.

What happens to Jews in one country affects them in other countries. Its contagious. It's like the bloody assassins of the president. One takes up after another. There's no question about it. Anti-Semitism has increased everywhere as a result of the attacks upon Israel. There's no way of understanding Israel in modern secular political terms. The idea of returning to a homeland after 1,940 years makes no sense as an outcome of Jewish history and the Jewish experience. The people who understood this were evangelical Christians.

One reason why I'm more and more apprehensive is that I think one of the great facts of our time is a widespread superstitious atheism about everything. In the nineteenth century the masses were credulous; the intellectuals were atheistic. In the twentieth century it's the masses who are all disaffected, secular, atheistic; and it's the few intellectuals here and there who have some other way of looking at things. My students, by and large, have no sympathy for, no grasp of, anything transcendental or religious. But given this part of the culture, the Jews are victims. The Jews are always the victims of a purely secular psychology. The Enlightenment philosophers like Voltaire were very anti-Jewish. America has been the only country uniquely without too much anti-Jewish hostility of a political kind.

And yet, people do hold on to their religious identity in a world which frightens them. More and more the wars in which we are engaged everywhere in the world are religious wars. It's self-evident in Lebanon, in Northern Ireland, and everywhere else. Whatever their origin, they are more deeply religious than they ever were before. And, of course, the "real" world is incredibly unreal.

12.

THE SCHOLAR AS CHANCELLOR

Gerson Cohen

I WAS BORN in 1924 in the old Bronx Hospital, to Russian immigrant parents. My mother came from Belorussia near Minsk, my father from Brest-Litovsk. My father was a militant Zionist who arrived, I think, in 1910, and soon after that he worked in sweat shops. My mother was sent to the first Hebrew teachers school for girls. They met at a Hebrew-speaking club in New York City, and it was understood that their offspring would be raised in the Hebrew language.

The only language I knew as a child was Hebrew. My father forbade Yiddish in the house. He called it "jargon." I suppose this attitude was formed out of several circumstances. Yiddish was the language of Bundism, of left secularism, and of militant Orthodoxy. No such ideology appealed to my parents who were observant, neo-Orthodox, but mostly Zionist in their point of view.

My grandmother spoke Yiddish but she was compelled to learn some Hebrew in order to communicate with me. She used to speak Hebrew by quoting verses from the Psalms, which she knew in Yiddish, translating them into biblical clichés.

Many years later when I was at Columbia, my attitude towards Yiddish changed completely. Max Weinreich persuaded me to become a member of the Research Committee of YIVO (Yiddish Institute). I am still by no means a Yiddishist and I have no nostalgia for "the world of our fathers."

Gerson Cohen was born in New York in 1924. He is a rabbi, biblical scholar, professor of history, and Chancellor of the Jewish Theological Seminary in New York.

I went to a public school, and my first memories go back to being put in kindergarten. At that time I understood a bit of English and the first child I encountered said to me, "You sound so funny, I want to cut your nose off." I burst into tears. Then I remember my mother acquiring books from the school and reading aloud with me, to overcome my foreign accent. Two years later, when I was about seven and a half, we moved to Perth Amboy, New Jersey. That was something of an ordeal. Perth Amboy was a small town, famous only for adoring Herbert Hoover and making Bakelite. But the whole town learned overnight that a family had moved in with two children and that all of them spoke a funny language. Also, on account of our having come from New York, the kids made fun of "Noo Yawk."

My mother used to make me sit in front of the radio during the Ford Sunday Evening Hour and listen to a man who, she felt, would teach me how to speak English properly. She was quite unaware that the teacher was W. J. Cameron, who had edited the anti-Semitic *Dearborn Independent*. He would speak, with his burly, rasping voice, about "the birrrrds in spring"—and I became quite a mimic—but we still used Hebrew in the house all the time.

It's interesting to me now how confined and parochial my experience first was. My parents were very protective of their Hebraism. Along with it went an intense Zionism that my father bespoke, coupled with staunch but selective Orthodox observance on the part of my mother. For example, I remember when my mother was stopped, with me, by a rabbi who said that any little boy who could speak Hebrew so well ought not to walk about with a bared head. When he left, I asked my mother what the rabbi meant. "He thought you ought to wear something to cover your head." And what did she think? "It's not necessary."

Without being totally Orthodox, we shared the Orthodox perspective. Therefore, when my parents sent me to a day school (then called a yeshiva), they insisted on one that was *Hebrew-speaking*. My sense of alienation at that yeshiva, apart from its shabbiness, and poverty, was based on the narrow Orthodoxy I encountered there. I missed the liberalism of my parents' home.

On the other hand, New York opened me up. My father, who by then was Assistant Manager at the Metropolitan Life

Insurance Company in Perth Amboy, left his job, became an agent, and moved us to Borough Park in Brooklyn. There, for the first time, I began to be happy. I was put into a good parochial school where I met kids of my own—how should I say—economic bracket. Generally, they were much more Orthodox than we were, but many other kids were less so. On the whole, they were more tolerant and more catholic in their interests. *I discovered intellectuality in Borough Park among children.* Punchball and Karl Marx were mixed together. What's more, it was an observant crowd. So, within another narrow and homogeneous neighborhood, I found that the Jewish horizons were broad and diversified enough to make it a very happy place.

I recall certain things that had a major impact on my life. One: my mother received a call from an aunt of mine who, by the way, was a graduate of the Jewish Theological Seminary. Her daughter, a pianist, happened to be ill. "She cannot go to an indoor New York Philharmonic concert. Would Gerson like to go?" I was all of twelve and I had never been to a concert in my life. I met my uncle downtown. We went directly to the balcony at Carnegie Hall. I remember Schubert's *Unfinished* Symphony— and all the rest of that concert. It was only forty-four years ago. First, Schubert's *Unfinished* Symphony, conducted by John Barbarolli, *before* he was *Sir* John, and then, I remember a little boy— with acne—by the name of Eugene List, playing one of the Beethoven piano concerti.

A few years later, I discovered that at the Brooklyn Museum on Sunday afternoons, you could hear the symphony—free of charge—*and* you could see soloists perform. I would run every Sunday afternoon, by myself, to listen to the symphony orchestra. I knew that symphony orchestras were for the rich, but this was one I could hear and see for nothing. I didn't fully appreciate the quality of that orchestra, but I enjoyed it very much. From then on I would always be able to hear great symphonies.

Another little boy at the yeshiva told me a very interesting secret. There was a radio station called WQXR on which you could hear symphony orchestras. Apparently the music percolated up to me, because I have been passionately addicted to it ever since. For a while I took piano lessons, at one dollar an hour, which was a compromise: the piano was first introduced to my brother (my parents called him an "uncontrollable child" because he wasn't getting *all* A's in his work). I used to sit in on his lessons, trying to understand how notes were read. Then, finally, my parents relented and gave me lessons for a couple of months. I never really learned much, but somehow, I always wanted to know what was behind the theory of composition. It still is an agony of mine.

My grandfather, for whom I am named, was apparently a man who liked to perform as a cantor. He was a Hasid who sang. I suspect that his musicality is in my blood. While my grandfather came from a *shtetl* in the province of Minsk, he did not hold a box at the Minsk Philharmonic. He had *Jewish* music. Grandfather would go every Saturday night to a *Melaveh Malke* (a joyous Sabbath gathering), where there was singing. In 1904, he was drafted by the Russian army and promptly assigned to the Tsarist Army Band. My wife always teases me that my grandfather played flute for the Tsar. We still have the music that he composed for himself.

Closer to home, an uncle of mine loved to chant as a cantor, and also to read the Torah liturgically (with proper musical notations). At seven I was proficient at reading Torah. And at the age of twelve I was virtually a professional. As a rabbinical student I sometimes made two dollars a week for "reading" the Torah. But I became most musically aware by going to the Brooklyn Museum on Sundays. We would cut past the Egyptian collection, the sarcophagi, and certain pieces of art. I became vaguely aware of the art world, but mostly of music. I have nevertheless always been thankful for the abundance of New York's museums and their resources.

At City College, I discovered the library. But of course, that was at the relatively advanced age of sixteen or seventeen. At seventeen, I entered the honors program for social sciences under Oscar Janowsky, and I was assigned an eye-opening topic. Janowsky suggested that I work on the Alliance Israelite Universelle, from 1864 to 1900. I began to use the (Jewish Theological) Seminary Library because somebody told me it had "the greatest collection of Jewish books in the world." I went to the catalog and found my topic: Ulpan l'Alliance Israelite Universelle. These bulletins, I noticed, were missing certain issues. So were the Archives Israelites which the French usually put out. Because of those lacunae, the New York Public Library, Jewish Division, was recommended to me. I soon became one of its regular visitors.

In fact, I spent some of the most thrilling moments of my life in the main reading room of the third floor of the 42nd Street Library. Why there? Because as part of J. Salwyn Schapiro's courses in college, I got interested in the apostates in the great eighteenth-century revolt against religion, those *philosophes* with whom Schapiro identified as incarnations of liberalism and its concomitants. Schapiro was a disciple of Condorcet. Since I read French well, I wanted to know what the French *Encyclopédie* was. I'm pretty sure its volumes were stacked on the top balcony of the north side of Room 300 of the main reading room. Imagine a little whippersnapper asking for books almost as tall as he was! They were brought down for me, and I had some of my best moments reading Diderot's *Encyclopédie*. I learned in the *Encyclopédie* that American Indians lived in a beautiful state of nature.

This literature intensified my feelings. I have to explain that. As a result of being in or near the alcoves at City College, one couldn't help but come across the Marxists, the Trotskyists and, on the other hand, the Avukahites (left-wing Zionists), all fighting desperately. Since I belonged to none of these groups, being interested by that time in rabbinics and Hebraism of the elitist cultural kind, I found liberalism in the French Revolution and in French literature an avenue for research.

In pursuit of that research, I was entangled in an interesting network: the Seminary library, the New York Public Library, and the Brooklyn Museum. At the Brooklyn Museum you could get concerts. At the Seminary library you could get almost all the Jewish books you might want. And at the New York Public Library you could get everything! Its Jewish division was excellent—with Joshua Bloch as librarian in my time. What a terror was Joshua Bloch! If he didn't like you, the books were unavailable. And he had very definite likes and dislikes. On the one hand,

The New York Public Library.   DANIEL ROSENBERG.

certain people were allowed to do things that outraged me: sit in the back, wearing yarmulkes while they ate sandwiches dripping over books! On the other hand, people he didn't like, even if they were quite moderate, he literally threw out of the room. For one reason or another, I was left alone. Abraham Berger, his assistant, took a shine to me, and we remained close friends for a long time.

No place else in the world could I have had such facilities: the Jewish Theological Seminary Library; the New York Public Library; Columbia, with its great Semitics collection and great Arabic collection; Union Theological Seminary, with its great theological collection and, as a matter of fact, its American history collection and its comparative religions collection. Then the YIVO collection, with its remarkable anti-Semitic files, as well as portraits and pictures and archives of East European life. And now, the Leo Baeck Institute on 73rd Street, with the greatest collection of German Judaica. And, by the way, a cellar into which I was taken when I became a librarian—the Lubavitcher Rebbe's library. It has, to this very day I presume, a vast collection of Jewish Sovietica, available only to the elect. I was one of them.

Then, of course, in New York you had access to book stores. *Book* stores! They are among the deepest influences in my life. I don't necessarily mean Doubleday or Brentano's. I'm talking about the old Fourth Avenue, where with a little luck you could pick up a prize for ten cents. And then you went down on the East Side, perhaps to Rabinowitze's, and you found rare Jewish books. Over Columbia's bookstore was the Ideal Bookstore, where the Epstein brothers would introduce you to old books and *you* could own an out-of-print book. You would haggle and bargain. One of the Epstein brothers said to me after the reprint industry began, "I'm making more money than ever before and enjoying it less."

At the Seminary I heard of the Hebrew Arts Council that Moshe Davis, Sylvia Ettenberg, and Zipporah Jochsberger had begun to cultivate. And I'd go, of course, to their plays. On one memorable occasion I was taken to a play that the Hebrew youth performed at the YMHA. They put on a *Hebrew* play. And that was a vital part of my awakening. It alerted me to the possible modernity of Hebrew which was after all not necessarily a phenomenon limited to two families in the United States. It was a play by Americans whose Hebrew pronounciation amused me because they spoke in an American accent, while mine was thoroughly Russian.

I spoke only Ashkenazic (Hebrew with an East European accent)—and when I get excited, even now I will slip into Ashkenazic. When I came to the Seminary I was put into the class of a man named Hillel Bavli who lectured on Bialik for two hours in Sephardic (Iberian- and now Israeli-accented Hebrew). I decided two things: this is beautiful, and it is modern; I want to be beautiful and modern. Overnight, I changed to Sephardic. My parents were shocked—for this conversion was a revolt against the house. But maybe it was also identification with an open form which meant carrying on the house tradition. I have since spoken Sephardic. I still pray a lot more comfortably in Ashkenazic.

It's true that yeshiva was thoroughly Hebraic. We would study Hebrew texts, and yet, no one there seemed to be interested in the *totality* of Jewish life.

Apropos of that totality, two major events occur to me. When

I was ten years old, I met a boy who had come from Palestine. He spoke Hebrew with perfect naturalness. Somewhat later, I met a Polish boy—I must have been about fourteen—who studied within the Hebrew secular system of Poland. He and I played ball together, talking away in Hebrew, from which I drew the following inference: New York City was a place where people, however isolated they were from the mainstream, did not need to be alone. Occasional encounters with children somewhat like myself enabled me ultimately to evoke—I would say, give full expression to—a lifetime commitment that basically began as a household pattern of Jewish education. My father conveyed his Hebraism, my mother a deep adherence to Jewish tradition. And from Rabbi Milton Steinberg I inherited the desire to see what was behind all that, and to study it critically.

About Steinberg: I had not yet actively connected with the rabbinate. What happened was that Yeshiva College offered me a scholarship in 1937. By that time my parents were getting into dire straits. The Yeshiva College offered me a full scholarship, with room and board. But my uncle was vehemently opposed to Yeshiva—"You have to go to City College." He hated Orthodoxy.

My mother of course wanted me very much to go to Yeshiva. She suggested that the dispute be refereed by Milton Steinberg, a man who had impressed her. Upon being asked, Rabbi Steinberg said that he would be glad to negotiate the matter. We came to him with our story. I'll never forget, it was in June on a Friday afternoon. Each of us presented his or her case, I for City College, my mother for Yeshiva. I indicated a concomitant interest in the Seminary College. And Rabbi Steinberg decided the case in my favor. Or, let's say, he set forth the options, along with his opinion that if I went to City College and the Seminary, I would not lose my Jewishness, but would be exposed to more worlds. Going to the Yeshiva, I would also retain my Jewishness but I'd have the whole world sealed to me. As a Seminary graduate, he was probably not above a certain tendentiousness himself. But he said to me, "Whatever you decide, I would like you to come and see me, and I will give you books to read and we will discuss them." I particularly recall his giving me two books: Fleming James' *Personalities of the Old Testament,* and Gizenga's *Grammar of the Hebrew Language.*

Gizenga floored me because the language I spoke was such a freakish thing, so far as the world was concerned, and here it had been reduced to scientific principles by a gentile! A German! That fascinated me. I was equally fascinated by Fleming James. His book I used to read—well, I was glued to it. I read it the way a kid reads pornography for the first time. Fleming James was a devout Protestant minister who wrote about the Bible from a biblio-critical point of view. And what I learned was the unspeakable thing that, according to scientific method, Moses had not written the Pentateuch. As a matter of fact, there was no such thing as the Pentateuch, the Torah. This shattered my world. I knew I would be going on to the Seminary to find out the truth!

Also, for a while, I was totally taken with Mordecai Kaplan as a teacher at the Seminary who constantly asked us to "unlearn" things. I came to Kaplan's class knowing a good part of the Bible by heart, and Kaplan exposed me to Bible criticism. Therefore, when I finally met H. L. Ginzberg, for a while I was going to become a Bible scholar. And I will confess that I have a manuscript of about 250 pages of a book that I hope to complete on biblical historiography. I'm not, however, really a biblical historian. For one simple reason: the tremendous linguistic baggage that one has to have, for instance, in Akkadian, Ugaritics, Phoenician. But that's the kind of interest Janowsky and others began to arouse in me.

I started to read *Speculum* in which there were articles on stained glass windows and illuminated manuscripts. I became aware of certain Midrashic (pertaining to ancient Jewish exposition of a biblical passage) substrata, Jewish themes in church windows. I was conscious of the Jewish artists in New York and, to a large extent, alienated from them because they were alienated from the Jewish community.

But this discussion evokes memories in me. For instance: I'm walking home from the library in Perth Amboy on a day I recall very well. I must have been ten years old. And as I was walking home, I passed a church. The most beautiful singing came out of it. I stopped to listen. Since I loved synagogue singing, and He-brew singing in general, once at home I quite innocently asked my father: "Do you know there is a church on the way to the library where they sing beautifully?" He said: "Do *you* know you are not permitted to listen?" "No." "Well, that's taboo for us."

I felt very guilty until twenty-five years later when a lady, who was head of the Interdenominational Program of the Jewish Theological Seminary invited me to a concert of the New York Philharmonic, featuring Miss Jessica Feingold. My heart fell when I saw that the program included Verdi's *Requiem*. We received the text of the *Requiem* in Latin, which I could read and translate. In a few seconds they began to sing "Kyrie Eleison, Christe Eleison," and I remembered my father's warning. But I was struck by the beauty of the music. Also I began to see that what I was reading in Latin was a Hebrew liturgy.

I now own at least two versions of Verdi's *Requiem*. I think I could sing any part on thirty seconds' notice with a clear con-science. In fact, I feel a little uncomfortable when I go to the Israel Philharmonic and hear "Stabat Mater" being sung in Latin on an Israeli podium, and they sing Mariology in Latin. But I have no inhibitions about enjoying church music.

About gentiles I knew nothing well into adolescence—except that they were the majority. I had very little contact with them until I came to City College. And there the contact was peripheral. I did, however, have one intense association. I was chosen, by the history department, to be a delegate to the Students' United Na-tions. I stayed at the home of a distant cousin who was willing to house and feed me on that Sabbath of the Conference. It re-quired no violation of the Sabbath, no note-taking or activity of that kind. Another delegate from City College was a black boy with whom I would occasionally eat. He belonged to a very dis-tinguished family in New York City. As we waited for an elevator during intersession, he said to me: "Gerson, you and I have com-mon interests. You are interested in saving the Jews and opening the gates of Palestine (this was 1943) and I am a member of a minority that has many of the same problems yours does. We could solve those problems of discrimination together. Why don't you join the Communist party?" To me that was unthinkable.

"The Communists want to destroy us." Not in his eyes. "That's a myth. Communism is the only thing that will save you." Those were the last words we ever spoke to each other, for both he and I felt that a deep chasm had opened between us.

But then, in *my* world, I learned that there were *our* Jews and what the family referred to as "Yehudim." I learned that these were "Deutsche Yiddin," German Jews, "Silk Stockings." They were essentially assimilationists. That much I *knew*. One of my great shocks was to find German Jews in the Jewish Theological Seminary who were not all out to assimilate *me*. I knew there were certain "good" Yehudim like Herbert H. Lehman, but basically they were impenetrable characters to me because, first of all, they were so rich. They didn't speak Hebrew. Or Yiddish, even. They went to Temple Emanu-El. Once as a child, I walked into Temple Emanu-El and I ran right out again. I didn't feel uncomfortable about visiting St. Patrick's, but the imitation of what looked to me like a Gothic Church, the temple, frightened me and I left it in a hurry.

I therefore realized that there were German Jews but I had no contact with them whatever until much later in life, and then as a result of my administrative responsibilities in the Seminary Library. Afterwards, some of my early suspicions were confirmed for me when I became librarian. At my first library board meeting I reported that the Yiddish press which we owned was falling to pieces because it was printed on pulp. I told the board that we needed a budget to microfilm all this material. And a very powerful member declared, "We have no money for that trash!" I was so shaken at the time that I didn't dare raise the question again. But I am sorry to this day that I didn't resign on the spot because I might have saved the collection that disappeared.

I don't suppose I can divorce my personal feeling from an institutional decision, though I made it in concert with all my colleagues. When I became the Seminary chancellor in 1972, we were confronted with a problem: the Seminary was unable to expand or to build facilities for its library, which had suffered a catastrophic fire in 1966. At that time I felt sure we were going to move out of New York, the more so after a dean of ours had been stabbed in broad daylight. Many people reproached me, arguing like this: "If you move out of New York, the Seminary will become a parochial institution." I am today convinced that that was true. My sense of desperation, however, probably did help. I went to Mayor Lindsay. The city was more responsive to our needs and that mood may also have induced closer cooperation with Teachers College, the Union Theological Seminary, and Columbia. A high-ranking Catholic prelate came to see me: "If you move the Seminary to the suburbs, you will die. It will choke you." He meant that if we moved to a suburban town, our young men and women would no longer have access to the sources of culture, and—above all—to metropolitan social life. I said to him: "Remember, we have boys and girls. We are not celibates." And he replied, "But you still need a lot of choices for mates, and here your students will have them." He was right. Our students do find a very rich life. So, in spite of all the *tzores* (trouble), we decided to stay.

I suppose New York City has been the formation of my life. Wherever I go, I gravitate to extensions of New York, but it is precisely this rich and various culture that makes—let me put it this way: When I was in school, soon after World War II, I had the typical religious rabbinical crisis. For a time, I thought of leaving. Will Herberg had just come in and asked me to give him private Hebrew lessons. I indicated to him that I was really suffering very grave doubts about my faith. Herberg was fascinated by what he called "an encounter with an unbelieving rabbi." As it turned out, I was not an unbeliever, but I was going through a crisis all right. Herberg introduced me to the works of Reinhold Niebuhr. As a result of that, I went across the street to a library of our foremost Protestant seminary—where we had borrowing privileges—and I read a lot. I met Niebuhr, Paul Tillich, and John Bennett. (I have since developed close ties with both Protestant and Catholic theologians.)

More important than any individual was this: that the Niebuhrian reinterpretation of Christianity exposed a new perception of Judaism, and Tillich's redefinition of faith made me examine afresh certain potential elements in Judaism, not of course from a Christological aspect. But as he examined Christianity, I began to explore Judaism. Niebuhr was saying that Christians should not try to convert Jews but that Judaism should be allowed to develop as a legitimate faith. Direct exposure to such currents of thought could only have happened at that time in New York City.

Kaplan had been most effective in breaking down any vestige of Orthodoxy that I had left. The Union Theological Seminary, with its books and teachers, plus men like Abraham Heschel, Meyer Rabinowitz, and Roger Scheinwold in my own school, put me on another track. All in all it was a broadening experience, liberating me from the intellectual Orthodoxy of my early years— and helping to resolve my crisis.

The Holocaust had one conscious effect on many of us. We regarded ourselves as "The Last," the saving remnant. The Holocaust didn't bring me any *Jewish* consciousness: I never grew up with any other kind. The Holocaust left me baffled. I have often said it taught me nothing about the Jews. I say it is an indictment of world civilization.

But I suppose the Holocaust did contribute unconsciously to my "crisis." When I was courting my wife, we went to the Hyde Park Library to peruse the Roosevelt Papers. Long before my friend, Henry Feingold, uncovered what he did, Naomi and I learned the truth in those papers. We were so shaken that I knew I could never deal with the subject dispassionately. I saw the passive role Roosevelt played long before it came out that six million Jews had died. I knew that as a twenty-three-year-old. In 1947 the trauma of my life occurred when the Yiddish Scientific Institute ran an exhibit of materials from concentration camps and there I saw a Jewish bar of soap—a bar of soap made of Jews. . . . The Holocaust really reduced me to a state of despair for the world.

The Holocaust did not bring me a new theology but a new anthropology. I became a great pessimist. I developed a terrible fear of the demons let loose, almost a Kantian, Platonic, or Maimonidean point of view. I feel very strongly and have great fears, which is why when some of the riots occurred in New York City—that burned out the retail businesses on 125th Street—I was deeply troubled by them and by the series of uprisings in cities throughout the United States where the Jewish retailers were literally driven away. And I was similarly alarmed by the teachers' strike of 1968 because it was one of a series of such strikes and I thought it was virtually a concerted effort to drive Jews out of the Civil Service. I have read that record elsewhere. Where the burgher or the lower middle class tries to rise by taking over functions which the Jews had filled because of historical circumstances, Jews were expelled from the mainstream of city life.

I think the American Jewish community is split, confused, and traumatized, but largely silent. To put that in perspective, we must remember that a great many Jews shifted completely to conservatism, which is basically the nineteenth-century liberal position. Jews were not liberals until about 1848, when they saw in liberalism the possibility of their own emancipation. Before that they had always been dependent on good goyim with power who supported law and order, to give them protection. They thought that with natural rights and with man in a state of nature, there would be a meritocracy. When one round of riots occurred, I remember the mayor on television enjoining us to understand the bitterness of blacks. I could only answer, "You have to understand *my* terrible traumatic reaction to a mass uprising that bore so heavily on Jews."

I took no stand on the teachers' strike. Instead, I went around the country and to Canada, lecturing on "The Sociology of Pogroms." I stressed the fact that there is a *pattern* to pogroms beginning in 411 B.C. with the destruction of the Temple at Elephantine, which repeats itself, let's say, in the Alexandrian riots of 37–39 of our era, 1096 with the Crusades, 1391 in Spain, and then 1648 and 1658 in the Gorodnitzky Pogrom. I have tried to teach my students that you cannot judge the structure of anti-Semitism in a pogrom by the Tsarist and Nazi experience, which are *sui generis* in Jewish history. Anti-Semitism is orchestrated by a government. You must distinguish between hatred of the Jew and an uprising against the Jew. They are completely different phenomena.

I believe that blacks themselves and Puerto Ricans and other minorities in this city realize the danger in such mass uprisings. The middle-class Jew and the middle-class black are sociologically the same. Ultimately a meritocratic framework will reassert itself. I also believe that open enrollment at the city colleges has proven to be bankrupt and will reverse itself.

Black-Jewish antagonism is abating. Top leaders of the Jewish community are able to work with men like Bayard Rustin and NAACP executives—the militant blacks denounce them as "Uncle Toms"—but they are making fresh overtures to the Jewish community, which is eager for cooperation. I doubt that there'll be serious trouble between Jews and blacks anymore.

I am nevertheless terrified of something I learned from Ibn Khaldun, an Arab philosopher of history. He firmly believed in *collective will*. And that collective will is sometimes expressed in fatigue. I am appalled by a general breakdown of morale and the widespread dedication to what have become truisms. Now, the challenge of any cultural leader is to make a truism a truth, to recapture the vitality underlying what has become a platitude, so that it is not just part of a catechism that we automatically recite.

When I discovered America, at City College, it meant a great deal to me. I feel very strongly about a healthy statement made by Daniel Boorstein in *The American Image of Europe*. He did not like a certain homiletical, platitudinous equation of the Jewish and the American traditions—"They're both the same." They're *not* the same. On the other hand, in consequence of the Second World War, the Holocaust, and the resurgence of ethnic groups, something good did happen. We began to abandon the Boston Brahmin yardstick and an obsolete melting-pot theory that made Anglo-Saxon Protestantism the only legitimate way of life.

There's an intense parochialism on the part of each of us, from which we derive our roots. And yet, at a certain level of our experience we can meet, whether it's in the concert hall, or in the library, or in the conference room of a university, and there express ourselves in the pluralistic tradition. I'm still thrilled to meet people of different cultures, faiths, and commitments, to enjoy a drink with them and exchange ideas—not necessarily agree—and often enough, find common cause with them. That's New York at its best.

In school I always gravitated toward students on the upper crust of academic work. One of them was Sidney Morgenbesser, then and now a brutal taskmaster in the use of words. He too provided a formidable challenge to my faith. On the other hand, Sidney had a great admiration for excellence in texts, and I like to think that I gained his respect that way.

Will Herberg was an enormous influence on a group of us in the forties. It was precisely because he claimed to be a master of Sovietology, a Kremlinologist and an expert on Communist theory as well as Christian theology, that his reassertion of Jewishness was so interesting. He wrote *Protestant, Catholic and Jew* in the Seminary. We regularly went to 213 Bennett Avenue where Anna and Will received us three times a week.

Jacob Taubes was a figure of some importance in these precincts—less to people like me than to certain editors of *Commentary* magazine. He used to give then lessons in Maimonides. The last I heard of him, Taubes was in the Free University of Berlin where he completely disassociated himself from the Jewish community, and became a Maoist. I don't know precisely why young men like Irving Kristol and Nat Glazer found Taubes so seductive. But one can speculate. These *were* people who had gone through their own political eschatology and theology and found them suddenly bankrupt. They were former Marxists, heirs to what's been called confessionless theology. It's even a universalist humanitarian point of view, and Taubes, who knew that language—which we did not—was able to say that true intellectuality by universalism could be found in the esoteric tradition which legalistic rabbis had suppressed: namely, mystical medieval philosophy.

Existentialism, when it was very modish, had very little impact on us and "Death of God" theology no effect at all. Why? Well, consider another incident that took place when we were contemplating removal to suburbia. Besides the Catholic dignitary, a *Protestant* bishop came to me saying, "You mustn't take the Seminary out of here because God dies here every day." And I told him, "We don't go where God dies; we go where Jews live." Then he apologized for the use of that metaphor.

In the cultural sphere, two technological revolutions happened in my life which were very good: first, paperback reprints and then, long-playing records culminating in cassettes. I have even found it difficult to look at the television *news* anymore. It's meaningless to me. My whole orientation is reading and listening to music. I know at the same time that Jews are said to be disproportionately represented in the mass media.

Simon Kuznetz wrote a splendid essay on Jews and economic life in the third edition of Louis Finkelstein's *The Jews*. Kuznetz contends that abnormal economic stratification for an abnormal group seeking survival is normal. Jews are always going to have an abnormal economic position. Consequently, they're always going to be different.

Always? Shall we say until the final redemption of all mankind in the spirit of Isaiah 2:11, there is always going to be Jew-hatred. It's just one of the things you have to contend with. I don't believe that all the Brotherhood Weeks and all the matchbooks handed out by the Brotherhood organizations are going to make us brothers. And Jews will remain economically marginal. Perhaps there are a lot of Jews in television, but maybe it's because Jews are pioneers. Remember that joke, in *The Graduate,*—"Plastics!" And everybody laughed. Jews are in plastics because historically they are in the front pews where there aren't yet any vested interests. You know, for many centuries Jews had a monopoly on glass manufacture in the Byzantine world. And they didn't reveal their secrets. That was a matter of survival. It still is.

13.

THE TEACHING OF
THE HOLOCAUST

Irving Greenberg

MY FIRST awareness of the Holocaust was subtly communicated to me by my parents from the very beginning, because they lost a lot of family. And they never talked to me about it, but I'd see my mother crying. That had to have left an impression. No one talked about the Holocaust except indirectly. Jewish people didn't want to hear about the Holocaust. But consciously and articulately it probably came in the late fifties or early sixties.

Then we went to Israel in '61. Our first child had just been born and I'm sure that's part of it. Somehow, my emotions crystallized. I spent one day a week traveling from Jerusalem to Tel Aviv, giving my lectures, and six days a week I sat and read about the Holocaust. I read everything. I used both the Yad Vashem (a Holocaust archive) and the university. Yad Vashem was totally disorganized in those years, and I didn't like it, so I ended up mostly in the university, taking books home and reading them. Reading in all the languages I could muster. My primary languages were English, Hebrew, and Yiddish, although I can read German and French too. It was a consuming thing, undirected because it was obsessive. It meant almost complete absorption. There I was in Israel and we had our child, who, I now realize, was my balance wheel. But to this day, my thinking, my theology, are very much

Irving Greenberg was born in Brooklyn in 1933. He is a rabbi, theologian, and author. He has taught history at Yeshiva University and is now a professor in the Department of Jewish Studies at City College, CUNY. Greenberg is director of the National Jewish Conference Center, where he specializes in Holocaust Studies.

related to the juxtaposition of reading about the Holocaust and walking around Jerusalem. The mixture of living Jews in a living community was exceptionally powerful. I experienced it as the living body of the Jewish people all out there before me, while I read about the dead body of the Jewish people. That's the reality. And the reality of how many survivors were walking those streets and the reality of their life. It was a tremendous exposure to the pain, a full awareness of the Holocaust. The survivors' lives suddenly became miraculous. By contrast, the news at my yeshiva had been couched in traditional religious terms. Now a different kind of religious news reached me. Suddenly Israel became a religious revelation. Before it had been a "Zionism of the *siddur* (daily prayerbook)" and a secular state. To me it became a fundamental religious and emotional experience. There was a true change in my thinking.

The other part of it was our child, our firstborn. We were wrapped up in him. I've always been a workaholic and a readaholic—so to be on sabbatical meant there was much more time with my wife and my son. That's where I see the balance wheel.

The Eichmann trial was just ending when I arrived in Israel. It had a powerful effect. I remember reading about the trial and following it. It's interesting how memories are starting to float up. I also recall meeting second cousins of my parents who came to visit us in the late fifties. They were survivors who didn't talk much but said enough. They did not describe much. Maybe it's the *misnagid* (traditionally Orthodox) tradition; maybe it was just too hard to handle. There was none of the brutal detail which I later read. I do recall the simple realization that there but for the grace of God went my entire family. Actually I had very large families on both sides, and they would have been dead.

As a result I came back and began to talk to my students about it at Yeshiva University where I was teaching history. I didn't really have the guts to teach a Holocaust course. I was talking about it a lot. Then students asked me, "Why don't you *teach* us about it?" because until then they had not realized how gripping the subject was.

I went to the Yeshiva faculty with a proposal, and couldn't get it through! Imagine, Yeshiva University! And when over a year of resistance had elapsed, and I couldn't get it through, I was chatting one day with the dean. He said, "You know, Yeshiva guys get into medical school." Yeshiva had a terrific reputation; its pre-med class was very heavy. "My son, the doctor." That syndrome. He went on, "One reason they take our kids is that we have credibility. We're not the same as a Catholic school, not so parochial. The Catholics are loaded down with theology courses. Here they say that's Mickey Mouse stuff. But we've got good solid science." He was convinced that a course on the Holocaust would be seen as brainwashing which might destroy Yeshiva's academic credibility.

You know how I solved that problem? By returning the next day with a question: "What would you say to a course called, 'Ideology and Totalitarianism in the Twentieth Century'?" And on that basis he approved it. At the height of this argument the faculty pointed out that other universities didn't teach the Holocaust. I checked the catalogues, and the truth is, only one had a course in the Holocaust. And that was Brandeis!

Well, I got the course, and began wondering what materials to use. New York had libraries. That was no problem. Both 42nd Street and Yeshiva were available. I think the 42nd Street Jewish division is first rate. I used it for many things, not just for the Holocaust. I didn't become totally concentrated on the Holocaust either.

What happened was that in the course of a widespread Jewish liberation process, I moved back from American history into Jewish religious history. To be fair, the whole experience of encountering neo-Orthodoxy had left me fascinated by the impact of modernization on religious values in general. I had kept that as an important part of my studies at Harvard. The interest was there, but as the Holocaust sank in, I became more and more interested in Jewish things.

It would be hard to call my preoccupation a religious crisis. It's like Milton or, in a way, it was like the old story about Jews: they never have an acute crisis; they have a *chronic* crisis. So what "sank in"? Let me put it this way: at ten I had gone through several intellectual and religious crises and came out with a kind of modified liberal Orthodoxy. The crisis of science and of psychoanalysis, also radical questions to religionists, made me more humanistic, more liberal. The Holocaust was far more radical. It challenged the whole idea of God in a fashion that made science and religion look like playthings. The shock kept deepening. It didn't go away. I think one ordinarily overcomes shock or develops protective numbness to it. But this shock drove me into looking for new categories.

Whether I found any remains to be judged by other scholars. In a sense, I was living both with the adequacy of modernity and of Orthodoxy, striving for some synthesis between them. When I got through, I felt that both were inadequate. The crisis broke up a lot of assumptions. It drove me to much more dialectical positions. For example, I am now in a state of continual tension with modernity. Although I do not see the Enlightenment as an unmitigated evil, I would say there's much merit in the conservative critique.

But there's a combination of elements including several social benefits. Historically, however, as the Jews became more at home in this country, they could afford to be (a) more distant to America, and (b) more critical of liberalism. It's a matter of timing. Jews were more fully accepted in the fifties, and could, therefore, be more distant and critical, even if that sounds like a paradox.

I really feel that modernity and the tradition were shattered. If you admit that, the only way you can stay liberal is by becoming very critical of your own ideology. So in a sense, I am deeply sympathetic to *Commentary*. Having said that, let me add again, I am very dialectical. I feel the mistake is in letting the Holocaust give you a unidimensional answer. Surely it's right to defend Jewish interests. If you make that affirmation after the Holocaust, it provides a position that you can take. But you can't affirm it *unequivocally*. I have argued that no theological statement or understatement can be credible in the presence of burning children.

If you say, "I believe in God in the presence of burning children," you also have to say that you're ashamed of it. Now, I would say the same thing about modernity. If you tell me that the Enlightenment is adequate or is really liberating, I believe that. You can say it in the presence of burning kids, but you should also be ashamed. After the Holocaust it's not so important which position you take, as long as you're ashamed of it. I groped my way to this dialectical or paradoxical position, but it hardly existed when I gave my first course on the Holocaust. I put it together myself. Enrollment was excellent, partly because I had a good reputation. Besides, talking to kids on this subject was absolutely gripping. One reason I had impact was like the golden goose: you touch it and then you get attached and someone touches you and gets attached, and so on.

What did I ask them to read? Elie Wiesel, of course. *Night* had come out early, but that book was utterly neglected. When I started to look for reading matter, there it was. Once more, *Night,* when I first read it, was a shock. It was ice cold. It took me years to realize that underneath the ice cold was white hot heat and that's the way Wiesel wrote.

When I started teaching the course, not only did I have to learn to control myself, but I also learned, for example, how to handle the question of Jewish resistance. For three years the kids immediately reacted by asking, "Why didn't they resist?" I was very upset and angry. I tried to prove that they *did* resist, and it was a disaster. After three or four years I had enough self-discipline to refuse to answer the question and to insist, "You keep reading first." I began to build many more personal eyewitness accounts. When you do that, the question answers itself. My mistake consisted in trying to persuade them instead of letting them live through the experience from within.

I'm sure I would have had trouble teaching my course somewhere else. "The Holocaust" was not a recognized academic course, let alone a recognized discipline. For resource material I had the booksellers and the Jewish libraries of New York City. Partly for the lack of an adequate literature we had to bring survivors in to talk. Their presence, their stories had a tremendous effect. In Oshkosh, or wherever, you couldn't do that, but New York had so many survivors with so many different experiences. And some of the kids were themselves children of survivors. Sometimes you'd have a kid come in with a parent or bring in an account from a parent who had never previously talked about the death camps. Of course New York had the largest concentration of survivors.

After all, talking to survivors was an important factor in the growth of my own thinking and feeling. In class, reactions have been extraordinarily diverse. They are perhaps analogous to the condition of faith in which there are moments when you believe and moments when you don't. The only way you can be a true believer is to be atheist half the time. You have to experience continual tension. You want to reconcile opposite attitudes and end up with a positive answer. Finally the solution I found lay in an empathetic reliving of the horror.

In '65 or '66 I had my first direct contact with Elie Wiesel. It was late, but I had read all his books and knew him in that sense. A friend and I organized a group of rabbis and scholars who met in Canada. It crossed all existing religious and secular lines. By then the Holocaust had been boiling for years in my mind. One day my friend remarked, "I know Elie Wiesel. Should we invite him?" I don't know why I never thought of checking out where he lived and visiting him myself. But I guess my *misnagidic* tradition, in which books are as real as people, accounts for it. Anyhow, I thought that having Wiesel was a great idea. He came. That was the first time I heard a personal account of the Holocaust. Now the only thing worse than writing about it is to betray it by total silence. Yet I think silence is the highest form of speech, and that's a dominant theme in his work. If you want to trip him up with logical categories, you can dismiss him, but in person and in his work he has acted out the profoundest dialectical tensions. Finally, anything you say is inadequate, because you're domesticating the ineffable, the inaccessible.

When I use the language of paradox, I offend people in the Orthodox community. My stand has caused a great deal of hostility over the years. There's a whole wing to the right of Orthodoxy that's furious at me. But within the community I found that it also broke down a number of barriers. I no longer saw the adequacy of just being Orthodox. I was prepared to continue Orthodox but I was not prepared to write off the rest of the Jewish people. That drove me across logical and theological lines in Canada in the sixties. I came to the conference with my tremendous load of the Holocaust. That was my contribution and I got a sympathetic, emotionally very powerful response from the group.

I met Emile Fackenheim, a Jewish philosopher who thought history had nothing to do with the Jewish religion. Fackenheim, a Reform Jew, reacted to the Holocaust as powerfully as I did. I sure as hell couldn't see him as "the other." I saw him as me. I felt closer to him than to a lot of the guys on my right. Down came the barriers. My reflections drove me intellectually and socially to a much broader community.

I'm convinced that prophetic voices are not responsible for action and power; they are responsible for the articulation of magnificent ideals. Jews have to protect themselves, but they must be morally aware and responsible for gentiles as well. Otherwise you're doing to them what was done to you.

Putting the Holocaust into the curriculum all over the United States is one of my main goals. It's happened on a volunteer basis in the New York City curriculum. But elsewhere in the United States adoptions are amazing. The Holocaust study has spread to Yuma, Arizona to San Antonio, Texas, El Paso . . . places you wouldn't imagine. The seed has spored. It's the process of dissemination. We're setting up conferences. In Pittsburgh we had meetings on the Holocaust to which the educational establishment was invited. The administrators ended up committing themselves to a course in their public schools, and we will do teacher-training for them. The spread is gradual, but now I would put it this way: There were many liberations in history, but the Exodus was cosmically perceived, and as a result of that Jewish incorporation it ended up reshaping the values not just of Jews but obviously of a big part of the rest of the world. To some extent, this proposition holds for the Holocaust and Israel. In other words they are not just decisive in Jewish circles, but they have dramatized a worldwide cultural crisis.

Obviously, other theories feed into this one. I also am convinced that neither religion nor ethics nor the modern paradigm will ever be the same. In other words, I think they're being worked over and fundamentally shaken up if not reshaped by this experience. The Holocaust is not everything, but to me it's one of the cutting edges. As Jews reflect on it, their thought will be mirrored by others reflecting on it.

14.

PSYCHOANALYST
IN NEW YORK

Joel Kovel

BOTH MY parents came over from Russia at a very early age; each was four or so. I grew up in an extremely Jewish neighborhood which itself was divided into various levels and segments. My own family was never Orthodox. When I was a youngster, and I am ashamed of this, we used to make fun of a few extremely Orthodox kids. There was a certain sentiment against the very Orthodox. The prevailing ethos was that of the Enlightenment. Not that I knew the word. It's just that in the forties the prestige of science had really taken over. And at the little school I attended, in a very special class of brilliant kids, everybody was going to be a scientist. We were all free thinkers. The children went to Hebrew School and developed a certain Jewishness, and boys went on to be bar mitzvahed. But the dominant attitude was skeptical, and we were scornful of the old time religion. In Flatbush and later on in Midwood, there were Orthodox outposts, but I myself became antireligious at a relatively early age.

As for my parents, they were split on the question of Judaism, particularly Zionism. On East 10th Street at that time Zionism was popular, even though in the larger world it was not. But I didn't know that. As a child in my immediate world some Socialists and many non-Socialists were Zionists. My father was an anti-Zionist while my mother was a rabid Zionist. They had ter-

Joel Kovel was born in New York in 1936. He is a practicing psychoanalyst and professor of psychiatry on the faculty of The Albert Einstein College of Medicine. Among his books are *A Complete Guide to Therapy* (1977) and *The Age of Desire* (1982).

rific arguments about it. So from the beginning my consciousness of the issue was subjectively determined.

Do you remember a group called The National Council for Judaism? It was a right-wing anti-Zionist organization led by Lessing Rosenwald. My father liked that outfit. Politically, he was very conservative. During the early thirties, which were also his early thirties, he moved in left-wing circles in the shadow of Max Lerner, Ben Shahn, and all the heavies. For reasons that are still not clear to me, around the time of my birth he started moving to the right. He was an oppositional man, the kind who, if everyone else favored something, he was against it. Since everyone in the neighborhood was a Zionist he would be an anti-Zionist. The neighborhood liberals and radicals reflexively made him a right-winger. I remember being handed Roosevelt literature on the street in 1944—FDR must have gotten every vote in the neighborhood except my father's. I don't know why they bothered to campaign in that district. Anyway, I brought some New Deal handouts home and he was enraged. My father worked as an accountant, so his primary contacts were with the commercial world. He developed a great admiration for businessmen and a great hatred for labor. I grew up with a living contradiction between my father and practically everyone else around me.

My parents quarreled. Mother didn't prevail. Father was the dominant one. He never repudiated religion but neither would he go near a synagogue. Only my mother wanted us to take part in Jewish activities. My father was an intellectual, interested in the arts, but part of his revulsion from people like Lerner and Shahn was a reaction against modernism. He liked Michaelangelo and the Greeks and the Romans, the Romans above all. I think it was part of his imperial right-wing mentality. The Romans had an empire and they built things. What rubbed off on me was a profound sense of contradiction, a feeling that there were tremendous puzzles in the world that stimulated me.

My mother was musical. She had, in fact, once been in the second chorus of the Metropolitan Opera. Both of my grandfathers were Orthodox. My father's father was decisive in teaching me how to read, and I used to play chess with him. But he died when I was quite young. My mother's father survived into old age. He used to sing and there was a great love of music between us. My mother also had a good feeling for music. My father hated music. Whatever mother liked, my father disliked.

There were great cultural resources in Brooklyn. However, up to the age of twelve, I didn't really use them. Resources in Brooklyn, for me, were people, and the life of the neighborhood, and being around very bright kids, and sensing an enormous amount of free-floating intellectuality. We were really clever, you know. We were smarter than our teachers and we knew it. In Brooklyn, while formal education was repressive, the students were rebellious. We had our own culture. All of us hung out on the street; that's where the life was. And then came a very important determinant in my life: we moved out to Long Island. I expected the same friendly sort of thing Brooklyn provided. Instead, nobody talked about anything. You wandered around, there was nothing to do. You couldn't walk on Coney Island Avenue or into the candy store because there was no street life. There was just a great gap. Ever since, I have hated suburbs. I like nature and I love the city. But suburbia was a terrible experience. I felt lonely out on the Island. I had been cut off from the very rich, highly self-conscious Jewish culture of Brooklyn. When we left it I felt estranged, which helped me develop a radical sensibility.

I thought myself a stranger first in Long Island and then at Yale, although I did form personal bonds at the university. But it soon became clear that those I felt most at home with were New Yorkers. We made trips to the city. There was a sense of life about Manhattan, a vivacity, a world swirling with ideas and actions, and a sense of freedom, unconstraint, excitement. There too I had to face the political dilemma caused by my father always pushing me to the right and others pushing me to the left. The benefit of that dissonance was that I learned to form my own opinions, which, however, remained dormant for a long time.

At Yale I also found a conservative environment which seemed to be made up of people who owned the world. Living in Long Island meant being exposed to the *embourgeoisement* of Judaism, which to me was its death blow. Traditional religion at least had some feeling left in it. And I could respond to that passion. In New Haven I attended some Jewish meetings. I tried to tune into that. But it seemed meaningless to me. I resolved the problem as a college student by picking up a few political threads. After all, we are constituted as believing creatures. The question is: what do we believe? The religious approach has certain attractions for me. But every time I see it organized and institutionalized, whether at Yale or in a synagogue, a radical streak in me rebels. Nevertheless, I somehow continued to identify with Jews. But in a nonrational way. It was mostly a matter of qualities associated with Jews: a certain kind of humor, a form of discourse, a sense of irony. By now these qualities have been assimilated into New York. Many of my college friends moved back and half of them weren't Jewish but they all had that style.

At any rate, I wanted to study medicine in New York, just as I had wanted to visit it whenever possible, leaving Connecticut to hang around, just to be there. It was a return to my experiences as a youngster. But I wound up in Manhattan, not in Brooklyn. I went to Columbia, which was worse than Yale in some respects. I found my apprenticeship as a physician meaningful enough, but the intellectual content of medical school was hopeless. And the atmosphere of Presbyterian Hospital, although not anti-Semitic as such, was rather cold, alien, and aloof. I did have some good experiences there. However, by graduation time, when it came to moving on, I didn't want any part of that institution.

As a matter of fact, for my psychiatric training, I wound up at the Albert Einstein College of Medicine, which, at the time, offered the best program in New York City. It was created at a fortunate moment in the early fifties. There was a substantial investment of money, with plenty of freedom to develop a good institution. Einstein inherited certain fruits of the Holocaust. An incredibly beautiful psychoanalytic culture had developed in central Europe. It was dispersed. Key figures ended up in New York: Hartmann and Kris and Lowenstein and many others. A number of these people were even brought to the United States through the influence of liberal Jewish American psychoanalysts. The psychoanalytic movement in America started slowly. It built a certain base mainly in Jewish circles, which in itself is a fascinating story. Then when the Holocaust came, this base was substantial enough to draw a large number of brainy people. These cultivated European practitioners met their American opposite numbers, not all of whom were philistines by any means. You had Americans like Bertrand Lewin who was from Texas, Jewish, and an altogether brilliant man. His kind would go over to Europe and study there because they wanted to escape parochialism and general stultification. When they came back, they settled in New York. They provided the nucleus of the New York Psychoanalytic Association. Then came the Holocaust and the Europeans migrated to this city. By the early fifties, you had the manpower; the people were there; you had prosperity; and you had specific cultural conditions that were making psychoanalysis acceptable in America. Institutions such as Einstein simply reaped the harvest. There was a man named Milton Rosenbaum. He came from Cincinnati, had a strong Jewish identity, and was deeply involved in the formation of a Jewish state from the beginning. But he was the founder of the Department of Psychiatry at Albert Einstein. He was instrumental in bringing out quite a few psychoanalysts. These people gave of themselves to the institution, starting in '55, and by '61 to '62 we really had a brilliant gathering. Einstein was the place to be if you were a young psychiatrist interested in psychoanalysis as I had become by that time.

It might be that my Jewish background brought me to psychoanalysis. Jews have always been drawn to Freud. Much psychoanalytic history was determined by Freud's uneasiness about his disproportionately Jewish circle. Thus, for instance, his flirtation—the romance—with Jung. Marxism, in this respect, resembles Freudianism. Both have particular relevance to the Jewish people as devices by which they can relate to something bigger than themselves. Both traditions have drawn from a peculiar position, that of the Jew as an outsider who comments upon and cultivates a special consciousness . . . who is wedded to the Enlightenment by a secret love affair with the mysterious tension that exists in this world. Many Jews have become straightforwardly involved with science, but those dialectical disciplines, psychoanalysis and Marxism, where the Enlightenment has made a step forward, many of us see as an attempt to overcome the past of the human race. I probably reflect the concrete history of Judaism with respect to the Enlightenment.

What do I mean? The commitment is to rationality, but with a full recognition of irrationality which, like the past, has to be overcome. The sense of history is very important. Although I despised my little Talmud Torah teachings as a kid, those teachings always boiled down to this: "You belong to a very ancient race that has had a mysterious and problematic history. It's been kicked around and has never stopped wandering. Which raises the question of history, the genetic question, namely, how did things come to be as they are?"

Be that as it may, the concentration of psychoanalysis in New York has been very important to me. As you know, Freud distrusted America. Part of the antipathy was irrational. Some things that America stands for are essential to psychoanalysis, particularly the fact that this society is willing to experiment. Freud worried, with reason, that his ideas would be trivialized in the United States. What has been missing from the American psychoanalytic tradition is precisely the kind of radical political sensibility that would protect it from vulgarization. Freud remained radical as a thinker, not as a practitioner.

When I entered the sixties, it was as a trained person, and psychoanalysis somehow seemed to be backward. That had a stunning effect on me. In the fifties, I had regarded Freudianism as the most radical and advanced kind of thinking. I was attracted to it for that reason. But much of my work in the last few years has consisted of wrestling with this problem of how a radical theory can become accommodated to existing social ends. There was a great deal of prestige for all of us who practiced in New York, but there was also a problem. By the time I got started, psychoanalytic institutions were hierarchical and top-heavy. It was a difficult time for younger analysts to make their way into teaching psychoanalysis. There was a saying that when you are forty you are just starting—and only when you reach the age of sixty is it possible to enter the council of the elders. There is something nice about being in a line of work where you feel you can continually develop, and where the advice of older people means something. I don't want to badmouth it. Many of the older people have a great deal to say, but there is something institutional about it that tends to produce closure. Psychoanalysis in New York and elsewhere has to struggle against the tendency to become a hardened system of achieved and codified knowledge.

At the end of my medical training I was assigned to the West Coast on a tour of duty in the United Public Health Service in Seattle. For me that was too much like a repetition of Long Island. It *was* beautiful. What with nature and the mountains, I almost stayed. I rather liked being out of doors. But I ran into indifference among the people I met out there. The things that mattered to me didn't matter to them. Then in the course of my time out there, I decided to get training as a psychoanalyst. I could see that the psychoanalytic community in Seattle, although it had quite a few good analysts, was totally isolated—tiny, fragmentary, out of touch with the larger world, lacking social weight. The Department of Psychiatry in medical school was plodding, in my opinion. I had spent a little time teaching there in the service so I got to know it. In one word, I was dreadfully bored. The place was just too bland. The sense of opposition that makes New York what it is was missing. I remember walking through the shopping centers; people looked the same; they were all lined up like a cross section of the consumer society. And at that time I was getting very radical politically on account of the Vietnam War, which awakened a lot of things in me from my childhood. That's when I got in touch with a lot of radical thought which had been sort of slumbering in me. I was a liberal throughout medical school. But with the war, I began to see how society is anchored in the everyday life of its people, and not just in abstractions about political economics. I could see that the everyday life of bland suburban enclaves was such as to bring people into line with a certain commodity-mindedness, calculated to make them happy, feed them, and deaden their sensibilities. I saw this in the bureaucratic smoothness of the Public Health Service.

I got interested in Herbert Marcuse, and was influenced by *One Dimensional Man*, as well as *Eros and Civilization*. This takes us to the mid-sixties. Then the question became: "What do I do with myself? I want to be a psychoanalyst. I am in this middle-sized city where there is no richness in psychoanalytic life." I was exaggerating. Seattle is a rather progressive town. It even has a great radical tradition. But I was locked in one dull side of that world. So coming back to New York, touching roots again, rejoining a brilliant psychoanalytic community was irresistible. It was enormously stimulating just to mingle with people I admired, who had exactly those qualities of mind, particularly complexity and irony, that I appreciated, and which meant a good deal to me. Coming back to New York immediately made sense to me again because of these human associations.

By then I was married and had three children. Their education was a problem, but fortunately I belong to the upper middle class, so I could afford to send them to private school. As for Jewish education, they've had none. They're not Jewish. My wife is Catholic, neither of us is religious, and our children receive no Jewish training. About Israel we have a number of complicated feelings. I am not an anti-Zionist but I am not a Zionist either. Emotionally, I care about Israel's survival; politically I care about Israel's retaining its original thrust. I have my differences with the American Jewish community, which tends to support Israel re-flexively, overlooking the fact that it has played a very problematic role in the system of states and nations. I am not willing to say, "Israel must be right because it is Jewish and I am Jewish and Jewish people were knocked about by the Nazis." But I would hope that Jews are not wholly assimilable. I don't think that *I* am. There is something about Jewishness that helps one to stand outside and look inside with clarity and detachment.

The marginality gives you perspective. That element in my Jewish background has been a source of strength for me. The problem with Israel is that it too gets incorporated into bourgeois American Jewish life. Just the same, in '67, I experienced a great sense of relief when Israel survived. The picture I got was of Israel about to be pounced on by monsters, and the outcome left me with a tremendous sense of joy. I knew my response was emotional. In '73, I was even more upset because I did not want Israel to go under. The Jewish forces appeared to be having much more difficulty than in '67. When they began to win, I found myself more than relieved.

Now, I'm not about to leave for Israel or to depart from New York, which has been good to me. Ultimately the question of why one stays is quite personal. A major reason for me is that

I form long-term relationships with patients. I have to stay with them. They are no longer mainly Jewish. It is, however, certainly the case that Jewish people are more predisposed to the analytic situation than many other groups. The analytic situation is easily assimilable to Jewish mores. The categories of Freudian thinking are there: looking at yourself, wondering about your motives, conceiving of yourself as someone divided into a number of different parts, feeling estranged. Historically, Jews are more aware of their alienation and more able to reflect on it. That, with their traditional premium on verbal discourse, tends to make Jews more congenial to analysis. However, once you get started, there is no Jewish syndrome: everybody has his own history. Jewish or gentile, it's the patient more than anybody else who has held me in the city. Also there are friends and contacts of all sorts. Colleagues more than institutions. I find that I make relatively little use of the great cultural resources of New York City. Much of my free time is spent reading, and you can get a book anywhere. Still, it means something to me that I can go to bookstores. I like the cinema. And I like the fact that there are fifty or sixty movie houses from which to choose.

But mainly I like . . . see, I really have three ways of life: as a psychoanalyst, as a teacher at medical school, and as a writer. As a writer, I have a publisher, and associations with editors. Being in New York City is a great advantage in that respect. There's direct contact. If you want a manuscript delivered, they send a messenger. You stop by the publishers; it is a local call. This makes a difference in the practical conduct of one's life as a writer. But then again, it is not absolute. Obviously one could go off to the woods and work; and there are so many distractions in the city that sometimes you wonder if it is worth staying. But I suppose the crucial factor for me has been the range of human associations. That goes for friends and colleagues, but also chance associations. To me the streets are a book.

I am a walker, a jogger, a bicycler. I am an observer. I am always watching the street. One of the books that was most important in my growing up was Alfred Kazin's *Walker In the City*. The book had resonance. It was not just about being in Brooklyn, but capturing the texture of human life at large.

And I believe New York's been good for my children. We enjoy Cuban-Chinese restaurants, going in and finding sixty or seventy different kinds of people. To me, that provides endless fascination. It's what I mean by the city being like a book, which is symbolic of what keeps me where I am. There *are* times when I feel like taking a few years off to sit in the woods and look at the hills. What actually happens is that I get enraged because of what is going on in the city, and the animosity directed at its inhabitants—which in a certain way is analogous to anti-Semitism. You could say that the New Yorker is to the country what the Jew was to Europe. Of course there is a type of New Yorker who considers himself culturally superior to others whom he treats with disdain. I think the disdain is not warranted. Some New Yorkers project nothing but bad qualities on the rest of the country. Like when I was putting down Seattle a while ago. Had I looked more closely, it would have been apparent to me that I was seeing my own faults. Why wasn't I making more of my life? Why wasn't I finding more friends? I blamed hicks and made a big social generalization about it. Actually, I was thinking of myself as a New Yorker trapped in the hinterlands.

But then, even America is not Europe. The structure of American society is fundamentally different from, say, Freud's Viennese society. Our situation includes blacks and third world people as scapegoats. I don't want to minimize the spectre of anti-Semitism, which is always there. Thomas Mann wrote about the demon that sleeps in the heart of the European soul. Periodically it strikes out at us. The demon is there, all right, but look, I wrote a book on racism. In our society, the main structural polarization has been white and black. I am ambivalent about American Jewry as it more and more joins the mainstream. On the one hand, that is good; it weakens the chances of anti-Semitism arising again, although the spectre is always there. On the other hand, I see this tendency as something related to my criticism of Israel, namely, that American Jewry has become much more conservative. When I was a kid, the idea of being a Jew and simultaneously being a radical seemed to make a lot of sense. That is not the case any more. Now we have a number of very conservative people who stand up for Judaism. In my lifetime there has been a significant Jewish move to dominant American ideologies. Now it's true that we got a conservative *Commentary* magazine, but there was also the Jewish vote for McGovern. Obviously, it's not a unitary phenomenon. But the shift to greater conservatism has a lot to do with structural changes like moving to the suburbs and enjoying unheard-of affluence. It may also reflect an attempt to become more white than other whites.

Albert Shanker personifies what's gone wrong with too many Jews—and also what's wrong with the American working class. When you get involved in real social and political struggles, you realize that there are contradictions at every point. You never find an absolutely clear issue. The enlightened person has to be aware of these contradictions. Therefore, any move is a difficult one. And that goes for ideas too.

For instance, the Holocaust has been burned into my memory; it is always with me. But my revulsion over Vietnam was easier to articulate. It came when I was already in my thirties. The impact of the Holocaust is *deeper*, but more remote. I can't so immediately become aware of it. I constantly try to incorporate those horrors into my understanding. Often I feel ashamed to live in the twentieth century. Probably the First World War must have been to Freud as Vietnam is to me and my generation. Each of us is thrown into history at such-and-such a time, when a certain configuration of events defines our problems. We can choose to ignore them, which most people do—at the expense of their humanity.

American Jews are afraid that the demon, the beast of anti-Semitism will return and take another bite. Since so many have been assimilated into the bourgeois world, it is very hard for them to think of the Holocaust in proper perspective. As history is indeed a series of holocausts, you have to ask, well, what is a holocaust now? Vietnam was a holocaust, and we did it; Chile is a holocaust, and we made that possible. I feel guilty about the atomic bomb. In 1945, when it went off, I was nine years old and at camp. I remember big headlines: "Bomb Dropped On Hiroshima." Everybody at the camp danced! There was a great celebration. Even for a child, such involvement in atrocities is of deep importance: later on when the time comes to play a real role in the world, he's afraid to think of his association with all that. I had to undergo a long process of reflection to unburden myself of that feeling. And simply to survive as a Jew when so many other Jews were killed also induces guilt. There has to be an ingredient of self-identification. The Jewish Holocaust was quantitatively so hideous that every human being can respond to it. But if it is not generalized and universalized, then a Jew like myself is untrue to the Holocaust. It is just like saying, "Let someone else be the victim. I want to join the aggressor." Even a touch of racism in the American context is a betrayal of Hitler's victims. One reason racism has become intense is that too many of us have been unable to come to terms with the Holocaust. And that's tantamount to joining the aggressor.

Another factor among Jews is their own uneasy position in the class structure. I alluded to it in discussing my experiences at Yale where I was in the presence of "people who really owned the country," knowing that while Jews didn't, they were moving up. It's the kind of thing that leaves you with a bad conscience in relation to lowlier members of your society. Now, very concretely, there are the cleaning women who work for Jewish housewives and are accused of being surly. Families wonder why. They pay good money and they're so nice to the help. Of course, that happens whether or not you are Jewish.

Where, then, does one seek identity? Universalism is really the task of every group. We should situate ourselves in history and try to overcome its rootedness in the here-and-now. I think the only way people can do that is to become aware of society in motion, which they have to do through their own experiences. This applies to "the woman question," to "the race question," and to "the Jewish question." It has to happen through what's real to you. What's real to Jews ought to include the Holocaust and, in the long run, their participation in history as victims, survivors, and perpetuators.

15

THE SPIRIT OF THE NEW YORK LABOR MOVEMENT

Victor Gotbaum

MY ROOTS are in East Flatbush, part of the Brooklyn Jewish ghetto. There you were really insulated, wrapped in a false sense of security, what with Jews to the left of you and to the right of you and across the street from you.

Much later I was impressed when my Chicago friends told me that right across the street there might be a Polish family and a Polish gang ready to get you. I never had that problem. Neither did most Jews raised in Brooklyn. When you went to school the minority would be two or three non-Jews per class. I can still remember their names—George Hart, Willie Valentine—but I can't remember the Jewish names because there were so many of them.

I went to work at the age of thirteen in a full-time job: I mean forty to fifty hours a week besides going to high school. But times were tough, the family was on relief, and I had no choice.

At thirteen I also had a "black market" bar mitzvah. There was no time and I had no patience to deal with the rabbi. So I didn't do my lessons. The rabbi would chase me, my old lady would chase me, but they could never track me down. Now my father was really an agnostic. He worked out a deal. Instead of

Victor Gotbaum was born in New York in 1921. He is nationally known as a labor leader and is Executive Director, District Council 37, American Federation of State, County, and Municipal Employees.

having my bar mitzvah on Saturday with everybody invited, we had it like 6:30 in the morning on a Thursday. I just repeated everything after the rabbi. I think my father bribed him with a couple of jars of pickled herring. Well, I got my bar mitzvah, a phoney one, to be sure, which was very unusual for a Jewish kid in Brooklyn. It was also unusual for such a kid to put in fifty hours a week, which is what I was doing as a short-order cook and a dishwasher. Who cared about child labor laws for a retailer or an operator of a little luncheonette? No one ever bothered about that. I got paid six dollars a week—and tips. So I gave Mama the six bucks and I kept the tips, which were minimal.

Oh, I was in poverty, but a kind of middle-class poverty— I mean, my father, a salesman, wasn't making any dough. We applied for relief and got it. But that was disgraceful. I remember one scene—just vague outlines of it. Relatives on my father's side, some of them in the house, were very upset with Mama because we were on relief. *A schandeh fun menschen!* (A deep disgrace.) Mama said, "What do you want me to do?" And the relatives didn't really know what the hell they wanted her to do. They either didn't have the resources or the desire to make up for the relief check. I keep remembering Mama's wild fights with the landlords when we didn't have the rent. But Papa wanted to keep up appearances. So we lived in pretty nice middle-class neighborhoods. I worked and went to school. I was very proud of my working. My brother worked. We had to work. No money. Mama truly bore the brunt of it. Socially, the really bad thing was not my working but the family being on relief.

At home, political discussion was also middle class. Papa would make strong noises on social protest. He was always angry at the bosses. I learned about—or became intellectually involved in—socialism, Marxism, communism, and Trotskyism only when, at nineteen, I met my wife and her family. True, as a boy I almost led a strike; I was a worker with strong sensitivities. But I can't relate any of my feelings to socialist cant. Once I had breakfast with Mike Sverdloff, who asked me, "Vic, how did you escape any of the movements?" And I told him, "Maybe I was the only worker you ever knew." It's the truth in jest because I didn't have the luxury of enough time for *movements*. Too much work to do. Anyhow, there was no strike; I only had to threaten it.

Papa was the manager of a company called something like Dye-craft. He had an exalted title, but made next to nothing. I worked there and sat around with some black workers and learned that they were getting two dollars less than everybody else. I couldn't believe it. They were grumbling. Theirs was a really simple statement on the merits of it—"We work as hard as all the others for two dollars less."

So I said, "You shouldn't do it."

"Why not?"

"We all work—and you guys get less for doing the same thing." A few of the white workers agreed that it was unfair. The grumbling got quite loud. We agreed that the blacks should ask for their money, and if they didn't get it, we'd walk off the job. I insisted we *all* had to walk off. My father called me in: I was his son and I was embarrassing him. "Papa, I don't understand it. Why are they getting less?"

So he smiled a little bit. "None of your business, none of your business."

But I wouldn't back away. I said, "Well, Papa, they should get it, and if they don't, it's unfair for me to get more."

He gave it to them; that is, he got the bosses to give it to them. And he was pleased. In fact, he talked a great deal about it afterwards, with pride. Maybe if *he* had been the boss, he would not have been so willing to yield.

All along it was taken for granted that I wouldn't go to college. My brother Irv went, and it was really very tough for him. He worked like a son of a bitch to make it. And even then Papa had to borrow a hundred dollars for tuition to keep him going in 1938. Around that time I was getting out of high school and wanted to continue my education. Papa told me, "I can't do it. You go into business with your Uncle Jack (who owned a power printing plant where my father was then employed). You're really not cut out for school." That was his rationalization, and I recognized it as such. I started to cry. I've cried so seldom, but it was such an unhappy moment, I cried and cried. Then I walked away and forgot about it. I was a printing press feeder, and I didn't go to school until I got out of the army.

In the army I suffered anti-Semitism very badly. Before that I'd had a little taste of it. I went to work in a plant in Rockaway, New Jersey, as an ordnance inspector. I found a room with another worker, and remarks were made about my being Jewish to the people who rented it. There was also an incident in that ordnance plant where one of the inspectors was an uptight guy named Maxie Weinstein. It spread around the plant that this Jew-bastard was screwing things up. I can't claim to have been entirely naïve about irrational group hostility.

Later I found myself in a reconnaissance group with many southerners but also a larger group of Italian New Yorkers who were as virulent in their anti-Semitism as the others. They weren't anti–New York: they were anti-Semitic. I have a strong remembrance of getting into arguments, but never into fistfights. None of them would take me on physically. About that I never worried—my size protected me.

One guy, Edgar Strauss, was suited to the army like I'm cut out to take over AT&T. He was a naturalist who loved flowers. Edgar never *put* his clothes on; he draped them on. He was a military misfit. Some smart lieutenant gave him a plot of ground and let him work it. But he was much too happy—and what makes the damn thing so paradoxical is that Edgar was thoroughly atypical, nothing like what the stereotypic anti-Semite would think of as a Jew. He didn't bother anybody. If they turned him loose among the flora and fauna, he loved it. He was picked on and picked on. I stayed with him and protected him, but then someone tried to bait Edgar into a fight and Edgar didn't fight anybody. I stepped between them as a neutral. I didn't say anything. The bully turned on me—with real hatred. The "you-Jews-sticking-together" thing poured out of him. I got a little angry and moved over to Edgar's side. "Look, you were picking on him," and pretty soon I got very angry. When that happened he backed off, and one of his friends walked him away from me.

There were many incidents like that, anti-Semitic statements about our cowardice and Jewish unwillingness to fight. I was deeply upset by it. Here we were fighting the Nazis, and then this madness in the United States Army!

There was another painful thing. One didn't know what the hell he was doing in the army, especially if he didn't understand Nazism. I didn't actually get caught up in the war until two weeks after D-day, when we landed and saw what the Nazis could do. We had been waiting for the St. Lo breakthrough. In reconnaissance, you have to wait for a breakthrough. When it happens, you go forward and feel out the area. One was a French town called *Robert d'Espagne*, Robert of Spain. We were met by women and old men. They were hysterical. Just before us, the SS troops had burned the bodies of all the younger men and then gone on. I was not prepared for that or for the slaughter of the Jews. How could you be?

This is an aside but—I recently met with the new Consul General of Israel, who's a Brigadier General. We were a group of labor leaders, Jack Schenkman and a few others. As "part of the family," they went on to criticize Israeli policy. I thought some of it outlandish, and as I listened, I wondered why I wasn't more critical. They asked me to talk, and I realized, "I guess I'm an emotional party-liner in this case. Since I helped to liberate Buchenwald, I feel Zionism as a *faith*. I can never be critical of Israel." I hear about over-centralization of the Histadrut (federation of Israeli unions) and of course it exists. But I apologize it away. When their terrible crisis is over they can go back to normalcy. Meanwhile, I knowingly apologize. Every time I hear a criticism of the bureaucracy or whatever, I answer: "Look, they're fighting for their lives." My response goes all the way back to Buchenwald, to a traumatic meeting with those I helped escape from the Holocaust.

I regard myself as a "cultural Jew," whatever the hell that means. I was never religious, and I mentioned before I was never properly bar mitzvahed, but something happened to me in the Army of Occupation. The war was over, and soon after we entered a little town in Germany I went to all possible religious services. Along came Passover, or maybe it was one of the High Holy Holidays. I'm not sure (that shows how religious I am). But I *had* to go, it was a compulsion, I had to go to a synagogue and be with other Jews. It meant traveling about a hundred miles, but that's where I met Jewish soldiers and Jews who survived the Holocaust. There was a young, beautiful Jewish woman—I think she came out of Schwannsdorf. We began a tough conversation. I asked her, "Where do you want to go? To Israel?" she said, "Wherever I can be a Jew, that's where I want to go." It was the main thing—perhaps the only thing— "wherever I can be a Jew."

All this was burned into my consciousness: the liberation of Buchenwald, meeting a person like her, and three Czechoslovakian Jewish women who escaped from a concentration camp, living off potatoes in the forests. I got to know those women quite well. I sent extra food to them. As American conquerors we had taken over a lovely guest house and the vicious Germans were now drawing water for—and very subservient to—us, and our men were sleeping with nice middle-class German women. My buddy George and I were friends of these Czech women while we were having a time with the German women who never said anything to us. One day, there was a little German boy, seven or eight years old. I was playing with him, he was seated on my lap, and I sang songs to him while my Czechoslovakian friends looked out the window. He ran off and they called me, crying furiously, "How could you be so nice—?"

I told them that this is my natural instinct.

"How can you not be nice to a German child? Do you know what they did to *our* children?"

So finally I said, playing it very cute, "How come you're not upset when George sleeps with their women?" It came out that sex was a vile act to them, something nasty and rotten: if you slept with their women, that wasn't pleasure or love. But, to play with their children was love. It saddened me to think that love for a child was something you should not express in relation to a *German* child. On the other hand, if you slept with a German woman, you were committing a vile act. Sex had become vile to the Jews. What a horrible society; what perversion of values.

Sarah and I were married just before I shipped out. Upon my return I did a lot of serious reading, and we agreed that we would both go to school. We both went to Brooklyn College. Later I got my master's degree from the School of International Affairs at Columbia. Like most of that college generation, after going through the crucible of war, I was quite mature. I joined the American Veterans Committee (AVC)—it was a political hotbed where I finally got my education in Stalinism and Trotskyism and liberalism. The American Veterans Committee taught me a great deal. It was there that I came to know Gus Tyler. And it was there that I first got to express my own leadership abilities: I became head of the AVC of Brooklyn College, then head of all its college chapters. I began to watch the tugs and the pulls between Communists and anti-Communists; guys like myself, and Peter Strauss, or Bernie Bellush, were caught in the middle; we didn't like the Communists but neither did we like the way some people fought them. Brooklyn was unique. I started as a freshman and finished in two and half years. I'd come to class in the morning and there'd be the Socialists, the Communists, the Trotskyists, the Schachtmanites; I would take ten leaflets on saving the world. It was there that I learned about the Stalinists' duplicity, their fanatical adherence to the Soviet line. . . .

By 1948 I was sophisticated enough not to be taken in by the Progressive party line. I voted for Norman Thomas—but with no background. My wife belonged to the Young People's Socialist League. I was also unaware of a specifically Jewish labor movement. Of course, we went to work at Unity House, and I knew the ILG (International Ladies Garment Workers Union) and thought of it as a movement with Jewish leadership. David Dubinsky was there, and I was very close to Sascha and Rosie Zimmerman. Sarah and I really loved them, and they went out of their way for young people. Some of the oldest memories I have are of Sascha letting us know what callow youths we were and giving us the benefit of his broad wisdom.

Backing up some—it was in the army that I got my education overseas, in a way. A whole world opened up to me in faraway places like France and Germany and Czechoslovakia and Austria. Probably from Papa's leanings, I was a worker and I was fascinated by the labor movement. So after graduating from Brooklyn College, I wanted to get involved in international labor affairs.

Frankly, I would have gone to work for the ILG as an education director or something like that. But I got to know those people too well and realized that under the modern facade of their organization they were basically contemptuous of intellectuals. Gus Tyler was held in disdain. I still have strong memories of Gus and Bill Gomberg, one of the first labor industrial engineers, sitting off in a corner, huddled together, very critical of all that was going on. I had had high visions of Gus Tyler and his activity in the AVC, but I got some cruel awakenings. For example: the '48 election, which as you know was a peculiar one. Besides Norman Thomas and Harry Truman, there were those crazies, Henry Wallace and a Dixiecrat candidate. I attended one political meeting in which Gus Tyler was very vile about all the candidates except Norman Thomas. Dubinsky went for Truman. And then Gus voted for Truman. Since I have a pretty good memory, I can repeat verbatim Gus' remarks about Truman. "Well," he said, "you must remember, we've got a responsibility. When you have tens of thousands of members, you can't give them impractical choices." And it dawned on me that after all he had no power. Dubinsky made the decisions, and men like Tyler followed suit. It was an unpleasant fact of life that I learned at Unity House.

I also learned then that though the ILG was one of the more democratic unions, its staff was held in contempt. The ILG used them, and was proud of them, with the understanding that they were not to be taken seriously. It was a great staff: Mark Starr, Gus Tyler, and several others, were extremely good people. I was tempted by one ILG job, but somebody's nephew got it. Oh, yes, there was nepotism.

After that, I accepted a job in the Office of International Labor Affairs where I set up programs for incoming trade unionists. You can't work in international union affairs without doing a stint overseas. I luckily got a job as Labor Education Specialist in Turkey. I had hardly any training in labor education. It was the McCarthy era, 1954, and some beautiful anti-Communists were turned down for that job because they were Socialists. My working-class background stood me in good stead—I didn't belong to anything. How the hell could you fault me? Being a leader of the American Veterans Committee was okay, especially since in my

Brooklyn days I fought the Communist faction. But I really got hired because—you could almost be amused by it if it weren't so tragic—many better-qualified guys were knocked out on account of their connections with the Socialist party. Consequently, there I was in Turkey as a Labor Education Specialist, doing a fairly good job. They wanted to renew my contract and add good plums to it. But an offer came from Helmuth Kern of the Meatcutters: would I be his Assistant Director of Education in Chicago? I jumped at the chance. It meant going into the labor movement full time.

Traditionally, the organizers and the administrators of American labor came from the ranks; the professionals were mostly intellectuals from outside the movement. Now look what's happened. No one's paying attention to it, but think about the ILG and the Amalgamated—and their incredible transformation. Four lawyers—legal intellectuals—heading up the needle-trades unions. Nobody has investigated that phenomenon. Jerry Wurf really didn't come out of the industry; he was a professional intellectual trade-unionist.

The old hostility of intellectuals versus rank-and-filers has abated somewhat, but necessity is the mother of cooperation as well as invention. With more sophisticated requirements, you need the intellectual. Old-time labor leaders, who are now getting on, used intellectuals for trappings. It was the thing to do. Now, it's more than the thing to do; there's a real need.

Recently, at the Central Labor Council, Harry Van Arsdale presented an emotional monologue to this effect: "We don't have enough education for our people." And he meant it. I may have my disagreements with Harry, but not on this matter. The gist of his talk was that we must have more scholarships for the kids, our members have to be better educated, we've got to set up more schools.

My experience with the Meatcutters union was schizoid. First, let me give you the bottom line: it's the only job from which I was ever fired. Helmuth Kern, the director, was an excellent technician and a good professional. But very rigid. Helmuth had hardly any rapport with the rank-and-file; he made up for it by doing a superb technical job. That kept him going with Pat Gorman, who can be quite volatile.

The main reason I felt schizoid was that we worked out of national headquarters. I dislike national headquarters in general. Too much bureaucracy. But I loved getting out in the field, dealing with local union leaders. Helmuth was a bureaucratic guy. I wasn't. You can see that by looking at my shop. Moreover, I was a number two man; he called the shots. I won't burden you with how it came about, but Pat Gorman gave me a raise over Helmuth's objections and I was out on the streets.

I got involved in the Jewish Labor Committee for the first time through David Schacter in Chicago. The Jewelry Workers' number two man, also Jewish, was an activist there. We worked together and I was very comfortable with him. But the Meatcutters did more for me. And my desire to go back into international affairs had diminished. I was getting hooked on the American labor movement. After some months, I caught on with the Cook County local of my present union.

Getting back to New York was just a question of trade union needs. Jerry Wurf was a tough, authoritarian leader. For years he had been running for president of the national union, apparently unaware of the difficulties gestating in New York. He had as his replacement a lovely guy named Charlie Taibi. When Jerry made it to the top of State and County, a palace revolution took place in which Arnold Zander was deposed, Jerry became president—and asked me to be midwestern director. Taibi was suffering from a terminal sickness. To make a long story tragic, it soon became apparent to Jerry, as the newly elected president, that his power base—the largest council in the union, the New York City Council—was in terrible trouble. He was in Cincinnati at an executive board meeting when he got some more bad news about New York. They had just lost an important election. As a result, the social service workers left the union. Jerry was very upset—here was his power base; he had built New York; it had catapulted him to the national union presidency. He called me in Cincinnati. Would I go to New York and work with Charlie? I must admit, New York to me was what a public service union should be. I learned a great deal from Jerry. He represented the militancy that we didn't have in Chicago.

Why? It was very simple. Jerry believed that public service unions were no different from unions in the private sector. And against incredible odds, he built District Union 37. To go there appeared to be as exciting as it was fascinating.

On the spot, I discovered it was not all roses; it wasn't even romantic—for all the obvious reasons. Among others, that brilliant guy Wurf had let a lot of strings unravel. And Charlie, very sick, was incapable of providing the necessary leadership. So it was a nightmare. Some staff people put in as much as ten hours a day. Others paid no attention to the job at all. So there were situations such as hospitals, with a steady decline in membership although the area was growing. To top it off, I discovered I knew nothing about New York. It was an entirely different ballgame. In my entire life I never went through a period worse than those two years. And the first year was a real chamber of horrors. I'd get up at seven in the morning and work until twelve at night. The Jewishness in me was my release: eleven or twelve at night I'd go to Ratners and get some blintzes, or prowl the Lower East Side, just walking through the neighborhood for relaxation. Then I'd go to bed.

Lots of people didn't like Jerry. He was a tough, aggressive, irascible character. Then I came in—and they didn't like me either. A strike followed the social service election, only a few months after I reached New York in 1965. I could see, from Mayor Wagner to the people around him, the labor movement, Harry Van Arsdale—they didn't like Jerry. At that time, the union *was* Jerry, and I was the new kid on the block. They could easily kick my ass in and I knew it. They had a right to do that.

I was putting in twelve or fifteen hours a day; my family remained in Chicago, creating a double difficulty for me. At the end of two years, I learned to survive. I learned about New York. But you can't ask, "What did I learn?" Success, rather the accident of two black people, did it. Otherwise you wouldn't be talking to me now. What was "the accident of two black people?" I'll explain, but I've got to lead up to it.

We went into a strike of the Department of Welfare (as it was called at that time). All of the forces converged on Jerry, who returned to lead that strike. I didn't even know if my behind was screwed on. I simply walked the picket lines—which I did very well, having mastered that art in a hospital strike in Chicago, among other strikes. My job was Jimmy Higgins rank-and-file work. And I had a lot of pride in doing it. I went from picket line to picket line. The workers had seen me and I felt good about that. Jerry, with one of his assistants (later on Dave Dubinsky came in), finally pulled us out of the strike, but we were terribly weakened. After that, one of the key locals was the Hospital Workers. At that time it was the biggest local in the county, but deteriorating. The Teamsters and our union had about 50 percent of the membership each, with both organizations afraid to take on the other. It was like Russia and the United States with the atom bomb: if you thought you could kill us, well, we could kill you. But the Teamsters understandably and justifiably saw a very weak situation. The tough top man—Jerry— was now in Washington. We were just finished with a strike that all but crippled us. They were gaining and we were losing members in the hospitals. They filed for an election.

About this time, I was no longer number two man. Charlie had resigned, I had taken over, and the election became my baby. The head of the Teamsters' local was a black former hospital worker named William Lewis. I had imported Lillian Roberts from Chicago. She was also a former hospital worker. But in my mind, Lillian is probably the best rank-and-file trade unionist in this country. She became the field general as I became head of staff. And what Lillian smelled immediately was that the workers didn't want war. They wanted a union, they wanted decent wages, they wanted peace.

Then, using an idea contributed by Carl Scheer (an old Socialist and Chicago UAW official) on career development, she also presented that to the workers. With my assistance Lillian worked up a positive trade union program. The Teamsters, although they were the favorites, fought a completely negative battle. They talked about Lillian as the "outsider from Chicago." They made nasty little derogatory remarks about Jerry and State/County. While they conducted this negative battle, we told the workers about wages, working conditions, career development.

When the election campaign started, we were about fifteen-to-one underdogs, and even that was fifteen and out: nobody was betting on us. It was a night and day business, with Lillian in the field and me figuring out all the angles. I told Jerry at one point that if we lost, I would leave. I didn't feel I could build a union on top of such defeat. Well, we won by six to seven hundred votes, and from that point on, the union really developed.

Things began to turn my way. John Lindsay, that uncharacteristic Republican, ran for mayor, and he won at about the same time I began to feel my power. To anyone who's knowledgeable about labor relations, this coincidence was important. Why? Well, I'm still the new kid on the block. And on this block along comes a new politician with no commitment to do favors for the Old Guard.

Alex Rose, president of the Hatters union, was never seriously regarded as a labor man. In other words, *I* was the union guy involved with Lindsay; Alex was the Liberal party man. In 1969—Lindsay's second race—the two people given credit for winning it were Alex Rose and myself. Lindsay, Rose, and I worked together. Quite an interesting team. Well, necessity is the mother of many things—even of bastard children.

Any other politico would have had ties to the Old Guard, the labor movement, and lots of other people. As soon as Lindsay came in, the Teamsters began to fight the results of the hospital election. Lindsay had it certified immediately. Had Beame beaten Lindsay, we might still be fighting that group because of Beame's debts to so many labor people.

If anybody can show me that Lindsay was a disaster, I'd like to see it. My only difficulty with him was that I had a very high level of aspiration for the guy. I thought John Lindsay had the equipment, but that he never realized his potential. I must say that he was as good as or better than most pols. My sadness is that he never fulfilled all that was in him.

Any honest analysis of our contracts at the time would show that Lindsay's were the same as those of everyone else. To point

The New York Hospital Strike of 1976.   D.C. 37; AMERICAN FEDERATION OF
STATE, COUNTY AND MUNICIPAL EMPLOYEES.

at the Lindsay contracts as being costly is pure nonsense. Lindsay
did give us impartial grievance procedures and the same honest
collective bargaining that had been achieved in other areas. He
didn't play the political game, fragmenting the unions as Wagner
did. Lindsay hired Herb Haber, a professional mediator, a pro in
labor relations. From that vantage point, his administration was
fine. In this period our unions flourished. Yet, it's said that they
hated him. That's simplistic. Look: the Firefighters didn't hate
him; curiously enough, the Teamsters didn't hate him; the Sani-
tationmen didn't hate him. Gotbaum didn't hate him. District 37,
the largest local, didn't hate him. Even the Transportation Workers supported Lindsay in '69. Van Arsdale never liked him—no
question about that. Al Shanker's antipathy stemmed from the
teachers' strike of '68 which was a very special case. Did Lindsay
go wrong there? Well, I think everything went wrong, and Lindsay went wrong with it. He tried to recoup but couldn't.

   When it came to trade union rights, I was on Shanker's side.
I thought those rights were being negated. On the community's

side, take Sonny Carson. Both Shanker and I had utter disdain for Carson but Shanker used Carson to play to his own fears in the Jewish community. I do think Sonny Carson was wrong, but I don't think he was the black community. I don't think the black community was ever really involved in that strike. It was the period of black nationalism and black anti-Semitism. I believe Shanker used that sentiment. It's where he and I parted company. Still, the Rhody McCoys, who are weak human beings, were used by the Sonny Carsons. And there I sided with Shanker because the Carson stuff was antilabor.

I felt Basil Patterson handled himself very well, and there were others like him who didn't join the antilabor crowd. As for contracts, transfer rights, and job security, I was with Al all the way. When he stopped dealing with the community and found a formula, we disagreed. You've got to remember that the teachers were 80 percent Jewish and he played to their fears, which is where I left him. Bill Michaelson, of Retail-Wholesale, and I went to visit him once. Basically, our approach was, "Al, we have no quarrel with you, but you've got to sit down and talk." He was a wreck. He wouldn't talk, he wouldn't do anything.

I think he was scared. This strong, tough, troubled leader lost some of my own very strong belief in him. If it hadn't been for Bayard Rustin, I doubt that the strike would have been settled. Shanker was still holding back, exhausted and uncompromising, when Bayard finally said, "Al, either your friends will make the peace, or your enemies will make the peace. Listen to your friends." Only then did Al finally negotiate the end of that strike. This has to be said even though we had lots of difficulties with Bayard. He's part of the labor establishment, as far as I'm concerned. But Bayard's role in the teachers' strike was excellent.

I don't know if the strike conservatized Jews in New York. It did raise their fears. The strike brought Jewish antiblack feelings and black anti-Semitic feelings to the surface. That wise men should have prevailed and moderates mediated was one thing. They didn't. Al prevailed, and it made him a power. In the black community men like Carson and Rhody McCoy are out. To their credit the Basil Pattersons, who are moderate, moved in and are still around as powers in the black community.

There's a myth that our union is predominantly black and Hispanic. The myth was perpetuated by those who wondered, "Why is Vic so concerned about the black community?" In point of fact the power base of our union is ethnically Italian. I'm speaking of blue-collar workers, the laborers, the sewage treatment and motor vehicle operators. They hold the power. Of course we have white-collar workers too. But power to bring this city to its knees is blue-collar, Italian ethnic.

Blacks and Puerto Ricans at that time made up about 30 percent of the union. We had set up education programs; we said that the Teachers union was fighting for its life. We had Basil Patterson and Sandy Feldman talk to our education people in a debate. We aired everything. All this with an executive board whose largest part was Italian-American. I got a unanimous vote from them on the union's policies. And I wasn't then that strong with the group. In '68, I had only been with the union for three or four years. And Lillian did a great job with that. Here was a black who really called it as it was, who supported the Teachers union in terms of its rights. She would say quite openly, "It's nonsense about the whole black community feeling anti-teacher. Most blacks want their kids in school. They want the strike to be over." So Lil was an enormous asset once again. I also took a strong stand in favor of community participation, not what they call "community control," but what I call "administrative decentralization." Anyhow, we survived that one, too. As for teachers in New York City, Jewish, black, or pink, those who are sensitive to the needs of lower economic kids have a future.

If only out of self-interest, the white establishment ought to be raising the standard of living among blacks and Puerto Ricans. They are going to be a big piece of the plurality of New York, and if you want to stabilize it, you *can't* keep blacks and Hispanics at lower economic levels. You've got to do something substantial for them. Education is one way. Whether you own a department store or want to keep your kids in the schools, or you are eager to restore peace on the block—I'm not a Marxist, I'm not an economic determinist, but I know enough about economics to realize that it produces the crucial frame of reference. If you don't raise the standard of living, if you don't help stabilize the black and Puerto Rican community, you're asking for big trouble. By now the percentage of blacks in our union is pretty high but we've got black leadership. We've got Lillian and Charlie Hughes and a black staff. How many blacks does the ILG have on its executive board? How many black staffers are they picking up? There's the big difference. It's not that you have a Chick Chaiken in charge. There's a theory according to which the thoroughly depressed or the thoroughly uninvolved don't make revolutions, which only come from those who take a piece of the action and taste it. I suspect that in the ILG they have blacks in their classes and courses, but I don't think they constitute any part of the power mechanism.

To understand that you've got to look at what is happening in the Ladies Garment Workers Union. It used to have a quarter-million members in New York. Are they half that now? I suspect that if they were growing, qualitatively and quantitatively, there would be more ferment. The depressed industry is an important factor. On the other hand, one of the nicest things I heard from Chick Chaiken was that he intended to reach out and start training black and female leadership. That would be a New York City phenomenon.

Here we have a tremendous source of social consciousness and I think we can document this in terms of what exists today—and this is where I get so pissed off at the anti–New York people. We have evidence in New York of social welfare and social conscience. It's no accident that our people are taxed 21 percent of their income. We do it because we believe in social services. It's no accident we have homemaker programs, bilingual programs, rates that are higher than any place else in the United States. That's our tradition. It's part of what Irving Howe wrote about in *World of Our Fathers*.

It's a tradition of nineteen hospitals for the sick poor, the highest monetary rate for people on relief, and of taking care of the aged. To me, this *is* New York. We may be vulgar, we may be dirty, but we have more sensitivity about those in need than any goddam city in the United States.

I was sick when Hugh Carey went to Washington and apologized for having too many hospitals here. I'm sick for those people who apologized that we are living beyond our means when we have to pay 1.1 billion dollars for welfare and Medicaid to take care of the nation's poor who are escaping deprivation in Mississippi and Puerto Rico and everywhere else. We could have balanced our budget five times over if we didn't take care of Puerto Rico and the South. And we should take care of them! As we took care of the Jew and the Italian and everyone else who came here. This is the tradition I love. This, to me, is New York. And we're supposed to be hard.

It's not happenstance that New York developed a needle trades tradition. And a social welfare tradition. And a social democratic tradition. (I'm accused of being a social democrat—and I guess that's what I am.) I don't think it's an accident that so many people came here and found roots in New York. I've always been conscious of it.

David Dubinsky built a union almost out of nothing and it got citizens politically involved who had no previous contact with the social democratic tradition. I'm talking of the initial stages. Dubinsky was a true pro, an all around trade-unionist. His professionalism gave him tremendous influence with George Meany. Some people, with reason, think very negatively of the Dubinsky-Meany relationship. That's half of it, mostly related to foreign affairs. The other half is that Dubinsky imparted his concern for social services and domestic reform to George Meany. When I waited on tables in Unity House I used to see Dubinsky and Meany playing cards and talking very animatedly. On such occasions Dubinsky gave Meany more than sterile anti-Communism, and for that we must credit him. He built a union that gave him power in New York and in national politics. It was no small achievement. If trade unionism transcends its necessary bread-and-butter operations we have the Dubinskys and the New York atmosphere to thank for a large part of it.

16.

THE RANGE OF
THE NEW YORK
INTELLECTUAL

Irving Howe

GROWING UP in the Bronx I didn't feel Jewish, nor did I *not* feel Jewish. "Feeling Jewish" is something that occurs to people only when they already see some alternatives to being Jewish. Growing up in a Jewish family that spoke Yiddish, as I did, made it all a natural environment. I had no distinctive consciousness that there was any choice or alternative. I knew there were non-Jews but that didn't mean there was any alternative for me. Once you say, "Do you feel Jewish?" that already implies a problematic element. You feel "a little Jewish," you feel "less Jewish," or "more Jewish." But if you *are* Jewish, if it's your condition, your fate, your natural existence, then the question of *feeling* Jewish doesn't arise.

The distinction between religious and secular Jews has probably been exaggerated in historical retrospect and by various ideologues at both extremes. I think a good many Jews were like my father, neither religious nor antireligious; that is, they went to *shul* on Rosh Hashana and Yom Kippur, they kept a kosher house, they held two Seders on Passover. I doubt that my father went to *shul* otherwise, and he certainly didn't lay *tefillin* (phylacteries). He didn't try to define his relationship to God, for that would

Irving Howe was born in New York in 1920. A founding editor of *Dissent,* he is a historian and literary critic and Distinguished Professor at Hunter College. His *World of Our Fathers* (1976) won the National Book Award in history.

imply a degree of self-consciousness and possible alienation which wasn't present. I think if you asked my father whether he believed in God he would have been a little puzzled because what he really believed in was the presence of God as a force within Jewish life. For him, God was someone you spoke to. Whether God actually answered or even existed was a different matter. When he went to *shul* it was Orthodox. Reform was for the goyim or for the Germans—they were the same thing. We lived in a neighborhood that was 99 percent Jewish (only the janitors were non-Jews). First we lived in the West Bronx, which was middle class, and then in the East Bronx, which was working class, even lower. Unemployment during the Depression was bad, very bad. We didn't live quite on the worst street in the East Bronx but we lived fairly close to it. The *shul* consisted of a little storefront or a loft run by a poor rabbi trying to eke out a living. I was occasionally sent to *cheder* in the afternoon, and like most kids I rebelled against it. Then if there wasn't enough money to pay for *cheder,* I'd drop out and my father would make a pass at teaching me a little Hebrew. My bar mitzvah took place in the storefront *shul:* I went through the ritual, my mother baked a honey cake, a *lekach,* and the poor old guys there had something to eat that day. So if the bar mitzvah wasn't any benefit to me, it was a benefit to ten old men.

One didn't even know about Conservative congregations; the only congregation was Yiddish-speaking Orthodox. Plenty of Jews didn't go to *shul* at all, like the socialist Jews who were antireligious. But the notion we now have of three or more denominations was entirely out of our ken.

Two childhood incidents were important in my development. The more traumatic one took place in kindergarten. Yiddish had been my first language, but by then I spoke English because I was out in the street. The street, far more than the schools, was the strongest factor in our Americanization. It acted as a "counter-culture" to the home. In the West Bronx, the street was not rough as it was on the Lower East Side. Once, when I went to kindergarten, the teacher held up objects to identify, among them a fork, and I, already trying to distinguish myself, yelled out "*guppel,*" the Yiddish word for it. The other kids laughed at me. (How cruel kids can be: they're getting ready to be grownups.) That experience is one of the most vivid memories of my life. I felt terribly humiliated. I remember running home to my mother, crying and saying that I would never speak Yiddish again. In fact I didn't for a good many years, which was probably one of my first conscious decisions.

The other incident occurred a little later, when I was nine or ten. I was a good baseball player, even captain of the team. We played baseball in an empty lot at the end of our block, and my father, who had a grocery store on the main street of that neighborhood, sometimes came to get me because I was late. He would yell after me, "Oiving, Oiving"—which was his way of pronouncing my name, no great cause for shame but so it seemed to me at the time. And I was already embarrassed in relation to the other kids, whose parents might not have pronounced their names any better, but some of the kids with whom I played came from families that were already more Americanized than mine. A very remarkable fact: some of them had parents who were born in America and I envied them that position because I felt that they were more rooted, more set in this world. So, when my father would come, wearing his grocer's white apron, I would go home, running ahead to avoid being near him. It's one of the first tokens of shame of which I've since been ashamed.

We moved to the East Bronx when I was eleven. It was a much more homogeneous area, almost entirely immigrant working class. The social distance between the West and East Bronx was enormous. Today the West Bronx looks like a terrible slum, but then it had new, white brick buildings and we thought it was beautiful. We moved to the East Bronx when my father's business failed. First he had one grocery store, then he expanded and had two, and then both failed. He was suddenly dead broke. So we moved in with my grandmother who had an apartment in an old tenement on Jennings Street near Prospect Avenue. That street looked pretty much like the Lower East Side; the West Bronx did not. The apartment had five rooms, one for my parents. There was an unmarried aunt and an unmarried uncle. The uncle had a room and the aunt slept with my grandmother in one bed. I had a cot in the same room. No doubt this arrangement accounts for some of my subsequent psychic malformations. When I finally got a room of my own, that was a tremendous conquest.

When the stores folded up, my father became a customer peddler. Customer peddling is one of the oldest immigrant trades, if you can call it that. I remember that my father had yellow cards for keeping his accounts. He peddled dry goods—sheets, towels, and the like—mostly in immigrant neighborhoods, Italian, Irish, Slavic. Women would buy the stuff on credit, paying him a dollar a week or so. One reason he worked with these immigrant women was that they felt uneasy about going shopping. He made life easier for them; also it was on credit. But that didn't work out very well for him. He had unpleasant incidents, he got annoyed, his feet hurt. So he became a dress presser. Through various finaglings he got into a shop. My mother became an operator in the dress trade a bit later.

One reason that I've always been strongly attached to unions is that they made an enormous difference in my own life. My mother made 12 dollars a week as an operator when she started working. That wasn't as bad as it sounds today, but it wasn't very good either—65 or 70 dollars by current standards. My father did a little better. They were barely scraping by, and it was rough. They worked in a seasonal industry where you didn't calculate your wages over a fifty-two-week year: at best, you worked thirty-five or forty weeks. Then came the big strike in 1933, and my mother's salary went up to 27 dollars a week and my father's equivalently at least. You can't imagine what this meant. Suddenly we could have meat more often for dinner during the week. Suddenly, for example, my mother bought me a couple of shirts; I've always had a thing about shirts which probably goes back to that time. All the garment workers went out on strike. It was a Jewish strike: the ILGWU was largely a Jewish union. It had been decimated in the twenties by internal faction fights with Communists and by the general difficulties of organizing. Then came a tremendous revival. The union moved from virtual nonexistence to control of the whole trade.

My folks were what we call *folksmassen*—ordinary people, you know—with a little bit of religion and a little bit of leftish feeling, but hardly political at all. My father may have voted for

Norman Thomas once, but afterwards, like all such people, he became a Roosevelt man. Anyway, once the strike was called, everyone accepted an absolutely unquestioned assumption: you had to go out. Even my mother, who had never been on a picket line before, went out. The idea of scabbing was as inconceivable as conversion to Buddhism. What is, I think, interesting is the deep sense of solidarity in relation to this strike on the part of people who were not active unionists. Maybe occasionally they had to attend a meeting but they never really participated in the union. They had no political ideology. Yet it was assumed that to scab was to sin. They just went out on strike and it helped. Life became a little better. I had a shirt and a regular allowance of 10 cents a day! The benefits were immediately tangible. And also the tone of life at home changed: the feeling of extreme pressure eased up a bit.

I don't think people develop a social conscience directly out of their experience. Some idea has to intervene. I had been poor and still was but I didn't have any *idea* that I was poor. I didn't know what that idea meant, though I knew what the experience was. The idea started to develop in high school when I really began to read. There were excellent teachers then, even in junior high school, some of them slightly to the left. Their jobs were considered plums—you made 40 dollars a week in regular pay and you could go to Europe every other summer. Things opened up through those teachers. And I began to read. One very strong memory of mine is that I began to pick up a magazine called *Today* in which Sherwood Anderson was printing reportage from North Carolina about textile workers. Afterwards it became a book called *Puzzled America*. The articles were very moving accounts, in Anderson's impressionistic style, of how wretched life was for textile workers. Now, I don't know if the life of the North Carolina textile workers was any more wretched than the life of the Jewish garment workers in the East Bronx; but it was to the wretchedness of the workers of North Carolina that I responded with great imaginative urgency. I remember shedding tears about their conditions while taking utterly for granted the conditions I lived in. But once this experience opened me up to the idea of poverty, I talked to my teachers about these reports of Anderson's and other things I read. Only then did my mind turn back upon the life that *we* were leading. I recognized that we, too, were in poverty.

In my way, I experienced "the trauma of sharply fallen circumstances." If you look at the careers of American writers like Hawthorne and Melville you see the pattern. For a kid, moving from the West Bronx to the East Bronx was an overwhelming change of circumstances. In the West Bronx I was gregarious, on the street, carefree, a baseball player. We move to the East Bronx and I don't go out of the apartment; I have great difficulty adjusting to "toughies" on the street. There were gangs that probably weren't so different from those in the West Bronx, but to me they seemed different. I yearned to get back. On Saturdays I'd visit my old friends. To save the nickel carfare I would often walk and probably waste more money on shoe leather. It was several miles from the West Bronx to the East Bronx.

At eleven and a half or twelve I began to read voraciously. Apropos of that, one incident stands out in my memory. When I got scarlet fever I sent my father to the library to bring home— I blush to remember—the collected poems of Milton, Wordsworth, and Keats. Just think: the librarian looks at him with considerable disbelief, for which I don't blame her. "What the hell's going on here—this man with a Jewish accent comes for the collected poems of Milton, Wordsworth, and Keats." But she gives them to him. I guess she has some idea of these crazy Jewish kids. And he brings the books home. I was laid up for about six weeks, and in a feverish condition I read just about all of these three poets. You know, the memories I have of reading certain poems like "Samson Agonistes" over forty years ago are more vivid than things I read a year ago. "The Eve of St. Agnes" is another. Keats' candied romantic diction made a big impression on me. Overall, such things disrupt the normal course of existence. They throw up elements of consciousness: they introduce uncertain or problematic factors into one's life.

In high school the teacher customarily pitched his class to the best kids. If you weren't good enough in a given subject, you didn't resent it because you felt it was appropriate that he should pitch it to the best kids. Whoever was good in English had his moment; somebody else got his in Biology. There was no notion of working for the lowest common denominator. Junior high was almost entirely Jewish. At Clinton we were mostly Jewish. Each class had a high sense of morale. I have no recollection of behavior problems or anything like that. Some of those teachers were at least as good as the people you now have in colleges and perhaps a shade better.

My folks' reaction to school was pretty typical. They had a kind of blind, sweet trustfulness. They didn't really know what the hell it was all about. There was something like a semi-religious faith that books were good. I don't know if they could have said why. There were no books in our house—none, literally none. But while books were regarded as intrinsically good, my parents also felt a great deal of shyness about school. When my mother had to attend a Parents' Day she was very hesitant about it. Nor was this unusual. To visit the school embarrassed my folks because they felt they couldn't speak English well and they were terribly respectful of teachers, really in awe of them. They'd come now and then but try to stay in the background.

Parents like that entrusted their kids to the schools: they said, in effect, "You Americanize them, you educate them, you transform them." They entrusted us to *goyish* schools with preponderantly *Jewish* teachers. Afterwards immigrant parents found that, by their standards, they had entrusted the kids too much and had lost them; but that's another story. The point I want to make concerns their total trust in the idea of schooling.

I met young socialists in high school. They were sons of ILGWU organizers. I was already susceptible to their political ideas, and so I joined the YPSL (Young People's Socialist League) when I was just fourteen. Overall I think it's significant that people don't move in a direct line. A certain kind of consciousness has to intervene; it enables you to generalize about an experience of your own that you previously took for granted.

In the thirties there were tremendous strikes. The ILGWU and the Amalgamated, which had been virtually paper organizations, now had 20,000 members. The ILG in those early days during the thirties couldn't even pay the rent on its offices and the telephones were disconnected. Imagine. And then suddenly mass expansion as a result of the Wagner Act, and the unions, at this point still somewhat socialistic, became a great force in the city. Also they became a force in the Jewish neighborhoods. There was a rise in morale, life became a little better, and as life becomes better there is more political activity, more radical consciousness. I think that, characteristically, radicalization occurs in times of improvement, not in times of despair. When I became a YPSL, I was in a good high school, DeWitt Clinton, where we had a little clique of twelve or fifteen kids. Then I got involved in a neighborhood group that met at the Workman's Circle headquarters. Thus began my distinguished career of uninterrupted political failure . . .

Jewishness was really very important in becoming radical before college. In the East Bronx at this time the Socialist party frequently got the second largest vote. Not when Roosevelt was running. In 1932, I think, Thomas came in ahead of the Republicans in some of the districts in the East Bronx, but never after that. In the vote for assemblymen, congressmen, etc., ours was the second party. But it was poorly organized: the Communists, on the other hand, were quite strong and tightly disciplined. I grew up in my early teens with the notion that one of the major interests and excitements in life was the street corner meeting, which has virtually died out as an institution. Any evening when you walked on Wilkins Avenue near Freeman Street station there was a street meeting, usually Communist, sometimes Socialist. When I became active in the YPSL, we would hold meetings of our own. I was an atrocious speaker. I would begin by yelling at the top of my lungs and lose my voice in five or six minutes. I was fourteen or fifteen at the time.

But there was one guy, an old friend named Irving Panken, who's now an organizer for the UFT (United Federation of Teachers). He was an extraordinarily brilliant speaker. In five minutes he'd have two-hundred people around him. I could lose those two-hundred in two minutes. The street corner meeting was a remarkable institution which formed part of Jewish life. When it was warm outside and there was nothing else to do, Jews would stroll about, listen, be interested, skeptical, and amused. For them, it was a form of entertainment. Of course, we had to know how to handle hecklers. At that, too, Panken was brilliant. He always knew how to shut them up, especially the major hecklers, who were Stalinists. Occasionally there would be a wise guy right-winger advancing the kind of arguments that Robert Nozick recently codified in a very learned book—such as, "Well, if Henry Ford worked for his money, why shouldn't his children have the right to the fruits of it?" We would then go off into a long explanation about surplus value and the like. This kind of contact provided training in many ways. Thus, although I was never good at speaking out of doors, it prepared me to speak indoors. Indoors I was a good speaker, outdoors not good—I don't know why. Panken, by comparison, was brilliant out of doors and indoors he was lousy.

When there was a strike in a little bakery shop on Hoe Avenue, about half a mile from our house, we naturally were on the workers' side. There was a meeting every night in front of the bakery. Once I got up and started yelling when there wasn't a soul in sight. August Claessens, who was an old Socialist agitator, came over, and when he started talking, in a quiet conversational tone, out of nowhere came a crowd. Anyway, about three or four days later, my father, whose attitude toward my political activity was very mixed—on the one hand, he thought it might get me in trouble; on the other, he was sort of proud, you know, his kid was a bigmouth—suddenly at dinner, with a certain sardonic touch, he said to me, "What do you have against the man who owns the bakery shop? He's a poor Jew, trying to earn a living and you want to ruin his business." I remember blushing and wondering how he knew. It turned out that one of his *landsleit* (immigrants from the same community) had seen me on the street corner and had stopped and listened. Then he called up my old man and told him about it.

The Jewish milieu was essential for such street meetings as we ran because there was a tacit code about disruption. The Stalinists would heckle us; we would heckle them, too. And yet, there was an unwritten understanding: no violence. That was very Jewish. The garment center was different, but in our neighborhood it wouldn't have looked good to break up a Socialist meeting. We Socialists never tried to break up meetings. We truly believed in free speech. And we had no sense of danger. A little later violence did emerge in different ways. But in 1934 or 1935, the Communists were trying to be friendly with the Socialists. When relations worsened, there would be a little shoving and pushing, but no rough stuff. I remember that one of our girls had her glasses broken jostling with a Communist lady, a Jewish woman. The girl burst out crying: her mother would give her hell and where would she get the money to have those glasses fixed? The Communist lady who had been denouncing her in the most vitriolic terms suddenly became a Jewish mother who forgot that she was facing an adversary. She offered to pay for new glasses. This is how elements of common experience undercut political differences.

If we spoke in Jewish neighborhoods, there was rarely trouble. Venturing into non-Jewish neighborhoods to expand your social base meant taking your life in your hands: in the Bronx the non-Jewish neighborhood meant the Irish neighborhood which was then heavily Coughlinite. (Father Coughlin was an anti-Semitic priest of the thirties.) Those people didn't like a bunch of sheeny kids coming in and telling them about politics. We used to wish we had an Irish speaker—not likely in the Socialist movement! And when we went up to Fordham Road, to a totally Irish area, we had good reason to be nervous. Later on, when I got more involved in politics, I would attend meetings in Manhattan which had essentially the same pattern. In a Jewish neighborhood you might get called *pisher* but you were all right. The worst that could happen was that somebody would throw a tomato, but you could hardly call that violence.

We roamed around the whole borough, but with some care. Why the circumspection? We didn't articulate the reason because I guess we felt uneasy about admitting that fundamentally we disliked leaving the Jewish neighborhoods. In later years when we made occasional incursions into Yorkville, which was a Nazi neighborhood, we were in for really serious trouble. We would go to Harlem without *any* sense of danger, walking the streets and entering the Apollo Theater on 125th Street quite often. Five or six kids would hold a street meeting in Harlem. I don't know if we made a dent in the listeners, but they didn't make a dent in us either: that's the significant part of the story. There was no violence in Harlem! Irish neighborhoods were much more frightening.

In political campaigns we thinned out the ranks. To have as many meetings as possible we'd send out a few kids to hold a street meeting and then we toured the speakers. A guy like Irving Panken would speak four or five times a night in different places. I'd be used as a kind of anchorman just to keep the goddam platform there. The school, the street, *any* place was an arena for political activity.

I entered CCNY in 1936. It was understood that a Jewish boy like me would go to college. How could it be otherwise when the central credo of the immigrant world was, "my son should not work in a shop"? That was the beginning and the end of all desire and all wisdom. A great many of my contemporaries went to college because it was free. No fees. Second, there was nothing else to do. The best we could expect was to work as a shipping clerk at 15 dollars a week in the garment center. My parents, who were there, had had a rich taste of it. The thought of my doing the same horrified them, and they were right—it was a wretched job. I was not very strong physically anyway, and I was bright! So I went to college. The cost of college came to about 30 cents a day: 10 cents carfare and 15 or 20 cents for food. It's true that sometimes I had to collect nickels for leaflets. One guy, an old comrade who now lives in Detroit—Martin Glaberman—used to bring enormous numbers of sandwiches. A leaflet cost about 45 cents—a ream of yellow paper 19 cents, a stencil a dime, the rest for ink. If we had to collect money for a leaflet we would borrow some of Martin's sandwiches and contribute the nickels. All of us took it for granted that college was an arena for political as well as intellectual activity. We assumed there was considerable connection between the two.

City College had those famous alcoves. In the first alcove we were all anti-Stalinists, which meant Socialists and Trotskyists or

Socialists like myself moving toward Trotskyism, and a small number of Lovestonites who were even then sort of in hiding, and a small number of right-wing Socialists. Stalinists had the second alcove, which was just a few feet away. The alcove was my home for four years because unless there was an exceptionally good teacher, I didn't go to class very much. After all, I had important business to attend to, political business. Frequently, I'd go to class, wait till they took the roll, then walk out and return at the end of the hour. Whether the teachers knew about this, or cared, I don't know. The atmosphere during the period I was at City College was intellectually intense. I had a fully formed "worldview." I thought of myself as a Marxist by the time I was sixteen or seventeen.

Morris Cohen and I brushed against each other—note my modest way of putting it—only I knew that we brushed against each other and he didn't. We were frightened of him because he was said to be the one guy you had to watch out for in debate. Your ordinary liberal professors would not come over like lions, while we were really sharp. The Stalinist teachers we tormented. Once I read a composition aloud in the class of a Stalinist teacher. It was about the persecution of writers in the Soviet Union. I kept reading until the guy was going out of his mind. But all he did was correct the punctuation. So that was fair game. Cohen, of course, was a brilliant and formidable figure. He thought of himself as a socialist, too. Or rather, he wasn't hostile to socialism. He was hostile to orthodox Marxism. He took on opponents from the right and the left; when he eviscerated the Communists we were beside ourselves with delight.

Even though we knew that a scrap with Cohen meant he'd tear us to pieces, we all adored him. Everyone did—except the Stalinists, and even probably some of them, too. He was, after all, for the students against that wretched, reactionary administration. He believed in freedom: even when there were excesses—like a riot or two a week—he still defended us. In 1937–38, in the antiwar strike, I was on the committee for our side, the Socialist-Trotskyists. He was the mediator between us and the Stalinists. For our speaker we wanted James Burnham, and the Stalinists said no. We went to see Cohen and I said, "Look, each side has the right to choose its own speaker; if they want to bring Joseph Stalin himself, we don't object. But they can't tell us whom we should choose." He said, "That's a good liberal principle." But then, after saying that, he turned to me and, with a really wicked grin and that Yiddish accent, he said, "Byt vy do you vant to bring such a bad philosopher to speak?" The idea that Burnham was a bad philosopher came to me as a bolt out of the blue.

There was one professor, Oscar Janowsky, who was known to be consciously Jewish, and we stayed away from him. Cohen maintained a distinct Jewish aura. We looked at that as an amiable eccentricity. It didn't matter much because with Cohen it was display, intellectual bravura, that counted. There was a decided rejection of Jewishness at this time. Our party names, the pseudonyms that we took, made that clear. There was deep, blind hostility to the Zionist movement—although it's interesting again that life was richer than ideology.

There was a left-wing Zionist group at City College called Avukah, led by Seymour Melman, whose political path has crossed mine for almost half a century. Seymour then, as now, had a fantastic tongue. He was young and strong and when he started talking you could hear him a mile away. He was our political ally, and in spite of disagreements about Zionism we worked together on concrete political issues. We were good friends because Avukah was moving toward us politically and anyhow they were nice kids. We would work together in anti-Stalinist campus politics. The Stalinists were very large; they must have had four or five hundred members including many professors. We had no professors. That was a handicap for us, but it also meant that we had to bone up intellectually. By 1937 there was an edict from the Young Communist League that they were not to speak to us—no more debates: "You don't talk to class enemies and fascists." That order put them in a very tough spot because the average wise-guy kid would taunt them with, "What's the matter? You afraid to argue?" We'd say, "Come on, talk with us." Or we'd invade their alcove and try to pick an argument.

When we made inroads into the Stalinists in 1937–38, the YCL got nervous and sent down Joe Clark, one of their big-shot leaders. Clark spent a month on the campus, and we gave him

Political rally at City College in the 1930s.   CITY COLLEGE OF NEW YORK.

a miserable time. His mission was to shore up the ranks against defection. We had regular meetings. Norman Thomas would come to speak; and Max Shachtman was always a great favorite because he fitted in so naturally with the wise-cracking style. It may have been '36 or '37 when I first heard Shachtman speak. He debated Morris Schappes. What an act of destruction! Schappes wasn't quick on his feet, although he was not altogether a foolish man. Max was young and vigorous. I never heard such a barrage of rhetoric, invective, wit, humor, polemical annihilation.

But the Jewishness at this point was suppressed, tacit, with elements of shame included in it and then rationalized by young minds. On Jewish identity—well, we regarded ourselves as internationalists, as cosmopolitans. No doubt we didn't understand the ordinary rebellion of adolescents that was going on within us. But politics gave that stage an ideological justification. Also, we

277

had large ambitions about winning over the American working class, and really that wasn't going to be done by a lot of "Jew boys." Jews would have to be content to play the background music. This problem existed in all the radical movements—Socialist, Communist, Trotskyist.

I was still living at home at that point. I *had* to live at home. Everyone lived at home. I didn't know one kid who left home. By now my mother and father were a little unhappy about my role in the movement. But it was too late because, although I lived at home, I really had emancipated myself at a very early age. By fourteen or fifteen I was on my own. There was nothing they could do about it. They blinked, and they hoped, and they deluded themselves, but finally the important thing was that I went to school and would get a college degree. (What I would do with it was another question.) I was no exception: Irving Kristol, whom I had, perhaps unfortunately, recruited to the YPSL, lived in Brooklyn, at home. There was no possibility of living anywhere else.

I felt some sense of conflict between home and school but, then again, the whole idea of escaping from Jewishness is itself a crucial aspect of Jewish experience. It goes right back to Salomon Maimon and no doubt before. I remember feeling ashamed of bringing my friends to the house. First, there was no space; it's hard for anyone to imagine what the space problem was like. There was literally no place to sit. You *had* to be on the street, or in school, or in the party office—which became a hangout: that's where we spent Saturdays, for example. I felt that my parents would be uneasy with my friends, and my friends would be uneasy with my parents because my parents would remind them of *their* parents. There was an unspoken understanding: we rarely went to one another's homes.

When I think of some of these things I still feel embarrassment and shame. But now I feel it in different ways. I felt embarrassed in relation to my parents, but also felt ashamed at feeling that embarrassment because I knew there was no intrinsic reason for it. The feeling was morally disreputable, but I couldn't help it. It could be described as virtually inevitable for any kid in an immigrant family. If you look at Hutchins Hapgood's book, *The*

Spirit of the Ghetto, you'll see that in 1902 he noticed the same thing. It's triggered when your father yells "Oiving" instead of "Irving." Things like that take on an importance you only later learn to regret.

Today, of course, I know that, morally speaking, my parents were probably better than some of the kids in relation to whom I felt embarrassment, and now I feel there was much that was inauthentic in the response that I was making. We had really no Jewish consciousness. If anyone had told us we were trying to hide what we really were, we would have laughed or sneered or become angry. We had a worldview and the fact that I was born Jewish was an accident; it wasn't really something major in my experience. But as I look back it's clear to me that in many ways it was major.

I know people in Detroit and in Chicago who seem to me to have come out much the same way. The intensity, the radicalism were there, too. But the street corner meeting was probably unique to New York. And I suspect the sheer thickness of Jewish life in New York was the crucial factor. You could virtually live out your whole life in New York, as my parents did, among Jews. The only contact with gentiles such people as my parents' generation had was with the schools, with the kids, or when they went to vote.

Within the movement some gentiles were certainly significant. And once we went to City College there were gentiles, though we Jews were the majority all the way through. But then there were experiences where it became clear to us that we were not the majority, once we began to roam around the city. Alfred Kazin describes that in his work. We found that the East Bronx was not typical, that there were large sectors that were not Jewish. The majority of teachers in City College were not Jewish. Authority and power in the city and the world were not Jewish. The closer we came to authority and power the more we had to learn the limits of the Jewish community. And, in fact, if you wanted to succeed, either in radical politics or in your own career, you had to get past the limits of the Jewish world.

This was then in my mind in *certain* ways. We understood that if we wanted to build a socialist movement in America we couldn't confine it to the East Bronx and the East Side. The whole dilemma of Jewish socialism which had been so strong in New York was that it could never get out of the Jewish community. So we understood that it was necessary to thrust out, and that was one of the things we talked about endlessly in the movement. I really had, I think I can say honestly, at that point no career ambitions in the ordinary sense. First, I had no expectations of *ever* having a job. I remember when we graduated from City College in 1940, I think I was sitting next to Irving Kristol and Earl Raab, and some men gave graduation speeches about "careers lying ahead of you," and we burst out laughing because it seemed so preposterous, so irrelevant. Not only were there few jobs, but a war was coming.

Even as I was a leader of the socialist and semi-Trotskyist group, I was also an English major because it struck me as the easiest major, where I could bullshit the most. But surely there was also some kind of native interest. I remember taking a course in Spenser. The man who taught it was a poor teacher. In general, the students were better than the teachers, who were overworked, you see. They taught fifteen hours a week. They were worn out. And the administration had hired a lot of palookas. It was a mediocre faculty, with a few stars here and there. I turned in a Spenser paper which was pretty crude stuff—a Marxist analysis of Spenser's *Epithalamion*. The teacher gave me a B − and wrote on the paper, "The trouble is you confuse a sunset with the decline of civilization," which wasn't a bad comment. Still, I was already sophisticated. Remember, we were "highbrows" and the Stalinists "lowbrows." Trotsky had taught us not to treat literature in crude political terms. I had written the paper in that vein. I knew it was no good; it was a lapse. On the other hand, I remember a course in critical theory where we read Aristotle's *Poetics* line by line for two-thirds of a semester. It was wonderful. I became deeply involved and wrote a hundred-page term paper on, of all things, Max Eastman's criticism—hardly worth all that space. The teacher understood what kind of kids we were and he was impressed. I got an A on that.

Even in literature I wasn't all that exceptional because I learned from the political milieu that people had intense cultural and intellectual interests which they tried to reconcile with politics. There was Noah Greenberg who became a distinguished musician, my first teacher of music, so to say, and a damned good one. We went to his house where he would rant and rave about why Schnabel was superior to Serkin. And if he ever caught me listening to a record of Serkin that was, almost, the end of our friendship. He was an absolutely brilliant music teacher and he was deeply involved in politics, in the Seamen's union. On Saturday nights we'd go to his house and listen to records, and he was wonderful about music. So you see, I wasn't all that distinctive in having other interests.

The anti-Stalinist left was very small and isolated, and just because it was an ideological sect it, far more than mass movements, had to feed upon intellectual issues. What else did we have? So, at the age of eighteen or nineteen I may not have read Joyce, but I was already sneering at YCLers for reading "proletarian" junk and doing so in the *name* of Joyce. Edmund Wilson's *Axel's Castle* made an enormous impression on us; I remember borrowing that book from a YPSL and saying, "Boy, this is it." And it was.

I read the very first issue of the anti-Stalinist *Partisan Review*. We felt that journal was a major accession to our side. Distinguished intellectuals, famous people, major writers. The first issue was a slam-bang issue that had stuff by Wilson, Delmore Schwartz's great short story, "In Dreams Begin Responsibilities," James Farrell, Philip Rahv, Lionel Trilling, and others. I read that issue from cover to cover, with passion.

One reason some of us were especially attracted to *Partisan* was that it gave us a formula for reconciling the two sides of our own experience. We had a formula for that, too, according to which you had to distinguish between a writer's literary work and his politics. You couldn't dismiss a writer just because of his politics. And we had another rationale, namely that T. S. Eliot, though reactionary, had many profound observations and insights into the decadence of society. And I guess we were basically right about that.

As for my living outside New York, well, that was a problem because the radical movements tried to do "colonizing." Young people would pick up and move to Detroit, Youngstown, Akron, or any other industrial center and get jobs in factories. You weren't forced to do it, but you were pressured. Some people resisted. I didn't get involved in it because when I was twenty-one I was editing the paper, *Labor Action,* for about three-quarters of the year. I was facile with the pen and I turned out vast amounts of copy, much of it more or less grammatical. Then I got drafted.

In small ways, I felt more Jewish in the Army. I encountered a few anti-Semitic incidents and insulting remarks, but there wasn't very much of that. It would be an exaggeration to say I was tormented by it. And I had my rationale. None of us denied that anti-Semitism existed; we simply had a different understanding of its cause and meaning. And its magnitude. Jean Malaquais, who published his *War Diary,* reported a lot of anti-Semitism in the French army. He was very upset by it. I remember liking the book but being somewhat puzzled by Malaquais' emphasis because I had not observed large-scale anti-Semitism; some, yes, but nothing very serious.

But could I conceive of living outside of New York? Actually, I did live away for about fifteen years, while always feeling that I was more or less in exile. Implicitly all of us were very attached to the idea of New York, but it didn't come into the open.

It does make a difference to me where I live now. The myth of New York makes the difference. By the myth I mean a group of interesting people. A myth isn't a lie; it's a reality that takes on a kind of enlarged character. After a while it became clear to me that I belonged to a generation called the New York intellectuals. These people don't necessarily have to see, or talk to, one another. They still have certain kinds of common experience.

These intellectuals did not think of themselves as merely literary, but rather as intellectuals who wrote about everything, often presumptuously. As we, in the New York literary gang, used the term "literary," it always implied a very wide scope. To be "literary" meant to write about politics, about society; we didn't mean just writing about poetry. In our sense of the term a literary man took the world as his province: he was an *homme de lettres.* We didn't use that phrase—it sounded pompous—but that's what we really meant.

Lionel Abel many years later said something with which we all would agree. He said, "Literature is too important a matter to be entrusted to literary critics." And he was quite right. Yes, we were all antiacademic. Science we didn't know about; that was a blind spot. Scientists seemed very dull and unimaginative. The socially conscious scientist was a creature who came on the scene only after the war. Science didn't figure in our imaginations at the time.

In some sense New York may well have been an impediment to certain kinds of career advancement. Not only I but others like me are so caught up with the idea of New York that certain job opportunities probably don't even come our way because people assume we won't leave. It *would* be terribly hard to leave. I've been away from New York and it's very boring. You can take the same group you find interesting here and put them in Stanford and they're not interesting. You can take a group of people from Stanford and put them here and they become more interesting. There really is a difference. That is, the atmosphere here shapes the people, it shapes one's life.

This sense of vitality was evident to us even in the Bronx. New York was the political center of the movement. This was where the brains were. And whereas various leaders would go out and become organizers in different cities, secretly—and perhaps not so secretly—they weren't very happy about it. It had to be done, but it too was looked upon as an exile, a matter of putting in your time, doing your duty. After the war, it was proposed that I go out to be the organizer in San Francisco. I really didn't want to go. New York was where the brains were. And it still is.

In some ways the city's gone down culturally. Still, New York happens to be the home of George Balanchine, one of the great cultural figures of our time. In my judgment he's as good as Picasso and Stravinsky. It's something to be able to live five minutes away from that genius, to go and see his work.

The ballet is a recent passion of mine. It's interesting to remember now how little connection we had in those early years with the so-called cultural advantages of the city. We never went to the ballet. I didn't see an opera until I was in my late twenties. We used to go to free concerts at the Metropolitan Museum. A man named Mannes, Marya Mannes' father, used to conduct. We'd sit on the stone there and listen. But if you had to pay, we just couldn't afford such things. One of the first great cultural experiences I remember was a series of three concerts by Arthur Schnabel when he did all-Beethoven programs.

I have been asked whether anything Jewish still holds me to New York. My whole life, I suppose. The whole style of life is Jewish-connected. The people I know, my friends. I have thought about what would happen to me if, heaven forbid, my friends were to go. Would the city still mean as much to me? Probably not. If Meyer Schapiro left for Florida or California, obviously the city would mean less to me. I don't see Meyer for three or four months at a clip—still the fact that he is here means a lot. If I need to know something, *anything,* I can always call him up.

But there aren't many minds like his coming up in the younger generation. It may sound vain and childish now, but we thought we should know everything. "Everything" didn't really mean everything, but it meant a great many things. I felt inadequate that I was not so hot in economics or that Delmore Schwartz would talk about certain kinds of poetry that I didn't know. We had, I'd say, a mania for range; that's why when I say literary intellectual I mean something other than a critic. We used to make fun of the guy who spent ninety-six pages analyzing a twelve-line poem, when in that space you could have analyzed the entire works of Dostoyevsky. Meyer, I would say, is the ultimate example of the whole idea of range and scope. On a more modest level somebody like Danny Bell lives by the same notion. Behind this is a very profoundly Jewish impulse: namely, you've got to beat the goyim at their own game. So you have to dazzle them a little. I remember as a kid hearing old stories about medieval disputes between rabbis and popes; it was taken for granted that the rabbis were smarter than the popes. The problem was how did the rabbi beat the pope in an argument without making it too obvious, so that the pope wouldn't cut his head off. In effect, without knowing it, we would repeat many of the same patterns.

Just as in some sense we were repeating Salomon Maimon and Heine.

I went back to Yiddish literature in the early fifties. When I was growing up there were Yiddish newspapers that served, you might say, as magazine-journals. I was able to read the Yiddish paper and sometimes I would read it on the sly because some of it was very amusing and because after I began to get a little more intellectual I found to my astonishment that I could get more out of *Der Tag* than out of the American papers. I didn't know a thing about the Yiddish writers. However, if there happened to be a story by Sholom Aleichem in the paper I would have read it. My father would have read it, too. He read the semi-Zionist paper. It had serials, often on a low level, but also literary pieces, stories, columns. It was weak on news, but strong on commentary, analysis, discussion.

In the fifties, when I started reading Yiddish literature as such, I loved it and saw its literary value. (And I suppose also that I might have had some small opportunistic motive: I noted it was something that nobody else was working on or paying attention to.) I wrote a little piece on Sholom Aleichem for *Commentary*. Then I got a note from Eliezer Greenberg, who became my collaborator over the decades, saying that he thought I'd make a good partner. I was struck by his charm and erudition, and we did make good partners.

I don't really know *exactly* why I returned to the Yiddish writers—for literary or Jewish reasons. The Holocaust was part of it, but with a delayed impact. At war's end we didn't know much about the Holocaust. *Commentary* only began to print very valuable material about the Holocaust in the late forties. It took a couple of years for a horror of such immensity to sink in. Also, it may be that by then I had become less ideological and more responsive morally. And perhaps things that had been suppressed started to come out. That's only speculation.

The dispute over Hannah Arendt's book about Eichmann played an enormous role in my consciousness, in our consciousness. And though I still have just as sharp an objection to that book, I also feel that unwittingly it served a great purpose. The book was like a therapeutic session where you discover that, welling up within you, there is a great mass of feeling that you have not known, that had been suppressed.

The book was an event. Suddenly Lionel Abel wrote a wild, passionate essay. We had an incredible *Dissent* meeting on account of which Hannah wouldn't forgive me for years. It was an extraordinary meeting, with Lionel pounding the table, excitement in the air. We saw Hannah's question as a point of honor, an issue that many of us had tended to evade. We had been slow in responding. But now, when she said that to some extent even the victims had been at fault—that forced our guilt to such an extreme point that we had to fight. The passions that Hannah Arendt's book aroused in us were overwhelming. I cannot think of anything since then that harassed me so much except perhaps the Vietnam War. You might say that it was a tacit recompense for our previous failure to respond. Some people taunted, us, "Ah, you've suddenly become Jews." Those people who *had* been involved had a right to taunt us. I remember Marie Syrkin who, although she was always a dear friend, teased me in a gentle way about this and laughed, but she was pleased that I could be bothered.

I would be lying if I said I was tremendously excited by the formation of Israel in 1948. It didn't, at first, touch me very much per se—it got to me only later, when it was in danger. I was for the state; I thought it was okay. But I wasn't so deeply stirred emotionally as I would be in the last fifteen years. There was another occasion, at Brandeis in 1960, that highlighted what was happening. I debated Oscar Handlin on the Eichmann kidnapping. That was also a wild debate, and at the end everyone was angry. I defended the right of Israel to take Eichmann out of Argentina. Handlin denounced it as a violation of international law. Brandeis University was hardly the ideal locale for his point of view. I had a peroration ready for the debate. I said I thought it was a great event that Eichmann had been tried in a court where Hebrew was used. Now I had no particular infatuation with Hebrew. What I meant was a Jewish language. I probably would have preferred Yiddish, but it wouldn't have occurred to me to say that ten years earlier.

I still don't think of myself as a Zionist—I'm not a Zionist—and I have no particular interest in living in Israel. My feeling about Israel is that if it were able to exist as a country among other countries, then some of the criticism that I have of what goes on there would come out more freely.

The growing interest in Yiddish must to some extent be stirred by the kind of thing I just talked about—the growing concern about the Holocaust. Sartre's essay, "Anti-Semite and Jew" made a strong impression on me because the idea (also put forward in an essay by Sidney Hook) suddenly struck me that Jews didn't have a choice! You *were* a Jew! That was the crucial fact which in a way the Holocaust made clear. I suppose there was a reciprocal relationship, that is to say, this new sense about being Jewish, which for me never took a religious form—it was a cultural, historical, national sentiment—this new feeling about being Jewish had a reciprocal relationship with working in Yiddish literature.

Looking back at my disillusionment with political ideology, it would be more correct to say that my politics changed and I became, I like to think, more humane, tolerant, and broadminded. If I'm right in using those adjectives, then it became easier for me to acknowledge things that a rigid ideology would deny. It became possible to say, "Well, look—this is part of my experience, I don't deserve any gold stars for this response, but I now feel a kind of natural piety and real loyalty."

17.

THE WRITER IN GREENWICH VILLAGE

Grace Paley

MY PARENTS, aged twenty or twenty-one, came here in 1905. They had children right away. It's a typical story—they brought the whole family over; then all the women went to work and put my father through medical school.

They worked in the garment industry. My aunts have sashes for being among the original members of the ILG. Their home was on Chrystie Street, where everybody comes from on the Lower East Side. They moved up, step by step. My father started his practice about 1918. He had big children already; I was born later. My brother and sister remember an impoverished family, very hard times, and many people in a small house, but by the time I was born my father had become a successful, hard-working doctor in a poor neighborhood. Originally, he thought we were moving into a nice Bronx neighborhood but, like a lot of the Bronx, it was built funny. Tons of brick were brought for the Bronx and left there in different places. And they tried to build it up. But between the First World War and the Depression, which hit too fast and too hard for anything to happen, it went down very rapidly. To me it was a poor neighborhood in which I felt very comfortable because we were well-off.

I was an important person on the block. It was like being

Grace Paley was born in New York in 1922. She is a poet, short story writer, and political activist. A member of the literature faculty at Sarah Lawrence College, her books include *The Little Disturbances of Man* (1973) and *Enormous Changes at the Last Minute* (1974).

the rabbi's daughter. I was protected in many ways, but I really lived on the street. The neighborhood was totally Jewish, *totally* Jewish.

My father and mother were Socialists. My father had been exiled to Siberia, but when the Tsar had a son he pardoned everybody under twenty-one. So my father returned, and mother, who had been exiled to Germany, came back too. Then they married, and migrated. They were always radicals, social democrats, actually. My grandmother spoke Yiddish and I chatted with her in my own poor Yiddish. My parents learned Yiddish in this country (father needed it for his practice), but mostly they talked in Russian, of which I've kept enough to know what's going on. Anyhow, they wanted me to be very educated. Most of the people I knew while growing up were on relief. It was the common experience of my friends. But even so the girls all went to school.

I didn't have very much to do with religion in our Orthodox neighborhood. Where my father practiced medicine, there was the *shul* in a house two doors away. As a small child I was intrigued by devout Jews. I used to take my grandmother to the synagogue, but she was already discouraged by her family. She had had many children, and all of them turned out to be irreligious. We observed no holidays except Passover. My parents thought of it as a great family holiday. My father would read—at top speed, he would go through the whole thing—and it was done; we had all the proper foods.

My father and mother were anti-Zionists, as were all the Socialists at that time. People forget. I had one Zionist aunt, and she was held in some contempt. But the secularism of my parents had absolutely nothing to do with the fact that we were Jews, and Jews for life. I took that to mean a whole ethical tradition. As a child, it meant the Old Testament, which the family liked. We would read and tell stories about it. And it also meant a recollection of common suffering—of pogroms, which had happened in all of their lives.

It was an insulated environment, to be sure, but with a pleasant side, producing an atmosphere where everybody around you was your friend. I grew up being very sorry for Christians. My idea was that there were very few of them in the world. And one should have some sympathy for their problem.

My father, who died at ninety, had read everything. He learned English on Dickens, which I think was common for that remarkable generation. My father-in-law, whom I met many years later, told me he *also* had learned English on Dickens. But my father read a tremendous amount of history and in many other fields.

I had more sympathies with the Communist party when I was a kid. My parents were strongly anti-Communist. And yet, my sympathies were with them, too. Mother would come back from different Popular Front meetings in tears. She'd be crying over what the Communists had done, how they had broken up meetings, this and that, and I would get very angry and be on her side then.

But about Depression times, I remember evictions on our block most vividly. Every day there were evictions, with families and furniture on the street. Otherwise, from my point of view, the street was full of Jewish kids.

As a child I couldn't have thought about that too much. But I did know one kid going to the Sholom Aleichem School to learn Yiddish. And then we were Falcons—Socialists' children under twelve—and there were YPSLs (Young People's Socialist League) and then YCL (Young Communist League) kids.

School was school. Most of the teachers were non-Jewish. I went to the library every Saturday. That's what you did. You'd get a lot of books, generally in the morning, and in the afternoon you'd go to the movies. My mother would take me or my cousins on Easter or Christmas and we'd go downtown. I didn't think people *lived* in Manhattan. I thought it was where you went.

Looking back at that place in that period, well, you know, I've written a lot about it. My general feeling is that it was very lively and very interesting: I can only compare it to certain Puerto Rican neighborhoods. Most Jews have now forgotten that way of living, always on the street, the women outside, sitting on benches or boxes, with their kids running around them. That life of the windows, the noise: it seems to me a very good way to have grown up.

In high school, I was very political; active in those United Front organizations like the Student Union. I didn't do a lot, really; I guess I just liked them. I was aware of the Nazis. In the early thirties, maybe even before, my mother read something from a newspaper about Hitler. My aunt said, "It's coming again." That's as clear a remembrance as I have of anything, being small, and of hearing that exchange.

We weren't so scared of Germans in Yorkville, but of the Irish in the South Bronx. That was Father Coughlin time. Those guys were crazy. They went around beating people up. I hated them, but they were a good twenty-five blocks south of us, a menace if we went near them. At the same time, it never crossed my mind that one would go into that area.

My last year in school, I had two fantastic English teachers, Mrs. Lafferty and Miss Rudin. They were wonderful. I did terribly well in English classes, and on the Regents exam. I had nothing to do with the school newspaper. That's where ghetto life really tells. I was scared stiff of those students who were running the newspaper. To me they seemed too brilliant, too classy. Being scared affected me in other ways. For example, I had been a very public child and fright made me much more private. I didn't decide about college; it was assumed that one went. I was fifteen when I finished high school. They said I had to go to college, so I went. Also, they thought since I was very kind, I should become a social worker. But they wouldn't have wanted me to *do* anything.

After one year in college, my mother told me I had to go to secretarial school, so I did. I can't bring myself to say I was kicked out of Hunter; I just ceased to go. I hated it. I did become a typist, but even that took me a long time. Then I got a job for a while at the New York Central Elevator Company. I couldn't do that too well, either. By then, I was writing poetry very seriously. My first real trip downtown (outside of the secretarial school on 42nd Street) was to hear W. H. Auden, who had recently come to this country and was giving a course at the New School. I was just mad about him. That was the highlight of my life. I attended the class every Thursday night. Auden taught, but I couldn't understand a word. He had trouble—you know, that accent, and his

The New School. DANIEL ROSENBERG.

lisp—I simply sat there in absolute awe of him. I wouldn't have missed a moment of it. Oh, God I knew everything he wrote inside out, all of his poems. Spender, too—and was I ever writing derivative stuff!

Auden asked us to show him poems. I said to myself, if I don't show him any, I may as well be dead. I showed him the poems. And he said to me, "I didn't know you used words like 'trousers' (in the Bronx!)." I said, "Yes, we do, you know." Then he said, "But 'sepulchre,' I didn't know that was a common American word." "Yes, we use that word." Anyway, *I* used it— that's how I was writing.

I hated working so much that I went to CCNY at night for half a year just to get my grades up. There I took a course in history and one in philosophy. Louis Feuer was my teacher. I did well there, and afterwards I went to NYU for a year. Academically, that was it. I got married. End of education. I never took a degree.

Many boys I played with as a child didn't go to college. Actually, the war was coming and a lot of them went into the army pretty fast. But a lot just hung around, and they were mostly political. For my own part, I remember feeling fear: what had happened in the old country could happen here. We "lived" with an uncle of mine all the time I was growing up. Actually, we had, and I still have, a family picture that included him. He was killed in a pogrom six weeks after that picture was taken. We were always aware of my father's younger brother. His fate belonged to the imagination of my life. He died in a town then called Yusefka. And in between it was called Stalina, now something else. Surely my aunt had that pogrom in mind when she cried about its "coming again."

We lived in Brooklyn for a couple of years, then in the Village, on 15th Street where I am now. When I was a young woman, my neighborhood was very interesting to me. Because of my old neighborhood, I've always had a strong sense of neighborhood, of where I am. After all, I had lived continuously in the house where I was born until I got married and left. That's unusual for a New Yorker. I'm very centered in that way. I can go anywhere but I always live in one place.

In my younger days this wasn't such a fancy rich neighborhood. It's very well-to-do now. The house across the street that someone bought for $10,000 when I was twenty-two years old is now sold for $110,000—or maybe more. But what was nice about the neighborhood when I lived there and the kids were small was the sense of community. I was active in the PTA, involved in the schools, and concerned about my kids' education—at least through junior high school. We kept Robert Moses from putting a highway through the park. That was the kind of problem I understood best, and which I know now why I felt with all my socialist background. All the large organizations I was in were too global for me. I felt unable to deal with them, not even wanting to that much. But my kids went to the day care center at Greenwich House. So we were involved in that. Keeping the Verazzano Expressway out of the Village: such things are important.

The Village has changed. It's gotten rich. But many young people who come here now probably feel very much as I did then. Who knows? I live here, we have this apartment, it's fairly roomy, there's rent control.

I have never considered leaving the city, not even when a number of friends moved into the suburbs. Such an idea never entered my mind or my husband's mind. I don't see that kind of life. I couldn't live there *now*. I love the street. It is everything to me; I like to go out and talk to people. There are men and women in our house whose kids went to P.S. 41 with my kids.

I gave a reading recently at the library near our home. The stories I read were about that earlier period. Quite a few women who were there knew they were part of my fiction, and they are still around. I have always wanted to understand the everyday life of ordinary people. Not out of ideology. The ideology may come later. But out of temperament, curiosity, nosiness, you know. Like, my husband was very angry with me because I'd gone up to Bedford Hills Prison to talk to some of the women. "You're always doing this," and "You're so tired," and all. But I had to go there, just out of curiosity, to see people. They interest me.

I write mostly out of my life with other women about a time when my kids were small and growing up. My kids in the day care center were with those women, and theirs were the lives I wrote about. I do not write about strangers. I think people I know are on the Upper West Side, too. But this is okay. I lived on 15th Street and Ninth Avenue for about six years—very important years for my children, from seven to twelve, like that. Again, it was a lot of street life, more than on this block. Here a lot of little boys run around for about three years, and then suddenly disappear. But our kids were out all the time. It was a house in which the Irish were going down while the Puerto Ricans and the Cubans who lived there were coming up. And there were some people like us. It was a funny mix of Jews and other Village people. I liked living there.

I don't think there's as much energy in Greenwich Village any more. Not in these nice neighborhoods. Oh, they've become so nice. The neighborhood is getting too "single class." There were always people in duplexes, but also people in funny little apartments, crummy places, and women trying to raise kids alone, even then, in little two-room places. There was always a mixture. It's getting too homogeneous. And that's not what this city is about. This is a very generous city. I doubt that another city of New York's generosity exists in the world. Partly we're paying for that generosity. New York has received the troubles of the whole country. Always. Trouble would hit the South, people came here; trouble would hit the Midwest, often people came here. They also went to Chicago and Detroit during the war. But we received half of Europe! We took them in, and English being the hospitable language that it is, received all their tongues. That's what New York is to me.

To this day I believe that sitting on a subway train, which some people don't like, is kind of beautiful; just sitting and looking at all the faces is a wonderful experience. And I'm not being mushy about this. The variety is fantastic. You see poorly dressed and well-dressed people; you get a sense of what's happening in this city and in the world. There was a time when you heard only Spanish. Now you sit in a subway train and you see all the same old faces, you see the regular people, all the people you know, and added to that in the last number of years are all the yeshiva people, the Hasidic people, and also now, the French language can be heard. You could study the history of the world by listening to the languages spoken in the New York subway. So you have some terrible French now working its way in that sounds a little like German. It's part of the subway culture.

In 1968 I was very close to the school, next door in fact. And not on account of my children, who were out of it. I knew every teacher backwards and forwards. I knew the principal very well. I knew that whole place. But I was not with the teachers. I thought they were making a big mistake. Their strike divided the world and divided me; I mean, I was divided in my sympathy. After all, my sister—whom I love very much—is a teacher. It's partly through her that I understand the development of the Jewish teacher in New York City. My sister and her friends and my sister-in-law graduated from school into the Depression. They were grown-ups who had to take teaching exams, or they went into social work. My sister-in-law was a social worker at that time, but she also got a teaching license. You see, I have been close to New York teachers all my life. I so vividly remember them taking home those exams. I've often wanted to write about it but have never had time. I remember their language being corrupted by those exams. They were practicing how to pronounce words all the time. It was designed to keep them out of teaching, out of the civil service.

These difficult oral exams were meant to keep immigrants out, to keep the Irish and other English-speaking people in. They didn't want "greenhorns and mockies" coming around, right? Well, I think all our teachers forget that tremendous efforts were made to keep them out. Among those efforts was a determination to fail them on their orals. I'll never forget my poor sister and her friends sitting around and practicing those goddam words! "Ig-no-MIN-y," "Ig-NO-min-y," they said. Then, "Ig-no-MIN-y, ig-no-MIN-y." I'll never forget how to pronounce *that* word. Those of us who were contemptuous of the whole thing used to call it the establishment of Hunter College English, and the wreckage, as far as I was concerned, of our New York tongue. A couple of women in my family still talk like that. Those oral tests were part of the merit system. Only merit consisted of speaking "well" so that when you spoke to children, they would learn proper English pronounciation, and all these little Mocky Yids would get over their singsong speech and speak correctly.

About the strike: it turned into a black-Jewish issue. That was the horror of it. I hated those guys who were making anti-Semitic statements. Some of them spoke in rage, and some were sorry later on. But they said it. And that was terrible. My feeling about a great many people I knew at the time was that they didn't do enough to point out that Jews were in the forefront of anti-racism. I felt that strike with great pain when surrounded by all that black anti-Semitism. Some of the black statements were real. If you go down on the Lower East Side all the landlords are Jewish. You can't deny it. People who talk like that always have to be reminded that Jews are in the forefront of antiracism. I have had Puerto Rican kids talking about Jews right at this table and I tell them: "Look you say one more word and you'll have to go out. I can't bear it, I just can't bear it."

But I thought the teachers were wrong (even though I was sorry for them). I thought that decentralization of schools was right, and I feel now that decentralization of this whole city is right. The city is too big. It should exist as a federation or something like that. There is a lot of feeling right now for decentralization. I'm thinking locally again—like, when I began to work in school before all this trouble, when the kids were small, in the early sixties or maybe even in the late fifties. I was a parent and a parent-citizen. When they were very small I worked in the park. And I would assume that other young people now are in the schools and parks.

As for my girl and boy, they did well in elementary school, pretty well at junior high, and really badly in high school—like Mom! They went on, and they dropped out, and then nothing. They did not get much Yiddishkeit (Yiddish culture). I feel bad about that. I didn't do what my parents did. But they understand that anti-Semitism means them.

One of the most important things in my life developed for me with the Vietnam war. What really happened was my meeting antiwar types who were not Marxists, above all A. J. Muste. That was an absolutely extraordinary meeting.

I didn't work with the Women's Strike groups; I knew them from the old times. I worked with the Quakers, but didn't like them too much either. We set up our own Peace Center in the Village. It was only local, again. But out of our local center, we developed a lot of action. We had very large events; for example, we organized the artists. The experience was very important. It turned my head around. How? By the corroboration of my localism, so to speak. We never had to join any large group, we never joined the Women's Strike, we Villagers contributed our share. We're not together very much anymore. But I became aware of different groups, like the War Resisters League. Up to that point I had not been particularly pacifist, but that's the direction my life took.

I always considered that I was interested in women. Now a lot of *young* women became feminists. So that's good too. But my head was not turned around by it. I mean, that was my bent. Without calling it anything, I wrote and thought about women and how they lived. But I did that all the time. My interest in women was always there, but the pacifism was different. It hadn't been there. But my hatred of violence was there. I'm talking about international violence. As for urban violence, well, this area is easier to live in than others. In a neighborhood that was difficult I might very well have another point of view. Oh, things happen here. People have been robbed in this very house. But in general, you don't worry about coming home at midnight. I walk my dog. I wouldn't walk her at three in the morning, but if I came home and I hadn't walked her, I'd go out at one-thirty. The reason is that even then there are people walking in and out, going back and forth. But that doesn't mean nothing could happen to me. I'm not naïve about it.

Does this sound like Jane Jacobs' thesis? In my opinion, she's right and she's wrong. I think, up to a point, the amount of violence in certain areas exceeds the amount of street-watching that can happen. But people don't resist enough. I don't mean fight back, but why have we stopped using the parks instead of taking them over from those winos, which we did a couple of times? That is what nonviolence can mean. We did that a couple of times. Another time a whole group of parents with children much younger than mine did the same thing in our park, which was full of winos. They simply went in and took over the park and for several weeks it was theirs. But then they would get scared and pull out. I think we can stiffen their backbones. It doesn't have "to come again."

18.

THE MUSIC OF
THE CITY

Barry Brook

MY FATHER came from Vilna, now in Poland, my mother
from the Ukraine. They reached New York and lived in various
parts of this city. Neither one was at all religious, but they were
political—my father in particular. He became a union official,
deeply concerned with the Socialist party and with the Jewish
workers' movement. He was a pocketbook framer, a craftsman
who applied the frame of a lady's pocketbook to the rest of it.
Accordingly, he belonged to the Ladies Pocketbook Workers
Union. I'm sure that there's still such a trade because the principle
of needling a frame on a handbag still exists, and there must even
now be an organized group of pocketbook framers, possibly rid-
dled by the same racketeers who took it over some time ago.

We moved around New York a great deal, if for no other
reason than to take advantage of every month's or every three
months' rent security. I was born in the East Bronx on November
1, 1918—and grew up in Pelham Parkway. We were medium
poor, as immigrant families might be. Until the Depression,
things went quite well, but after that life got rather rough for us.

There was no doubt about our Jewishness even though we
seldom went to the synagogue. My father read Yiddish papers;
he even wrote for one. What he wrote was music criticism, which
the editor used more as filler than anything else. Father was a

Barry Brook was born in New York in 1918. He is a professor of musicology and an
executive officer in the Ph.D. program in music at CUNY. He is author of a number of
works in musicology.

music lover who, however, never studied music. Otherwise, he argued more and more vociferously with those who read *The Freiheit,* a Communist daily. He was anti-Stalinist. His attachment to organized labor came out of an ideological commitment. All along he was a passionate music lover with a great ear, and great gifts, a man who listened intelligently despite his lack of technical background. My father sang in Lazar Weiner's large chorus. Weiner conducted. His son, Yehudi, a close friend, is now at Yale. But Lazar Weiner made a real impact on me and on many others.

Elementary school was quite run-down, no doubt a fair place, but I don't recall having any great love for it. While I was in junior high school, we moved up. Up and away. Up in the world. We got into a new apartment house and I went to a nearby public school. There I was quite happy, and had a number of good friends. The junior high school was run by a famous principal named Angelo Patri. Most people only vaguely remember that name, but in my time Angelo Patri was known as a marvelous educator. He had striking white hair which helped make him a wonderful father figure for everybody. The school was right off Fordham Road, not far from Fordham University. It was an extraordinarily good school. And there, for the first time, teachers made a vivid impression on me. It was an honor to go to this school! We were admitted by competitive examinations, and felt that to be there was very special.

My parents discovered I was musical in my fourth or fifth year. They had no piano because neither of them played. My father would have been delighted to see that I've stayed with music. I certainly wanted to become a musician and I seemed to shine a bit. My high school, DeWitt Clinton, had relatively modest musical training opportunities, and I took advantage of all of them. I played the piano and learned instruments in the orchestra and for the band. I took the theory classes, which were rather inadequate. I was very much interested in literature at the time, so I was on the school paper and wrote for the school magazine. I was equally interested in French. And those three areas have from that time on been central to my whole life. I think if they had had vastly more music, I'd have missed none of it. But because they didn't, I found outlets in French and in the school newspaper.

I started private lessons on the violin, and after a short time changed to the piano. Since our economic situation was pretty bad, I got personal scholarships from teachers. One woman who was my teacher for a number of years taught without a fee (except for the first couple of years when my father had enough money). She said it didn't matter, never asking for payment. Later on, when I taught piano, I did the same thing with some kids.

Whenever a concert took place on the radio we heard it, and later on there were records. We went to band concerts in the park, and my father was always one of those who would enter a contest the Goldman Band had, to guess the anonymous pieces; he'd usually come out first or second.

All through high school I took advantage of the twenty-five cent Philharmonic student ticket, which involved getting to the Philharmonic office on 57th Street and waiting on line from eight-thirty in the morning every Friday in order to buy a ticket for the afternoon concert two weeks later. You could *only* get tickets two weeks in advance. But at ten o'clock—the office opened at nine—everything was sold. You had to be there early. This deal was just for students. I always managed to find the twenty-five cents—although sometimes it wasn't easy. Besides the twenty-five cents you needed carfare, an additional cost quite a few of us had to calculate. On that line, there was a whole flock of people who later became important in music, and many whom I knew for years thereafter. Noah Greenberg, for one. As a matter of fact, I probably met him then; we became very good friends at that time. Another guy, John Barnett, became the conductor of the National Orchestra Association, and remained in that position for nine or ten years. Yet another one was Jonathan Sternberg. And there were several people who went on into singing.

This was the period when Toscanini conducted the Philharmonic, and week after week, year after year, we all sat up in the last two rows of Carnegie Hall where there were wonderful acoustics. And we had our scores. We didn't realize then what a tremendous effect this experience would have on us. It was way back there that I learned all of the repertoire Toscanini performed. Of course, there were other more venturesome conductors around, but Toscanini profoundly influenced my musical knowledge and heightened my enthusiasms. This was the case with Noah, and other friends as well. We used to spend many, many hours listening to music, talking about music, fooling around with music. The Saturday morning sessions were equally important, although not quite as exciting; we heard esoteric music, the chamber music that we couldn't otherwise hear, art music, and art songs. Then we started going to the 58th Street Music Library on Saturdays in order to listen to records. It was the only place really that you could get to listen to records easily for free. And we had a racket. We would sign up, one of us for nine, another for ten, another for eleven, and there was only room for two or three in the booth. Noah, Bob Levenstein, and I were specialists in this operation. Bob, who not only was a very good pianist but a boyhood chess champion, went into the public school system and stopped performing at an early age. Somehow, and I think most regrettably, his career didn't seem to progress. I imagine the library had special endowment funds. It was run by a battle-axe of a woman who loved to show off this extraordinary library. And with reason—because in addition to having thousands upon thousands of scores, which somehow managed to get stolen by earnest music students, including a number that I returned on the death of a friend (I won't say who, but his wife asked me to perform this errand—and I'm talking about hundreds of scores), it also had a rental library for anyone who wanted to have them for amateur or school orchestras. It had tables where music copyists spent hours upon hours, every day, taking things down and copying them out for publishers who put out works that originated in other editions. They were copying for republication. It was unusual and remarkable. I was drawn there because of the great riches the library held. It was like a great museum. It had scores, recordings, and books about music. I spent a good deal of time there. I took out a lot of books. I don't know if it was unique in this country, but it was surely exceptional. Few graduate schools of music had this kind of facility, maybe because there were so few graduate schools. Some conservatories had libraries, but those, for instance the Third Street Music School, were relatively modest. You couldn't get the scores of an opera by Rimsky-Korsakov, or an obscure chamber work. This was a 58th Street Library function. Those in charge understood the importance of gathering a large library in a musical city such as New York.

I went to Manhattan Music School after leaving my piano teacher who had taught me for so many years without payment. She belonged to a group of teachers who had their own philosophy; they used to meet once every several months and give concerts, with students of the various teachers performing. I attended Manhattan School through my high school period, and did a great deal in theory and keyboard harmony. It was good training, and I got involved with excellent people who also happened to be well known. You could continue only if you passed examinations . . . it is still the case. At that time there were more opportunities in an expanding economy and in a country where more schools were being built and more orchestras were being created.

Right after high school I entered the City College of New York. Once again, there wasn't much music study because the department was very meager, and so I concentrated on French literature and kept busy as president of the French Club. But I took everything that was offered, and I apprenticed myself to the then new head of the music department, who was an organist. I learned some organ on the marvelous Skinner organ they had in the Great Hall. What an instrument! It was fantastic and thrilling to touch—with scads of ranks of pipes. Although I also played bassoon in the orchestra, by then I was convinced, and had been even in high school, that I didn't want to be a performer. My piano teacher was very unhappy about that. But in my high school yearbook, I indicated that I wanted to be the French Schumann, someone who combined composition and writing about music with French. One way or another, although I stopped being a composer, I realized most of that dream.

At about the same time I developed a relationship to art museums in New York City. We had a group of nine or ten people, including two artists, one future architect who already knew his calling, several musicians, a self-styled poet or two. But my serious interest in painting came quite a bit later. I went to look at that time mainly because my friends who were emotionally involved thought it was important.

Radicalism was part and parcel of it. The same people were leftists. Noah Greenberg was very much of a Trotskyist. Arguments never ceased. Let's say that I was not among the most committed, but I was radical enough to be suspended from high school, in 1933 or thereabouts, for helping to lead an antifascist peace movement. With a bunch of other Jewish kids, I was trying to escape from my ancestral past. Politically, my thinking ran the same course as that of most juvenile radicals.

My father remained a staunch Liberal party member. He couldn't bring himself to vote for the bourgeois Democratic party. We had some friction over politics, none over music. I think he respected some of the esoterica that attracted me. I don't recall his ever being terribly interested in contemporary music after, say, *Pierrot Lunaire*. But he had a feeling that this music was important. He himself couldn't respond to it very strongly. He was a Social Democrat in politics, a forward-looking human being, not a radical. And that moderation was evident in his musical preferences. I mean, he adored Mahler, for example. He liked early Schoenberg. But after all, there was then so little of the later Schoenberg available to us. He respected Schoenberg and liked Stravinsky. He was forward-looking, all right, but he didn't live long enough to see where the new music was going.

When I was a kid, I can't even remember, and I can't believe that I was interested in contemporary music, but even in high school and from then on, I was eager to hear it. By my mid or late teens I was involved in all kinds of concerts devoted to or including contemporary music where one found many of the same people I spoke of before. Among them some were beginning to be interested in music that was not part of the standard 1700–1900 literature. I was influenced by this group and did go to performances of new music.

When I graduated from City College in 1939, the country was deep in the Great Depression. I took an FBI examination. My name appeared on a list from which many census people were chosen, and I was among them. I worked at the Census Bureau for five or six months. There I began to get promotions, and within months I had a high post at double salary.

Washington was a strange place for me. I had a nine to five job, I lived in a boarding house with people of various religious and social backgrounds, whom I enjoyed precisely because, to me, they were new and different. We generally had terrible food; our one big joy was a great meal on Sunday. I had no piano and I wasn't practicing. I did go to concerts a bit, but the period was really a vacuum.

I was waiting for something to happen. And it did, some months later, when I was appointed a fellow at City College. That enabled me to come back the following year to start my master's at Columbia. I was out of limbo! I was back doing what I thought was important. And I gave up what was then, for a kid my age, a very good salary—certainly more than my father was making. I must say that my parents didn't mind at all. I came back and moved in at home because it was very close to City College and I could pursue my studies at Columbia while serving as a fellow.

In musicology my most important mentor was Paul Henry Lang, who is still my friend and, so to speak, my professor. Erich Hertzman was another. He may have been Jewish, though I never knew or cared. He got here from Germany in the thirties. I presume it was to escape the Nazis. A host of musicologists arrived for the same reason. Karol Rathaus was a composer who taught at Queens where, after the war, he hired me to teach. Musicology in this country became a mature discipline because it was enriched by a number of distinguished European scholars. Alfred Einstein was undoubtedly the most conspicuous Jewish case in point. On the other hand, I believe that a Jesuit-trained Hungarian Catholic named Paul Henry Lang was *the* outstanding musicological professor in this country at that time. Lang left Germany before the Hitler era and others afterwards came over for ideological reasons. Bartók was not Jewish, Stravinsky was not Jewish, and yet they came as well. So it was not only the Jewish influx, but it was also the intellectual one. Granted all that, in musicology proper the influence of Jews was probably dominant.

Einstein was very actively Jewish. I could name quite a few

other people from a large number, including another colleague at Queens College, Morris Schwartz, who was a *wunderkind* as a violinist in Germany, and also studied musicology. He got his degree with Paul Henry Lang.

As World War II approached I was shocked by events like the Hitler-Stalin Pact. It raised profound or, rather, profounder doubts in my mind about the USSR. I already had plenty. I was not a believer in the Trotskyist view, but I was sufficiently in contact with its devotees to distrust Stalin on all counts. I knew about the show trials. They were a major turning point. But my reaction to the pact was an instance where being Jewish won out over my not too powerfully radical views. I had a low-intensity view of a future world that had to be better. The Hitler-Stalin Pact *shocked me as a Jew*. It was a pact with the butcher of the Jews. And that ended *any* positive feeling I could have had for Stalin. My consciousness as a Jew increased. It's still there. But there's no doubt that the climactic moment for me occurred when Stalin became Hitler's ally.

After the war and my stint in the army, I applied for a job at City College, where there was no opening. But I found one at Queens. Rathaus was chairman, and he gave me a job. I had already done a dissertation on French sixteenth-century secular music at Columbia, and I was still involved in French music. Well, I got my job at Queens College in '45, and I'm still there. I mean, nominally, on detached service. Most of my time goes into the graduate center as executive officer in charge of training doctoral students.

After the war, I entered into the swim of going to concerts and conferences. I had not really done very much. I wrote some program notes and a few unimportant articles. I attended meetings and concerts. So I felt very fortunate to get a Ford grant which enabled me to go to France and gave me the opportunity of gathering material for a dissertation on the eighteenth-century symphony, which I thought I was going to do with Paul Henry Lang. It made more sense, once there, to do it in France at the Sorbonne with Jacques Chaillet, who was the head of the Institut de Musicologie at the Sorbonne. Paris had nearly all of the source materials I needed, the U.S. virtually none. It was, after all, a dissertation on the French symphony. And in the course of that first year, I also traveled all around Europe, gathering materials from other libraries.

I did not have much opportunity to deal with the French musical life of the time. It was very weak. That was partially due, I believe, to the war and its aftermath, but also to the fact that France had never really regained its important position as a center of music. I was there for one year at that time, and for four subsequent years, with various aids and grants. I felt very much at home in Paris. I'm sure that the presence of personal friends helped a good deal. I would probably consider living there if New York did not exist. I didn't use to mind a year in Paris, but no more. The last time I was there for a year, both my wife, Claire, and I felt that while it was not quite the Paris of old, New York was still New York. The ferment—musical, artistic, intellectual— is still here. The people I find interesting and fascinating and stimulating are here. It's a great place to live. For one stretch, from '45 to '54, I was a suburbanite in my then-wife's parents' home, first a mansion on Millionaires' Row in Brooklyn, and then in a house in Hempstead. I was delighted to get back to Manhattan. It doesn't frighten me at all—though I choose not to walk in crazy neighborhoods late at night. Living and working in Manhattan is stimulating, not scary.

New York is full of composers. The number of composers per square mile in this city is greater than any other place in the world. We know many of them, and they're always visiting with us. New York is still a city where more concerts occur than any place else in this country. Not more than in London, where music of every kind is played and played well. But I didn't find I liked London enough to stay there. I prefer the excitement, the ferment, and the people of New York. You can't duplicate it anywhere. And I am at home in many cities of the world. I've spent significant amounts of time in Vienna, Berlin, Munich, and other culture capitals. In a sense New York has it all. I suppose that's what one means by this city's cosmopolitanism.

To me the irreplaceable people are creative, productive, fascinating to talk and listen to. We have an interesting circle of friends. First, there's a small group we see very frequently. In a way, it resembles the small group that existed in my middle and late teens. The cast has changed. The quality of movement and excitement is similar. Who are these people? They include Andrew Porter, the English critic now working for the *New Yorker,* and David Hamilton, who was a critic on the *New Yorker* and is now critic of *The Nation* and a freelance writer. Porter is English, but David Hamilton is American, although his father was English. Such men represent a continuity in mood and interest and involvement and creativeness. Those earlier times were comparable in their concern for the creative life, their excitement over a new piece or over a great performer, their enthusiasm for something unique or special. Toni Greenberg, who is Noah's widow, has been a close friend of ours for all these many years. Another is an Italian observer of this scene, rather than a participant himself. His name is Floriano Vecchi; he owns the Tiber Press; makes greeting cards. That is the "inner circle" of friends who see each other very often. There are a number of others like Elliott Carter, Charles Rosen, Yehudi Wyner, various performers, composers, some painters. We call them our family. The association is that close.

It would have been more difficult to set up a doctoral program elsewhere than in New York City. The presence and abundance of creative types—that's immensely valuable. So are institutions. A doctoral program takes advantage, for example, of the Metropolitan Museum of Art, which has a great instrument collection. We were able to bring in the then curator, now curator emeritus, Emmanuel Winternitz, to be a regular visiting professor who gave his classes at the museum, which has been a very important adjunct to the kind of work we do at the graduate center. We try to make it as broad and as interdisciplinary as possible.

The Lincoln Center Library is the second greatest music library in this country, and one of the world's great libraries, although in the area of source materials, where most doctoral candidates do their research, one has to go for Western music to European museums and European libraries. We do that by finding fellowships for the students or getting microfilms and bringing them back.

The very nature of the City University and its many colleges made it possible to bring together a varied and very gifted faculty in various areas. We reached out for visiting professors from Europe to handle things that were not completely covered by our own faculty. But the total faculty of the City Colleges by itself is so rich that we are sure to have an outstanding program. In composition, we have several important composers, like George Perle, Hugo Weisgall, Robert Starer at Brooklyn, Mario Davidovsky at City College, and Jacob Druckman, who's a prize-winner. We have the ambiance of New York in the performing world and also in the scholarly world, the library world. It makes a difference.

Apropos of the performing world, one wonders why so many Jews of my generation are to be found there. Part of the explanation certainly has to do with a deep drive to achieve something extraordinary. When Menuhin, for example, was a rising star, I recall my mother saying, "Well, you know, he's only a year older than you." I told this to Menuhin when I saw him recently and learned from him that a great many kids about my age had been told the same thing. My mother meant that I should be practicing more. I had talent, too, and should be working harder to achieve—like Menuhin. I'm sure that was a good part of why kids of Jewish immigrant families were taught music. There were a number of other famous performers; performance was seen as a vehicle of upward mobility: you could play rather than become a businessman. My parents didn't push me. I believe they were very happy with my aesthetic goals. My father never objected. My mother was sometimes concerned about whether I could earn a living in music, though, and she made occasional pointed remarks about how I might better be devoting myself to more lucrative pursuits.

The kids who are filling our conservatories now and looking to become soloists are doing so pretty much the same stupid way that too many did years ago. The difference is that then, only the very good ones could continue. Now, many seem to continue and work for concert careers that they can never achieve. Now you can go to a conservatory and work your head off while the teachers lead you to believe the whole world is waiting for you to play a Tchaikovsky concerto. It isn't. There may be an opportunity for one or two in the whole country. I believe that intensive training for nonexistent careers is wrong. It has nothing to do with reality. Most people should be trained to make music so that they can enjoy it in an amateur way and not dream of becoming soloists, which is a road open to very few of them.

If you want to go into music, New York provides alternatives other than performing and writing. For example, my wife Claire, also a native New Yorker, is in publishing—she's the music editor at W.W. Norton. New York is still a magnet for anyone interested in music. I don't believe that the musical or literary art worlds have yet participated in the middle-class exodus from the city (although many have homes in the country, as we do). The Upper West Side is still a place where the many types of people in music congregate. We like to be close to the concert halls. It's nice to be able to walk to Lincoln Center *and* to Carnegie Hall. Where else but in New York would we have so much music within earshot?

19.

"THE ARCHITECT
FROM NEW YORK"

Percival Goodman

MY PEOPLE got the hell out of Germany and came here in
1848. I was born in New York seventy-five years ago. My mother
divorced my father when I was seven years old, and we never saw
him again. He didn't do much of anything except use up our
money, so that by the time he left it was pretty sparse. Mama got
herself a variety of jobs. For a long time she sold ladies' clothes
and became one of the earliest travelers in that business. As a
result, she disappeared for long periods of time.

I left home when I was thirteen. By then I had decided either
to build bridges or paint pictures. Uncle Ben, who happened to
be my mother's sister's husband, recommended me to an architect
friend. By age eighteen, I was designing large buildings.

In those days, to be a licensed architect you didn't need spe-
cialized schooling. I left my uncle's office because in the first place
he was a relative and in the second place, he wasn't paying me
enough. I went to work for John E. Peterkin, a charming Englishman who took a liking to me especially after he discovered
that I had certain abilities which his office could use.

The major building I designed for Jack Peterkin was called
40 Park Place, a forty-story office building. In the early stages of
its design, I was called into the conference room. I thought some-

Percival Goodman, an architect and city planner, was born in New York in 1904. His
works include many religious and community buildings for Jewish organizations throughout the United States, as well as numerous New York City and state buildings and projects.
He is coauthor, with his brother Paul, of *Communitas* (1947) and *The Double E* (1977).

thing terrible had happened. I knew that the promoters were discussing the building. I had prepared a whole set of drawings. So I arrived at the conference room and there was Jack Peterkin: "Percy, Mr. Stevenson and the rest of the group here want to ask a couple of questions about the building." I answered the questions, he thanked me and I left. That was that. The next morning, a telephone in my little cubbyhole rang. It was Jack Peterkin. Could I come to his office? I went over, convinced that my job was gone, I had flubbed it. But no. Jack was even pleased about the way I had handled myself at the meeting. But, "When you left the room, Stevenson said, 'Hey, Jack, what's this? Robbing the cradle these days?' Percy, why don't you grow a mustache? Why don't you start smoking cigarettes? Why don't you at least *look* older?" That very day, I started growing a mustache and I bought a pack of cigarettes. I promptly got sick on the cigarettes and smoked them for the next fifty years. I did quit a number of years back and now try to convert everyone else to abstinence.

It never struck me that doing the things I did was unusual for a kid of my age. It only occurred to me thirty years later . . . Oh, my God, if that happened now I'd be shivering in my boots. But then I didn't know enough to be scared.

My American architectural education, such as it was, took place at the Beaux Arts Institute of Design. The BAID had been founded by Beaux Arts architects, among them my Uncle Ben, who'd gone to the Ecole de Beaux Arts in Paris. He and one of his friends ran an atelier, and an atelier signified the system by which young French architects were trained. The BAID consisted of a number of ateliers, some of which were called free ateliers. As in France, some were not connected with any school. Others were limited to schools throughout the country in a national network, with programs written in New York and examined by New York architects. New York was the architectural center of the United States. Insofar as it reflected European influence and as a rich banking center, New York exerted *its* influence throughout the country. Chicago was much more modern, with Louis Sullivan and later Frank Lloyd Wright. The West Coast was also important. I'm talking about 1900, in that time.

The atelier system was customary. Later on, everything in this country got bureaucratized. It started with Franklin Roosevelt, for whom I had profound admiration. But he bureaucratized the U.S. through WPA and all his other alphabetical agencies. And until the end of World War II you no more needed to register as an architect than you did as a businessman or a painter. Schools of architecture existed, but that didn't mean you had to get a license from the state in order to practice. It all started among doctors and lawyers in the nineteenth century, but architecture was quite late and was part of the general bureaucratizing of every profession from mortician to real estate dealer.

The city struck me as being not a big apple as such (some idiot invented that term in our time) but as *a nice big oyster*. All you had to do was get your knife in and turn it and there was the nice big oyster to eat. It seemed to me that no matter where you turned there were tremendous opportunities. I was terribly lucky as a kid. All the people I met were helpful.

I guess you might say the aesthetic impulse was in the family. I left home shortly after my brother Paul reached any kind of age at all. He was seven years younger than I. He had just been born when Pop disappeared. Then, when I was thirteen years old, Paul still was a little boy. I didn't really get to know him until he was twenty-one or twenty-two years old.

We were all involved in the arts. Even my father was "artistic." My sister worked for MGM and could have been a topnotch Hollywood writer if she hadn't had Paul to support and to worry about and to throw all her affection into. My sister, who never married, is two years older than I. She took over the mother role and sacrificed a good part of her life for Paul. Alice was a tough Broadway girl. She started at MGM as a typist and then got a job in the story department. Of course, Alice was brighter than either of her brothers. There's no question in my mind that she was more talented than both of us. She could type ninety-seven words a minute and take a great many words in shorthand. In very short order, Alice *became* the story department of MGM, working, however, for a guy who took all the credit. She did the research, studied law, found things out, wrote synopses.

Paul was a real New York boy—City College and all the rest. It's obvious in the fiction: read his stories and poems, you'll find New York at the center. I'm a New Yorker too, but I never loved this city the way Paul did. I loved Paris. But New York has many charms. When I go to other cities in this country, I realize that New York's the only place I want to live . . . in America. I can walk from the Upper West Side to Fifth Avenue or to 42nd Street or to 14th Street. How the hell can I go about like that anywhere else? I was in San Antonio a few weeks ago, giving lectures. There you walk two blocks and the city disappears. After that, all you see is highway. Chicago is a pain in the ass, too. Boston is pretty good because it has certain urban qualities. Those qualities mean a lot to me, probably in part because I am a Jew.

How can I put it? The Jew until Israel came along was willy-nilly a city guy. It's the life he was forced into and accounts for the kind of creature that he became. My daughter, on the other hand, is living in Oregon on a farm with very few amenities. My son works in television, and he's very fond of the country.

I have lived in this city all my life, except for the Paris years. I do have very strong feelings about it. I was born in Greenwich Village and that neighborhood is precious to me. I get sick to my stomach when I see what Washington Square Park has become. In the good days, you wandered through the park to see people, and you weren't afraid to go there after dark.

I'm a Jew in the big city now as I was then. And yet I was brought up without any religion at all. When you had a Reformed German-Jewish background like mine, you wanted to assimilate. That's basically how things were. And it turned out all my good friends were non-Jews. Very few Jews were involved in architecture. I can explain why with no difficulty at all. The building trades, the engineering and architectural professions, were more or less integrated as three parts of a common endeavor. And it was not Jewish. Jews came in only as real estate speculators. They were very late in gaining acceptance as architects, except for some who built tenements. But they were people I wouldn't spit at, because I was a "superior type of architect." So I had very little professional or personal contact with Jews.

Much later I met Frieda Warburg and Louis Finklestein, who was then president of the Jewish Theological Seminary. I met them through a lawyer for the Warburg estate. Mrs. Warburg was in the process of giving her mansion on 92nd Street and Fifth Avenue to the Jewish Theological Seminary for the purpose of creating a museum of Jewish objects. This was right after the Second War. Mrs. Warburg didn't know whether it would be feasible to convert the mansion. She wanted everything to remain as it had been during her marriage. I was given the job of gently altering the house into a museum which she wanted to call the Hebrew Museum, then the Judaic Museum. Finklestein played along with her ideas, but when it came to that he said, "It's got to be the *Jewish* Museum." That was my first such experience. It prompted me to ask a lot of questions. Hitler had already led me, like many other Jews, to wonder: "Where do I belong?" and "Who the hell am I?" I was very gung ho for the Second War and I paid my "debt" insofar as I could. Also, I began to do a little reading: I found out about Anne Frank.

Finklestein didn't push me, but he helped. The man was amazed that I hadn't been bar mitzvahed. "Who's not bar mitzvahed?" And he had very simple things to say: "Maybe the Sabbath isn't such a necessity, but it's very good to sit down one day a week and do quiet thinking." I tried it, and this led not in any sense to being religious, but to a definite feeling that there were certain Jewish things to which I reacted. I couldn't understand why I should react in a sympathetic way when I read a book, for example, by Bashevis Singer, or when I heard a Jewish joke and it sounded funnier. When I read Freud, it was the Jewish part, as I ultimately discovered, that made sense to me and the other parts that did not. One insight followed another. It's hard to pinpoint what mattered most.

Nothing specific—unless it was the museum—precipitated my awakening. It didn't happen overnight. From 1933 on, with the impact of Hitler and a touch of radical politics, I felt a gradual opening of doors. The upshot was, well, that I am Jewish. It had nothing to do with religion. Rather, I concluded that you're Jewish as a monkey is a monkey.

A conference was an important turning point for me. It dealt with the big move of Jews out of New York into the suburbs and a major trend toward building synagogues. This took place before the fifties, in 1946 or '47. The Union of American Hebrew Congregations sponsored the conference. I was invited and I accepted because I had something to say. My topic was "The Holiness of Beauty." Out of that talk, I became an instant expert on synagogues. The speech apparently conveyed what people wanted to hear on "the holiness of beauty" and the importance of designing Jewish places of worship that represented not what Christians or Moslems or Asians thought proper, but what an American Jew might think proper. What I meant by my beautiful title was actually suitable to what we were driving at. And I felt and I still pretty much feel that the imitation of churches and even of old synagogues is a great mistake. Most of all I was pushing for what I considered to be a modern architecture. I felt, and my brother agreed on this, that the act of creation is a holy act. Paul continuously wrote of the creative spirit—and I've taken it over from him, that along with the belief that when you're touched by this spirit, you're engaged in an act of prayer. Of course, Kafka said the same thing.

It's the spirituality of Judaism that interested my brother and me. We did a number of articles together on synagogue architecture. Paul spoke biblical Hebrew, not fluently but well. He had been to Hebrew school. The Jewish theme appears repeatedly in his stories. It works very well in "Parents Day," for example, and in "The Breakup of Our Camp." We did *Communitas* during the late days of the Depression. With nothing else to do, it kept our minds busy. I sketched out a city. In fact, it was for the World's Fair of 1939. I tried to sell Otis Elevator Company on a great scheme for what a city ought to be like, using lots of elevators and escalators. Those idiots didn't go for it. To this day I don't understand why. I developed the idea of an urban utopia, of Zion, to a fairly extended point. During the Depression what bothered me was this: how is it that so many people don't have a piece of bread to eat? That really seemed to be crazy. The whole society had to be operating at top speed to give a guy a loaf of bread or a roof over his head. I developed a scheme which I thought would come to grips with this problem. It was a dual economy scheme.

Shortly before the war, I was involved with the army and navy as a civilian on a couple of things in Washington. I'd see Paul occasionally; and he was, of course, in his usual state—not making a dime. He was a pacifist; a homosexual; all kinds of things which could only add up to trouble; and he was always in hot water. Anyway, I began to talk to him one night about my scheme. One of Paul's brilliant characteristics was his ability to put things together. He scratched his head. "Do you know, that might not make a bad book. If you had that city of yours, the consumer city as you call it, for the first part, and for the last part you had your insurance scheme; and if you put something in the middle, like a nice socialist community, that'd be a pretty good book." I said, "Hey, that's not a bad idea." He said, "Let's do it." So we started working. I would rough out a part and send it to Paul, and he'd take it to pieces before reassembling the whole thing. He finally wrote the book because he was the professional writer in the family. Seventy-five percent of the ideas were mine, but Paul was able to arrange them logically. *Communitas* looks better to me now than it did then.

In *Communitas* we concluded that there was no future in luxury as such. Every society that concentrated on luxury went down the drain. Basically, both of us, although we liked conveniences and comfort, were opposed to big thick padding on things, and diamond rings, and Rolls Royces. They just weren't our style. We didn't consider them desirable and, as it's turning out, the world can't afford 'em anyway. That's what my second book (*The Double E*) is all about: the world can't afford these things; therefore, we'd better get smart and live without them.

Maybe this country, and New York City in particular, would have been spared some of its urban agony if *Communitas* had been taken seriously. My proposition in a nutshell was that you could take all the office buildings and put them into one air-conditioned cylinder. People don't depend on daylight anyway. They depend on artificial light and artificial air. I designed a cylinder which was twenty-five stories high and three quarters of a mile in diameter. It would have provided enough space for all the department stores and all the office buildings in a city half the size of New York. Our consumer city only projected what already existed, not what

Frank Lloyd Wright or Corbusier or Kenzatangi or any of the city planners had arrived at. Great populous cities are a nineteenth-century phenomenon. They developed because of the steam engine and the factory system which required a vast concentration of labor. I don't think we have that necessity anymore.

What I have in mind is much more than decentralization. When Wendell Willkie said we live in "one world," he spoke the truth. And Lewis Mumford put it much better than Willkie. He said that for a long time the village was the world; now the world is a village. On the one hand, we have this tremendous village with six billion people in it—six billion people, that's how many human begins we will have in another twenty years! What do you do with a village inhabited by six billion people? The only way you can deal with a village like that is to have a lot of little neighborhoods. And the smaller the neighborhood, the better it operates.

Seven or eight years ago, Senator Proxmire asked me to come down to Washington to give some testimony on cities. Now Proxmire is a pretty anti-city guy. He's always been that way. I spoke of trying to find out what an efficient city size would be so that the government might put some real money into a national survey of cities. You'd take New York, then a city like Cleveland, another of 300,000 of 200,000 and so on. Well, Congress didn't follow that up, but there's been some work done on it, and the conclusion that many of us have reached is that a city of 150,000 is most efficient from the point of view of taxes and also, curiously enough, from the point of view of culture. In *The Double E*, I've got a little discussion of that. So, for example, Florence had 245,000 people in it when Michelangelo and Leonardo lived there. Not that size alone will do. I mean, go to a city like Syracuse and, you know, nothing happens in a place of that sort. Go through the whole country and you find little places and big places that are really terrible. Go to San Francisco, that's great, or New York, and that's great, too. But actually only *parts* of those places are great. Brooklyn is zero; the Bronx is zero; Staten Island is zero. So where are great things happening? They're happening in a small area. If you took the number of people who make them happen, you'd probably find a half-million. The rest of them could drop out of sight and culturally, nobody would know the difference.

Universities contribute a great deal, and they also have their faults. My first academic job was at New York University. When I came back from Paris I was the only person in New York talking modern architectural language. Students were beginning to catch an undercurrent of new things. And I was invited to give lectures at NYU when it had an architecture school. I'd been in Paris on account of winning a big prize and that set me up for four years, from 1925 to 1929. Those were the days of Hemingway and the whole expatriate scene. They were beautiful times. A dollar was worth five dollars—among other things. For me it was absolutely wonderful. The totality of Paris.

I still get a bang out of every visit to Paris. Upon my return, I opened an office. NYU offered me a job to lecture at the night school, and then that closed up. So my friend Whitman and I decided that we would run an atelier in the French style. And we did and it was very good. But that also folded. And then during the radical days, a group of my former employees and students came to me, and we started the Design Laboratory, based on the Bauhaus, which by that time had been closed up by the Nazis. That was pretty good until the Commies got really busy at it. The situation became more and more sticky. You couldn't move with these guys who were constantly shouting about the fact that you weren't getting enough class consciousness into your work. So that ended. Then there was a hiatus.

I got my first opportunity to do a synagogue in—would you believe—Lima, Ohio. I knew Lima, Peru, but I didn't know Lima, Ohio. Nevertheless I built a small synagogue there which was very successful from their point of view, meaning it was built at half the budget the local architect had proposed. It suited them; it was not imitative, and it seemed to me to be authentically Jewish. *I was inventing the tradition, if you please.* That is to say, being a modernist, I strove to understand what the Jewish service was all about, what these people were trying to do that was neither

Catholic nor Protestant, and tried as best I could to express that difference in the materials which were available—steel, concrete, and the rest. I'd been in Temple Emmanuel, Central Synagogue, the Little Synagogue Around the Corner, and all of them struck me as irrelevant. They were exactly what I didn't want to do.

I started out with Reform Jews, but also I built Orthodox synagogues. If you go to 62nd Street and Fifth Avenue, you'll see an Orthodox synagogue of mine—the Fifth Avenue Synagogue.

On this subject the question of Jewishness as such is central to my thinking. First there's the Torah and what the Torah represents. But let me suggest a larger example. Shortly after the synagogue in Lima, Ohio, I was given a Reform Synagogue in Providence, Rhode Island called Beth-El and because of that, I was given the Baltimore Hebrew Congregation. They were both very large, old German Reform temples. The Providence rabbi, who is still a good friend of mine, had no notion about what a synagogue should be. The rabbi was a real old-time Jew who had no feeling whatsoever about aesthetic shape. Neither did the members. Anyway, I designed their building on the basis that they had a fine site, a congregation with an adequate amount of money to build the kind of synagogue that should be built, and I had a free hand because they didn't know what I was about. The old building they had was in Roman style, and that they knew was "out." But what was "in," they had no feeling about at all. So I designed a building in what I felt was appropriate form for the site and for these people. Again, it was successful, meaning it was within the budget, so none of the people who were worried about money could complain. It was hailed as a very important building for the Jews of Providence, and as I got to know people like the rabbi, I began to learn more and more.

Then I was invited to Israel in 1950 to be a judge in a competition for the design of a monument for Theodor Herzl. At first, I didn't want to go because I'd come to the conclusion that monuments were not for Jews. A setting, yes, but a monument, no. Prior to this Jerusalen episode, I had been asked to design a New York memorial for the six million Jews of the Holocaust. On Riverside Drive at 80th or 82nd Street, you'll see a plaque in the ground which is a piece of property given by La Guardia to

The Fifth Avenue Synagogue, designed by Percival Goodman. DANIEL ROSEN-
BERG.

the Jews of New York in memoriam. I designed a monument for this place which was to serve as background for a religious service. My notion was that once a year, as we had Polish day, Puerto Rican Day, Columbus Day, St. Patrick's Day, there should be Jewish Day, and on this day, people wouldn't march, they would walk carrying a Torah, two Torahs, an Ark, and they'd walk over to Central Park, where a couple thousand Jews would gather and someone would recite the Kaddish (mourners' prayer) and say, "Can't we be brothers?" or something of the sort. That would be the memorial. Our estimable parks commissioner, Bob Moses, being Jewish, and therefore an anti-Semite, destroyed the project. I thought there should be no monuments because, to my mind, their use is not the way Jews memorialize. They memoralize with *words*, with the service. That, throughout history, is how we've memorialized. We don't memorialize with buildings, with stones, with concrete; it's not in our tradition. Jewish history has not allowed us to build monuments. Therefore, we have no history of monuments. No tradition of monuments. What we do have is a tradition of oral memorializing. Every Jewish service ends with a spoken memorial for the dead. This was on my mind when I accepted the Israeli invitation. I fully intended to oppose the monument. By refusing to go, I couldn't accomplish anything. Once there, I reviewed each project and pointed out why it was unsuitable, till finally everyone might agree with me. And none of the projects was accepted. Whether that was my influence or simply a reflection on the projects, they were all judged unsuitable.

I had positive ideas too. I said, "You want to celebrate or memorialize Herzl? Well, the whole country is a memorial to Herzl. You can have a Herzl Street, or a Herzl anything you please. That's a memorial."

In Israel, a group of nutty Orthodox men came to me: "We hear you're a great synagogue builder. We want to rebuild the temple in Jerusalem." I told them that one was enough: "When the Messiah comes," I'd do it again. Seemed to me fair enough! But just going to Israel gave me the feeling that they were on the wrong track. Why, the minute I landed at Lod Airport there was a busybody stamping passports . . . something that is not Jewish. Hadn't Jews had problems enough with this sort of thing? Documents! I felt that Israel should be open, that the UN ought to be in Jerusalem, that the big Israel export should not be refrigerators, turnips, or oranges. It should be peace. That's what the world needed, and needs most of all. If they had gone into the peace business, Israelis wouldn't have the problems that bedevil them.

I've been back several times. If I'm invited to participate in a dialogue, I go. If you don't go, you're a coward. So you've got to go and say your piece. Israel's no homeland for me. I've got a homeland. The Jew is *not* somebody from Judea, not any more. Two thousand years have made the Jew an international being. That's what he must realize. All the energy of our international community should not be given to making commodities. There should be a place that manufactures *peace*; I think that's what we need. It should not be a "homeland." Now, a spiritual center, that's something else.

Christians sometimes have a clearer idea about all this. When William Blake writes of Zion, he's really using the language that I try to talk. Zion is an image, a utopia, something we aspire to. It isn't a question of daily business. One sees a university in Jerusalem, not a shoe factory with material goods to export. The Jew is a creature of the Diaspora plus two thousand years of the Torah, and all its ramifications. He's carried that tradition with him in his books. That's what we're all about.

In 1945 or 1946, a friend of mine named John Moore had been teaching at Columbia and he had a problem. Someone supposed to teach a city planning course didn't show. John asked me to fill in for him. I went up to Columbia (I was currently popular) and I stayed for twenty-five years. There were no other Jews on the architecture faculty. Meyer Schapiro was, of course, in the art history department, but I was the first in architecture. I enjoyed the experience. It only meant three afternoons a week, plus occasional committee meetings. I had no academic pretensions or desires. I wasn't competing with anyone. My students came mostly from other schools to do master's degrees. I was pretty much left alone, another one of those lucky circumstances. I was a maverick, but they accepted me because I was no threat to them.

Until the last years, to get me to a faculty meeting wasn't

easy. Everyone knew I had a full-time job in my office. Working with graduate students was something I did for fun. In 1968 came the revolution; I got involved in those last years. My little group of fifteen to twenty guys, with a big sprinkling from the under-developed countries in Africa, looked to me for guidance on questions of technology, whether and how far to follow the American lead, etc. At Columbia it didn't happen but the so-called revolution destroyed another great school.

When Paul went to City College, so did every intellectual in New York who was worth a damn. Paul, who was idolized by the militants for awhile in the sixties, became very sour. . . . Things weren't going the way he wanted them to.

All in all, there's much to be heartsick about. I'd prefer New York City to be like it was when I was young. And I'd like lemon meringue pie to taste the way it used to taste. Basically, I'm lamenting the loss of my youth. Still, some changes are demonstrable—and they're for the worst. I like to walk in Central Park; it's very difficult to walk in Central Park. That symbolizes all kinds of things. I suspect that New York *is doomed*. Every time it's ready to declare bankruptcy, they throw a little more money into it. What for?

For a simple economic point of view, there's no purpose in New York any more. As a culture center, it's going down the drain. The number of theaters that have been closed is one indication. The fact that other cities, thank the Lord, are beginning to develop a cultural life of their own means something. That's only part of it. Economically, New York is not viable. It has to go, hat in hand, to the government and the government has to lend this city money. Why? Because they couldn't conceive of New York going broke. The large Hispanic—black population we have is not composed of urban people. What kind of city is this that has so many people who are not urban? There were manufacturing jobs for the earlier immigrants, many of which don't exist any more. What can these people do? A tremendous number of them sit on stoops drinking beer, living on welfare.

And that's not a reasonable way to manage, to grow, and advance in a city.

Apart from our work, what keeps me and many of my friends in New York? Well, there's the Natural History Museum, the Museum of Modern Art, you can include Columbia as a piece of territory and you've nearly got it. Maybe the Brooklyn Museum, if you're interested in its Egyptian collection. I know there's a treasury greater than that, only I sense less of it these days. I used to go to the 42nd Street Library after work. John Peterkin's office was at 50 East 42nd Street. I'd have dinner at the Automat and spend the evening in the fine arts section of the Public Library. Now that I know more, Avery Library at Columbia strikes me as better. Avery's the best architectural library in the country, maybe in the world. Art historians and architecture historians draw heavily on that library. At present I'm working on the first big translation of a French classic history of architecture. I suppose I should be working up at Avery. I'd find more reference material there than in my own books at home. But that isn't the way I like to work. I'm not a scholar. To anyone with a passion for architectural scholarship, Avery's indispensable.

Now, my brother was and was not a scholar. I'm sure there will be biographies to come about Paul. But I can tell some things about his life: My brother wrote his first publishable story at the age of sixteen. In 1960, he wrote *Growing Up Absurd*, the one book that really sold. But including at least the first year's revenue from that book, Paul and I figured out one day that he had averaged twenty-five dollars a week in his working life. Nothing could shake Paul's confidence in himself because he never bothered about his own self. What he bothered about was the fact that people weren't listening to him. There came a time when they did listen. And when that happened, he began to say, "Eh, they're a bunch of *schmucks*. They listen to *me*." I think Paul was a great man, and as time goes on his particular importance will grow. It will not be the importance of a sociologist but of an artist. I believe that *Empire City* is one of the first-class novels of the twentieth century.

The title tells you a lot—it's very hard to separate him from the city. In *Empire City*, you can read a version of Paul's notion of me, of Paul's notion of Paul, and of Paul's notion of my sister Alice. We're all in that book. Paul, who wrote *The Lordly Hudson*, one of the best American genre poems, knew our Hudson River, not so much the Hudson that's out there, but more like the Hudson seen from 133rd Street.

Paul was *sui generis*—he also belonged to a specific group that included Delmore Schwartz, Harold Rosenberg, Ben Nelson—and maybe ten more people. What brought it to flower? How did we get an efflorescence of Jewish novelists? Why Bellow and Mailer and Roth? There's no question that a seed will germinate in a certain kind of soil. Look at Paris, for example, during the time of Lipchitz and Soutine and Chagall. Jacques Lipchitz was a very good friend of mine. I asked him about this. And his answer was, "You come from a place where you're not supposed to make images. Suddenly, you're in a place where you can make images . . . the shackles are *off* and you make your images." You see other people doing it and what was pent up in you is allowed to burst out. Something like that took place on the New York Jewish literary scene. Not that it has to be literary or aesthetic at all. You get poor guys with a pack on their back and forty years later, they're millionaires or billionaires. They see an opportunity where no one else sees it, and they jump in. I suppose the same sort of talent did that. Jack Kaplan is the only *rich* millionaire I know—probably worth 200 million dollars. Jack started out when he was fourteen years old selling newspapers in Brockton, Massachusetts. How did he come to have 200 million? To my mind, it took as much genius as there is in writing a great novel. The reward is not so lasting, but, nevertheless, there it is. When Jack Kaplan tells me what he did, I'm just as amazed as when a writer tells me how he went about composing a book. At certain points in history a number of people have a feeling for the right thing at the right time, for putting down the right word at the right moment. Paul was part of that.

I think my brother was a great man because he almost never compromised. Paul lived in cold water flats for a good part of his life and he wouldn't change a line. No editors could get him to. They tried; he just wouldn't. Black Mountain College was important to him for the free environment it provided. But then: "Paul, have you been making advances to this young man?" It happened in Chicago, too. Paul liked an academic life; he was a good teacher. I don't think he would, by preference, have been peripatetic. But every time he settled down, suddenly, there was a blond-haired young man who created problems. That was the story of Paul's academic career. He was uncompromising even on issues that didn't seem important to me. Like refusing to wear a necktie when coming to a dinner party without one could only offend others. He had many quirks that made material advancement impossible for him throughout most of his life.

Paul and I were pretty close. His bisexuality didn't bother me. You see, he believed in the family. He was an antiabortionist, for example. Idiotic of him, but he meant it. He believed in the family and was a *paterfamilias* as well as a homosexual. Somehow he had to compromise this position. It was not hard for him to do because he felt there was a difference between duty and pleasure: your duty was to have a family and your pleasure was to have a boy. He adored his son Matthew. The heartbreak for Paul of Matthew's death probably shortened his life. I blame the FBI or the CIA or whoever it was. Matthew went to Cornell where he was a brilliant student in biology, and he refused to register for the draft as a protest against the Vietnam War. Paul supported him to the hilt. And chances were that Matthew would be arrested because he refused to compromise at all. Matthew was Paul in spades, the kind of kid who fasted one day a week because it was good for the soul to do that. Unbelievable boy with an utterly gentle disposition and a brilliant mind. So, up in New Hampshire, unfortunately there's a mountain that Matthew climbed to get some huckleberries. It's Mt. Percy. He went up 2,000 feet and fell 300 feet down until a rock hit him. But he was an expert climber. The only explanation I can think of is that his mind was on his being pinched by the FBI or whoever was after guys like him. I blame them. He was twenty-two years old, a young man who would have carried on in the best tradition of Jewish intellectuals.

As for myself, during the last fifteen years, I've been trying to help civilization by finding a use for unwanted things. You know, all these things here in my office are picked out of garbage cans. These are packing crates, and so forth. I enjoy doing those and I like to paint and make sculpture. My wife Naomi is of the opinion that we really ought to move out to East Hampton. But I have difficulty in closing up the practice. That's the problem.

It's really very difficult to say what you want to do. My problem, in a nutshell: my sister died; in the course of events, I would be the next. Seven years after I've died, Paul would die. Well, Paul done me wrong. He died first. We were going to do a book together and it didn't come out that way. So, I really feel that it was a great mistake because I think Paul had much more to offer than I did in the years that were left. If it's a case of apples and oranges, his apples were better than my oranges, or vice versa. So it's a difficult thing to say. My problem is that while I never doubted my capacity, now I get nervous about what I design. I never used to ask myself whether I ought to be doing this, that, or the other thing.

I'm finishing another book and when asked about a memoir I think again of Paul. The problem with having a brother who wrote extremely well is that you have a lot of hesitancy about writing. For example, several years ago, I was invited up to Springfield, Massachusetts by a Unitarian Church to be interviewed to design a building. I took the train up there, I got out at the station at dusk, and found you could walk to the Unitarian Church. As I walked in the dusk, I saw a handsome tower and profile of a building, and I found out that that was, in fact, where I was going. So I went inside, and the inside was as good as the outside. And there was the building committee waiting for me. We began to discuss what they had in mind and what I had done, and what I should be doing for them if I did it. As I looked around the room, I saw that the windows were by Tiffany, the kind of thing I don't like too much, but these were beautiful examples of what Tiffany could do. So then, having looked around and heard what they said, I said, "Why do you want to move out of this building?"

"It's not suitable for us."

I said, "By the way, who designed this building? Do you know? It's really an interesting building."

"A fellow named Richardson designed it."

So I asked them, "Do you know he's a great American architect?" They professed to know, but still it was not the building for them. I told them, "Those Tiffany windows are very important."

But their question was, "What would you do if you designed a new building for us?"

I said, "I couldn't design a building as good as this one. And I don't think those windows ought to be moved out of this building."

I didn't get the job. I told Paul about this and he wrote a marvelous story called "The Architect From New York." Now the problem with writing a memoir is that when I see how I told the story and how Paul wrote it, believe me . . . I like beautiful words and the way they string together. It's one of those things that really gives me a bang. Just as I like beautiful buildings and beautiful girls. It all fits together.

20.

THE RABBI'S DAUGHTER
AS JUDGE AND HUMANIST

Justine Wise Polier

I CHANCED to have been born in Portland, Oregon because my
father, Stephen Wise, then a very young rabbi, chose to leave his
home in New York City to explore the Northwest for awhile.
He intended thereby to be more than "the son of Rabbi Aaron
Wise"—and to enlarge his understanding of America. Father first
went out to the West Coast in 1899, visiting California, Oregon,
and Alaska. Then he agreed to be the rabbi of the Reform temple
in Portland. He and my mother were engaged at that time. They
agreed that after their marriage they would move to Oregon. I
think his six years there were the happiest and most important
part of his formative phase.

Portland was still part of the American frontier, with lots of
shooting—and very few educated people. My father was asked
to join a luncheon club of university graduates where he met a
small group of intellectuals, among them the great lawyer, Dick
Montague, and a young Episcopalian minister. One day the young
minister asked him home to lunch. There he found his friend's
mother presiding in a very cold and austere fashion. Afterwards
my father and his friend went for a walk in the Portland woods.
They talked about their dreams and hopes. Suddenly the minister
stopped and said, "Wise, do you know what happened this morn-

Justine Wise Polier is a lawyer, humanitarian, and retired judge of the New York State
Family Court. She was born in Portland, Oregon in 1903. A pioneer in legislation on
children's rights, she has received a Distinguished Service award from the city of New
York (1973) and many other awards for service in philanthropic and community service
organizations. She is author of a number of books on the law and the family.

330

ing? I told my mother I was bringing a young rabbi home for lunch. She looked at me and said, 'What do I do with it? Bake it, broil it, or stew it?'"

At that time there were terrible attacks on the Chinese. The Exclusion Act was passed; Chinese people were fingerprinted. My father battled on their behalf. There was also the question of open prostitution and the involvement of criminal elements in houses of ill fame, and he openly took them on. And on that account his life was threatened. Then came a much more basic issue: the exploitation of children in mines and factories. He began his work on behalf of child labor laws. He and my mother subsequently went to see many textile mills in the South.

Later he helped to establish the National Child Labor Committee. But while still in Portland—incidentally, I was given the National Award by that committee, which would have pleased him—he became the first Commissioner for Child Welfare in the state of Oregon, a nonpaid position, while he remained as rabbi. And then my father was offered a senatorship, actually a nomination on the Republican party ticket which was a shoo-in. After a long struggle with himself, he rejected the opportunity. That was a major decision for him. While in Oregon, he, along with others, asked Louis D. Brandeis, who was then a celebrated lawyer, to take the case on minimum wages for women that became famous as Muller vs. Oregon. And in this period he started to lecture in universities, the commencement of a long trek through academia in America. My father saw these six years in Portland as a period of wonderful, personal happiness: he did a tremendous amount of reading, and at the same time felt the pulse of America while coming to know many of the most important leaders of his day. The whole experience gave him drive and direction. Translating his beliefs and principles into the American reality and doing it explicitly as a Jew was the role he saw for himself.

He kept developing that theme throughout his life. It went right on. He filed a famous suit with my husband as his counsel against Columbia, of which he was a graduate, because of its discrimination against minority groups prior to the enactment of the Fair Education Practices Law. He also served as a member of the Truman Committee on Equality in Education.

In 1905 he was asked to preach trial sermons at Temple Emanu-El in New York. They had heard that he was a great young Jewish orator. He came on and everybody was most impressed. The leaders of Temple Emanu-El offered him the pulpit. My father felt that he could only accept on his own conditions. One, unheard of in those days, was having a private secretary; two, working with poor Jews on the Lower East Side; third, and most important, having complete freedom of the pulpit. The first two conditions were met. The third came up and Louis Marshall cried, "Freedom of the pulpit? The pulpit is always subject to control by the Board of Trustees." Seligman, a banker who'd been a friend of my maternal grandfather, was conciliatory: "Oh, I'm sure Rabbi Wise can explain what he means . . ." and gave father a kick under the table. Father said, "Yes, I can. It means that I would have to speak out against child labor in your copper mines, Mr. Guggenheim. It means, Mr. Marshall, that I would have to attack your partner, Mr. Untermeyer, who is tied into the corrupt Tammany Hall machine. It means that I would have to. . . ." I've forgotten what other things. He always told us that mother was standing behind the curtains shaking her head, against his yielding. And father wound up with, "Gentlemen, I think you now know what I mean by 'freedom of the pulpit.'" He went back to Oregon and wrote an open letter, which became famous, on freedom of the pulpit.

Father also made up his mind that the time had come for him to return to New York, the center of Jewish life. There he would start his own synagogue. He came east with my mother, my brother, and myself—my brother was a year and a half older than I, and I was three. We lived in my grandfather's home. My father began to work without salary and slowly got together a group of people who shared his beliefs. They started the Free Synagogue.

Within two years, mother and father bought a little house on the West Side, which shocked my mother's family because that was déclassé. If you lived between Madison and Park Avenue, where my grandfather's house was, at 68th Street, that was considered very definitely on a different social and economic level. And, of course, by that time, father had also become strongly identified with the Zionist movement, which was also unacceptable to the wealthy German Jews of New York. Many of my mother's friends, including the Schiff, Warburg, and Loeb crowd, regarded him as a stormy petrel.

Early on, I felt the tension between East European and German Jews. We went to Germany when I was nine. That's my first recollection of the tension. My father had a sabbatical year. He was going to take us to Egypt and Palestine, but typhoid broke out in Italy and the Middle East. So our parents left my brother and me in Munich. They put me in a German day school and my brother in an academy. I lived in a pension with a maiden aunt. My mother's cousins lived in Munich—one was a judge, one was a lawyer, one was a banker. They were wealthy—very assimilated—and I sensed the discomfort they felt because their cousin was married to a rabbi. I began to feel their appreciation for my mother and complete lack of appreciation for my father, whom I always adored. Father's mail went to their home while he was abroad. I remember their being amazed that father got letters from the White House from Woodrow Wilson. That almost made him acceptable.

I resented the whole German ambience, the pension, that rich family. They didn't appreciate my beloved father. So at the age of ten I ran away and used my pocket money to send a cable saying, "I will not stand it another minute" to mother and father. They received it and sent word that I was to be brought immediately to Naples, where they would meet me. When I got there I buried my head in his shoulders and wept for about two hours. He was ready to kill the whole German nation! Anyway, that's my first personal memory of this cleavage that I really felt. And, of course, I also heard tales, many of them about some of mother's former social friends asking her to a party without father and her saying, "Of course not!" I remember her telling us about being married by old Rabbi Kohler, and his taking her aside and saying, "Your young husband has a great future if he will give up this *meshugas* of Zionism." And mother, who had been brought up in a completely non-Jewish world, had never been in a synagogue until she met father, saying, "I want him to do whatever he believes is right." I sensed a lot of this as a child.

One of my earliest memories was of father having a distinguished "colored" leader (before we got to "Negro," before we got to "black") for dinner. We lived in a house on West 90th

Street, with a living room, a dining room, and a foyer in between. Father and mother always had my brother and myself join them at dinner no matter who came. I remember holding my father's hand and seeing a very distinguished tall man with white hair (I have no idea who he was) telling father, "I'm sorry, Rabbi Wise, but you cannot ask me to sit down to dinner with a colored man." And my father simply answering, "Oh, I'm so sorry. May I take you downstairs and help you get your coat?"

We went to Sunday school and we usually went afterwards to synagogue to hear father preach. And we met Jews from all over the world, whether they were escapees from Tsarist Russia or residents of the Lower East Side, or from far-flung educational circles, or leaders of the NAACP. Father was one of the signers for the call to establish the NAACP in 1909, which made people say, "What are you doing? Reducing the Jews to the level of the nigger?" He suffered terrific attacks on that. But he persisted, never deviating, always going his own way.

New York was considered the world center of Western Jewry. And so it was. But when father went to Poland before the war, he came back telling us how deeply moved he had been by the intellectual and moral leadership of Jews in that country. This made him feel that American Jews were far too parochial and too arrogant in claiming that they could decide what should happen in Eastern Europe instead of trusting the Jews who lived there to determine their own life and fate. He objected to the view that because you had money and the privilege to give, you could also impose your thinking on people who lived in a different part of the world. That attitude was consistent with his feeling about the democratization of Jewish life in America. He always resented the power of the purse. To him it was a disease of our life in this country that the Jewish *balabatim* (wealthy people, with power) should presume to speak for their fellow Jews without really searching them out and seeking to understand them. That was a major motivation for starting the American Jewish Congress.

When I grew up, I went to Bryn Mawr for two years, got interested in social and economic problems, and transferred to

Radcliffe. In mid-year, sensing that I wasn't close enough to people, I moved out of that blue-stocking world and found a job as a resident in the Elizabeth Peabody House, the old Settlement House in Boston. Then I wired my parents that I had moved. Father immediately came up—and found me living next to the Charles Street jail. While he was concerned, he felt I should be able to do whatever I considered to be right. So I combined teaching foreigners English and working with the people in that part of Boston, while I finished my year at Radcliffe. After that I came back to New York, enrolled at Barnard, and got involved in a research study on what happened to women following industrial injuries, how workmen's compensation related to the real loss of earning power. Economics was my major, but I took philosophy with Dewey, educational psychology with Kilpatrick, and I didn't go to my graduation because I did not wish to receive a diploma from the hands of an arch-conservative, Nicholas Murray Butler.

Instead, I went to Europe. After that, to experience labor conditions first hand, I joined four friends in the textile factories of Passaic and Paterson, working the night shift first in a cotton factory, and then tried to work at the Botany worsted mills. They had a "gestapo" in those days: searched your house when you weren't there, found out who you were, and although I attempted to conceal my identity, they discovered it and fired me. When asked what my father did, my reply was, "clerical work." My mother? "housework." Education? "I finished high school." Technically honest. Very clever—and all to no avail. They caught on to me very quickly.

My best friend who was there with me, the granddaughter of a bishop of Maryland, who married a Sephardic Jew to the horror of his family, had had the same experience in the Acheson-Hardin handkerchief mills. And so had two other friends, Sy Whitney, a descendant of Eli Whitney of Yale, and Roland Gilson, who was similarly discharged. Well, after that I began to study race relations in industry with Bruno Lasker, and went on to learn more at the International Labor Office in Geneva. The Jewish labor movement was inactive at that time in the textile mills. Sidney Hillman and David Dubinsky were starting to move in—but theirs was not a *Jewish* labor movement: it was the ILGWU and the Amalgamated. I also worked at adult education in Passaic, which is where management had its labor spies. At the end of that summer I met father and mother in London. Father respected my good intentions but he wondered why I didn't get myself to law school and learn something about people's rights. He gave me four beautiful folio volumes of Blackstone, which I still have. So I wrote to Yale Law School, and they admitted me. During my second year at Yale, a strike developed at Passaic; I commuted between Yale and Passaic to help with the strike. The conditions were horrendous. Father was tremendously helpful in organizing a group, in getting Senator Borah interested, in involving Sidney Hillman, and in coming out to address the strikers, as I did, in a less important way. The president of Yale was very disconcerted by my behavior.

At the end of my second year, I married a young Yale professor, Leon Arthur Tulin. We had a lot of fun working together. After graduation I did a study on workmen's compensation. A year later we moved to New York and my husband became an associate professor at Columbia law school. Then he became fatally ill. He died of leukemia when our son, Stephen, was four years old. Those were terrible years. After Leon's death, I once again wanted to be independent. So I moved down to Greenwich Village and I took a little apartment for ninety dollars a month. Soon I was the first woman referee in the Department of Labor for Workmen's Compensation. And out of that came a study on the Medical Care of Injured Workers. I was also active in the Women's Trade Union movement.

When LaGuardia came in as mayor (1933–34), I was asked to direct the division of the Corporation Counsel's Office in Workmen's Compensation. I discovered that doctors' bills were paid only if 50 percent of their take went to Jimmy Walker's brother, Dr. Walker! I set up a program by which city workers could choose their own doctors and get impartial testimony. Then, with the guidance of Walter Gelhorn, legislation was drafted so that the new system could be applied statewide. After four or five years in that field, I did a study on welfare for the Mayor's Committee on Unemployment Relief, challenging procedures which were harmful to families who had to seek welfare. After the report was published, LaGuardia sent for me to ask whether I'd like to be on the bench. I didn't think I wanted that. "Well, would you like to be on the Domestic Relations Court?" That didn't much interest me because I had been told that the judges were rubber stamps for probation officers. He said, "Why don't you go up and take a look?" I told him, "If I were to be a judge, I'd rather be a magistrate." Magistrates handled labor cases and at that time, labor injunctions were pervasive. LaGuardia exploded, "That's just like you! I offer you a higher position and you want a lower position with less pay! Go take a look!" I went and took a look. The first case I saw and heard ended with a judge pronouncing that unless a man and woman who were not married and had a child got married within ten days, he would take the child away. I came back and told LaGuardia that I would like to be a judge of the court but I would only stay for a couple of years, or long enough to do a study. I was sworn in.

I was fascinated by the work but at the end of six weeks we had trouble with WPA. Where General Hugh S. Johnson, Roosevelt's economic tsar for the country began the program in New York City, I began to get reports about how he pretended there were work programs but actually people weren't paid promptly and had nothing to live on. They went from Home Relief to WPA, but the projects weren't real, the tools were not there. LaGuardia asked me to meet with General Johnson and the Commissioner of Welfare, Charlotte Carr, who had been Labor Commissioner for Gifford Pinchot in Pennsylvania. Johnson demanded that we take 100,000 people off welfare until they accepted work. We negotiated, and it was agreed this Miss Carr would find 10,000 people a week to register for work. Still, he openly attacked people on welfare as loafers. I wrote an open letter to General Johnson, saying he had no right to cover administrative errors by this kind of attack on welfare people. I called a press conference and gave a statement to the press at the same time that LaGuardia received it. He demanded that I withdraw it. I refused and he said he was ordering me to do it "as Mayor of New York," and that if I did not comply, he wouldn't reappoint me. I said that was up to him, but I could not do what he was asking. This was a matter of conscience. Anyway, my term expired and he did not reappoint me. I went to Lake Placid (where my child was) for a two-week holiday, and resolved to look for a job after that.

Back in New York, one day just after breakfast with Louis Weiss, a distinguished lawyer and senior partner of Paul, Weiss, and Garrison, the phone rang and it was Charles Burlingham, the Dean of the Bar, an old friend who had published the Sacco-Venzetti documents. He said, "The Mayor came up to Connecticut and asked me to recommend somebody in your place. Felix Frankfurter was there and he wanted to know what LaGuardia meant. LaGuardia's response was, 'I have got to have discipline in the judiciary'—at which we hit the ceiling." They had a long talk. The next day, I got a call from the Mayor, who asked to see me and sent his chauffeur. When I got to his house, LaGuardia opened the door himself. "Come in . . . I could have expected this from Robert Moses but not from you." And he proceeded to tell me that the trouble was that, like my father, I said whatever I wanted to and didn't care about the consequences. And I answered, "Yes, but there is a difference between you and my father: no matter what I do, he has confidence in and stands behind me."

Well, the dialogue went like this: "Do you want to be a judge?"

"Yes, I'm fascinated with the work and would like to continue."

"Do you want a year or ten years? Ten years from you or nothing! Come up and have breakfast with me day after tomorrow."

I went to his house and he swore me in. This ended another episode. But instead of staying ten years, I stayed for thirty-seven!

When I first went on the bench, there was a very small, good group of judges, whom LaGuardia had appointed. It later became more of a political football.

I think that I first ran into the terrible discrimination against black children in the court system. I would be told by probation officers, "There is nothing we can do about this little boy who's black, and Protestant, unless he commits a felony or becomes twelve years old; then we can send him to a training school." I was so horrified that I collected a group of twenty cases and went down to LaGuardia. He sent me to see Bishop Manning. I went with my beloved friend, Dr. Marion Kenworthy, founder of the child guidance movement, whose background was Episcopalian. We arranged for the temporary use of some property recently bequeathed to the Protestant Episcopal Mission Society (Wiltwyck). So, Wiltwyck School got started. Then Marshall Field got interested and provided funds for professional staff and to build a school and gymnasium. When the war came the Society decided that they needed to put their money into chaplaincies rather than children.

This happened in 1941 when I was serving as counsel to Mrs. Roosevelt in Washington. Those were war days. She asked me what she could do for me when I was leaving (I had to come back because my husband, Shad Polier, was going into the service), and I said, "Well, there *is* something. We should form a nonsectarian, interracial board that will carry on the work at Wiltwyck for the children of minority groups." So she helped form this new group, and we took over the school with the generous help of Mr. Field and some other friends, including Adele Rosenwald Levy. A few years later, Shad drafted the first law in this country stipulating that voluntary agencies in receipt of public funds could not discriminate against children on the basis of race. At first it was a city law, weak, but the first in this country. Did New York City make it possible? I now think it was a combination of the city and a group of citizens who assumed leadership and made other people understand. In this instance, my husband's knowledge of constitutional law and concern for human rights and my experience in the Children's Court were helpful. We began working on it. And it was our good fortune to have Stanley Isaacs on the City Council. He led the battle for the enactment of the Brown-Isaacs Bill. This would not have been possible without sympathetic support from larger groups within New York City and in other places. Minority children were either treated with benign or malignant neglect or sent to the wrong place.

Another problem in New York City came from the fact and the custom that everything for children was done on a sectarian basis: the Jewish agencies took *their* children. One of my first fights with the Jewish Child Care Association involved a man who regarded himself as a descendant of Ethiopian Jews. He went to a little Black Jewish synagogue. The Jewish Child Care Association said they didn't want to take his child. And I said, "You've got to take him! You say you take Jewish children, and this man has brought up his children Jewish. You've got to take him!"

Then, of course, there were constant battles with the Catholic Church. The first important opinion I wrote in *that* field was a fascinating one, which really got me into trouble with the Church. I had four kids before me, whose father was Turkish Moslem and whose mother was Irish Catholic. They had been married by a Protestant minister. During a period when the couple was fighting, the mother took the oldest child, a boy, and had him secretly baptized in the Catholic faith. Later, when they had another battle, the husband had a Moslem ceremony in the house and the second child, a girl, was inducted into the Moslem faith. At the time the parents came before me, charged with neglect, they were terribly deteriorated people. I found that the boy who had been baptized Catholic was tall, black, and swarthy, fifteen years old, and wanted to live with a Moslem uncle, who was a very good person. The girl, who had been "baptized" Moslem, was blonde and blue-eyed like her mother, and loathed everything Moslem, including her father, whom she accused of trying to molest her.

After doing a lot of research, looking into English law, the Louisiana law, the New England law, I found that the children should not be bound by religious ceremonies, especially when they occurred without the consent of parents, but by what was in their best interest. So I placed the "Catholic" boy with the Moslem uncle and the "Moslem" girl with a Catholic agency. The *Brooklyn Tablet* thereupon came out with a big spread: "Daughter of Rabbi Wise Turns Over the Child of Christ to the Bearded Prophet Mohammed!"

Next, I got a call from the Cardinal's office that a certain distinguished lawyer wanted to see me. I said I'd be glad to see him at my home. He came down and told me the Cardinal was very disturbed that I had undermined the role of baptism. I told him the facts of the case and asked, "What would you have done if you were a judge who had to determine what was in the best interest of the child?"

"Well," he responded, "I don't know what you did that was wrong, but why did you have to write an *opinion*?"

"Because I spent a week or more in the Bar Association and found that every decision on these cases had been without an opinion. If I had to spend all that time in research, I felt I should set forth the law as I understand it and the basis for my decision."

Also, in those days—under our law—although probation officers were public servants, only a Protestant probation officer could serve a Protestant child, a Catholic probation officer a Catholic child, a Jewish probation officer a Jewish child. And only Negroes could serve Negroes. Judge Hubert Delany, a wonderful judge, and I opposed that practice.

The Church had long taken the position that if parents couldn't look after their own children, then the Church was the only appropriate parent-surrogate, and that therefore, there should be no public facilities. This went back to the days of John Purroy Mitchell, an outstanding Mayor of New York. He had a great Commissioner of Social Welfare—Kingsbury. Kingsbury found a canceled check which had been paid by the City of New York to the Catholic Orphan Asylum in New York (no longer in existence). It had been endorsed as "Peter's Pence" in Rome. In other words, it hadn't been used for the children; it had been sent to Rome. As a result, there was a great commotion and the Catholic Church sent out word that every priest was to speak against the reelection of Mitchell. He was defeated. (He then joined the air force, and was killed in World War I.)

The Church's constant opposition to public services continued even when the sectarian agencies could not meet the needs of children. Being on the Foster Care Commission of the City of New York as well as being a judge, I took the position that voluntary agencies, which were sectarian, could be used if they could provide prompt and appropriate services to a child. If not, there was a basic responsibility of the public welfare agency to provide such services.

The Jewish agencies provided the best coverage for their children. The number of Jewish delinquents was very small compared to the others—not necessarily because they were less delinquent but because more preventive and supportive services were available.

There's a great deal of difference about what happens to a child when he gets into trouble. If there's a reputable parent or social agency that says at least they'll take care of him, they are more likely to be referred to an agency. This is true at the point of arrest; then later, at the probation intake; and even later, when a case is before the court. Everything moves more smoothly and there are more voluntary placements. When there were appropriate private facilities, the court didn't have to shop around. Where there were few voluntary services for any group such as Protestant Negro children, the statistics on delinquency increased.

Intervention on behalf of children was a credit to the Jewish community, whose policy developed at the turn of the century when Commissioner Woods proclaimed that the doors of New York should be closed to Jewish immigrants, for they would commit "larceny, arson and sex attacks," and alleged many of them were mentally deficient. That was his statement in or around 1910! Commissioner Woods wanted to close the doors against Jews who would "undermine" American society. Every new immigrant group has always been under attack. So there were many, many problems in this whole field. Finally, a few of us were able to force the city to begin to develop public services to complement and supplement the voluntary services, but they continued to be and are still inadequate.

All this time I was deeply involved in endless discussion and constant meetings about the fate of German Jewry. In 1933 father called the first great meeting against Hitler at Madison Square Garden. For that he was strenuously attacked. I can still remember that Herbert Lehman pleaded with my father not to hold this meeting. The official line of the American Jewish Committee at that time was that if Stephen Wise condemned Hitler, the blood of the Jews of Germany would be on his head. And I remember his pacing the floor, wondering what was right, and his getting a cable from a man named Weiss in Germany, who had been Chief of Police, a Socialist, and a Zionist. His message urged that the meeting be cancelled. The following summer I met my father in Prague. We were having breakfast in the Hotel when there was a call that Dr. Weiss was downstairs and would like to meet Rabbi Wise. He came upstairs. It turned out that Dr. Weiss had been arrested and detained. He had been forced by the Gestapo to send the message to father to stop the Madison Square meeting of protest against Hitler, and wanted to apologize for his message. "It didn't *solve* anything, but that Madison Square Garden protest stopped some of the terror for a short period."

During this tragic period, there were incessant efforts by my father to move our State Department to help rather than mislead the public about what was happening to Jews in Germany. There were constant trips to Washington, the travels to embassies, to Christian groups at the Union Theological Seminary, where a few prominent German Jews had visited and insisted that they could handle the situation. They agreed that America should do nothing. These people, most of whom were later killed or arrested (a few managed to escape), included the editor of the *Frankfurter Zeitung*. It was a lonely course for my father, with no substantial sums of money, with hostility from the American Jewish Committee, with resistance from rich German Jews. Father had the vision to see that what was happening in Germany was going to affect the whole world and lead to war, but few listened. The Committee felt that the approach to the problem of Hitler must be through *Shtadtlonim* (people with access to the seats of power). As a matter of fact, Roosevelt once said to father, "Why are you so exercised on this? Max Warburg of Germany says Hitler will not hurt the German Jews."

There was "nothing to fear." Finally, father decided to hold that first mass meeting. The Committee would not participate. Bishop Manning, John L. Lewis, Senator Wagner, Father Ford were among the speakers, but the Committee would have no part of it. Like a beggar he pleaded in place after place. It was just an endless misery. Nahum Goldman, his coworker in the World Jewish Congress, often accompanied father to Washington. One day, father and Nahum took the five o'clock train to Washington, going from embassy to embassy, to the State Department, ev-

Rabbi Stephen S. Wise addressing an anti-Nazi rally in New York City, 1933.   AMERICAN JEWISH CONGRESS.

erywhere, and then they had no place to sleep. Not a room to be had. At last the Mayflower put up two cots in their billiard room for him and Nahum.

Finally the Secretary General of the World Jewish Congress got a clear message through to father about Nazi plans to exterminate the Jews. Father went down to the State Department with that document. They held up their response for two months, then denied that there were such plans.

In Paris, father got word that his affidavits were not being honored by the Marseilles consul; Jews who escaped were being held there, and if the Germans came they too would be destroyed. Father rented a car and drove to Marseilles, went into the consul's office and said, "I understand you are not honoring my affidavits."

The consul protested, "No man could honor as many affidavits as you've signed."

344

Father replied, "I will remain in your office until you call President Roosevelt and ask him whether my word is to be honored." He just sat there until the consul yielded. But it wasn't just one consul. Later he found out that his letters had been opened—whether by the Germans or by our consular service in Switzerland wasn't entirely clear—as well as material from father and Nahum to representatives of the World Jewish Congress, including Gerhardt Riegner, who had escaped from Germany and was heading this work: they did fantastic work in Switzerland. I don't think anybody looking back can realize the extent to which these few men were isolated, or how utterly anti-Semitic and dishonorable the State Department was, or how fearful Jews were here, afraid of stirring up trouble which might affect their position. Nor was there any apparatus for breaking through to reach the public.

Revisionist historians who blame father for not alerting the world have no appreciation of the atmosphere in which he had to live and work. His situation was like that of a dissenter in the Soviet Union today.

I think he hoped against hope that FDR would do something. There was no other person to whom he could turn. And President Roosevelt was not on the best of terms with father until about 1936. After all, Stephen Wise and John Haynes Holmes had attacked *Governor* Roosevelt for not ousting Jimmy Walker, and father supported Norman Thomas in 1932. After the election, he called to congratulate FDR and asked to meet with him as soon as possible, but there was a rift that had to be bridged. Samuel Rosenman was never very friendly and he was very close to Roosevelt. So were the Warburgs. A few years later, Henry Morgenthau was helpful when father went to him with a plan to put money in Switzerland as a bribe to Nazis who would let Jews escape. Henry proposed that they go over to the President and see if he'd agree. The President threw back his head and laughed, "Of course you may. They'll never live to get that money."

You also must remember that the Church and the Pope at that time were most unfriendly. When Pope John, then Bishop in Turkey, wanted to contribute money to help Jews escape, the Pope refused.

My father was surrounded by fear, by the accommodation of the Western world to Hitler in hopes of placating him, and by isolationism in America. Also there was the feeling that Jews would cause a world war, the hostility and the duplicity of the State Department, plus a great deal of open anti-Semitism spread by Father Coughlin and many others. Walls of loneliness surrounded the few Jews who spoke and tried to act. A sense of impotence was pervasive.

My father helped set up a U.S. Committee to admit Jewish children from Germany, with aid from Clarence Pickett, Marion Kenworthy, Marshall Field, and others. Mrs. Roosevelt offered to help, as she always did. The Wagner-Rogers bill was drafted to admit 10,000 Jewish children above the quota. The antagonism was unbelievable. Father pleaded with the tongue of angels before the Senate Committee, but American Legion Auxiliary people objected: "What? Admit Jews into our country who are born with hate in their hearts?" And the bill was defeated. The 10,000 Jewish children were not saved. Who can reconstruct the climate of those days? I don't know whether anybody ever will. Cardinal Spellman refused to associate himself with the efforts to save 10,000 Jewish children. We had to go to Bishop Sheil in Chicago for leadership in the North. A few wonderful Catholic bishops in the South rallied to the cause. It is hard for young people today to grasp the situation of those days.

The full horror of what was going on reached me just before the war. My father went to Paris to meet the first Jews who had escaped. When he returned he was charged with exaggerating. To his warning that there would be a world war if the abominations were allowed to continue, the response was that he was histrionic, an exaggerator, a demagogue.

There were allies among the Zionists, but they were of no great help in gaining a hearing or combating the isolationism in this country. One faced a deadly combination of isolationism, together with virulent anti-Semitism and general indifference to the fate of Jews.

Father fought for relaxing the immigration quotas, once again with very little support. There was the same desperate loneliness, the same lack of instrumentalities, the same lone voice, with just a few friends. It was heartbreaking—simply heartbreaking!

And as I look around today, I'm not at all sanguine that the world hasn't again forgotten. Do leaders in this country have a real sense of responsibility for Jewish survival in Israel? Moreover, there's strange combination on the left in Jewish life—a crowd trying to tell Jews whose lives are on the line what they should do in Israel. I find leftist Jews, like I. F. Stone, identifying with those who would be perfectly willing to see Israel destroyed. I find pacifists and people who are disillusioned about America's role in the world, withdrawing the hem of their garment from the defense of Israel. That includes some of my friends in the civil liberties world. Again, I find too many Jews apathetic, unaware of what they are allowing to happen, not as deeply committed as they should be. And I'm afraid I also find the Orthodox playing a most dubious role about Jewish survival. This too is a grim period for the Jewish people. To avert another Holocaust (and I don't say it has to come), we must do a tremendous amount of work.

My father, happily, did live to see the establishment of Israel. As a matter of fact, Truman sent him the pen with which he signed the recognition of Israel, which my father gave to my oldest son, Stephen. There is more to the story. Right now, I'm having trouble with some Jews in Federation who argue that Jewish agencies should concentrate their efforts on helping Jews and not accept so many nonwhite children in residential facilities; that the Jewish atmosphere is diluted. I said to one of them the other day, "You know, it's a strange thing that a former president of Federation dares to tell me privately that Jews are uninterested in the blacks. Well, my father was condemned for lending his name to the creation of the NAACP. Little did he think that at one point later in history, when two more votes were needed for the recognition of Israel, it would be Walter White of the NAACP who would get those votes!" I'm not saying you should support blacks because of what they might do in return, but surely one should realize that what one does determines whether other people will respect you and your beliefs.

After all that has happened in my lifetime, I now see Jews who think they can be insular in this world! Look at New York City. Like few other great metropolitan centers, it has become the refuge of a tremendous number of blacks and Puerto Ricans who have suffered from terrible discrimination. They come with few skills and poor education. The Federal government has refused to take its responsibility for them as U.S. citizens. New York City has had to bear an unconscionable and disproportionate load compared to other cities. Then there's been the enormous growth of the suburbs, not only for living but for industrial life. Many with money move out, creating a concentration of people without money. We are faced with basic economic and social problems which only a different kind of Federal government, one with a sense of responsibility, can possibly begin to remedy. No city is an island unto itself, any more than Jews are an island unto themselves.

There's a feeling in other parts of the country that New York is where the elitists live. They say: "New York does more for people and look at them now. We have done better." Washington has played into this resentment against New York and so intensified hostility to the poor and fostered basic racism.

Would I ever consider leaving the City? No, indeed! I love it. And I don't believe in running away from problems.

PART THREE

FROM BEYOND THE HUDSON

21.

AN ACTIVIST CRITIC ON THE UPPER WEST SIDE

Midge Decter

I WAS born in St. Paul. So was my mother. My father came to the U.S. from Poland as an infant and he grew up in New York on the Lower East Side. He went to St. Paul as a young man who had to make a living. In St. Paul an uncle of his had discovered that middle-western Jews lacked seltzer. Supplying them would obviously be very profitable. He sent for my father. I don't think that business lasted very long. Apparently, the Jews of St. Paul were not much interested in seltzer. They don't have it, at least not as a staple of the table, to this day.

To grow up as a Jew in a place like St. Paul, you had one of two possibilities. Either you passed, which very few people did because it was a small town, or you were totally conscious of being a Jew all the time, in one way or another. Jews went out with Jews, Jews hung out with Jews, Jews socialized only with Jews. When my children were growing up in New York, my mother would come to visit, and when they talked about their friends, she always asked them, "Is so-and-so Jewish?" Not knowing what the question meant, they always said, "Yes." As New York kids, they thought that everyone was Jewish, or that no one was. They simply assumed that they were members of the majority culture.

Midge Decter, a writer and social critic, was born in St. Paul, Minnesota, in 1927. She has worked as an editor on *Midstream* magazine, *Commentary, Harper's, Saturday Review,* and others. She has also been a senior editor at Basic Books, Inc. and is author of several books, including *Liberal Parents, Radical Children* (1975).

As for St. Paul, one's entire life—or none of one's life—was led within the Jewish community. It was either/or. You did not date a gentile boy. Certainly by twelve you were not going to parties together, because that could lead to marriage.

The center of the Jewish culture in which I grew up was Zionism. My parents were Zionists, so were their friends. Zionism, indeed, was the basis of their social world. In high school my own Zionism took on a rather snobbish and rebellious cast. The idea of going to Palestine—an idea with which I played—was partly based on getting away from home. Of course, it wasn't serious. It was posturing. It merely signified escape. In fact, I had really contradictory ambitions. One was to be in New York—that was clearly serious—and the other was to be in Palestine and die on the barricades.

I enrolled at the University of Minnesota in 1946. In 1947 I dropped out and came to New York with the idea of entering the Jewish Theological Seminary. That, too, was in some measure an excuse for coming to New York. It was something my mother and father were willing to sponsor. After all, my argument ran, at the Seminary I would be "getting a Jewish education." The Jewish Theological Seminary had four schools: the Rabbinical School, the College of Jewish Studies, the Teachers Institute (a daytime school), and the School of Jewish Studies, which consisted of popular classes, like the New School. I went to the Seminary's College of Jewish Studies at night. And then I transferred to the Teachers Institute, not because I wanted to train to be a teacher but because classes were in the daytime. In order to be there, I had to take education courses, which were awful, like "How to Make Maps Out of Papier-Mâché," which they actually taught at the Seminary.

An interesting thing about the Seminary was that there you encountered Hebraism, a phenomenon of American Jewish life which has been very little noted or recorded. It has not, alas, found its Irving Howe. There were a crew of Hebraists teaching at the Seminary. I don't think most of them were really particularly religious—mildly observant, but not "really religious." Piety didn't bring them there. They were there to keep Hebrew alive!

There was something called the Chug Ivri (a Hebrew-speaking club). The Hebraists published a newspaper called *Hadoar*, as well as a children's publication, *Hadoar Lanoar*. They were a tiny, passionate band of devotees. Many wrote poems in Hebrew. There was a professor at the Seminary named Reuben Wallenrod, who had written a novel in Hebrew about the Catskills. Theirs was a kind of madness, not unlike the madness of those early Hebraists who went to Israel and insisted on talking Hebrew and forced their children to talk it and were probably speechless for a long time until they actually became articulate in Hebrew.

Hebraism pervaded the atmosphere of the Seminary College. These Hebraists—who were really, I suppose, the second generation of Maskilim ("enlightened ones")—were our teachers. They were rather comical, but also very touching and very moving. A passion of that kind is irresistible—to get caught up in that! I had gone to Hebrew School for eight years or so, and I knew no Hebrew. In the end I never really got beyond the stage of reading painfully with dictionaries. It was all homework to me. I never could really just sit down and read. As a consequence I never really got to know much of the Hebrew literature. My relationship to it was only that of a schoolgirl. Then I encountered these Seminary Hebraists. There was Zvi Scharfstein, an educator, and Hillel Bavli, a Hebrew poet. They were my first teachers. Bavli taught Hebrew and Bible. He had once known Bialik. The great event in his life was that Bialik had commended him for a poem. He talked about it endlessly. Things like that were all these Hebraists cared about. They brought their children up to be bilingual. In class, of course, these bilingual children made life very hard for the rest of us. They were also a kind of joke, because there was a big ideological commitment to speaking Hebrew at the Seminary, and the Hebraist leaders among one's fellow students would insist that one do *everything*, from tying one's shoe to eating ice cream, in Hebrew. I happened to find this useful because I was learning the language. It was a very good way to learn fast. There were people who absolutely insisted on talking Hebrew to you all the time, as they did to one another. Well, they were like all people with a harmless obsession. They were Americans, like the rest of us, and the amount of self-consciousness that went into discussing that flavor of ice cream to buy, in Hebrew, was formidable.

At the Seminary I encountered brilliant minds like Sidney Morgenbesser. He was already a graduate, but he was a friend of people I knew, like Moshe Decter, so I got to know him and, ah, to meet somebody like that was terrifying. He knew everything. He had read every book ever written.

Then, in my own class, there was a gang of brilliant young men in the Rabbinical School. Since the Rabbinical School was for advanced education, they had all gone to college somewhere, many of them to Yeshiva College. In the end, a certain number of them ended up having academic rather than rabbinical careers. Morgenbesser was one. Izzy Scheffler was another, and Red Weisberg, who became a dean of Brandeis, and a couple of others. The sad ones—a few of them were really sad—were the rabbinical students who took courses at Columbia with a fantasy of escape and then did end up in the rabbinate, out of cowardice, or out of being unable to make it academically, or out of discomfort with the big world.

Anyway, this particular gang of students were very, very smart. At least in my eyes. I was a dumb hick. I didn't know anything. I was totally uneducated. And they were so . . . first of all, they seemed formidable because they knew so much. Moreover, most of them already had acquired the manners of my generation of academic philosophers. That is, their most rewarding intellectual experience was to catch someone, anyone, out in error. So their whole mode of relating to you was to wait until you should say one word, then, "Hah! What does that mean?"

There was something particularly Jewish about the quality of this brilliance. It is what I call the "Jewish disease." The Jewish disease, I think, must have originated with the study of Talmud. It is an affliction which makes it necessary to know absolutely everything, before you are allowed to say one word on any subject whatsoever. This particular disease flourishes in the lives of certain professional intellectuals and academics—not to say scholars. For some people it proved to be quite incurable. They could never write anything because somebody might come along and say,

The Jewish Theological Seminary.   JEWISH THEOLOGICAL SEMINARY.

"Aha, but you didn't read this" or "Aha, you're wrong!" And for them that is the worst possible fate. I associate this with Talmudic scholarship, though it may come from somewhere else in the formation of the Jewish psyche. But it is true about Talmud scholarship that you have to know everything before you can say even the first word. And not only that, but they're all standing there waiting to kill you for error. Now, analytic philosophy turned out to be absolutely perfect for young men who had cut their teeth in this tradition. Absolutely perfect. Because the main thing those analytic philosophers were doing all the time was waiting to catch one another out and close in for the kill. Naturally, the effect of this was to make their field extremely sterile. What is more sterilizing to the mind than the fear of error?

I think you don't find this disease much any more. The climate for it is gone. That's probably much too glib and facile an observation, but this particular outlook seems to me to derive very largely from the intellectual tradition of Jewish Orthodoxy.

355

If those guys had been born twenty-five years later their families would have seen to it that they went off to Harvard. But they mostly grew up in poor Orthodox Jewish homes where the idea of being a rabbi seemed respectable. There was a kind of fear or hesitation about the big world and a sense of shyness about venturing into it on all their parts. They'd grown up in this very parochial atmosphere, and all of them showed signs of it, even those who finally left. It took them awhile: they didn't feel at home out there.

The people I'm talking about were by no means the majority of Seminary students. They were around within a spread of only a few years. In fact, I heard later that the Seminary had so much trouble with these friends of mine—so few of them had stuck to becoming rabbis—they decided to change their admissions policy.

Mostly these young men treated me with condescension, except that being a girl made it easier for me to get around them. When you're a girl, you can always claim your own special mode of perception and apprehension: "They may know all that stuff but you know things they don't know." I could, and frequently did, play that swampy kind of game. But they did indeed condescend to me all the time.

But I may give the wrong impression. Until my first marriage I was totally immersed in that world within the Seminary and I enjoyed it very much. I had never before been in a place where what people did was sit around reading, talking until two o'clock in the morning, arguing, yelling; which wasn't so much the atmosphere of the Seminary—it was the atmosphere of that particular, rather disruptive, gang of mine, I guess.

After I got married and went to work, I met another Jewish gang, a very different sort from the Seminary gang. That was at *Commentary*, where I eventually got a job. There were Irving Kristol, Nat Glazer, Robert Warshow, and Clem Greenberg. Elliott Cohen was the editor, but those three, Warshow, Glazer, and Kristol, all of whom became my friends, were most important to me. They were extremely Jewish without much actual formal training. At *Commentary*, because I'd been to the Seminary, *I* was the big expert. My new friends had been radicals who became pro-American because of World War II, and then afterwards they went to work at *Commentary*. They were quite young. They had been radicals of the City College type, though Bob Warshow had gone to Michigan. I think it could be said that they were more anti-Communist than they were merely pro-American. They had looked upon the face of totalitarianism and were finished with their early flirtation with radicalism. And they were getting interested in Jewish matters. They were studying, they were trying to learn. They got hold of a young professor from Europe named Jacob Taubes to teach them for awhile. To me they represented a vastly different experience. They were intellectuals who lived in—or you might say they were creating—an intellectual community, and therefore they were not *exclusive*. They were *inclusive*. They were very welcoming.

They did not have the "Jewish disease." They were both productive in themselves and the goad, or inspiration, to productivity in others. They were journalists, after all, not scholars. They were very open to one and to the world. They were full of intellectual appetite. So their mode, unlike that of my earlier friends, was to include people of all kinds, to be interested, to try to enlarge their society.

What had happened to them is fairly simple to describe. There was the Holocaust. They had been radicals, Socialists, Trotskyists—though none had been a Stalinist. To put it much too crudely, Hitler taught them that they were Jews. Hitler and Stalin had also combined to make them serious in a new way about being American. As radicals, they had been more or less internationalist in their feeling and in their ideological commitments. Then came World War II. There was Hitler and Stalin and there was the United States of America. They were Jews *and* they were Americans. You remember there had been a fantastic debate conducted in *Partisan Review*—Dwight Macdonald against Philip Rahv and William Phillips. The issue of that debate was whether one should or should not support America's going to war against Germany. Philip Rahv, as I don't have to tell anyone who ever met him, was a very formidable radical intellectual. Well, when it came to the assertion that World War II was merely the imperialists' war, he said, "Nonsense." Because Philip Rahv's primary commitment was to being an ordinary *mensch* (man) and to being a Jew. That was true of him at any crisis point including, as I remember, 1967. I think that's probably also true of William Phillips, at that time his coeditor on *Partisan Review*. The *Commentary* crowd, who were younger than the *Partisan Review* people I'm referring to, certainly felt that way. They had fought in the war or worked for it. They were Jews and they were antitotalitarian. Those two feelings were very much related—how, after Hitler, could they not be? If they were antitotalitarians they made a commitment to American democracy, and if they were Jews they made a commitment to being Jewish. They were serious people. So they studied Judaism. They never really learned very much, I think, at least not by the standards of those earlier friends of mine. Nor did they ever become observant, though they played around with it a little. All of that formal seeking passed. In part they had just wanted to study, and Taubes was the sort of man who was only too willing to play the guru. They had a profound influence on my political thinking, these people. Their Jewish business I didn't take seriously, and, for obvious reasons, it didn't interest me all that much. I was more or less amused by it at the time.

The organized Jewish community had almost no part in my interest in things Jewish. On leaving the Seminary, I ceased going to synagogue and I still don't go. I didn't go to synagogue (a) because I was not religious, and (b) because I felt much too familiar with the rabbinate. I still feel that way. There's now a younger generation of rabbis, but at one point I personally knew the entire Conservative rabbinate of the United States. I knew them entirely too well.

Later, of course, my lack of connection to the organized community gave rise to a great problem for me. What to do about the education of one's children? You never find a satisfactory solution to that problem. I didn't want to send them to a synagogue school. And I certainly didn't want to send them to a yeshiva. What I wanted, I eventually realized, was for them to end up where I was in relation to all this without having to go through what I had gone through. I didn't want to send them to a religious school. But I did want them to have my sense of Jewish existence. They had to learn about it somehow. Why? I cannot deal with this matter coherently. I hate, I *hate* Jewish ignorance—more than any other kind.

The children did grow up Jewish *and* skeptical. If I had been living in St. Paul with them I would certainly have sent them to a Talmud Torah (Hebrew school). I would have had no choice. Living in New York meant living in a Jewish culture anyway. The problem of overcoming ignorance in New York is far more a matter of giving one's kids books to read and telling them it is important to understand—it's not so much a *spiritual* problem as it is in other places. Yes, you can give them books to read anywhere, but New York means living in a Jewish society. Elsewhere you have to create the Jewish society. I told you that story about my mother saying, "Is this friend Jewish, is that friend Jewish?" and their saying "yes" about every kid who went to their school even though a large number of them were not. They just took it for granted that they were living in a society of people like themselves. And it was quite largely true that they were.

Like all young hotheads, particularly young Zionist hotheads, I used to be contemptuous of the organized Jewish community. Of course, the feeling has abated. Partly just because I grew up and got older, partly because I learned better. I have learned to be more respectful of middle-class people, and I am deeply respectful of the Jewish middle class and upper middle class in the United States for their communal behavior. They command my moral and social—though not aesthetic—respect. But then, I'm much less interested in the aesthetics of people than I was when I was young. I take this as a sign of maturity and good sense in myself. The Jewish middle class is often unlovely perhaps, but entirely admirable. For instance, if you think of the incredible amount of money that the American Jewish community has raised, it's breathtaking. I don't think it's vulgar. I don't think it's awful. I think it is breathtaking and admirable that people give away their money the way American Jews do, even if it means they need to have their names on plaques or buildings, and all that. What's bad about having one's name on a plaque rather than a three-masted schooner? In any truly moral accounting of vulgarity, why would the latter not be a good deal more vulgar than the former?

Moreover, I don't have any great sentimentality about the wonderful old days on the Lower East Side. It is a pity about Yiddish. That is a great loss. But I don't think Jewish idealism has been lost, as certain Socialists among us are nowadays claiming. This idea that the Jews have moved to the right annoys me inordinately. How many years' worth of abuse did the Jews take from black leaders before they quit giving them their money? And now we'll be giving them money again. I mean, how much kicking around, how much insult did they tolerate? As it happens, the Jewish-black friction hasn't directly impinged on me because I live in what may be the one truly integrated neighborhood in America. And I live among "sophisticated" people, black and white.

We take reasonable precautions for safety; of course, there are all kinds of safety measures and rules in our house, and it does sometimes get me down. But that's not a black-Jewish matter. That's white-black or rich-poor. There's a difference, a difference, by the way, that is choking us to death, between what everybody says about reality and one's actual experience of it. And the "official" line I am referring to in particular here has to do with the alleged growth of Jewish bigotry as part of the alleged white backlash. That idea simply doesn't reflect my experience. There happens to be a terrific lot of black lawlessness in the city of New York, particularly on the part of young blacks who victimize old people and children. And that is terrible. It makes life very bad. What is more, I don't believe anybody who says he knows what to do about it. But—I don't feel the problem particularly as a Jew, nor do I respond as a Jew. I think it's absolute nonsense for people to talk about something called Jewish bigotry and to bemoan the fact that American Jews are going to the right, and so on.

One source for this idiocy was the fact that a lot of Jews voted for Nixon in 1972, more than had normally voted Republican before. But as anybody with the least political understanding knows, this was not because they were moving to the right. It was because they were voting against McGovern. If you were simply to say, even with the hindsight of post-Watergate, that McGovern meant left and Nixon meant right, then you wouldn't have understood anything that was going on. Jews voted against McGovern because (by and large) they thought he was not good for Israel. And because, like vast numbers of "square" respectable liberals, they didn't like black militants and women's libbers, all of whom McGovern got stuck with, courtesy of the 1972 convention. If you identify a noisy political hustler like Willie Lee Brown of California as virtue, liberal virtue, well, then, okay, you can be my guest and say the Jews went to the right.

In New York City crime is a big problem. And the bad mood of people who go around saying it's intolerable to live in New York adds to it. I mean, the hatred of New York which infects the *mood* of New York does a great deal by itself to spoil the quality of life in the city. But this hatred is, or was, pure fad. Lately, I have begun to notice that it's the political fad to love New York, especially in its fiscal crisis. It is because of our glorious history of compassion, we hear from the columnists of the New York *Post*, that we're in this kind of trouble. So now we are all supposed to love ourselves. Once more, it's pure fad. The reality actually hasn't changed very much—except for the crime, that's all.

The departure of the white middle class from this city doesn't actually much affect my life. If I lived in Flatbush, I guess it would. My mother-in-law, who lives in Brooklyn, twice had to move out of what had become for her the old neighborhood because each time she settled in somewhere, it ceased to be safe. That was traumatic for her. She doesn't move easily or travel well. Most of us don't, I think. She moved from one neighborhood to another, and as soon as it really became her neighborhood she had to move out. She didn't know that she was experiencing the exodus of the Jews from Brooklyn. But that's what she was experiencing. Now she's in Brighton Beach. And as she says, there's no place to go now but straight into the Atlantic Ocean. I didn't experience any of this because I live in Manhattan. My friends are around. Our neighborhood has *improved* since I moved into it.

That reminds me of another discrepancy between the official line and experience. People keep saying that New York City is going down the drain, bankrupt, swarming with the unemployed, the poor, on the point of depression. . . . Try to get into the Palm Restaurant, where you can't eat for less than twenty-five dollars a head, some time. One night recently we were taken to dinner in a little neighborhood establishment on 72nd Street. The place was jam-packed; it was an ordinary week night in a residential neighborhood. It was a terrific little French restaurant; I'm sure it was very expensive indeed. What I'm talking about is the fact that everybody walks around exuding well-being, and talking apocalyptic talk.

Now the *schadenfreude* elsewhere in America about New York is really terrific. But, after all, many people hate New York precisely because they're still dying to come here twice a year. Just as in the literary world there is by now a whole tradition of essay-writing devoted to attacking a mythical entity called "New York." That means, in plain English, "New York Jews." Even if the writers in this genre don't say "Jews." They say things like, "In New York nobody pays any attention to Iowa City novelists." And you know "they" means the Jews who are alleged to have all the magazines, all the publishing houses, and so on. It's because of the Jews, of course, that the aggrieved writer is not Ernest Hemingway.

This does sound, at least faintly, like Weimar. Jews *do* own the networks and a couple of the major newspapers. But the networks and the two big liberal newspapers in no way represent or ever speak for ordinary Jews. Nor do they even represent Jewish interests. And yes, it's true that there are a lot of Jews around nowadays in publishing and in the entertainment world. There are and always have been. On the other hand, the "outlanders" who complain of Jewish control of New York—who stops them from writing or publishing? Certainly no one in New York, Jew or gentile, who are engaged in a never-ending search for new talent, new "products."

I look back with nostalgia on the intellectual life of the 1950s. I think there are many people who, if they were really honest, would agree with me. That intellectual life got radicalized in the

1960s, and was turned into dross. *Everything* got politicized: art, criticism, history, popular entertainment, sex, and too much more. It was more stimulating and less doctrinaire in the fifties. There was more discussion, less self-righteousness, and fewer moral epithets in place of arguments. I know that I am talking about the McCarthy era, but the period did not belong exclusively to the late lamented senator. There was McCarthy, but intellectual life of a high order was also going on. This life engaged more serious people, more seriously trying to figure out what they thought, with minds more alive than at any time in my experience. The people who politicized argument in those years were the Communists and their fellow travelers, and one simply stopped arguing with them after a while because it was useless. One of the real arguments of those days was about totalitarianism, whether it had a historical precedent or not. This one arose from Hannah Arendt's book. "Are we in an unprecedented situation or is this like medieval times?" This kind of argument, in which the fifties abounded, enriched one's life.

Later, to be sure, it got to be very much a matter of position-taking. I take my position against you and you take your position against me. I characterize your position and you characterize mine. By the middle sixties that seemed to be all there was. I think the blacks had much to do with bringing on the bout of position-taking. But whatever the reason, virtually all conversation on public issues came to be politicized in a way that didn't add anything to one's life or mind. You were judging people on the basis of whether you agreed with them or not rather than on the basis of whether they were first-rate or not. It was happening all over. "Whose side are you on?" turned into the most important question that people asked one another. It absolutely poisoned New York intellectual life.

I'm not enchanted with Israel. However, I think it's absolutely irrelevant whether I'm enchanted or not. I went to Israel and I thought, "It doesn't matter whether I like this place or not. It is mine. And everything that happens here happens to me as well as to these people. So I can like it or not." It's as if somebody says to you, "Do you like your family?" Well, that's both a pointless and unanswerable question.

I was absolutely passionate on the question of establishing the state of Israel. But I didn't get there until very, very much later. And when I got there I found it fascinating—and uncomfortable. No part of Israel matched London, where I instantly felt, "Ah, this is one of my good places." In Israel I felt on edge all the time.

The survival of Israel is absolutely essential to me. Why is it absolutely essential? Because I have the feeling that if Israel doesn't survive this time, it's the whole ball game as far as the Jews are concerned. I can't logically justify this feeling. I just have it. If Israel goes, that's the end of the Jews. Besides, it's such an outrage to me as a human being that the world could allow that country to go down the drain. Not *allow*, but *contrive* it. If the Israelis go down, it will not be on account of their own failure but by the contrivance of everybody else. Henry Kissinger *contrived* that the Israelis should lose a war which they had, in fact, won. It's an absolute outrage. It's impossible for me to say that if I weren't a Jew I would be outraged, because I can't conceive of not being a Jew. I don't know what that means, to say "if I weren't." It just outrages me beyond the place where I am a Jew. And as a Jew I think the destruction of Israel would be the end of the whole thing. It's not *supposed* to come to an end. There can't have been that much accumulated suffering over so many centuries just to wipe us out at the end. Am I just expressing a kind of mystical ethnicity? I'm extremely skeptical of concepts like "mystical ethnicity." But whatever the source of my feeling and belief, there it is. The Jews are a mysterious people. They're impossible to understand or to deal with by rational categories.

The most important single remark about Jewishness that was ever made to me came from Shlomo Katz, whom I worked for on *Midstream* magazine. Now while I was at *Midstream* the Sinai War of 1956 broke out. The British and the French and the Israelis went to war in the Sinai and Eisenhower said, "Back off." They had to back off. I came into the office one morning having just read the story in the *New York Times*, and in my rage I began to yell at Shlomo: "Jews are impossible; I can't stand them; why don't they disappear? Who needs them? They don't need themselves, and nobody else needs them, so why doesn't everybody just call it off?" And he said, "You're right, you're absolutely right. I'm going to take a shave and a haircut and assimilate."

At *Harper's* magazine, I did feel quite Jewish, but that was already the time in which everybody was talking about his own ethnic origins. It was not like today's preoccupation with ethnicity, but that was the time when everybody was thinking a lot about where he came from. Willie Morris, the editor, was talking about himself as a cracker, and I was talking about myself as a Jew. It was the cultural fashion for everybody to come in and lay his childhood on the table. Yes, I was very Jewish then at *Harper's* and I felt very Jewish.

But that was '67 to '70. It was just beginning. Being Jewish got to be a big issue, for the world in which I lived, again in '68, on account of the teachers' strike. Before then there was certainly the issue of black anti-Semitism and the Jews' relationship to the blacks, but it hadn't become an issue that could be objectively identified and talked about. I think the teachers' strike was *the* event that announced "Jews and blacks are now polarized." And so was the Jewish intellectual community within itself. *I* underwent a polarization all by myself, I can tell you, with respect to people like Nat Hentoff on the one side and the *New York Times* editorial board on the other. It was a very big experience that could have been traumatic except—it worked in reverse for me. I learned something very important for myself, about the way to behave.

Albert Shanker became Public Enemy Number 1. He was not only called racist, but was identified as the leader of the Jews. The teachers were Jews and, it was said on the left, they were bad news. Shanker was vilified in the press—especially in the press that mattered to him, that mattered to me. You know, the liberal community press. He was absolutely vilified and he didn't give a damn. Because he was a man pursuing his own end as he saw it. Winning was what interested him. He didn't turn blue if the liberals attacked him; it truly didn't affect him in the least. This was a very important lesson to me. You could survive. You could be called bad names by Nat Hentoff and survive very handsomely. It gave me great confidence in the idea that what you were supposed to do was conduct the battle you thought you had to conduct, and to hell with public relations. Now, what I just said doesn't sound like any big revelation. In fact, it's a big piety. But thinking such a thing and actually watching the way it works in the life of an actual flesh-and-blood person are two different matters. You don't necessarily alter your behavior, but your feelings can be totally altered. He set a terrific example.

The most important thing about the teachers' strike of 1968 was that it embodied the new policy of the WASP establishment, and it was an anti-Jewish policy. The WASP establishment, as represented in this case by the Ford Foundation, by McGeorge Bundy, by John Lindsay, said to the militant blacks, "We are going to buy you off, and we're prepared to throw the Jews to you. Because as far as we're concerned, it's either the Jews or you: there isn't enough to go around. So now we choose you." They could not succeed in doing that, certainly not in the city of New York, where you can't throw the Jews to anybody because here the Jews are a very important force. They are numerically important, they are politically important, they are culturally important. And because in this instance they were led by a man who was not nervous about what the goyim were saying about him. Or what would be said, or what would appear in public. He didn't care. He didn't succumb to traditional Jewish nervousness, which used to become particularly intense when faced with the McGeorge Bundys of this world. Shanker didn't have to look like a good guy. From this, I drew more than one moral. There was a general political moral, and there was a very personal one for me, which was, on the one hand, the Jews don't have to care what the gentiles say, and I don't have to care what the goddam Village liberals say.

What emerged from the '68 teachers' strike was a message sent to the Jews. Up to that point, we had really come to believe that anti-Semitism was more or less finished. I did. That there was no such thing any more. And the teachers' strike was a reminder that there was a specifically Jewish interest, that anti-Semitism did exist, that it had been suppressed because for a time it had been deemed no longer respectable. The blacks had once more made it respectable. Jews may have been declared the blacks' enemy. One thing I can tell you for sure is that left liberal Jews were *my* enemy. Specifically, those who said you have to sacrifice Jewish interests.

Some Jews were torn within themselves. I wasn't. I did not believe in the model school district. I do not believe in school decentralization. I think the blacks are getting ripped off just as badly as the Jews were in that situation. Therefore I was not torn in the least.

There's still a division among Jews on this question, but it's no longer significant—if only because the blacks themselves are refusing to allow themselves to be spoken for by the militants and because people who spend all their time merely contemplating their own moral virtue, like the Jewish left, tend to have a short attention span. But anti-Semitism did once again become respectable in America. That is our legacy from the days when the words "social justice" tripped hourly from every tongue.

22.

THE SOCIOLOGIST ON THE CUTTING EDGE

Joseph Bensman

I'M THE son of a shoemaker who spent sixty years in middle America, never really learning English but conducting his business exclusively with a non-Jewish clientele by communicating with an idiosyncratic assortment of words and gestures. He came to New York in 1900, worked a year in garment shops, had some *landsleit* (immigrants from the same community) in Sheboygan, Wisconsin, saved enough money to move there, and then became a peddler. He traveled in the outskirts of Sheboygan, selling and sometimes exchanging fruit for junk. He came to Two Rivers (where I was born in 1922) and discovered a town with no shoe-maker! He went back to Sheboygan and bought shoemaking equipment. The salesman ostensibly taught him how to repair shoes. He could be called a religious man who, however, worked on Saturdays and drove to Sheboygan for the holidays. He existed in spite (or because) of almost no contact with the town, a man who got along with his customers but, underneath, harbored real resentment against "beer-drinking and time-wasting goyim."

I was the youngest of ten children living in a house my father would not relinquish in the thirties so that we could qualify for relief like most of our neighbors. He wanted the welfare, but evidently wanted even more to keep the house. When I first wan-

Joseph Bensman was born in Wisconsin in 1922. He is the author of several books in applied and humanistic sociology, among them *Small Town in Mass Society* (1960) with Arthur Vidich, and *Dollars and Sense* (1967). He is professor of sociology at City College and the Graduate Center of CUNY.

dered beyond its immediate confines, and at least through high school, I continuously experienced anti-Semitism in ways that I suspect the New Yorker can't imagine. I had no supporting group for me in my Jewishness. So I was a kike and a Christ-killer. My nickname was Yosky—their distortion of Yascha, which my mother called me. From four through twelve I belonged to delinquent gangs whose activity ranged from raiding gardens to breaking and entering railroad cars and stealing aluminum and other metals. At one point we were as close to the reformatory as you can get without actually being thrown into one. Yet I was always marginal, never wholly accepted, *in* but not *of* the group. I was the gang's "intellectual." If they needed me to figure out a way of planning a break-in, I was good for that.

I lived in a working-class neighborhood. In school I met middle-class kids. My brothers and sisters taught me how to read before I went to school, and from kindergarten on, my nose was always in a book. There was no cultural or educational tradition in the family, except the notion that if I turned out to be pretty smart they'd *shep nachas* (gain prestige) from it. But my bookishness did not exactly endear me to the neighborhood kids. I remember one stealing my hat and then beating the hell out of me because I was a lousy kike. At least that was the reason he gave. In one case around 1937, my assailant was a German kid. One of the parents of my best friend was a Bohemian who, whenever he got drunk, would call me a Christ-killer. I surely knew that I was Jewish.

I went to *cheder* for a while but did not get bar mitzvahed. Attending the *cheder* cost fifty cents a day—and in my eleventh year we couldn't afford that sum. The family lived on fish and potatoes. Two Rivers was a fishing town, and we grew our own potatoes.

I kept reading away, cultivating my father's kind of resentment, which I directed at middle-class kids who comprised the gangs our gang fought. Within a working-class gang one developed class consciousness, particularly in the form of hostility toward well-mannered snobs. I suppose I always resented kids whose stock-in-trade was manners, poise, and a feeling that they owned the world. From the age of four on, I knew I was smarter than most of those kids; but I simply could not discover a sensible basis for their self-confidence, the poise and the manners which allowed them to think they could push everyone else around. I must have been thirty-five before I realized that they were just as nutty as I was, but covered themselves with a facade of manners I had not been able to penetrate.

By the time I reached seventh grade, I was half-mockingly called "the professor" by my classmates. Since I had emerged from a lower-class environment, I became a hero of working-class kids. I could put down the middle and upper class just by virtue of my vocabulary. In eighth grade, I had committed the minor offense of throwing a pen at a pupil's foot and missing it by half an inch. The teacher was so shocked at this that she made me memorize the Constitution. As a result, I recited the Preamble in class and thus became a boy orator. This thrust me into a political and social science tradition I had not previously known to exist. I went out for debate and for extemporary speaking which made me a big *macher* (big shot) in the high school. I depleted the city and the school libraries. Their books enchanted me much more than homework. I did well, I think, as an act of defiance against the system.

When I became a boy orator my picture began appearing in the local press, and with that I got hints of recognition at home. The pattern of my family, and it's my pattern also, was never to let the other person know that you're impressed. So I was teased and put down for my accomplishments, but even in that act I recognized that they were praising me.

I learned at an early age that my father had a brilliant mind with absolutely no possibility of using it in his American ambience. He was far more original than any of the teachers I had. Once when we were debating the issue of unicameral legislatures in state government, he asked me about it. It was clear that he didn't know these words. I spent twenty minutes telling him what we were debating. It was totally outside his own experience. Just the same, in his broken amalgam of languages, he remarked, "Well, when you got legislators in two houses of different size, in the large one you can get local interests represented that you couldn't get in the small one." Now that was brilliant. We had batted this problem around for six months and in minutes he presented a stronger case than any of us could formulate.

But my father's greatest influence on me consisted of his resentment of the stuffed shirts and middle-class "respectables." On one memorable occasion he talked about a peddler who was the cantor, the most religious man in *shul*. This peddler had a son who owned the local pool hall. He described the son as a typical greenhorn: a man with a five-cent cigar, knife-edged pressed pants, shined shoes, holes in the toes of socks, and dirty underwear. His total image of society lay in that description. He was sure that anybody who made two thousand dollars more than he did had to be a *gonif* (thief). I think I internalized his whole attitude, and that it's as good a basis for sociology as any.

My father was an honest artisan. His ambition for me was to be a tailor and to earn a respectable living in the local tailoring shop. Of course I had no interest in it. I was a high-flying debater, who had been reading at such a high level that what to do next was altogether unclear.

While I was a senior in high school, I thought I might become a village freak, the kind of small town intellectual at whom everyone else laughs and jeers. That year, I joined the community discussion club. We were then debating the third term for Franklin Roosevelt. I was pitted against the Vice President of Hamilton Manufacturing Company—the Vice President of Public Relations—a very smooth guy who made all the firm's speeches. Everyone there, bankers, lawyers, businessmen, thought that Roosevelt was either insane or a Communist. I was well prepared, making an innocent historical speech in which I concluded that Roosevelt had to be elected *because* he was antibusiness. In the question period I cited numbers, statistics, laws, legislation. I had more evidence than anyone present. To me it was exhilarating because here I was fighting the whole goddam establishment. Also, I knew that in the very act of winning, I was done for in Two Rivers. There were maybe half a dozen people there who, although they would not publicly support my argument, congratulated me after the meeting. They would help me get to col-

lege, to make something of myself, but would take no risks themselves. This group understood that I did not fit in either the upper-
or lower-class life of a small town.

My family as a whole and each member individually had the
same problem that I did in matters of sociability. I certainly didn't
focus on my Jewishness. I went away from it, to escape it. For
instance, I was an honorary Rotarian, which meant that for four
weeks I'd go to Rotary meetings. There again I'd get into political
arguments with businessmen. Intellectually I overcame them, but
at all other levels I was still a kike. For example, along with
everyone else, they served me a pork dish. I didn't mind eating
pork. We were kosher at home, but I ate crabs and bullheads with
my friends when we caught our own fish. When they served me
pork, I started to eat it. This was the first time I ever had pork
as part of a prepared meal. Then these people remembered that
I was Jewish. They embarrassed me by ordering something else
for me which was equally *tref* (non-kosher). I was humiliated not
because they served me pork, but because they reminded me of
its religious significance. That kind of thing happened all the time.

The junior college at Manitowoc, which was all of seven miles
away, propelled me into the midst of a whole new population.
There my academic accomplishments might have pulled me in the
direction of being acceptable in Manitowoc polite society. I was
president of the class in my second year and was invited to join
the De Molay Society which, however, struck me as being a
goyishe zach (a gentile thing). For me, being middle class and being
gentile were the same thing. But in those two years I got some
validation of the fact that I was a smart kid. Maybe I needed it.
I went to the University of Wisconsin at Madison for my junior
and senior years. There, for the first time, I met New York Jews.

Three days after my arrival at the university, I was sitting at
the Rathskeller when I encountered the Communists—the YCL
(Young Communist League) of the University of Wisconsin.
Now I had read Marx. I knew a hell of a lot about revolutionary
socialism, but I had never met a Communist, and meeting the real
living species did interest me. At that time the party line was
Yalta-Teheran coprosperity. They immediately wanted me to attend the YCL convention. I wanted to talk to them about how

their gathering related to Marx and Engels and revolution. But they didn't want such talk; hence I didn't want to go. I never did get involved with them. But for the first time in my life I had had dealings with an "intellectual" community, and it happened to be pretty heavily Jewish. My qualifications for entry into that community went back at least to high school. But I was all alone until this experience produced contact with an organized group.

At the same time, through a high school friend from Two Rivers I joined a YMCA discussion group. The next year I was put in charge of the group and met another guy who became my roommate. He had a City College B.A. and was doing his graduate work at Wisconsin. This fellow had been a Trotskyist and was a strong anticommunist. By my senior year, I too was an open enemy of the Communists, joining the ideological war against them. In that same year I became a protégé of Hans Gerth, a non-Jewish German refugee.

The student-stimulated culture was dominated, like its politics, by Jewish students from New York. I found hostility to the New York Jews almost everywhere for exactly the same reason that I provoked it: bad manners, argumentativeness, being too smart and too radical. They populated a separate world within the undergraduate universe. It was a world of unspecialized intellectuals who avoided narrow academics and concentrated on politics. The New Yorkers made me feel my own limitations. They had theirs too, but within a context of sophistication, practice, and intellectual competition. I had learned mainly from books, they much more from their social milieu.

I knew Marilyn, my wife-to-be, as the friend of a friend at Wisconsin. But after I'd been drafted into the army and came back on a furlough we had a whirlwind courtship, a war romance. Then I went back to the army, started writing letters, and proposed by mail. Most of the girls I knew represented the eastern radical type. Marilyn was a stunning girl with qualities rather different from those we thought of as eastern and radical. She was athletic, enthusiastic, an outdoors girl, danced well, and was also an egghead.

I supported the war, not just as a Jew but out of hatred for Hitler. We knew about *Krystallnacht* and concentration camps but not about death factories. As a GI, I wasn't going to take shit from anybody. So when I had a civilian teacher in the army school who was anti-Semitic, anti-Roosevelt, and antiwar, I denounced him for propagandizing in class and had him put on the carpet. When another guy sounded off with anti-Semitic remarks I shut him up by saying, "You could get a Section 8 for that." I was a fighter, but not a monomaniac. Lots of personal abuse was built into the system. I understood that, but I also realized that anti-Semitism was illegal.

I had a dream after three weeks of basic training, a magnificent full-color dream in which I was an executioner chopping the heads off all my friends. I, the executioner, was doing this with military precision, discipline, and detachment. I woke up in a sweat and decided: that's enough of this army shit. From then on I became a kind of special goof-off, that is, I complied with every rule in such a way as to make a mockery of it. In little symbolic acts I was sabotaging military chicken shit—and getting away with it. A couple of times people tried to punish me and I immediately asked for their court-martial because by then I had developed a defense which is part of my permanent character. Basically, it consists of a vast, formal respect for the rules. You do everything legally; you even overdo it; and the more you comply, the more you defy the establishment. I still do that all the time. I use legalism as a means of survival. I perfected my technique in the army. I was frightened by the whole goddam system. I had read Max Weber on bureaucracy but I didn't thoroughly understand it until I experienced army life with its mindless precision and caste privilege. After my military experience I was ready to become a revolutionary.

It never happened. Almost as certainly my intensive reading of Max Weber made me an antirevolutionary. Bureaucracy, not socialism or capitalism, was the problem. In this sense I took Weber more seriously than Gerth did. He was a Marxist-Weberian and I responded to those aspects of Weber which were antiestablishment, that is antibureaucratic, whether capitalist or socialist. The army is not private enterprise. And what did I see? Stupidity, anti-Semitism, ignorance, and a more than incipient form of bureaucratic totalitarianism. I said to myself, "If this is a form of socialism, then socialism is no solution." The lesson I drew is that specific policies, not formal structures, are crucial. The problem wasn't solved by capitalism and it could be turned into a greater disaster by socialism. The Russians had developed a kind of socialism and it exhibited every imaginable disease.

And then there was National Socialism, which was not socialism at all but an abomination, an unmitigated evil, an assault on civilization itself. I was aware of the Nuremberg laws from the time of their passage as well as the major events leading up to World War II. But I found the imminence of European war uppermost in my mind. Erich Fromm's *Escape from Freedom* was a very important book for me. Fromm asked: How is it that the most civilized nation on earth could become the most brutal nation? He offered a partial answer, and his question is still important; but in 1942 it was a major concern to me. Anyhow, my interest was focused more on the Germans than the Jews. And with that interest, one expected the worst.

When information on death camps became available, during the war and afterwards, we were appalled, depressed, shocked, and silenced. In its direct and immediate impact, the Holocaust was overwhelming. I had friends who were among the first American soldiers to visit those camps, and after the war they told us as much as they could. But what they had seen at close range was almost too horrifying to talk about. And yet, this obscene culmination was more or less what I had been led to expect. Precisely because somewhere in my mind, I had half-expected it, I was partly insulated from the shock, the sheer horror of it. But the slave labor camps in Russia took us by surprise. As early as 1936 we had read Ilin's book called *The New Russian Primer*, which described the Russian Constitution as similar to the U.S. Constitution. It carried the promise of liberation and redemption, but turned out to be no more than salesmanship for a document that never got more than lip service.

I had read about the show trials, and had become very much of an anti-Stalinist. And yet, knowing all about them and Stalin's awful purges and the dispossession of the so-called kulaks, one never expected the death of millions. So when, beginning in 1952, we were exposed to incontrovertible data on Soviet slave labor camps I was particularly horrified. At some perhaps half-conscious level, one expected Hitler's death camps but not Stalin's massive slave labor camps.

I came back to Wisconsin after the war, completed an M.A., and entered Columbia for my Ph.D. I was a rebel at Columbia, detached from most of the teachers, and only a little closer to C. Wright Mills, who had also been a protégé of Gerth. But I did some work for him, we kidded around, and I generally confirmed my view that he was as shoddy a Marxist as he was a Weberian.

Columbia meant less to me than just being in New York. There I felt I was *in the world* and that Wisconsin had been hopelessly parochial. I could now enjoy a continuous rediscovery of dance and all the other arts. In Wisconsin, I had known music and painting; I learned literature. I was not altogether unprepared for the riches New York City had to offer. But they were different in kind from the hothouse exposure available on a midwestern university campus. I frequented museums and galleries and concert halls—and I reveled in the absence of any self-consciousness about it. This was different from Wisconsin, where you went to a concert, a gallery, or a show feeling that it was something very special indeed. I used to go to first night showings at Madison dressed like a bum, unshaven and seedy in old clothes. In New York I didn't feel the need for striking such poses. What's unique about New York is that you don't have to take a bath just to participate in the arts, even as a spectator.

Yet, it didn't take me too long to discover the kind of salon character of much intellectual life in the city. The underside of all that I admired was filled with personal politics, factionalism, intrigues among cultural and intellectual circles and elites. This reality has kept me marginal to most intellectual, academic, and aesthetic communities. They always make me acutely uncomfortable.

I finished the course requirements at Columbia, then I taught at the University of Syracuse for two years. There I collided with the academic gentility and parochialism that always make me squirm when I encounter them. I was back in the hothouse. From Syracuse it took four and a half hours by car to reach New York where we went as often as we could. We had no extra money, which made it all the more like suffocating in the sticks. Now *I'm* from the sticks, but after one year in New York I had the sense that anywhere else was the sticks. In my mind the sticks came to mean those places in which lace curtainism predominated. Syracuse was such a place.

After I lost my job in Syracuse, I went back to New York, took six months on the GI Bill of Rights, and did nothing much, though supposedly I was working on my thesis. Finally, I got a job at the Voice of America through a college friend who had been Leo Lowenthal's secretary in the Institute of Social Research. By dropping Leo's name to the personnel manager, who was three steps below Leo, I got hired. I worked primarily through people who had been in the Bureau of Applied Social Research. When I was at Columbia these people seemed to me to be "soap salesmen," survey market researchers. But I was hired at the Voice to learn the techniques of survey research, which I did, and to work with dopes at the higher levels. This judgment did not apply to Lowenthal: I admired his academic work, particularly his book on the sociology of literature.

Once I attended a meeting between the heads of our department and those of the Russian bureau of the Voice. I knew the meeting had political overtones; they were jockeying and struggling for position. My job was to write the minutes, designed to help us learn about the larger organization. I wrote a nearly exact summary of the meeting, perhaps heightening the differences and the issues somewhat. It turned out to be a nice sociological document, which was the last thing they wanted. The governing "ethic" was that no one could edit our work without our approval. Another person, two grades higher, was given the job of editing my work, but had to get my okay on it. She took out all of the sharp angles, the conflicts, the differences. I more or less sadistically forced her to explain every change. She sympathized with me, but had her job to do, and she conscientiously performed it. Then my minutes were moved to a higher level where even more conflicts were removed; the final report was love and roses, consensus, cooperation, and positive accomplishment. I made stabs at bureaucratic sabotage like this one, which, however, had no consequence at all—except to feed my sense of righteousness.

After a budgetary reduction in force I went to work in an aircraft factory whose environment was anything but strange to me. I'd previously had my share of experiences inside such places. The brutality, the noise, and the playful aggression were familiar enough. I certainly didn't like being there, but I had to make a living and I had the skills to do it as a result of my army experience. I was there one year, until a lay-off.

Whereupon I went through "the snowball phase" of job seeking. People would refer me from one place to another place to another. At last, I heard of a job in an advertising agency. I had an interview with a vice president, who reviewed my considerable research experience, while I faked even more. I got the job. In this agency I was the third Jew they had ever hired. All were employed in the research department. No doubt we made it as highly trained technicians with a special mystique imputed to us.

During my interview the V.P. had asked me what kind of work I was doing. "The phenomenology of industrial administration." My interviewer was a Ph.D. in psychology who had never heard the word phenomenology. He asked me what it was. I told him that it pertained to the qualities of meaning associated with administration. "Well, does it have any application to advertising?" I modestly replied that I didn't know advertising so well, but would venture to say that all of it had qualities of meaning susceptible to phenomenological inquiry. Hence my second and third-hand encounters with the philosophy of Alfred Schütz got me into advertising just as motivational research was sweeping the field. Of course phenomenology and motivation are not the same thing, but my interviewer didn't know that. His definition of the job I was seeking was that of a psychologist. So I had to use projective testing without ever having studied it. I couldn't wait, with an imminent deadline, to get the standard tests. I "invented" dozens of techniques which already existed, deducing what they must be from shop talk with friends and peers in other agencies. They all worked better than the standard tests because, lacking the standard tests, I made up new ones to fit the specific problem.

About Jews in advertising: this is a big topic. Briefly: Ad agencies were willing to hire Jews in possession of certain techniques, which by the accident of postwar training, they had. Those techniques were most important to account executives for whom the major problem was and is self-presentation, in other words— how to deal with and sell ideas to WASP businessmen. It must have been 1964, just as I was leaving, when our agency got its first admittedly Jewish account executive. (We were fairly sure another one had been passing as a gentile.) Catholics preceded Jews in top spots by about ten years. We didn't have any Jewish clients, primarily because we dealt only with giant monopolies . . . Colgate, Ballantine, Reynolds Tobacco.

My boss was a five-foot-two tyrant who demanded total subservience and who, as soon as he got it, treated you like dirt. I was constitutionally incapable of being subservient. As with Leo, I treated him like an equal. The difference was that I got the advertising boss out of jams. We worked well together at an official level. He was a good salesman and I was a good technician. As far as he was concerned, my work was good, but the one thing I would not do was give him deference. And the one thing he had to have was deference. My personal style was not to be hostile, but to be friendly and equal, which he found insufferable. Whenever I made a mistake, he would try to court-martial me. He was a former colonel. . . . Whenever he made a mistake, I'd remind him of it in a very gentle, pleasant way. We had this battle of wills for ten years. Meanwhile, I got raises, making it hard to leave. I wasn't sure which of us would go crazy first. Actually, he went crazy first. But he was the boss!

There comes a time when, just on the basis of your salary, you are constrained to take your work seriously, and for me—in advertising—that was impossible. I was expected to act as if our business made sense, and I had something like a breakdown. It came in my tenth year as an ad man. It was perhaps precipitated by my working a hundred hours a week. Then, when Peter Berger decided to edit a book in the field of occupational sociology, he asked me for an essay on advertising. I delayed doing that essay for about six months. It meant summing up and winding up a whole decade of experience. I was close to 100 percent in the company's profit-sharing plan, after which there would be no unusual premium for staying on. Came the breakdown. During that period I went briefly into psychoanalysis, but I started writing my essay, which assesses advertising primarily as work with its own peculiar form of ethics. I had an absolutely wonderful mad, euphoric time writing it. The essay lent an air of finality to one long chapter in my life.

Then came an offer from CCNY which I welcomed because it meant liberation from the madness of Madison Avenue. I no longer had a crazy boss, nor was I under constant pressure to produce immediate results. Teaching was easy, even with the full load—twelve hours, four nights a week. For two days a week I worked as a consultant, and wrote a great deal, including half a dozen books and more articles than I can remember. I didn't think too much of City College but I wasn't required to think too much of it. In my time the college wasn't a great place that went downhill. It was a crummy place that went downhill. As of, say, 1960—65, one could have said the students were better than the faculty. This would have been even more the case around 1950. After '65, however, the faculty became better than the students, but not because the faculty improved.

In California, where the student rebellion began, the students may originally have had some legitimate grievances. But there and every place else, as soon as the "revolution" erupted, faculty jumped in, first to lead and control it, and then to redramatize their youth. Once these people were rejected by the students as being too old, too ideological, conservative, and dominant, *they* rejected the students. It's important to remember that the students first rejected them. Where I taught, the basic demands were those of the blacks to make City College into Harlem University, a term the revolutionaries used. But let me emphasize the point that just as soon as the student rebellion became a national or an international affair, somewhere between '66 and '67, the faculty made it their revolution. Once that happened, professors organized students for their own rebellion. At City, by 1968 we had faculty caucuses whose avowed purpose was to take over the college. Their first objective was to "get" the president. Later on students were organized partly by the faculty and partly by radical youth organizers. Some faculty members felt that the student rebellion was the wave of the future, and that they needed to be brokers mediating between the past and the present by becoming leaders of the institution and of a new society. Many were instant radicals.

At the Graduate Center (citywide headquarters for Ph.D. programs), there were grantsmen who had worked indirectly for the CIA and the military services who, up to that point, had been apolitical. Such people became spokesmen for the student radicals and for the wave of the future. Gutlessness was their common characteristic. These men and women felt sure they were going to be the winners. They jumped on the bandwagon. But, being lousy social scientists, they jumped on the wrong one. Some used it for the sake of promotion, others for tenure or for keeping their jobs. They organized little mobs of students, to use directly and indirectly as a physical threat to other professors. And so we had, in the two institutions that I know directly, and in the half-dozen I know indirectly, a kind of terrorism practiced by gangs of students sometimes standing outside or in a room next to which a faculty meeting was being held for the purpose of making academic decisions. They were there in order to intimidate the professors.

At City College demands for open admission, for special black and Spanish ethnic orientation programs exceeded all others. In 1969 or thereabouts, President Gallagher announced a plan for open enrollment which would take five years to implement, bit by bit. The youth rebellion came after the announcement of that plan, by those who expressed impatience over Gallagher's gradualism. In talking to kids after it was all over, I learned that the black caucus was composed of less than a dozen blacks. There was also a white caucus that joined with the black caucus; it was made up of a couple of faculty members and a few students. A white faculty radical would negotiate with the black caucus, and present demands to the president and to other faculty as a spokesman for the blacks. His students were almost all white. In addition, another faculty caucus was formed about a year and a half before the outbreak. In this one there were white radical professors not particularly geared to the black issue who wanted to make City College "relevant." They were out to get Gallagher, who himself had been generally recognized as a good friend of the blacks at City, a pacifist, a liberal who had headed a Negro college in the South. In our department seven or eight radical professors helped organize student terror. I responded primarily to the terror, real and implied, not to the issue of open enrollment, or black versus white, but simply the threats, the indecency, the lying and cheating. . . .

What first shocked me was the mendacity. One guy wanted to negotiate with me. Not that I was in any official position to negotiate with him, but he thought I had influence. Every time he told me anything, it was a lie. I have some instinctive caution or chronic inability to believe unclever lies. So I checked everything he said, and found I was being fed a bunch of lies, all in connection with political reorganization of the university. I was offended. The clumsiness of these lies was a blow to my pride. There was also something else. You could sit in a class and listen to a lecture by an activist who had just been radicalized and patently didn't know what he was talking about. He was teaching but hadn't had time to do the necessary reading. Now, I know the material, and my mind is not completely closed to all aspects of Marxism, but it does offend me that young men should passionately preach its problematic tenets without even having done their homework.

Neither was I opposed in principle to open enrollment. I came from a university that provided open enrollment, and I thought it was great. The Wisconsin system allowed anybody to enter the university, but did so without lowering standards. Fifty percent of the freshmen class flunked out by mid-term. This was open enrollment *with* academic standards. Anybody could enter. Not everybody *did*; but anybody *could*. That's open enrollment. It doesn't mean you have to kidnap people who sorely needed remediation and guarantee them college degrees after a four-year period when they'll need just as much remediation. As it turned out, open enrollment at City College was an immediate boon to the white ethnics. I sensed that it would not be that much of a boon to the blacks, and it never was.

Just before the explosion at CCNY I had been doing work at Bedford-Stuyvesant on the value of college-bound programs. What we found by analyzing all students in high school was that 50 percent of the black junior class dropped out in the eleventh grade, and 50 percent dropped out in the twelfth grade. So that if open enrollment applied to high school *graduates*, it wouldn't affect the blacks very much, but it would affect white ethnics. Without something like SEEK (a large-scale remedial program) as a means of qualifying blacks for the equivalent of a high school diploma, open enrollment wouldn't work to their advantage. Yet City College could not continue to operate as it had in the past for too much longer partly because as Jews moved up the middle-class ladder their children went to private schools, ideally to Harvard. For them, Harvard became the City College of the seventies.

The next several years at City College were a total disaster. One problem had been the spirit that animated its new students who on account of the hubbub were dragooned into college whether or not they wanted to go. College admission was redefined as a right, and that right existed apart from motivation and qualification. Some students were pushed into college to validate the principle of open enrollment. I would guess that most students did not know why they were there or, once there, what they ought to be doing. The clear, if unstated, demand they made was: "Entertain us. We are here to enjoy our rights." They did not recognize that a certain amount of work might be incumbent upon them. They were not aware of what a college is. Combined with a high degree of militancy, the product is a witch's brew, expressed as follows: "If I'm not getting anything out of this, *you're* doing something wrong." If a teacher says, "You ought to do some reading," or, "You ought to learn to read and to write," he's making an unconscionable demand. So, that happened, and a hell of a lot of faculty members were miserable while "teaching" was turned into a euphemism. Yet I try to find in each class students

I can inspire to do some real work and who can learn from that work. I'm not too successful; though I think of myself as a good teacher, in the role of a Shakespearian actor in the Borscht Belt.

I would say that, strangely enough, all of these issues of nine or ten years ago, are present right now beneath the surface. We're still fighting them out. Everybody who participàted in the youth revolution on any side is in some way marked for life. At a very subdued and subtle level the same issues are always being fought. They constitute the battle against inequality, privilege, and exploitation where there is never a final victory. If you win on one issue, that victory will perhaps produce a new elite that has to be fought again: there is no final resolution. Thus mine has become a pragmatic approach, I believe that there is no end to the struggle, no utopian final solution, whether that of Hitler or that of Stalin. This means that I'm certainly not likely to be taken in by any radical solution that will solve all problems in one act, or by a conservative acceptance of things as they are which says there is nothing to struggle for.

I was disgusted with those of my colleagues who yielded to short-term pressures for a final solution. In business you don't expect too much of people because they have to survive economically and no one professes to do much more than those jobs that are presumably designed to increase profits. In the academic world where higher ideals are emphasized, everybody proclaims them. Once you got tenure, all you had to do was work along the lines of your self-determined scholarly or academic interest. You're pretty largely free to pursue your own demons. Yet the percentage of honest men in academic life is no greater than anywhere else. But the university, which has greater institutional freedom, might allow one to be an honest man. Therefore, it's more disenchanting to see crooks, charlatans, operators and goof-offs in a university than it is to see them in advertising or in any other field. The contemporary college is becoming a sewer, and I would guess most of the faculty have lost even the ability to look above water-level. So they mostly seek petty favors and little means of surviving. They may be desperate but they find a way to dissolve their desperation by beating the system to get out of a course, or brown-nosing somebody into a promotion. So there is a kind of creeping mediocrity so embedded in my college that if I spend more than four hours there at a time I get nauseous. I also get nauseous at those people who know better, and let things slide because to act on their knowledge might offend someone.

There are worse things I could be doing, but are there worse things that could be happening to the university? It ain't gonna get better, it'll get worse. Today, it's not only a financial crush, I think this kind of creeping desperation, creeping madness, is cumulative: we've had a president who would reform the world from City College, a sychophantic administration, and a faculty that has adjusted itself perfectly to madness by complacency or by developing countermadness, which is just as bad. But it still doesn't mean everyone has to go mad.

At City College, the issues were not primarily nor even largely focused upon anti-Semitism. There were, of course, some anti-Semitic graffiti in the toilets; and some black militants have charged that white Jewish professors repressed and discriminated against the black masses and students. There were charges of Jewish elitism. But many of the radicals were Jews. And some of *them* were anti-Semitic.

I don't think I responded to these issues as a Jew. I have never been religious. Nor do I very often think of myself self-consciously as a Jew. I am reminded, and all my life have been reminded, that I am a Jew. So I cannot escape, nor do I attempt to escape, my Jewish identity. At the same time, the marginality that I have unfailingly experienced, and in which I exult, is partly based on being a Jew and partly based on a lower middle-class background that makes it impossible for me to accept middle-, upper- and, even lower-class things as they are. Nor am I any more receptive to the cant and clichés that justify things as they are. But there is still the experience of being a Jewish ethnic. There is an experience of some kind of Jewish elitism. That is, I can identify with Jews as intellectual disturbers and creators. I accept that, I suppose, primarily because we have all been brainwashed into that position, and that we've all been victims of our Jewish ethnicity. But this state of affairs is inherent in the Jewish tradition.

Finley Hall on fire during the student strike of 1968 at City College. "THE CAMPUS"—CCNY.

Georg Simmel could only have had European Jews in mind when he introduced the concept of marginality. It is no mere myth that we are still wandering Jews in the Diaspora, still in exile, even in America, even in Middle Eastern exile.

In 1973, I took my first trip to Israel, which sharpened some ethnic pride and brought old fears to the surface. The pride is in what the Israelis have accomplished while turning a desert into a garden. I've been in other arid areas, southern Yugoslavia, Egypt, and North Africa, and seen forbidding physical environments. I can well imagine what the Israeli pioneers did with their own work, their massive effort, the self-exploitation and the exploitation of world Jewry. Even their will to survive makes me proud.

The fear I share with all Jews is that Israel may not survive. But here again any civilization may collapse, from without or from within. In Israel the dangers are external. In the United States the dangers are internal, as they were prior to Hitler's Germany and prior to Soviet Russia. The totalitarian states of the left and the right are evidence of this descent into barbarism. The possibility of barbarism and brutalization lies deep in the human psyche, as Freud and Marx have separately taught us. But the pressures that turn that potentiality into an empirical reality are economic, political, and social.

And there's still the problem that for me will always be symbolized by National Socialism. It is easier to understand Hitler than it is the acceptance of Hitler by a plurality of the German people. It is above all the combination of madness, opportunism, and gutlessness that troubles me. Wherever turmoil exists, that combination is deadly. We are always living on the edge of barbarism, brutality, and madness. In Israel, the edge is external. In most countries it is internal. Of course, Israel has its share of corruption and crime, plus a host of other problems. But the accomplishment remains; and this has given me some sense of Jewish identity.

Yet I am not committed to Israel in any one-dimensional way. I'm committed to this country, at least in the sense that only its stupidities can make me really angry. I'm committed to my work, though I'm critical of my profession; I'm committed to my friends, and to the universalism of Western culture, and to an intellectual tradition that I see being sold out every day by its practitioners.

I guess, in all of these criss-crossing and contradictory traditions, I'm a marginal man who accepts his position. But this acceptance may be the decisive component of my Jewish identity.

23.

THE EDUCATIONAL
CRITIC IN NEW YORK

Diane Ravitch

GROWING UP Jewish in Houston was a lot different from
growing up Jewish in New York City. My father was born in
Savannah, Georgia, the youngest of nine children of Polish immigrants. His father arrived as a boy just before the Civil War
and was conscripted into the Confederate Army (as a drummer
boy, so the family legend goes). My mother graduated high school
in Houston, after arriving as a ten-year-old from Bessarabia. She
and her sister and mother reached the United States in 1918, possibly on the first boat that returned at the end of World War I,
according to her recollection. They made their way to Houston,
where my grandfather had been working as a tailor. My father
passed through Houston as a traveling salesman, met my mother,
and they married in 1930. Eventually they had eight children, and
I was the third. As soon as Prohibition ended, they opened a small
liquor store, in which both of them worked the rest of their lives.

My brothers and sisters and I went to the Houston public
schools. The feelings of Houston when I was growing up, especially in the 1940s, was very small-town. I rarely wore shoes
except when I went to school. We raised chickens and pigeons in
our back yard and grew most of our own vegetables. In my
elementary school, we were one of only two Jewish families in

Diane Ravitch was born in Houston, Texas in 1938. She is professor of philosophy and
social science at Teachers College of Columbia University, and is a frequent reviewer and
contributor to education journals. She has written *The Great School Wars* (1975) and *The
Revisionists Revised* (1978).

388

the school. I can remember some anti-Semitic name-calling, but I don't recall being much bothered by it. When I was about twelve, we moved to a neighborhood where there was a large Jewish minority. The junior high school—Albert Sidney Johnston Junior High—was probably 20 percent Jewish, which was quite a lot, since Houston's Jewish community was not much more than 3 or 4 percent of the population: non-Jews referred to the school as "Albert Sidney Jewstown." The same thing was true of the high school, San Jacinto, where Jewish students (though very much a minority) tended to stick together, to run student publications and to take a disproportionate share of academic honors; San Jacinto was derisively called "San Jew-center High." Again, I don't think too much offense was taken at this sort of anti-Semitism, though I can't say exactly why. Jews and non-Jews were friendly, but most of the dating and parties broke along religious lines; there were Jewish country clubs, Jewish secret sororities and fraternities, and friendship networks related to which temple one attended.

The school's program was rather routine and uninspiring. With few exceptions, everyone took the same courses, which were the same year in and year out. We were occasionally subjected to a barrage of right-wing propaganda, which we learned to take with a grain of salt; I was severely reprimanded when I refused to listen to Douglas MacArthur's farewell address to Congress, which was piped in to every classroom over the public-address system. I remember another day when, at a birthday party for the American flag (!), one student baked a chocolate cake seasoned with Ex-lax. I loved that irreverent quality in my classmates, though I now see that it was expressed in some fairly destructive ways, like drag racing at high speeds late at night (which I did fairly well) and widespread cheating in school (I helped several of my classmates make it through difficult subjects). Since there was no ability-grouping in the Houston schools, unlike those of New York, the students ranged in every class from very smart to very dumb. The range of competence among the teachers also was wide; a few were gifted, many were pedestrian, and some were pretty awful. Among students, there was no great respect for academic achievement, but rather for beauty (among girls) and athletic prowess (among boys). To be branded a "brain," especially if female, was something of a social handicap.

As I grew and started reading seriously, I become attached to a Reform rabbi, who was about the only person of learning that I knew. The community at large was materialistic and anti-intellectual, as was my family. There were few books in my house. As a teenager, I earned about ten dollars a week writing a gossip column for a neighborhood newspaper, and I used most of it to subscribe to the Great Books Club in Roslyn, Long Island. Books were a wonderful escape. Sometimes, if I wanted some peace and solitude (which can be precious in a household of eight children), I would climb a tree and read a book that the rabbi recommended. I didn't know it then, but the rabbi was quite a controversial man. He was at that time a leader of the anti-Zionist wing or Reform Judaism. I knew next to nothing about Israel. I was aware of its existence, but dimly. There wasn't anything like the intense involvement that one gets growing up in New York. I don't think I ever met anyone, as I was growing up, who had been to Israel or who had any interest in going there.

In Texas, Jews experienced great insecurity about whether they had dual loyalty. It meant a lot in Texas to be patriotic, and there always seemed to be some doubt about whether Jews were fully committed as Americans. The Houston Jews I knew tried extra hard to show that they were as patriotic as non-Jews. I recall a strong sense that it was gauche to seem *too* Jewish. As a child, I was embarrassed that my grandmother, who had been born in Bessarabia, never learned to speak English. She lived in Houston from 1918 until her death in 1967 and only knew a few words of English. She spoke Yiddish, as did my grandfather and my parents. They used it as a secret language to communicate with each other without the children knowing what they were saying. My parents did not want us to learn Yiddish; it was the language of the Old World and of a rejected past. My mother was ashamed of having been born in Europe, though when I eventually learned the story of her trip here, I thought she should have been proud of her perseverance and courage. When she and her mother and sister set out for America, they had tickets on a German steamship line. By the time they got to Marseilles, the war had started, and their tickets were worthless. The girls were placed in an orphanage, my grandmother scrubbed floors, and they survived through the charity of the local Jewish community. Eventually, they were able to complete their trip when the war ended. I thought it was a wonderful story, but my mother was not proud to have been an immigrant.

My Jewish education was limited to Sunday school in our Reform temple. We learned a smattering of Jewish history. I was so poorly educated as a Jew that I didn't know how poorly educated I was. At college, I came across an article by Milton Himmelfarb in *Commentary* (I was surprised to discover a Jewish magazine of ideas). It had to do with certain Jewish traditions like love of learning and social activism. I thought to myself, "So *these* are Jewish traditions." *I didn't know that.* The Jews I knew and grew up with didn't seem to be distinguished from non-Jews in either. There was no evidence of intellectual drive among the people I went to school with. My family was more liberal than most Texans (my parents always voted Democratic), but I didn't associate that with our religion. The main emphasis among Jews seemed to be on succeeding, assimilating, being very low-key on Jewish issues in order not to antagonize non-Jews, and becoming just as Texan as other Texans. Our parents dinned into us the importance of being Jewish but never communicated why. The reasons seemed to be largely negative. I recall my father warning us that we could never run away from being Jewish, that in the end "the goyim" would still call you a "damn Jew," no matter how much you tried to deny it. There were obviously contradictory tensions, since we knew that it was important to be Jewish but also important not to be *too* Jewish in behavior or language.

My rabbi's wife had gone to Wellesley, and was influenced by that. She told me that Wellesley was a good school. I only knew I had to get out of Texas. I had to get away from there because I felt a keen sense of aloneness. I thought I was a very strange person. The rabbi said, "Go to Wellesley and you will find other people who feel the same way you do." As it turned out, I'd have to say that my education, or at least the important part of it, began after college. But it may be a tribute to Wellesley that I left still eager to learn.

Most of my friends at Wellesley were non-Jews, but I had long since internalized my parents' admonition about the importance of being Jewish. So, while my Jewish education had been deficient, my Jewish identity was nonetheless secure. My sense of political activism grew stronger at Wellesley, though the dominant atmosphere was one of political apathy. As editor of the college newspaper, I felt personally responsible. for making the college administration as uncomfortable as possible. They were really quite decent people, and there was not an awful lot to be agitated about, but leading the charge against official smugness seemed to be the institutional role of the editor of *News*.

During the summer of 1959, I worked as a copyboy for the *Washington Post*. It was both exciting and spirit-dampening. On the one hand, I was working on a major daily in the heart of the nation's most intensely political city, close to some great writers and editorialists as well as to some who would eventually make their mark (like Tom Wolfe, a fledgling reporter, who wrote background stories for Nixon's trip to Poland without leaving Washington). On the other hand, I enjoyed the excitement at a distance, since my job consisted largely of errands, typing, pencil-sharpening, and the like. While my career didn't take off in the summer of 1959, my personal life did. I met my future husband that summer, despite the fact that I often worked a shift from three p.m. to midnight. We were married a few weeks after my graduation from college in 1960, and we settled in New York City.

I worked in the Kennedy campaign of 1960, and after the campaign, began job-hunting. I recall going to employment agencies and being asked, "How would you like to be a gal Friday at an advertising agency?" I never wanted to be a gal Friday anywhere. Meanwhile I was trying to be a housewife, which I didn't know much about. While the job-hunt was on, an odd circumstance steered me towards magazine journalism. One day I read the obituary of Sol Levitas, the founder of the *New Leader,* and a laudatory editorial in the *New York Times,* describing him and his magazine. I thought to myself, "That's the place I want to work." So I called and asked if they had any jobs. They said,

"Jobs! Sol Levitas just died. We have no jobs. We're in chaos. But why don't you come down, maybe you can help out."

I went down to the office on East 15th Street, and it *was* in chaos. But they did need help. The new editor, Myron Kolatch, asked me to start work and talk about salary later. I was so eager to do something that had some content that I jumped at the opportunity. We eventually settled on a token salary, something substantially less than the minimum wage, and I entered into what amounted to apprenticeship training. I worked at the *New Leader* off and on for about five years, interrupted by a year in Georgia when my husband was recalled into the army during the Berlin crisis, and by the birth of two sons. While I worked there, I did almost everything that could be done on a magazine. It was a small staff, generally only three people, and everybody did everything. I cut and pasted, I wrote headlines, I edited copy, I sold advertising, I even wrote some book reviews.

Aside from the practical experience I gained, I learned a good deal of history and politics while I was there. In addition, I was constantly exposed to first-rate writers. Stanley Edgar Hyman was the magazine's literary critic, John Simon wrote movie reviews, Daniel Bell and Irving Kristol were columnists. Among the writers were men like Erich Fromm, Theodore Draper, and Sidney Hook. Several of those whom I worked with during that period went on to brilliant careers in journalism and letters, one as art critic for the *New York Times,* another as editor of the *American Scholar*. Myron Kolatch was and continues to be a careful editor, and a journalist of the highest integrity. All in all, my years at the *New Leader* provided a valuable education. For me, the magazine was an introduction to a world of ideas of which I was scarcely aware. For the first time, I was immersed in debates that had been raging among intellectuals since the 1930s. I knew relatively little about the antagonists, since neither the debates nor the debaters had been part of my education in Houston or at Wellesley. I felt sometimes as though I was present at a game where you couldn't tell the players without a scorecard, and I didn't have a scorecard. I knew there were teams, but I couldn't tell who was on which team. It took a long time, longer than the time I spent at East 15th Street, to find out who was who and why they argued. Eventually, I found out that most of these arguments were traceable to who sat in which alcove at City College. I didn't come equipped to understand anything about New York City intellectual history and I felt woefully inadequate, which reinforced my own sense of provincialism.

While I was working at the *New Leader*, I wrote a few reviews which were published and began to write articles, which were not published. It is good that they didn't get published, even though it disappointed me terribly, because I really did not have a clear sense of who I was and what I wanted to say.

At the *New Leader* one saw much coming and going, a great commotion. It was stimulating. Neither in my home nor in my college life, even though Wellesley was a good school, was I ever in a Jewish intellectual atmosphere. The *New Leader* did provide that, although I think it was less ideological than *Commentary* or *Dissent*. I'd come up against one person after another with a really terrific education. That made me feel my provincialism all the more keenly—and spurred me on.

In 1966 our two-year-old son died of leukemia, after an illness of six months. Our older son was then four years old. For all of us, it was a horrible period. I had another baby the following year, another boy. The trauma of losing a child affected me deeply in many ways. I thought hard about what to do with my life, and resolved to do something, to find a professional activity that I could commit myself to. Soon after our baby's first birthday, I went to work on a part-time basis for the Carnegie Corporation, in a job that permitted me to choose my hours and work at home.

One of my Carnegie assignments involved writing a report on the Ford Foundation's school decentralization experiment in I.S. 201 in East Harlem, Ocean Hill–Brownsville in Brooklyn, and Two Bridges on the Lower East Side. I came to the project with a certain amount of knowledge because of my friendship with Preston Wilcox, a black activist who had been deeply involved in the battle for community control at I.S. 201 in 1966. I had learned a great deal about parent and community attitudes by attending meetings in East Harlem as his assistant, by long discussions with him, and by helping him organize the papers generated during the controversy. I was sympathetic to the idea of parent participation and community control; in one of the first articles I published about schools, in 1967, I urged "radical decentralization" of schools. Thus, I approached the Carnegie assignment as a sympathetic advocate of school decentralization. Soon after I finished my report to the foundation, the city's schools were plunged into the famous three-month teachers' strike, which resulted from the struggle between the teachers' union and the militant governing board at Ocean Hill–Brownsville.

During the teachers' strike, I decided to write a long magazine article about decentralization. Since I had interviewed most of the major actors as the crisis was developing, I thought I had a good vantage point. After some preliminary research on why the schools had been centralized in the 1890s, I thought I had a terrific piece. I sent a query to the *New York Times* Magazine, but they were not interested. By the time I received the rejection notice, I had already discovered that there was no good history of the New York City schools. I became determined to write a book, and though I didn't realize it at the time, I had stumbled onto the work that I had been looking for. In the course of writing the book, I had the good fortune to get to know Lawrence Cremin of Teachers College, one of the most distinguished historians of education in the country and also an extraordinarily generous person. Initially, he provided advice and guidance; later, he was a source of tough criticism. In time, he was the sponsor of my dissertation.

In the course of writing what eventually became *The Great School Wars: New York City, 1805–1973,* I became critical of my initial ideas about community control and decentralization. The book ended up, I hope, fairly balanced. I came to see that there were always problems, some perhaps stemming from human nature, and that there were no simple solutions; that whereas centralization didn't solve the problems of its time, neither did decentralization; that, in fact, there are no panaceas, especially where something as complicated as education is concerned.

During my research I published an article in *Commentary*

which more or less spelled the beginning of my career in the academic-intellectual world of New York. The article was about Ocean Hill–Brownsville. I had never before published an article in a journal like *Commentary*. And I was absolutely devastated by the response to it. I felt that I had discovered something important, basically that the high hopes aroused by Ocean Hill–Brownsville among very fine people were not justified. Prominent people had gone out to Ocean Hill and come away as converts. I said that the kids were never given a reading test. How could the school claim it had resolved the reading problem? When the experiment was concluded, and they did give tests in there and other districts, Ocean Hill–Brownsville students got the lowest reading scores in the entire city. That was fairly serious. And then there was stuff from the state evaluators about missing money, massive absenteeism, and a lot more that had gone on without being reported.

So I was attacked and got involved in sharp exchanges. That was an introduction to controversy and I can't say that I enjoyed it. At any rate, I have learned since then that if you say what you want to say and you make people angry, it's okay, but you have to know what you're saying and anticipate what the response will be, so that when it comes, you'll be prepared to take responsibility for your position. No one likes to be criticized, but if you get yourself into a controversy, you have to do it knowingly. When I wrote that article in 1972 I was quite naïve. I was still Texas provincial and didn't quite understand that I was walking into a lion's den. One doesn't just lightly tell a lot of people that they've made a big mistake.

To those who lived through it, the teachers' strike of 1968 will always be remembered as a seismic event, and certainly a cataclysmic event in terms of relations between Jews and blacks. The relationship had begun to deteriorate earlier, particularly when black nationalism and the community control movement emerged in 1966. Jews had been partners in the civil rights movement so long as it appealed to universalism and to assimilationist ideals; I think many Jews were stunned by the separatism and particularism of the black power movement; it repudiated much that the integration movement stood for, and there was a good deal of open religious and racial animosity, including appeals to violence and hatred. The breakdown of the partnership between Jews and blacks was probably inevitable because it was such an unequal relationship. The fault was not simply with black anti-Semitism, though it did exist; the problem was that Jews, in their eagerness to do good, were too often paternalistic, condescending, and domineering. Even if none of those attitudes were present, the fact remains that one side of the partnership was always giving and the other side receiving, which breeds resentment rather than gratitude. Certainly in retrospect it seems unwise that Jews should have played important policy-making roles in black organizations, as so many did. Their intentions may have been the best, but the effect was to emphasize black dependency on Jewish good will and money. Jews deluded themselves into thinking that they had a unique community of interests with blacks, which explains why so many were hurt, bewildered, and angry when the civil rights movement changed from being interracial in character to being black self-interest organizations.

I understood the anger of blacks and the need many blacks felt to control the institutions that affected them. But I never thought it was right to understand or tolerate anti-Semitism. Racial polarization became worse when responsible public officials and editorialists were reluctant to criticize black extremists. State and city officials were so fearful of a racial conflagration that they retreated from any possible collision with trouble-makers. As a result, the children in some of the community-controlled schools were exposed to black nationalist propaganda, to racism, and to anti-Semitism. School officials knew this, but they were afraid to do anything about it. The Ford Foundation's role in all of this was not one of which they should be proud. They began with what seemed to be a good idea, then succumbed to the mau-mauing; they kept the money flowing to some irresponsible people for fear that, if they didn't, "blood would flow in the streets" (as they were warned and as they believed). Some of the records from the project, maintained by Ford money, were kept in a double filing system (I would rather not say where). One set, available to re-

searchers, had the good news, the other set, not available to outsiders, contained confidential reports on chaotic conditions in the
schools.

What happened? It seemed to be a perfectly reasonable idea
to "give the schools to the people." But when a particular group
of people take over, you find that "the people" aren't taking over:
individuals do, and they are not "the people." They are individuals
with their own interests and opinions. In fact, you replace one
group of self-interested people with another group of self-interested people. In the end, you have to judge them by their deeds,
not their rhetoric. As I pieced all this together, it was like a de-
tective story. When I talked to state education officials about the
Ocean Hill–Brownsville district, the center of the turmoil, they
insisted that I protect their anonymity and then recited stories
about malfeasance and misbehavior that I had no way of verifying
(although the financial reports were quietly released). When I
pleaded for documentation I was told, "We have confidential reports from our observers that will never become public." When
I asked why I was told, "Because it would be too devastating,
too controversial. We can never release them." The teachers' strike
is long past now, and I hope some day that someone will use the
Freedom of Information Act to open those files, if they still exist.
Strange things were going on, like people being locked in closets.
I don't mean children, I mean the state evaluator.

At the time a good many people, in the foundations, in government, and in the press became convinced that decentralization
was a sure cure for the problems of the schools. I could understand
their view since I once believed it myself, but I never understood
why so many continued to cling to it long after contrary evidence
had come in. It was as though they had created the myth and were
then afraid to backtrack from their own invention. As I dug deeper
into New York school history, I was struck by the similarity of
the rhetoric surrounding both centralization and decentralization.
The schools were decentralized in the late nineteenth century, and
reformers said many of the same things that were later said in the
1960s about centralized schools. The reformers' claims for the
benefits of centralization were often precisely the same as the
claims later made for decentralization.

Of course, a significant difference in the crisis of the 1960s was the racial and religious aspect, and we are still living with some of the consequences. There was a sustained effort, for example, to bring more black and Puerto Rican teachers into the schools and into administrative jobs. But it moved too slowly, and it turned into an attack on traditional methods of hiring, and specifically to an attack on civil service testing. But just as it is wrong to make an objective test the sole measure of a teacher's competence, it is wrong to have no objective measure whatsoever. We have moved far in that direction under the prodding of the courts and the Justice Department towards racial quotas. Not long ago, a Justice Department official addressed top school administrators in New York and told them, "We don't care how you pick your teachers. We don't care if they are good or bad teachers. All we care about is that the teachers you select must reflect appropriate ratios of ethnic, racial, and sexual groups, and no group must be over-represented." What this means is that the federal government believes that competence is not the most important factor in hiring or promoting teachers, but race, sex, and national origin matter more. Following these criteria won't make the schools better, and they might make them worse. Personally, I continue to be an unreconstructed liberal of the early sixties. I believe that race and sex should be irrelevant. People ought to be judged by their ability to do the job.

There have been some salutary effects from these events. Many Jews like to believe that there is not a specific Jewish interest and that they (unlike others) are concerned only with the higher good, the public interest, or something well beyond any parochial self-seeking. I think the lesson has been learned during the past fifteen years that Jews, like others, have group interests which they ignore at their peril. Not all group conflicts can be harmonized, and many such differences between Jews and blacks emerged in and around the New York City schools. Blacks had a self-interest in reducing the importance of tests and pressing for racially-based hiring, while Jews had (and still have) a self-interest in preserving racially and religiously neutral policies. Blacks and Jews are in direct conflict over the issue of quotas, and I see no way to avoid the differences; if quotas were strictly imposed, Jews would be eligible for only 3 percent of whatever they sought, which would be particularly obnoxious precisely where Jews are "over-represented," as students, as professors, and in the professions generally. There is no way of obscuring the fact that Jews have thrived where opportunity was wide open and unrestricted by race or religion. This was the central theme of the civil rights movement until the mid-1960s, which is why Jews felt that they had a vital stake in its success. So long as the movement was universalist, it included Jews and everyone else who wanted a society without barriers based on race, sex, religion, or national origin. When the civil rights movement abandoned universalism and became a black self-interest movement, there was no place for Jews anymore, except as cheerleaders and spectators.

What has now happened to the city schools? A large number of minority students came into the New York City schools just when the trend in education was to abolish requirements. The prevailing notion was not to tell anyone what to do, to let students grope their way towards what they wanted.

It's a tragedy. I don't think anybody puts much stock in decentralization nowadays. But affirmative action is probably here to stay. After all, there's already a national association of affirmative action officers. They are making good money. And there are thousands of them. One thing decentralization has done (and I think I saw it before most people did) is this: it has made citywide protest almost impossible. In the old days, there was no trouble organizing citywide protests against an action taken by the central school board. Decentralize and you can't do that. However, history has taught me not to despair over transitory phenomena. I intend to keep writing and acting with the historian's belief that ideas make a difference.

24.

THE NEW YORK
PUBLISHING WORLD
Ted Solotaroff

YOU MIGHT say I was born into a repressed Jewish life, my parents having developed a strong emotional resistance to their Jewish roots. My father's father was one of the early Sons of Zion and went to Palestine, I surmise, in the late 1880s. His father was a railroad contractor in Russia and they took a lot of money with them to Palestine, where they soon lost it all investing in orange groves. My father's mother, Bathsheba, became a governess in Palestine to support the family. She worked for Baron Rothschild, no less, who in time sent her to study midwifery in Paris and Geneva. Bathsheba was a very lively, pretty, intelligent woman as well as a natural linguist.

Her husband was named David—implications everywhere! David spoke seven languages, including Arabic. He was a student of the Koran but he could not make a go of it in the primitive rural life of Hadera and Rishon-Le-Zion. As a privileged young Jew in Odessa, he'd been to the gymnasium and was raised, in the family parlance, "to wear silk stockings." They came to the United States but he couldn't make it here, either. Initially they settled on the Lower East Side and then in Yonkers, where Bathsheba did well as a midwife, but then my grandfather, sulking in the New World too, I suspect, invested in a glass business in Elizabeth, which he left to a partner to run while he drank tea in

Ted Solotaroff was born in New Jersey in 1928. He is a writer, editor, and critic, and is a frequent contributor to literary magazines. He is a founding editor of the *New American Review* and author of *The Red Hot Vacuum* (1970).

the back of the store with the other Jewish intellectuals of Union County. The partner, of course, stole him blind, and after he left, my father had to quit high school to keep the business going. He never got over that and seemed to blame his mother and Zionism rather than his father for impoverishing the family and depriving him of an education. It was my grandfather's wish that I be named Theodore Herzl.

My mother came from a devout family. Her father moved the family from Yonkers because he was afraid his sons would grow up badly among the goyim and settled them on a farm in New Jersey so they'd be safe from the false gods. My mother's family grew up on a farm outside New Egypt, about twenty miles from Lakewood. My mother's father knew no more about farming than my other grandfather knew about the glass business. So the sons were influenced after all by the gentile farmhands, who taught them to farm. But Poppa maintained his little *shtibele* (side room of a synagogue, used for public prayer) among the aristocratic farmers of Highstown and New Egypt. His cronies from New York would come down regularly to pray with him and discuss Talmud. My mother hated her life on the farm, including the religious strictness which made them such outsiders. But she dearly loved her pious parents and tried to see that I got a Jewish education, though she was not observant, except in certain sentimental ways.

The most important fact of my Jewish education was that my Hebrew teacher was said to have played on the Austrian Olympic soccer team. I thought he had terrific biceps, but there was little else in my life to support any kind of Jewish interest. Hebrew school was mostly a drag—learning to pronounce and then to chant words you didn't understand. It was what I had to do instead of playing ball with my friends. The only pay-off was the bar mitzvah in which you got to star in Temple for a half-hour and then collect lots of presents.

Judaism then was a sort of strenuous blank to me but I did experience a lot of anti-Semitism. I lived on the outskirts of Elizabeth in a pleasant suburban neighborhood called Elmora—a lot of Catholics and Protestants, relatively few Jews. There's a story that was told about me—I was six or so and a local judge, Judge

Waldman, started quizzing me in the local candy store where the few Jews around would congregate. He said, "Are you a Jew?" and I said, "I'm a Jew and I'm proud of it." Coming out of the mouth of a six-year-old, this was apparently a big item. So, curiously enough, although there was little Jewish content as such to my background—my two grandfathers were dead before I was five—there was a fierce kind of ethnic identification. Now, where did this come from? . . . Probably my uncles, the farmers I spent a lot of time with as a little boy. They communicated a strong feeling that they were Jews, and I suppose I picked it up from them.

In junior high and then in high school I got more involved with Jewish boys of my age. Elizabeth was an industrial town with a heavy working-class population, lots of Italians, Poles, Irish, etc. Jewish kids tended to hang together in the melting pot of the local high school. I joined a Jewish fraternity, and in general associated with other Jewish boys. That was when I began to have trouble in school. I was not diligent. I was more of a street kid than most of my friends who were already looking for signals to Harvard, Yale, Columbia, and so on. They had high aspirations, got high grades, and were intensely competitive. I was an 80 to 90 (percentile) student and felt that the other kids really had a leg up on me.

When I reached the eleventh grade, we moved to Roselle Park, a town outside Elizabeth, which was almost entirely gentile. The high school there was much more relaxed. Whereas at Thomas Jefferson in Elizabeth virtually all of us studied Latin for four years, at Roselle Park I was the only boy in the third year Latin class. And in that school I flourished; it was a real breakthrough. It got me out from under the psychological handicap of feeling that I couldn't compete with my Jewish friends. Well, in the middle forties I graduated from Roselle Park High School with honors but with no encouragement or money to go to college. So I went in the navy for two years. After that, I got the GI Bill and took off for the University of Michigan.

Ann Arbor in 1948 was like City College with trees. It was radical and, in some areas, Jewish. I was prepared for that partly because we lived in summer boarding houses where I'd run into older Jewish kids, and many of them were at either Michigan or Wisconsin. They made the middle-western academic life seem more reachable for me than Harvard, Yale, or Princeton, which seemed to me more like the Elmora Country Club. I did apply to Yale, though, and had an interview in New Haven after I got out of the navy. The interview was something to remember. I was from Roselle Park and I didn't know how to dress for such an occasion. My idea was to put on something called a "loafer jacket." Mine was powder blue, and, like all the other guys in Roselle Park, I wore pegged pants. I would tuck in the tips of my collar to get the "Oxford" look, and put on a tie that looked like scrambled eggs. That was my "good" outfit. I was interviewed by a man who looked as if he had just stepped out of the corporate loan department of Morgan Guaranty. Oh, the trouble he had pronouncing my name, barely able to bend his mouth around all of those syllables. He stared at me and I could tell that what he saw was some kind of New Jersey zoot-suiter with high college board scores. Why would I choose Yale? I told him I hadn't exactly chosen it yet. I had been accepted at Michigan and thought I would try an Ivy League school. Did I know anyone who had gone to Yale? Yes, someone in my high school class. What were my career plans? I said I was going to be a labor lawyer. Why that? "Because I'm a radical and want to work for the Political Action Committee of the CIO." The more I went on, the more distance grew between us. But he obviously had had doubts from the moment he laid eyes on me.

My adolescent politics were mostly shaped by an uncle who was a dentist. You see, my big escape route from Elizabeth and from my father's anti-intellectualism was in the direction of two unmarried aunts who lived in Manhattan, off Riverside Drive. Whenever I could, starting at age thirteen or fourteen, I'd come to New York for a weekend. I'd go to their apartment or to the home of my Aunt Belle's boyfriend. His name was Adrian, né Abe, and he was a cultivated dentist. He also worked on my teeth. Adrian was a gregarious man whose office was in his apartment. His waiting room was also his breakfast nook, and he sometimes practiced in his bathrobe, Russian style.

There would almost always be clever, impressive people at

Adrian's. While they waited to have their teeth fixed they would talk about fascinating subjects such as Trotsky, Kolchak, Deniken, and the Red Army. I "found out," from their determined point of view, soon learned that the Russian Revolution hadn't spread throughout Europe only because of capitalist intervention, aided by terrible White Russian generals who killed Jews. I took it in, because the only people I knew with ideas were my Uncle Adrian and his patients and my Aunt Fan.

New York also meant going to the theater and talking with my Aunt Fan. She taught English in a Jewish day school, and was the most important single influence in my life. I dedicated my first book to her. She got me to read Russian literature when I was fifteen or so, and it was then that I really became interested in books. She gave me an anthology of Russian short stories. The first story I read was "The Seven Who Were Hanged." What a revelation! *Adam Bede* and *Silas Marner* and *Ethan Frome* and the other fiction and plays we read in school were all about *them*, about the gentiles or about the old-fashioned America on whose margin I lived. But here was Andreyev—plus half a dozen other authors—writing about real people. They certainly weren't Jews, but they spoke to me as though they were. Their names were strange but not the dark music of their lives, made up of yearning and melancholy, just as I was. I plunged into Russian literature.

For all that, I still wanted to be a labor lawyer. In Ann Arbor my freshman adviser was a philosopher named Irving Copilowich. He later shortened it to Copi. Copi wondered why I wanted to take so many political science and economics courses my first semester. I said I wanted to enter law school in three years. He asked me, "Have you ever read any philosophy?" I said, "When I was in the navy I read something by a philosopher named Plato," which I pronounced "Platto." "Platto, hmm. Have you ever heard of any other philosophers?" I had. "There's a guy I've been meaning to read named Nietzsche." Copi was curious: "What do you know about him?" "Not very much. I thought he was Japanese." Copi recommended that I take the humanities course.

I took the humanities course, and it was like throwing a fish into water. I read Thucydides, Herodotus, Homer, Greek tragedies, Aristotle, annotating almost every speech or paragraph.

Then I wrote my first short story, which won an award. By the second semester I'd forgotten about labor law.

I had two older roommates, both veterans, both very active in the American Veterans Committee. I got straightened out by my roommates during the great political struggle of that year within the AVC, which was undergoing a strong challenge from the Communists. The big issue, I think, was whether Communists could serve as officers. There was some red-baiting on the one hand and plenty of Stalinist demagoguery on the other. Many of these veterans felt that the future of the United States was being fought out in their organization. How powerful an influence would the AVC be? Could it afford to take in Communists and expect to have any credibility? In the midst of this, my roommates made me aware of the Moscow trials, not to mention the Hitler-Stalin pact. I began to learn about people like Thomas Masaryk. There were a lot of skeletons in the Communist closet and a good deal of blood on their history, particularly Jewish blood.

Whatever remained of my radical opposition slowly turned into literary opposition. You didn't have to be anti-American to be an outsider. You could be something fancier. You could be an existentialist.

I began reading *Partisan Review* fairly early on in college and there too I learned a lot. In fact *PR* became a kind of higher version of the indoctrination I'd been getting from my roommates about Stalinism, while introducing me to my new gods—Sartre, Camus, Kafka, et al. In my senior year or thereabouts I fell under the spell of Isaac Rosenfeld, whose stories and essays I had discovered in *PR*. He became a model for me. I wanted to write like him. There was a special wit, forthrightness, humanity in Rosenfeld's voice that worked on me as the Russian writers had in my adolescence.

The University of Chicago offered me a scholarship, but I turned it down and came to New York because to be a writer in 1952 meant you had to be alienated, and to be a graduate student didn't seem to me a sufficient basis for that condition. My special figures were Joyce—"silence, exile, and cunning" was like a motto pasted on my forehead—and Kafka, as well as Rosenfeld, who was writing like Kafka and touting the marginal vision in a more local way. So I came to New York and worked as a waiter for four years. Every so often I walked past the *Partisan Review* offices, hoping to see someone brilliant and famous like Delmore Schwartz come out. Most of the time I lived on Macdougal Street where I didn't get to know very many literary people; mainly I mixed with the Italian waiters who lived there and who helped me to get jobs in "joints" owned by "the Syndicate." Meanwhile, I tried to write very polished Flaubertian paragraphs. I later put this experience into an essay, called "Silence, Exile and Cunning," about the *meshugas* (craziness) of trying to be a writer in those years when we were much more conscious of our literary values than of our daily experience.

The daily work I did was my way of making contact with the working class: I found it at 80 Warren Street, where unemployed waiters went to get temporary jobs. I lived in that temporary waiter ambience for several years, down and out in New York—which I felt one had to go through to be a writer. It was a curious mixture of alienation and identification with cultural aspirations. (I still have that.) I felt that there was still a secret life of the masses and that it had been given me to locate it.

Was this related to "Jewishness?" Jewish character had come to mean what you might call a full heart. As I saw it, the Jewish writer was one who had a particular compassion for the common life. I kept thinking of a line from one of Rosenfeld's stories called "The Hand That Fed Me." The hero falls in love with a Russian girl on the welfare line and he writes to her, "Be kind to the unfulfilled." Since I felt very unfulfilled, it was easy for me to thrill to that statement. Jewishness was not my bag at the time and yet it signified, more or less unconsciously, a certain ethic that I was trying to join to a modern art that came from the gentiles. The art rested on a kind of impassivity, as in Flaubert and Joyce and Eliot. God Himself was impassive. Your relation to your work as a writer was as impersonal as possible. I tried to write detached prose and at the same time write about the common life. My notion of art was tinged with a Russian Jewish sentiment which did not at all consort with the Christian detachment of Eliot and

Joyce and Flaubert. I was trying to plug an AC appliance into a DC socket, the Jewish ethos of concern into the Christian art of detachment. Rosenfeld too wrote about this dilemma. He says at one point in his journal, "When will I appear on the page as I actually am?" Faced with the same problem, I kept on polishing my subtle stories about the buried life. I wrote perhaps five stories in four years, and all of them were repeatedly and perfunctorily rejected.

At the end of that period, my wife got pregnant, and I decided that though it had been all right for my father's son to be a waiter it wasn't all right for my son's father. And I had another line going through my head: "Too long a sacrifice can make a stone of the heart." I could feel that happening. I was becoming a successful and cynical waiter. I had to do something else.

I heard that Rosenfeld was teaching at the downtown center of the University of Chicago. Partly because of that, I enrolled at the university in the master's program in English. I was very shy: meeting Rosenfeld was like meeting Gandhi. I began to make friends with friends of his so that somehow we would be thrown together. But just as that was about to happen, he died. It was about nine months after I came there and so I never got to know him.

If I had, I might well have fallen under his spell and example as a highly developed Jewish intellectual. As it was, something not very different happened in Chicago. In 1958 I was writing my dissertation on Henry James, like many good Jewish boys of the fifties, and suddenly like the surprise witness at a trial, came these familiar voices, those of Singer, Bellow, Malamud, Roth, the last being someone I actually knew from the university. They were putting into literature what I had formerly considered unworthy of literature: i.e., my common heroes, except for myself, were not Jewish. They spoke to my personal experiences, mainly what it had meant or, better, might mean, to grow up Jewish. It was enormously exciting to me. And not very different from what Rosenfeld had been doing. Rosenfeld was like a secret taste, a secret affinity. No one knew much about him except as a contributor to little magazines. But Bellow by then had won a National Book Award and in 1958 Malamud won one and a year or two later Roth did. My first published essay was a long review of "Goodbye Columbus," called "The Jewish Moralists: Roth, Bellow, and Malamud," which was mainly about the role of suffering in reaching moral truth; it turned upon *Seize the Day, The Assistant,* and a couple of Roth's stories.

So, again, this was like reading the Russians when I was sixteen years old. Here I was in graduate school studying American and English literature from an Aristotelian point of view and writing a dissertation on *The Bostonians.* I'd fallen into a kind of fascination with gentile literary culture, with that elegant *otherness*—trying to relate to it, even to become part of it. I was particularly interested in Lionel Trilling, who functioned as a guide, for young Jews like myself, to the Anglo-American literary tradition and to the higher style of criticism. He also was reassuring politically. Reading him you felt that you hadn't betrayed your heart by abandoning your radicalism, which was suspect anyway, for "the tragic sense of life" and "moral realism." Trilling could show you the true way to Henry James; he came to seem like the best model for the academic I was becoming: a Jewish Matthew Arnold, full of graceful energy and high public concerns.

At that point I think an important change occurred—namely, that just as the Russian writers in my adolescence gave me a personal stake in literature, so these Jewish writers and critics in the late fifties gave me a personal stake once again. They surfaced for me, and for everyone else, too: those I've mentioned, along with Kazin and Howe and Harold Rosenberg and Leslie Fiedler and Delmore Schwartz, as well as a lot of younger fiction writers and poets. Once you looked, there were a lot of Jewish writers.

Around this time, 1959, the *Times Literary Supplement* asked Roth to write an article on the Jewish role in American letters. Philip said he didn't know much about that subject, but he had a friend in Chicago who did. He had liked my essay on Bellow, Malamud, and himself. So Alan Pryce-Jones wrote to me asking if I would do him the great favor of contributing a 3,000 word essay to the *TLS.* There were professors of mine who would have killed to get a letter to the editor printed in the *TLS.* And I was being asked to write 3,000 words! In point of fact, I didn't know much about the subject either. However, by now I knew how to get around a research library. I took my three by five cards into the stacks where I read *Commentary* and *Midstream* all the way back to their beginnings. I also came upon an essay by Leslie Fiedler called "The American Jewish Novel and the Breakthrough," which gave me my theme. I simply broadened it to cover the breakthrough of American Jewish writing in general in America. I was guessing much of the time and guessing wrong some of the time. I put Richard Chase into the same generation as Norman Podhoretz and Steven Marcus, referred to Sholom Aleichem as "Aleichem" and to Karl Shapiro as a Catholic convert. All wrong. At the same time, the essay was full of passion, discovery, excitement; it *was* a breakthrough, at least for me. I had broken through the heavy WASP overlay of literature symbolized by my daily connection to Henry James, to a tremendous pride, affection, interest, and curiosity about how literature was being made out of being Jewish. The piece was full of that feeling. I guess I was the star of the issue, notwithstanding all my mistakes, and the essay was widely read in New York. It probably marked the first time that names like Howe and Podhoretz and Marcus, Roth and Fiedler and Herbert Gold had appeared in the *TLS*. Norman Podhoretz, who had just taken over *Commentary,* particularly wanted to know who the author was. When he discovered that I was the author, he tried me out with a book review and then offered me a job as an associate editor, which I almost immediately accepted and left the academy. He later told me, "You didn't know what you were talking about, but you guessed right 90 percent of the time, so I figured you'd probably make a good editor."

Commentary was very exciting. For two years or so I loved it. There was another young editor named Harris Dienstfrey, a representative of the new breed, who was also from the University of Chicago. Harris had the audacity to say that maybe Walt Kelly was a more important figure in our culture than Charles Dickens. I began to learn about American popular culture from him, as I did about the New York literary/political culture from Norman, Midge Decter, and from Sherry Abel who was the managing editor. The early sixties were good years at *Commentary*. The magazine's point of view was a strong but flexible one. It assumed that the old *Commentary* had pretty much exhausted the "hard anti-Communist" position, that we were in a new decade with an opportunity to articulate new issues and new perspectives, mainly from the liberal left.

Under Podhoretz, *Commentary* became less Jewish, but there was still plenty there for me to discover. The second book I reviewed was André Schwartz-Bart's *The Last of the Just*. I became aware of the realities and enormities of the Holocaust. Schwartz-Bart and Elie Wiesel had something to do with it, as did *Blood From the Sky*, a novel by Peter Ravicz, a Ukrainian Jew. His main figure is a sophisticated, elegant Ukrainian Jew with a symbolist's imagination. Because of his wits and blond hair and refined manners he is able to somehow survive most of the Occupation. Finally he is found out by the one unalterable identifying mark of the Jew which also proves to be his ultimate resource. I could identify very directly with a man who wasn't simply a victim or survivor, who for all his disguises is reduced eventually to a kind of utter nakedness. I'm not blond, but I certainly understood that idea of someone whose Jewishness seems marginal to him but who nevertheless discovers that it has determined his fate.

At *Commentary* I struggled to fit in. I mean their "less Jewish" was still, on my terms, very Jewish indeed. I felt I had much to learn; also that I was being put in touch with my two mysterious grandfathers, one of whom had named me. I was given a lovely piece translated from Yiddish to edit. It was titled "Three Brothers," and was a memoir by a leading Yiddish writer about his family as a kind of microcosm of the Enlightenment and its impact on the learned Jews of Eastern Europe. The author's father was a well-to-do and highly civilized Rumanian whose life had remained centered in Judaism. His oldest son went to Germany to study medicine and returned as an emancipated European, a "Spinozist" as he called himself. The second son, the author, became a lawyer, but retained his faith and cherished his Jewish culture, more or less living out the father's example and dream. The youngest son became a religious fanatic, driven to extremes of piety and austerity that carried him as far beyond the family pale as his oldest brother had been. This memoir, twelve to fifteen pages, was finely felt and tersely expressed. At least in my imagination. For it had not been translated very well and read woodenly. The more I got into editing it, the more I began to rewrite it, which one sometimes did at *Commentary*. I put it "through my typewriter," as we said, trying to maintain the thought, the spirit, but rewriting it in a way that made sense to me. I don't know how I managed to do it; I mean, I didn't know anything about Spinozists or about Jewish pietism. Yet the author spoke to me and spoke to me. It wasn't like editing so much as taking dictation. I finished editing it and gave the piece to Sherry Abel, a wonderfully tough, sweet woman who was sort of a combination of Virgil and Beatrice to me at *Commentary*. An hour later, she came into my office with tears in her eyes and said, "Ted, buried deep down in you is the soul of a Yiddish journalist."

All of which was part of finding a voice, a certain kind of sensibility which was all right to have at *Commentary* because that's what the magazine was in business to cultivate; a broadly Jewish point of view that was also American and contemporary and so felt confident enough to poke its nose into anything that interested it. Like my six-year-old self, I was again "a Jew and proud of it."

It was a rich, difficult experience that lasted six years. After the second year or so, my relations with the magazine and with Podhoretz became more problematical. Dienstfrey left because, as he put it, there wasn't enough oxygen. I think he felt cramped and a bit stifled by the strict and intense conception of what the magazine should be. That was pretty much defined in practice by the habitual question, "Is this a *Commentary* piece? Is this a *Commentary* short story?" What was meant was a matter of tone as well as of substance. In the course of giving it the *Commentary* look the prose did tend to become homogenized. I was a party to that. At first, I didn't feel there was anything the matter with the editorial process, which I felt was in the spirit of clarity, economy, readability, and also of cutting out the bullshit of cant and jargon. Let me try to explain this a little bit because, in a sense, it taught me how to be an editor.

Podhoretz himself is a very clear, distinct, economical writer. His prose always drives toward a point; he's not really interested in the graces of expression or in the richness of texture; he's interested in making a case as decisively as he can. Those values were carried over into the way and spirit in which we edited. Now this standard did not begin with Norman. *Commentary*, a magazine which initially carried a lot of writing by Jewish scholars and social scientists, must always have required extensive editing. Otherwise, it would hardly have been readable. Secondly there was *Commentary's* role as a conduit and clarifier between the New York intellectual, broadly understood, and the Jewish community out there in America.

Still, as time went on, my relation with Podhoretz became strained. This may have been nothing more than the inevitable frictions and wariness between two ambitious young men. I wanted more scope and responsibility and didn't get it. He wanted more unflagging commitment from me and didn't get it. I think I also represented a part of himself—the literary part—that he wanted to overcome in order to become the completely political animal he is now.

It was about this time that the Cuban missile crisis occurred and with it a noticeable shift in *Commentary's* politics. I always felt it was at just that point when *Commentary* began to close up its "opening to the left" and resume the hard line which was to grow harder from year to year. A lot happened to Norman and he has now written about it himself, but I think that his intellectual style never changed much at all. He was always someone, even as a young literary critic writing about Camus or Faulkner, who felt most sure of himself when he was hacking away at the prevailing opinion, the conventional wisdom. To be in an adversary position gave him energy and purpose which, at least as a writer, he didn't seem otherwise to have.

As for the magazine's politics, I noticed that people like Glazer and Moynihan commenced to be as influential as Paul Goodman had been two or three years before. But it was really only with the Vietnam War that I developed a strong negative feeling about the magazine's politics. They were expressed pretty much at that time by the headliners, particularly Oscar Gass, who was a trenchant, adamant hawk. I don't mean to suggest any great ideological struggle, which I was in no position to make, but my decision to leave coincided with our bombing of North Vietnam, about which Podhoretz and I sharply disagreed. I'd become a loner on the magazine.

I was offered a job at the *Herald Tribune* editing its book section. Podhoretz in fact recommended me for the job, as I remember. That was typical of him: in any personal matter, he was always a *mensch* (a man). And, let it be said once and for all that my important education as an editor came from Podhoretz and that learning to be an editor from him was like learning to be a football coach from Vince Lombardi. One learned the fundamentals, including how to persist, which is what editors mainly do, after they have set their course. A few weeks after I went to the *Trib*, for example, it was struck. I had to keep putting it out—it was syndicated—without its staff for about five months. It was a trial by fire, to say the least, but from working with and watching Podhoretz, I didn't have much fear of fire. On the other hand, I had lost any desire I might have to emulate him and I ended up doing something very different from what he does.

I left the *Trib* after nine months or so to start the *New American Review*. My policy there was partially a reaction to the *Commentary* editorial syndrome. *Commentary* was a very heavily edited magazine which in the last years added to my other tensions with Podhoretz. I'd run into more than one contributor who protested, "You say you're making my manuscript into a '*Commentary* piece,' but what you're really doing is taking me out of it and putting yourself into it." One friend had written a review and I, in my desire to see it published, had drastically rewritten the opening paragraph. He said that I had not only changed his voice, but his point of view as well, and so he had taken no pleasure at all in seeing the review published. I didn't agree that I had changed his point of view, only clarified and strengthened it, but still his reaction brought me up short. Then the objections of other writers began to get to me. I was writing myself and I knew that if anyone did to my prose what I was doing to others', I would surely be pissed off. This, in time, led me to my main principle as an editor, which I still fall back on in the difficult situations: treat writers as you expect to be treated when you're on the other side of the desk. This meant not accepting any writing that I wouldn't be willing to publish as it was: i.e., that my "editorial suggestions" were only that, that the writer was free to choose which he would take and which he wouldn't.

Secondly, I decided to put the initiative with the writers rather than with the editor. Instead of arranging for almost everything in the magazine to be written along predictable lines, I'd let the writer tell me what he really wanted to write about. Even on *Commentary* it had been the surprises that created the most tension and interest in its pages, such as the two years or so in which Hans Morgenthau, a regular columnist, took a stand on the way the magazine was edited and against the way it was heading politically. I found myself secretly agreeing with him in his hassles with Podhoretz and also welcomed them because they made working on the magazine more interesting again.

When I started the *New American Review*, one of the strong directives I gave myself was to try to create a national magazine, rather than my generation's version of *Partisan Review*. Part of this directive was personal. I had been educated in the Middle West, at Michigan and Chicago, and felt that much of that experience and what vision it had given me had been more or less unemployed in the years at *Commentary*. As I can see now there has been a kind of pattern in my career, a moving out from and then a return to what you might call home: home being represented by New York Jewishness, the flow of my people's history in me and through me, what I think of as my grounded side. The other side is the more open, indefinite, new experimental one that leads into otherness—the America that is not New York, the experience and perspective that is not "Jewish," that has little or nothing to do with my people's history and sensibility—i.e., the New Criticism, the Chicago criticism, Hemingway, James, the French symbolists, Lao Tzu, you name it. In the late sixties I wanted to strike out again in the direction of otherness, which presented itself as the America of the antiwar movement, of the counterculture, what I called at the time "the imagination of alternatives" which seemed to me a kind of last-gasp attempt to restate the democratic tradition and to reorganize the party of humanity before the rational maniacs of the warfare state took over for good.

So, as is often true of anything creative, which I think *NAR* was, it was the result of a number of things coming together: the opportunity to do a different kind of magazine—essentially a "little magazine" that had to survive in the mass market; the opening up of political and cultural consciousness; and finally my own felt need to be moving on and out. All of these are complex developments. But I can see now, in retrospect, that the editorial style of *NAR/AR*, which I came to think of as "wise passivity," in which I let the writers instruct me in what the important issues were, came partly from my sense of the age, that of a cultural revolution in which a lot of answers were turned back into questions; partly from the paradoxes of editing a paperback literary magazine which would have to be national in tone if it was to succeed at all; and partly from a reaction to the *Commentary* knowingness. There's the joke about the Jew who runs out of the prayer house shouting "Jews, Jews! I've got the answer, give me a question!" After six years of being told the answers, I was ready for some questions.

Hence, it's no accident, as they say, that the writers I came to depend on most to articulate the questions were themselves in reaction to the New York/Jewish syndrome—such as George Dennison, Eric Bentley, Philip Roth, Richard Gilman, Susan Sontag, Stanley Kauffmann, Milton Klonsky, Alfred Chester, Gil Sorrentino, etc., or almost completely removed from it, such as Michael Rossmon, Conor Cruise O'Brien, Robert Coover, William Gass, Benjamin DeMott, Robert Stone, Harold Brodkey, Theodore Roszak, Max Apple, etc.

Which provides one of the ironies of being regarded all along as one of the members of the New York Jewish establishment. Over the years I've encountered a lot of negative feeling about that, not unlike the anti–New York talk that surfaced a few years ago when the city was on the verge of bankruptcy and the general wish of the country seemed to be to saw off New York and let it drift out to sea. In literary matters, New York is perceived to be the corrupt and corrupting center of things which operates through a kind of conspiracy made up mostly of Jews. Some wise guy will saunter up to me at a reception after a lecture at Anthracite State and say, "My name is O'Brien. Will you read a manuscript by me?" But usually the question is a bit more veiled, i.e., "What's it feel like to be part of the New York establishment?" My answer is "It's pretty much like not being part of the New York establishment." I'm not being fatuous. When my own book was published, for example, it was not reviewed in *Commentary,* or *Partisan Review,* or in the *New York Review of Books.* "We" are also supposed to control the *Times* Book Review, but the first four books I edited at Harper and Row that were reviewed there were badly and unfairly panned. That's about as much as I can report about the allegedly concerted backscratching that is said to be our favorite pastime. I may see people with whom I'm supposed to be in league once or twice a year, if then. No doubt a certain sociology is at work which brings Jews into publishing, but there's no concerted effort I've detected to create a Jewish influence, much less dominance. Jewishness is probably much less pronounced and coherent than WASPishness was when book publishing was in the hands of the Harcourts and Scribners.

The careers of publishers like Bennet Cerf, Donald Klopfer, Harold Guinzberg, Alfred A. Knopf, Max Schuster, etc., suggest a pre-war Jewish presence. Occupationally, we are the sons of these people. But our social origins are generally different. On the whole, they came out of the German-Jewish class. The "Jewish influence" on publishing of their period was mostly, I suspect, an openness to Europe and to other literatures besides English and American. Those of my generation who have made their way in publishing, well . . . some of them are directly related to their predecessors, but mostly we are from the Russian-Jewish background, though by now mostly third generation. While I do not believe there is any such thing as a Jewish establishment, I think many of us do share certain assumptions about the importance of literature as a kind of conscience of society. Also, perhaps, an alertness to issues, which Jews seem to carry in their DNA, understandably so. But the formation of an unspoken point of view, if there is one, could occur anywhere. In fact, most Jews I know in New York publishing grew up elsewhere. We gravitated here because this is where publishing is and where the action is, such as it is.

That is, if you're an editor. If you're also a writer, perhaps you're better off elsewhere. I often feel that, particularly in the last few years when I've been trying to write fiction. The temporal dimension of experience, on which fiction feeds, is all awry here. Life here is so present-minded, perhaps because its character is so much hustle and hassle. Yet I stay and have no real plans to leave. Partly that's because two of my kids are still here and my main means of earning a living is here. But there's something else too. New York is still the place where my two aunts lived and the Upper West Side is still the place where I feel most at home in America. Settling in New York must have been my destiny— even though it superficially happened by accident. I would have gone to the University of Washington from Chicago if I'd not written that article in the *TLS*. But I willed myself to write that article because I sensed a kind of destiny at work. "The soul of a Yiddish journalist"? In the past years, I've experienced similar promptings, which I'd rather not go into just yet but which have led me to study Hebrew and to prepare myself to join a *minyan* (a quorum of ten for prayer).

Perhaps this latest phase—a return to Jewishness, a reconnection to my inward, "grounded" side—began with a trip I made to the Soviet Union four years ago. I hated the Soviet system but felt so deep a connection with the Russian atmosphere, as though I were returning home to the place where I'd spent my earliest years. I was startled to see how much I'd identified as Jewish turned out to be Russian, including the word *nu*. You go to GUM, for example, the department store in Moscow, and it's just like being back at Klein's. Perhaps Klein's didn't die; perhaps they just moved it to Moscow. Go downstairs in GUM and you're in Klein's basement. But of course, there was much more than that. There was the creaturely feeling, the affection and irony, the shrugs and winks Russians use to communicate; and that was like second nature to me. There were also the immediate affinities I struck up with so many of the writers and editors I met. Going to the theater to see "The Cherry Orchard" or "Mother Courage" was like dreaming—the familiar turning strange, the strange somehow familiar. In America I'd never understood what it meant to have roots. In Russia I did.

A similar encounter within myself occurred in reviewing Irving Howe's book *World of Our Fathers*. I read it like an amnesiac who had just received the blow to the head that brings everything back. I'd often wondered about all those tropisms, as it were, that Jews of my generation share. My own Jewish background is so meager. How do I account for that? I grew up in essentially a gentile world in a family that had more or less turned its back on Judaism. And yet, the deepest experiences of my life continue to be related to being Jewish. Howe's book was so tremendously important because it provided the missing link, as it were, specifically Yiddishkeit, which flowed down to me in all sorts of clues and cues—political, social, cultural—that had shaped my parents', aunts', and uncles' ways of thinking, feeling, being. It could be in the shock of recognition of reading Rosenfeld and the others. Or it could be in my feeling for Russian literature and culture which Howe pointed out had a strong influence on Yiddishkeit. Or it could be, as I'm discovering in my passion for Hebrew, one that I've not felt for any other language.

At the same time, simply to say "Okay, you're a Jew!" after all and define myself accordingly would hardly account for all my sense of myself. I also grew up playing first base rather than in prayer. My boyhood idol was Lou Gehrig, the writer I first emulated was Hemingway. I guess you could say I have a powerful immediacy about being American and a powerful hauntedness about being Jewish.

INDEX

Abel, Lionel, 283, 286
Abel, Sherry, 410, 412
Action party, 201
Adamic, Louis, 123
Adams, Franklin P., 141
Adams, Henry, 202
Adler, Jacob, 181–83
Adler, Luther, 184
Adler, Stella, 184
Adorno, Theodore, 82, 121
Agee, James, 199, 200
Albert Einstein College of Medicine,
  9–10, 237–38
Alcoves, at City College, 274–75, 394
Allen, Red, 100
Amalgamated Clothing and Textile
  Workers Union, 254, 270, 336
Americana (musical), 144, 146
American Dilemma An, Myrdal, 103
American Image of Europe, The,
  Boorstein, 224
American Jewish Congress, 334
American Scene, The, James, 197
American Society of Composers,
  Authors, and Publishers (ASCAP),
  149
American Veterans Committee
  (AVC), 252, 406
American Workers party (AWP), 164
Anderson, Sherwood, 268
Andreyev, Leonid, 405
Ann Arbor, Michigan, 403–4
Antioch College, 85
Apollo Theater, 98–99, 273
Apple, Max, 416
"April in Paris," Harburg, 145
"Architect From New York, The,"
  Goodman, Paul, 329

Arendt, Hannah, 70, 71, 79, 85, 108,
  119, 124, 125, 200, 285–86, 363
Arlen, Harold, 106, 107, 144–46,
  148–51
Armory Show, 199
Armstrong, Louis, 105, 111
Asch, Sholom, 61
Ascoli, Max, 201
Atkinson, Brooks, 93
Atomic Energy Commission, 5
Auden, W. H., 291–92
Avery Library, 12, 325
Avukah, 276
Awake and Sing, Clurman, 7, 185
Axel's Castle, Wilson, 281

Bab Ballads, Gilbert, 141
Baeck Institute, 12, 215
Bailey, Buster, 97
Balanchine, George, 283
Baldwin, James, 58, 103
Barbarolli, John, 212
Barnard College, 335
Barnes, Clive, 177, 192
Barnett, John, 301
Baron, Salo, 84
Bartók, Bela, 305
Baumann, Ken, 124
Bavli, Hillel, 216, 353
Beame, Abraham, 258
Beaux Arts Institute of Design, 312
Begin, Menachem, 131
"Begin the Beguine," Porter, 148
Bell, Daniel, 284, 393
Bellamy, Edward, 114
Bellow, Saul, 3, 83, 200, 202, 326,
  408, 409
Bellush, Bernie, 252

Benchley, Robert, 142
Bennett, John, 221
Bensman, Joseph, 5, 11, 17–18, 368–87
Bentley, Eric, 416
Berg, Alban, 93, 96
Bergelson, David, 53
Berger, Abraham, 215
Berger, Peter, 379
Berlin, Irving, 106, 148, 149, 184
Berliner Tageblatt, 114
Berry, Chuck, 97
Berryman, John, 203
Bialik, Hayyim N., 353
Billy Budd, Melville, 125
Blake, William, 20, 323
Block, Joshua, 214–15
Blood from the Sky, Ravicz, 411
"Blues in the Night," Arlen, 146
Blumenthal, Nachman, 66
Bolger, Ray, 145
Boorstein, Daniel, 224
Borah, William E., 336
Borkenau, Franz, 117
Brandeis, Louis D., 168, 331
Brandeis University, 229, 286
Braude, Zev, 61
Braude Schools, 61
"Breakup of Our Camp, The," Paul Goodman, 316
Brice, Fanny, 139
Brodkey, Harold, 416
Bronowski, Jacob, 185
Brook, Barry, 10, 11, 299–310
Brooklyn College, 252
Brooklyn Heights, 198, 199
Brooklyn Museum, 11, 212, 213, 214, 325
Brooklyn Tablet, 340
"Brother, Can You Spare a Dime?" Harburg, 144, 145
Brown, Lew, 149
Brown, Willie Lee, 361
Bundy, McGeorge, 366

Burlingham, Charles, 338
Burnham, James, 164–66, 275–76
Butler, Nicholas Murray, 335

Cagney, Jimmy, 191
Cahan, Abraham, 178
Cain, James, M., 95
Caldwell, Erskine, 103
Call It Sleep, Roth, 203
Call of the Wild, The, London, 34
Cameron, W. J., 211
Cannon, James, 163
Capote, Truman, 203
Carey, Hugh, 262–63
Carnegie Corporation, 394–95
Carnegie Hall, 212, 301
Carnovsky, Morris, 190
Carr, Charlotte, 337
Carroll, Earl, 144
Carson, Sonny, 260
Carter, Elliott, 308
Cassirer, Ernst, 125
Catholic Digest, 55
Central Labor Council, 254
Cerf, Bennett, 417
Chagall, Marc, 200
Chaiken, C. 262
Chaillet, Jacques, 306
Chandler, Raymond, 95
Chase, Richard, 410
Chester, Alfred, 416
Chevalier, Maurice, 35
Chiaromonte, Nicolo, 200
City College of New York, 11, 142, 386, *illus*.; alcoves at, 274–75, 394; Bensman on, 380–85; Brook at, 303, 304–5; Cohen at, 213, 214, 217, 219; Paul Goodman, at, 324; Howe at, 274–75, 279; Kazin at, 195, 197, 198; Morgenthau on, 85–86; Paley at, 292
Claessens, August, 272
Clark, Joe, 276–77
Cleaver, Eldridge, 58

Clurman, Harold, 6–7, 176–93
Cohen, Elliott, 356
Cohen, Gerson, 6, 12, 14, 210–26
Cohen, Morris, 4, 275–76
Coleman, Professor, 142
Columbia University, 3, 5, 11, 12, 84, 132; Bensman and, 376; Brook at, 305; Cohen on, 210, 215, 221; Goodman on, 323–24, 325; Kovel at, 237
Commentary, 14, 172, 225, 244, 391; Decter and, 356–57, 358; Greenberg and, 230; Howe and, 285; Ravitch and, 394, 395–96; Solotaroff and, 410–15, 417
Communist party, 166, 171, 271, 290
Communitas, Goodman and Goodman, 316–17
"Conning Tower, The," Adams, 141
Coover, Robert, 416
Copernicus, Nicholas, 125
Copilowich, Irving, 405
Copland, Aaron, 185
Coser, Lewis, 4
Coughlin, Charles Edward, 15, 273, 291, 346
Crane, Hart, 9
Cremin, Lawrence, 395
Crouch, Stanley, 104
Crouse, Russell, 141

Davidovsky, Mario, 309
Davis, Moshe, 216
Dawidowicz, Lucy, 68, 70
Dayan, Moshe, 80
Dearborn Independent, 211
Debs, Eugene Victor, 162, 196
Decter, Midge, 5, 7, 14, 18, 351–67, 410
Decter, Moshe, 354
Delany, Hubert, 341
DeMott, Benjamin, 416
Dennison, George, 416
Design Laboratory, 319

DeWitt Clinton High School, 184, 270, 271, 300
Dickinson, Emily, 199
Dienstfrey, Harris, 410, 412
Dietz, Howard, 143
Dissent, 133, 286, 394
Dostoyevsky, Feodor, 34
Double E, The, Percival Goodman, 317, 318
Draper, Muriel, 199
Draper, Theodore, 393
Druckman, Jacob, 309
Dubinsky, David, 9, 162, 168–70, 170 *illus.*, 173–74, 252, 257, 263, 335
Duke, Vernon, 145
Dulles, John Foster, 128
Duncan, Isadora, 188
Durbin, Deanna, 150

Eastman, Max, 280
Eban, Abba, 129
Einstein, Albert, 4
Einstein, Alfred, 305
Eisler, Hans, 191
Eldridge, Roy, 97
Eliot, T. S., 281, 407
Ellington, Duke, 102, 105, 110
Ellison, Ralph, 103
Émile, Rousseau, 114
Empire City, Paul Goodman, 325–26
"Encounter in Haiti," Gold, 53
Encyclopédie, Diderot, 214
Enemies: A Love Story, Singer, 36
Eros and Civilization, Marcuse, 240
Escape from Freedom, Fromm, 375
Ethics, Spinoza, 34
Ettenberg, Sylvia, 216

Fackenheim, Emile, 233
Farrell, James, 281
Faulkner, William, 95, 103
Feingold, Henry, 222
Feingold, Jessica, 219

Feldman, Sandy, 261
Fervent Years, The, Clurman, 185
Feuer, Louis, 292
Fiedler, Leslie, 409, 410
Field, Marshall, 16, 339, 346
Field, Mrs. Marshall, 80
Fields, W. C., 151
Fifth Avenue Synagogue, 320, 321
　illus.
58th Street Music Library, 10, 302–3
52nd Street, 96, 97–98, 99 *illus.*
Finian's Rainbow, 151, 152 *illus.*
Finkelstein, Louis, 226, 315
Finletter, Thomas, 80
Finely Hall, CCNY, 386 *illus.*
Fitzgerald, F. Scott, 9, 198
Fitzgerald, Robert, 200
Flaubert, Gustave, 34, 407–8
Ford Foundation, 366, 397–98
Fortune, 199, 200, 201
Foster, Stephen Collins, 107
Foster Care Commission of the City
　of New York, 341
Frank, Anne, 315
Frank, Leonhard, 90
Frankfurther, Felix, 338
Frankfurt Institute, 121
Free Synagogue, 332
Freud, Sigmund, 177, 238, 239, 315
Fried, Arthur, 150
Friedman, Philip, 62
Fromm, Erich, 375, 393

Galbraith, John, 199
Gallagher, Buell, 381–82
Galsworthy, John, 34
Gannett, Lewis, 197–98
Garfield, John, 190
Garland, Judy, 150
Gass, Oscar, 413
Gass, William, 416
Gear, Luella, 145
Gelhorn, Walter, 336
Gershwin, George, 106–7, 142, 146,
　148, 184

Gershwin, Ira, 141–42, 143, 145
Gerth, Hans, 373, 374
"Get Happy," Arlen, 147
Gilbert, W. S., 141
Gillespie, Dizzy, 98
Gilman, Richard, 416
Gilson, Roland, 335
Ginzberg, H. L., 218
Glaberman, Martin, 274
Glasser, Joe, 104
Glatstein, Jacob, 15, 51
Glazer, Nathan, 225, 356, 413
Goetz, Gus, 93
Gold, Herbert, 53, 410
Gold, Michael, 203
Golden Boy, 188
Goldman, Nahum, 343–44
Goldman Band, 301
Goldwyn, Sam, 150
Gomberg, Bill, 253
"Goodby World," Glatstein, 15, 51
Goodman, Alice, 313
Goodman, Benny, 100, 104–6
Goodman, Matthew, 327
Goodman, Paul, 8, 200, 202, 313,
　314, 316–17, 324, 325–29, 413
Goodman, Percival, 8, 11, 19–20,
　311–29
Gorman, Pat, 255
Gorney, Jay, 143–44
Gotbaum, Victor, 8–9, 15, 17,
　246–63
Granz, Norman, 104
Grappelli, Stephan, 97
Great Gatsby, The, Fitzgerald, 198
*Great School Wars: New York City,
　1805–1973, The,* Ravitch, 395–96
Greenberg, Clem, 356
Greenberg, Eliezer, 285
Greenberg, Hayim, 51
Greenberg, Irving, 6, 9, 13, 227–33
Greenberg, Noah, 281, 301, 302, 304
Greenberg, Toni, 308
Greenwich Village, 7, 52, 98, 110,
　293–95, 314, 407

Group Theater, 185, 191–92
Growing Up Absurd, Paul Goodman, 325
Guinzberg, Harold, 417

Haber, Herb, 259
Hadoar (newspaper), 353
Hadoar Lanoar, 353
Haggin, Ben, 189
Halley, Rudolph, 171
Halpern, Ben, 57
Hamilton, David, 308
Hammerstein, Oscar, 148
Hammett, Dashiell, 95
Hammond, John, 104
Hampton, Lionel, 100
Hamsun, Knut, 34, 35
Handlin, Oscar, 286
"Hand That Fed Me, The," Rosenfeld, 407
Hapgood, Hutchins, 278–79
Harburg, Edgar "Yip," 7, 20, 21, 137–54
Harburg, Max, 138
Harlem, 98–101, 102, 110, 273–74
Harper's, 174, 365
Harris, Jed, 182
Hart, George, 246
Hart, Moss, 148
Hawkins, Coleman, 97, 98
Hebrew Arts Council, 216
Hecht, Ben, 92
Helphund, Sam, 161
Hemingway, Ernest, 319
Henderson, Fletcher, 97, 105–6, 149
Henry, O., 140–41
Hentoff, Nat, 365, 366
Herberg, Will, 221, 225
Herbert, George, 205
Hertzman, Erich, 305
Herzl, Theodore, Foundation, 52
Heschel, Abraham, 206, 222
Hesse, Hermann, 109, 114
Hill, Herbert, 173–74
Hillman, Sidney, 335, 336

Himmelfarb, Milton, 391
Hirschfeld, Al, 90–91, 93
Hitler, Adolf, 35, 76–77, 117–18, 120, 163, 188–89, 208, 357, 387
H. M. S. Pinafore, Gilbert and Sullivan, 141
Hofmannsthal, Hugo von, 177
Holiday, Billie, 101
Holmes, John Haynes, 345
Hook, Sidney, 164, 287, 393
Hooray for What? Harburg, 150
Hospital Workers Union, 257
Howard, Willie, 139
Howe, Irving, 3, 6, 7, 8, 10, 133, 179, 187, 262, 264–87, 409, 419
Hughes, Charlie, 262
Humphrey, Hubert, 83
Humphrey and Weidman dancers, 144
Hunger, Hamsun, 35
Hyde Park Library, 14, 222
Hylton, Jack, 97
Hyman, Stanley Edgar, 393

Ibn Khaldun, 224
Ibsen, Henrik, 34
"Imaginary Jew, The," Berryman, 203
"In Dreams Begin Responsibilities," Schwartz, 281
Institute for Jewish Research, *see* YIVO
International Ladies Garment Workers Union (ILGWU), 8–9, 162–63, 167–74, 252, 253, 254, 262, 267, 270–71, 288, 336
"In the Shade of the New Apple Tree," Harburg, 150
Invisible Man, Ellison, 103
Isaacs, Stanley, 339
Israel, 18–20; Bensman on, 386–87; Decter on, 363–64; Goodman on, 322–23; Gottbaum on, 250; Greenberg in, 227–28; Howe on, 286–87; Kazin on, 205; Kovel on,

Israel (*Continued*)
  241; Morgenstern, Soma, on, 91;
  Morgenthau on, 78–80; Pachter
  on, 129–32; Singer's view of,
  35–36, 39
Israel Philharmonic, 219

Jacobs, Jane, 298
Jacobs, Paul, 173, 174
Jamaica, Harburg, 151
James, Fleming, 218
James, Henry, 9, 197, 198, 408, 409
Janowsky, Oscar, 213, 276
Jewish Child Care Association, 340
Jewish Daily Forward, 7, 27–30, 31
  illus., 83, 161–62, 168, 198
Jewish Frontier, 51
Jewish Historical Institute, Warsaw,
  65
Jewish Labor Committee, 255
Jewish Press, 83
Jewish Theological Seminary, 6, 73,
  213–18, 220–21, 315, 352–56, 355
  illus; Library, 12, 213–14
Jews, The, Finkelstein, 226
Jews Without Money, Gold, 203
Jochsberger, Zipporah, 216
John XXIII, pope, 346
Johnson, Hugh S., 337
Johnson, James P., 106
Jolson, Al, 139
Jones, LeRoi, 58
Journal of Commerce, 127
Joyce, James, 42, 406–8
Judenrat, The, Trunk, 70–71
Judge (publication), 142
Jung, Carl Gustav, 238

Kafka, Franz, 20, 92, 316, 407
Kalmanovich, Zelig, 67
Kampf, Louis, 202
Kaplan, Jack, 326
Kaplan, Mordecai, 218, 222

Katcherginsky, Shmerke, 69 *illus.*
Katz, Shlomo, 5, 6, 7, 15, 16, 22,
  45–60, 173, 364–65
Kauffmann, Stanley, 416
Kaufman, George S., 149
Kazan, Elia, 191
Kazin, Alfred, 3, 7, 9, 11, 14, 18–19,
  194–209, 242, 279, 409
Keats, John, 269
Kelly, Walt, 410
Kenworthy, Marion, 16, 339, 346
Kenyon Review, 85, 203
Kermish, Joseph, 66
Kern, Helmuth, 254–55
Kern, Jerome, 106, 143, 148, 149
Kessler, David, 182
Kibbutz Ein Harod, 49, 50
Kibbutz Lo'hamei ha ghettaot, 66–67
Kissinger, Henry, 80, 91, 92, 124,
  198, 364
Klemperer, Otto, 96
Klonsky, Milton, 416
Klopfer, Donald, 417
Knopf, A. A., 417
Kohler, rabbi, 333
Kolatch, Myron, 393
Kovel, Joel, 9–10, 234–45
Kracauer, Siegfried, 121
Kris, Ernst, 122
Kristol, Irving, 225, 278, 280, 356,
  393
Kronenberger, Louis, 200
Krutch, Joseph Wood, 189
Kuznetz, Simon, 226

Labor Action (newspaper), 282
Ladies Pocketbook Workers Union,
  299
LaGuardia, Fiorello H., 336–37, 338,
  339
Lahr, Bert, 139, 145
Lam, Herbert, 164
Lane, Burton, 144, 151
Lang, Paul Henry, 305, 306

Lasker, Bruno, 335
Last of the Just, The, Schwartz-Bart, 411
Latimer, Jonathan, 96
Lawrence, D. H., 176
Leaves of Grass, Whitman, 199
Lederer, Emil, 117
Lehman, Herbert H., 168, 220, 342
Lenin, 189–90
Lerner, Max, 235
Levant, Oscar, 148
Levenstein, Bob, 302
Levitas, Sol, 392
Levy, Adele Rosenwald, 339
Lewin, Bertrand, 238
Lewis, John L., 343
Lewis, Sinclair, 34
Lewis, William, 257
Lewisohn, Ludwig, 92
Lieberman, Elias, 159
Lieberman, Max, 159
Life Begins at 8:40, 145
Lifton, Harry, 142
Lifton, Robert Jay, 142
Lillie, Bea, 145
Limon, José, 144
Lincoln Center Library, 11, 308
Lindsay, John, 221, 258–59, 366
Lipchitz, Jacques, 326
List, Eugene, 212
Lodge, Henry Cabot, 128
London, Jack, 34
Looking Backward, Bellamy, 114
Lorca, García, 83
Lordly Hudson, The, Paul Goodman, 326
Lowenthal, Leo, 377
Lower East Side, 6, 137–38, 140, 153, 179, 194–95, 256, 288, 297
Lubavitcher, Rebbe, 12, 19, 40, 84–85, 215
Lubetkin, Ziviah, 66
Luce, Henry, 200
"Lydia the Tattooed Lady," 146

MacArthur, Douglas, 389
McCarthy, Joseph, 363
McCoy, Rhody, 260
Macdonald, Dwight, 200, 357
McEvoy, J. P., 144
McGovern, George S., 360–61
McKay, Claude, 55–56, 103
MacLeish, Archibald, 199
Magid, Simon, 156
Mahler, Gustav, 177, 304
Mahler, Raphael, 62
Mailer, Norman, 3, 83, 92, 200, 201, 326
Maimon, Salomon, 278
Malamud, Bernard, 3, 83, 408, 409
Malaquais, Jean, 282
Malthus, Thomas R., 41
Manhattan Music School, 303
Manhattan Project, 4
Mann, Thomas, 243
Mannes, Marya, 248
Manning, Bishop, 339, 343
Marcus, Steven, 410
Marcuse, Herbert, 240
Marquis, Don, 141
Marsala, Joe, 100
Marshall, Louis, 332
Marx, Groucho, 146
Marx, Harpo, 148
Masaryk, Thomas, 406
Mayer, Louis B., 104, 151
Meany, George, 263
Meatcutters Union, 254–55
Meet the People, 150
Mehring, Walter, 20
Meir, Golda, 49
Melman, Seymour, 276
Melville, Herman, 9, 125, 198
Mendele Mokher Sefarim, 35
Men of Ideas, Coser, 4
Menuhin, Yehudi, 309
Merton, Robert K., 4
Metropolitan Museum of Art, 284, 308

Michaelson, Bill, 260
Midstream, 52–57, 54 *illus.*, 173, 364, 410
Milano, Paolo, 201
Mills, C. Wright, 376
Mills, Irving, 104
Mills Brothers, 97
Mitchell, John Purroy, 341
Mitropoulos, Dimitri, 177
Molnár, Ferenc, 89
Montague, Dick, 330
"Mood Indigo," Ellington, 97
Moore, Big Chief Russell, 107
Moore, John, 323
Morgan, Frank, 151
Morgenbesser, Sidney, 224–25, 354
Morgenstern, Dan, 7, 21, 95–112
Morgenstern, Soma, 7, 21, 87–94, 109
Morgenthau, Hans, 5, 7, 13, 16, 17, 19, 75–86, 415
Morgenthau, Henry, 345
Morris, Willie, 365
Moses, Robert, 293, 322, 338
Moynihan, Daniel P., 413
Mumford, Lewis, 318
Muni, Paul, 184
Murray, Albert, 109, 110
Museum of Modern Art, 11, 325
Muste, A. J., 164, 297
My Life and Times as a Physicist, Rabi, 5
"My One and Only" (song), 147

NAACP, 173, 347
Nagel, Ernest, 4
Naked and the Dead, The, Mailer, 92
Nathan, George Jean, 185
Nation, The, 189, 308
National Child Labor Committee, 331
National Council for Judaism, 235
National Orchestra Association, 301
Natural History Museum, 11, 325
Nelson, Ben, 326

New American Review, 414–16
New Leader, 392–94
Newport Jazz Festival, 10
New Republic, The, 189, 198–201
New Russian Primer, The, Ilin, 375
New School for Social Research, 122, 198, 291–92
New York Daily News, 93
New York Daily World, 141
New Yorker, The, 5, 308
New York Herald Tribune, 197, 414
New York Jew, Kazin, 198
New York Philharmonic, 301
New York Post, 107, 361
New York Psychoanalytic Association, 238
New York Public Library, 12, 72–73, 214–15 *illus.*, 229, 325
New York Review of Books, 201, 417
New York Times, 93, 365
New York Times Book Review, 417
New York University, 160–61, 293, 319
Nick's (jazz club), 98
Niebuhr, Reinhold, 221
Nietzsche, Friedrich, 46
Night, Wiesel, 231
Nixon, Richard M., 360–61
Nozick, Robert, 272
"Nueva York," Lorca, 83

Oberlin College, 85
O'Brien, Conor Cruise, 416
Ocean Hill-Brownsville, 394–96, 398
Odets, Clifford, 186–87, 189, 191, 203
Office of International Labor Affairs, 253
OK, Pilnyak, 27–28
OmniAmericans, The, Murray, 109
One Dimensional Man, Marcuse, 240
On Native Grounds, Kazin, 9, 198, 207
Oppenheimer, J. Robert, 4
Original Dixieland Jazz Band, 98

Origins of Totalitarianism, The,
  Arendt, 119
Ornitz, Sam, 203
"Over the Rainbow," 146

Paasche, Max, 114
Pachter, Henry, 4, 5, 7, 16, 17,
  113–34
Page, Oran (Lips), 99–100
Palace Theatre, 139
Paley, Grace, 7, 8, 288–98
Pan, Hamsun, 35
Panken, Irving, 271, 272, 274
"Paper Moon," 146
"Parents Day," Goodman, Paul, 316
Parisian, The (magazine), 142
Parker, Dorothy, 141–42
Partisan Review, 199, 204, 281,
  357–58, 406, 407, 417
Patri, Angelo, 300
Patterson, Basil, 260, 261
Peabody House, 335
Perelman, S. J., 145
Peretz, Isaac Leib, 33, 178
Perle, George, 309
Personalities of the Old Testament,
  James, 218
Peterkin, John E., 311–12, 325
Phillips, William, 199, 357, 358
Pickett, Clarence, 16, 346
Pilnyak, Boris, 27
Pinchot, Gifford, 337
Pins and Needles, 162
Pinson, Koppel, 68
Podhoretz, Norman, 83, 410–14
Poe, Edgar Allan, 34
Polier, Justine Wise, 7, 15, 330–48
Polier, Shad, 339
Pomerantz, Seymour, 68
Porgy and Bess, Gershwin, 106
Porter, Andrew, 308
Porter, Cole, 106, 148
Powell, Adam Clayton, 173–74
Pozo, Chano, 98
Pratt Library, 11, 160

Princeton, New Jersey, 132
Progressive party, 252
Protestant, Catholic, and Jew. Herberg,
  225
Protestant Episcopal Mission Society,
  339
Proxmire, William, 318
Puck (publication), 142
Puzzled America, Anderson, 268

Queens College, 306

Raab, Earl, 280
Rabi, Isidor Isaac, 4–5
Rabinowitz, Meyer, 222
Radcliffe College, 335
Rahv, Philip, 199, 281, 357–58
Rathaus, Karol, 101, 305, 306
Rauschning, Hermann, 123
Ravicz, Peter, 411
Ravitch, Diane, 5, 11, 21, 388–400
Reinhart, Django, 97
Reisenweber's, 98
Reporter, The, 201
Riegner, Gerhardt, 345
Ringelblum, Immanuel, 62
Riviera (jazz club), 98
Roberts, Lillian, 257–58, 261, 262
Robeson, Paul, 122
Robinson, Jackie, 100
Roche, John, 82
Rockefeller Center, 153, 200
Rodgers, Richard, 106
Roebling, J. A. and W. A., 199
Rolland, Romain, 184
Rolling Stone, 203
Roosevelt, Eleanor, 16, 339, 346
Roosevelt, Franklin D., 14, 15, 30,
  149–50, 188, 222, 235, 268, 271,
  313, 343, 345, 371
Rose, Alex, 258
Rosen, Chalres, 308
Rosenbaum, Milton, 238
Rosenberg, Alfred, 67, 68, 70
Rosenberg, Harold, 204, 326, 409

Rosenfeld, Isaac, 200, 406, 407, 408
Rosenfeld, Paul, 185
Rosenmann, Samuel, 345
Rosenwald, Lessing, 235
Rossmon, Michael, 416
Roszak, Theodore, 416
Roth, Phillip, 3, 83, 92, 203, 326, 408, 409, 416
Rousseau, Jean Jacques, 114
Russell, Pee Wee, 107
Rustin, Bayard, 224, 260

Saidy, Fred, 151
Saint Paul, Minnesota, 48–51, 56, 351–52
Samuelson, Paul A., 4
Sartre, Jean Paul, 17, 131, 287
Satan in Goray, Singer, 33
Schacter, David, 255
Schaffer, Louis, 161, 162–63
Schapiro, J. Salwyn, 214
Schapiro, Meyer, 4, 7, 195, 284, 323
Schappes, Morris, 277
Scharfstein, Zvi, 353
Schatsky, Jacob, 67
Scheer, Carl, 257
Scheffler, Izzy, 354
Scheinwold, Roger, 222
Scheitz, Alfred, 378
Schenkman, Jack, 250
Schildkraut, Davie, 104
Schlesinger, Arthur, 176
Schlesinger, James, 80, 84
Schnabel, Artur, 248, 281
Schneerson (Lubavitcher Rebbe), 84
Schner, Tsvi, 66
Schnitzler, Arthur, 177
Schoenberg, Arnold, 304
Schopenhauer, Arthur, 41
Schubert, Franz, 212
Schuster, Max, 417
Schwartz, Arthur, 143
Schwartz, Delmore, 199, 200, 203, 281, 284, 326, 407, 409
Schwatz, Morris, 306

Schwartz-Bart, André, 411
Seeger, Pete, 114
SEEK, 383
Serkin, Rudolph, 281
"Seven Who Were Hanged, The," Andreyev, 405
Shachtman, Max, 277
Shahn, Ben, 235
Shanker, Albert, 244, 259, 260, 365–66
Shapiro, Karl, 410
Shaw, Artie, 104
Sheil, Bishop, 16, 346
Sholom Aleichem, 33, 141, 285, 410
Shylock, 182 *illus.*, 183
Sicher, Dudley, 156
Simmel, Georg, 133, 386
Simon, John, 393
Simon, Neil, 187
Sinclair, Upton, 34
Singer, Isaac Bashevis, 7, 13, 14, 27–44, 201, 315, 408
Singer, I. J., 27
Socialist Call, 164, 167
Socialist party, 166–67, 271
Solotaroff, Ted, 3, 5, 17, 401–19
"Somewhere Over the Rainbow," 146, 150–51
Sondheim, Stephen, 148
Sontag, Susan, 416
Sorrentino, Gil, 416
Speculum (publication), 218
Speier, Hans, 122
Spellman, Francis J., 16, 346
Spender, Stephen, 292
Spinoza, Baruch, 34, 43
Spirit of the Ghetto, The, Hapgood, 278–79
Stalin, Joseph, 357, 375–76
Starer, Robert, 309
Starr, Mark, 253
Starting Out in the Thirties, Kazin, 202
Stein, Andrew, 84
Steinberg, Milton, 217

Sternberg, Jonathan, 301
Stiles, Ezra, 198
Stone, I. F., 347
Stone, Robert, 416
"Stormy Weather," 146
Strasberg, Lee, 186
Strauss, Edgar, 249
Strauss, Peter, 252
Stravinsky, Igor, 304, 305
Strindberg, August, 34, 35, 42–43
Student Union, 291
Sullivan, Arthur, 141
Sullivan, Louis, 312
"Summertime," Gershwin, 147
Sutzkover, Abraham, 67
Sverdloff, Mike, 247
Syrkin, Marie, 286
Szajkowski, Zosa, 68
Szilard, Leo, 4

Taibi, Charlie, 255–56, 257
Tannenbaum, Frank, 84
Tarbut schools, 62
Tatum, Art, 101, 106
Taubes, Jacob, 225, 357, 358
Taylor, Cecil, 110
Teachers' strike, 6; Cohen on,
    223–24; Decter on, 365–67;
    Gotbaum on, 259–60; Katz on,
    56–58; Paley on, 295–97; Ravitch
    on, 396–400; Tyler on, 173
Temple Emanu-El, 220, 332
Tern, Jurgen, 127–28
Thalia Theater, 139
Third Pillar, The, Morgenstern,
    Soma, 87
Thomas, Norman, 252, 253, 268,
    271, 277, 345
Tiber Press, 308
Tiger at the Gates, 190
Tillich, Paul, 221
Times Literary Supplement, 409–10
Today, 268
Toller, Ernst, 21
Tolstoy, Leo, 34

Tomashevsky, Boris, 139
Tomorrow, 189
Tompkins Square Library, 160
Tompkins Square Park, 140
Toscanini, Arturo, 301
Trilling, Lionel, 3, 204, 281, 409
Trouble in July, Caldwell, 103
Truman, Harry S., 253, 347
Trunk, Isaiah, 5, 12, 21, 61–74
Trunk, J. J., 72
Tsivian, 162
Tstcherikover, Elias, 67
TSYSO, 62
Tulin, Leon Arthur, 336
Twain, Mark, 34, 178
Tyler, Gus, 8, 11, 13–14, 155–75,
    252, 253

Unfinished Symphony, Schubert, 212
Union of American Hebrew
    Congregations, 316
Union Square, 52
Union Theological Seminary, 12,
    215, 221, 222, 343
United Federation of Teachers, 271
United Nationals, 128–29, 130 illus.,
    132
Unity House, 252, 253, 263
University of Chicago, 200, 408
Upper West Side, 7, 310
Uriel Acosta, 181, 183

Valentine, Willie, 246
Van Arsdale, Harry, 254, 256, 259
Veblen, Thorstein, 23
Vecchi, Floriano, 308
Verdi, Giuseppe, 219
Vers de Société, Wells, 140
Victoria, Hamsun, 35
Village Voice, 105
Voice of America, 377–78

Wagner, Robert, 256, 259, 343
Walker, Jimmy, 345
Walker in the City, Kazin, 242

Wallace, Henry, 200, 253
Wallenrod, Reuben, 353
Waller, Fats, 97, 106
Walter, Bruno, 177
War and Peace, Tolstoy, 92
Warburg, Felix, 168
Warburg, Mrs. Felix, 315
Warburg, Max, 343
War Diary, Malaquais, 282
War Resisters League, 298
Warshow, Robert, 356, 357
Washington Post, 392
Washington Square, 314
Weber, Max, 16, 374
Wein, George, 104, 111–12
Weiner, Lazar, 300
Weiner, Yehudi, 300
Weinreich, Max, 67, 210
Weinstein, Maxie, 249
Weisgall, Hugo, 309
Weisman, Max, 204
Weiss, Louis, 338
Wells, Carolyn, 140
Wharton, Edith, 9, 198
"What Is This Thing Called Love?"
    148
White, Walter, 347
Whitehead, Alfred North, 1
White Rose Bar, 98
Whitman, Walt, 9, 198, 199
Whitney, Sy, 335
Wiesel, Elie, 231, 232, 411
Wilcox, Preston, 394
Willkie, Wendell, 318
Wilson, Edmund, 281
Wilson, Teddy, 100
Wilson, Woodrow, 333
Wiltwyck School, 339
Winchell, Walter, 193

Winternitz, Emmanuel, 308
Wise, Stephen, 6, 7, 15–16, 78,
    330–34, 342–47, 344 *illus.*
Wizard of Oz, The, Harburg, 150
Wolfe, Tom, 392
Women's Strike, 297, 298
Woollcott, Alexander, 141
Workman's Circle, 271
World Jewish Congress, 344
World of Our Fathers, Howe, 179, 262,
    419
WQXR, 132, 212
Wright, Frank Lloyd, 312, 318
Wright, Richard, 103
Wurf, Jerry, 254, 255–58
Wyner, Yehudi, 308
Wynn, Ed, 139, 150

Yad Vashem, 12, 66, 67, 71, 227
Yentl, Singer, 42
Yeshiva University, 9, 217, 228–29
Yiddish Scientific Institute, 222
YIVO (Yiddish Institute), 12, 14, 63,
    67–74, 210, 215
YMHA, 216
Youmans, Vincent, 144
Young, Andrew, 107–8
Young Communist League, 276–77,
    290, 372–73
Young People's Socialist League,
    208, 252, 270, 271, 290
Youth Movement, 114, 115

Zander, Arnold, 255
Ziegfeld Follies, 145
Zimmerman, Sacha and Rose, 252
"Zlateh the Goat," Singer, 43
Zuckerman, Yitzhak, 66

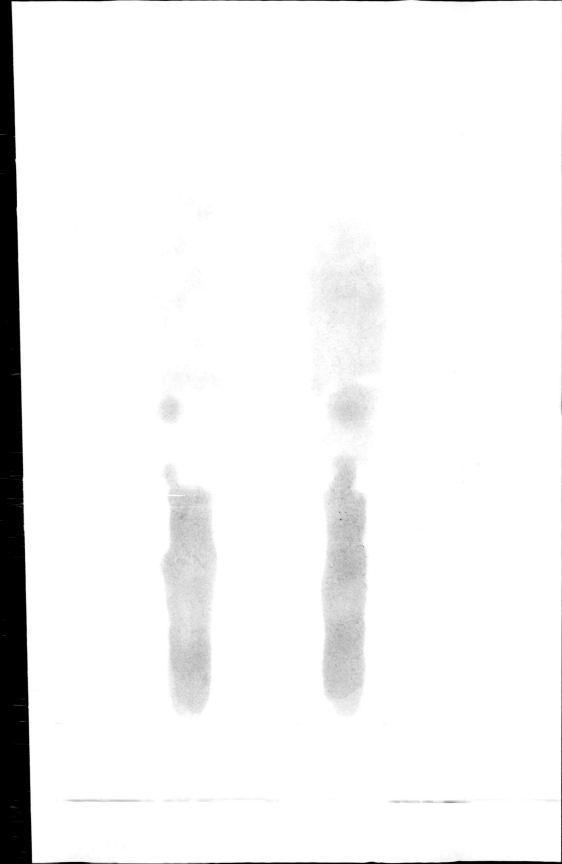